ICC/ANSI A117.1-2003

American National Standard

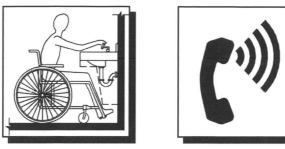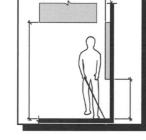

*Accessible and Usable
Buildings and Facilities*

2003

Standard &
Commentary

INTERNATIONAL
CODE COUNCIL®

2003 ICC/ANSI A117.1 Standard and Commentary

First Printing: June 2008

ISBN: 978-1-58001-697-1

COPYRIGHT © 2008
by
INTERNATIONAL CODE COUNCIL, INC.

PRINTED IN THE U.S.A.

American National Standard

FOREWORD

(The information contained in this foreword is not part of this American National Standard (ANS) and has not been processed in accordance with ANSI's requirements for an ANS. As such, this foreword may contain material that has not been subjected to public review or a consensus process. In addition, it does not contain requirements necessary for conformance to the standard.)

Development

The 1961 edition of ANSI Standard A117.1 presented the first criteria for accessibility to be approved as an American National Standard and was the result of research conducted by the University of Illinois under a grant from the Easter Seal Research Foundation. The National Easter Seal Society and the President's Committee on Employment of People with Disabilities became members of the Secretariat, and the 1961 edition was reaffirmed in 1971.

In 1974, the U.S. Department of Housing and Urban Development joined the Secretariat and sponsored needed research, which resulted in the 1980 edition. After further revision that included a special effort to remove application criteria (scoping requirements), the 1986 edition was published and, when requested in 1987, the Council of American Building Officials (CABO) assumed the Secretariat. Central to the intent of the change in the Secretariat was the development of a standard that, when adopted as part of a building code, would be compatible with the building code and its enforcement. The 1998 edition largely achieved that goal. In 1998, CABO became the International Code Council (ICC).

2003 Edition

New to the 2003 edition are criteria for elements and fixtures primarily for children's use; enhanced reach range criteria; transportation facilities; additional provisions for assembly areas; and an addition and rearrangement for accessible dwelling and sleeping units. These new criteria are intended to provide a level of coordination between the accessible provisions of this standard and the Fair Housing Accessibility Guidelines (FHAG) and the Americans with Disabilities Act Accessibility Guidelines (ADAAG). Illustrative figures are numbered the same as corresponding text to simplify the use of the Standard. Unless specified otherwise, figures are not part of the Standard. Should a figure appear to illustrate criteria that differ with the text of the Standard, the criteria stated in the text govern.

ANSI Approval

This Standard was processed and approved for submittal to ANSI by the Accredited Standards Committee A117 on Architectural Features and Site Design of Public Buildings and Residential Structures for Persons with Disabilities. ANSI approved the 2003 edition on November 26, 2003. Committee approval of the Standard does not necessarily imply that all Committee members voted for its approval.

Adoption

ICC/ANSI A117.1–2003 is available for adoption and use by jurisdictions internationally. Its use within a governmental jurisdiction is intended to be accomplished through adoption by reference in accordance with proceedings establishing the jurisdiction's laws.

Formal Interpretations

Requests for Formal Interpretations on the provisions of ICC/ANSI A117.1–2003 should be addressed to: ICC, Chicago District Office, 4051 W. Flossmoor Road, Country Club Hills, IL 60478–5795.

Maintenance—Submittal of Proposals

All ICC standards are revised as required by ANSI. Proposals for revising this edition are welcome. Please visit the ICC website at www.iccsafe.org for the official "Call for proposals" announcement. A proposal form and instructions can also be downloaded from www.iccsafe.org.

ICC, its members and those participating in the development of ICC/ANSI A117.1-2003 do not accept any liability resulting from compliance or noncompliance with the provisions of ICC/ANSI A117.1-2003. ICC does not have the power or authority to police or enforce compliance with the contents of this standard. Only the governmental body that enacts this standard into law has such authority.

Accredited Standards Committee A117 on Architectural Features and Site Design of Public Buildings and Residential Structures for Persons with Disabilities

At the time of ANSI approval, the A117.1 Committee consisted of the following members:

Chair. . . . . Kenneth M. Schoonover, PE
Vice Chair . . . . Edward A. Donoghue, CPCA
A117 Committee Secretary. . . . . Lawrence Brown, CBO

Organizational Member . . . . **Representative**

Accessibility Equipment Manufacturers
Association (AEMA) (**PD**) . . . . Kevin Brinkman
Gregory L. Harmon (Alt)

American Bankers Association (ABA) (**BO**) . . . . . . Nessa Feddis
American Council of the Blind (ACB) (**CU**). . . . . . Patricia Beattie
Krista Merritt (Alt)

American Hotel and Lodging Association
(AHLA) (**BO**). Kevin Maher
Jerry Gross (Alt)

American Institute of Architects (AIA) (**P**). . . . . . . Mark W. Wales, Associate AIA, CBO
Larry M. Schneider (Alt)

American Occupational Therapy Association
(AOTA) (**P**). . . . . S. Shoshana Shamberg
American Society of Interior Designers (ASID) (**P**) . . Samantha McAskill, ASID
Barbara J. Huelat, ASID, IIDA (Alt)

American Society of Plumbing Engineers (ASPE) (**P**) Robert H. Evans, Jr., CIPE/CPD
Julius A. Ballanco, P.E. (Alt)

American Society of Safety Engineers (ASSE) (**P**) . . Dr. William Marletta, PhD, CSP
John B. Schroering, P.E., CSP. (Alt)

American Society of Theatre Consultants (ASTC) (**P**) . William Conner, ASTC
R. Duane Wilson, ASTC (Alt)

Association for Education & Rehabilitation of the Blind
& Visually Impaired (AERBVI) (**P**) . . . . Billie Louise "Beezy" Bentzen, PhD
Builders Hardware Manufacturers Association, Inc.
(BHMA) (**PD**). Michael Tierney
Richard Hudnut (Alt)

Building Owners and Managers Association
International (BOMA) (**BO**). . . . . Lawrence G. Perry, AIA
Ron Burton (Alt)

Disability Rights Education and Defense Fund
(DREDF) (**CU**) . . . . Marilyn Golden
Logan Hopper (Alt)

International Association of Amusement Parks and
Attractions (IAAPA) (**BO**) . . . . John Paul Scott, AIA, NCARB
International Code Council (ICC) (**R**) . . . . Kimberly Paarlberg, AIA
Phil Hahn, AIA (Alt)

International Sign Association (ISA) (**PD**) . . . . Teresa Cox
James L. Chapman (Alt)
Muhammad Kahn (2nd Alt)

Little People of America, Inc. (LPA) (**CU**) . . . . . . Tricia Mason
C. Angela Van Etten, J.D.

Montgomery County Department of Permitting
Services (MCDPS) (**R**). . . . . Shahriar Amiri, CBO
Thomas Heiderer (Alt)

National Apartment Association (NAA) (**BO**). . . . . . Ronald G. Nickson
National Association of Home Builders (NAHB) (**BO**) . Jeffrey T. Inks
Richard A. Morris (Alt)

National Association of the Deaf (NAD) (**CU**) . . . . . Don Sievers
Nancy J. Bloch (Alt)

National Conference of States on Building Codes
and Standards (NCSBCS) (**R**) . . . . Curt Wiehle

National Electrical Manufacturers Association
(NEMA) (**PD**) . . . . Rein Haus
                                              Scott Edwards (Alt)
    James Shuster (2nd Alt)

National Elevator Industry, Inc. (NEII) (**PD**) . . . . . . Edward A. Donoghue, CPCA
    George A. Kappenhagen (Alt)
    Barry Blackaby (2nd Alt)

National Fire Protection Association
(NFPA) (**R**). . . . . Allan B. Fraser
    Ron Coté, PE (Alt)

New Mexico Governor's Committee on Concerns of the
Handicapped (NMGCCH) (**CU**) . . . . Hope Reed
    Anthony H. Alarid (Alt)

Paralyzed Veterans of America (PVA) (**CU**) . . . . . . Carol Peredo Lopez, AIA
    Mark H. Lichter, AIA (Alt)

Plumbing Manufacturers Institute (PMI) (**PD**) . . . . . David Viola
    Barbara C. Higgens (Alt)

Self Help for Hard of Hearing People, Inc.
(SHHH) (**CU**) . . . . Brenda Battat
    Timothy P. Creagan (Alt)

Society for Environmental Graphic Design
(SEGD) (**P**). . . . . Kenneth A. Ethridge, Jr., AIA, RIBA
    Ann Makowski (Alt)

Stairway Manufacturers Association (SMA) (**PD**) . . . Tim Moss
    David Cooper (Alt)

U.S. Architectural & Transportation Barriers Compliance
(Access) Board (ATBCB) (**R**) . . . . Marsha K. Mazz
    Scott J. Windley (Alt)

U.S. Department of Agriculture (USDA) (**R**) . . . . . . Larry B. Fleming
    Samuel Hodges, III (Alt)

U.S. Department of Housing and Urban Development
(HUD) (**R**) . . . . Cheryl D. Kent
    Louis F. Borray (Alt)

United Cerebral Palsy Association, Inc. (UCPA) (**CU**) . Robert Dale Lynch, FAIA
    Gus Estrella (Alt)

United Spinal Association (**CU**) . . . . Brian D. Black
    Dominic Marinelli (Alt)

World Institute on Disability (WID) (**CU**) . . . . Hale Zukas

Individual Members

Todd Andersen (P)
George P. McAllister, Jr. (P)
Jake L. Pauls, CPE (P)
John P. S. Salmen, AIA (P)
Kenneth M. Schoonover, PE (P)

Acknowledgment

The updating of this standard over the past 5 years could only be accomplished by the hard work of not only the current committee members listed at the time of approval but also the many committee members who participated and contributed to the process over the course of development. ICC recognizes their contributions as well as those of the participants who, although not on the committee, provided valuable input during this update cycle.

INTEREST CATEGORIES

Builder/Owner/Operator (BO) – Members in this category include those in the private sector involved in the development, construction, ownership and operation of buildings or facilities; and their respective associations.

Consumer/User (CU) – Members in this category include those with disabilities, or others who require accessibility features in the built environment for access to buildings, facilities and sites; and their respective associations.

Producer/Distributor (PD) – Members in this category include those involved in manufacturing, distributing, or sales of products; and their respective associations.

Professional (P) – Members in this category include those qualified to engage in the development of the body of knowledge and policy relevant to their area of practice, such as research, testing, consulting, education, engineering or design; and their respective associations.

Regulatory (R) – Members in this category include federal agencies, representatives of regulatory agencies or organizations that promulgate or enforce codes or standards; and their respective associations.

Individual Expert (IE) (Nonvoting) – Members in this category are individual experts selected to assist the consensus body. Individual experts shall serve for a renewable term of one year and shall be subject to approval by vote of the consensus body. Individual experts shall have no vote.

Category	Number
Builder/Owner/Operator – **(BO)**	6
Consumer/User – **(CU)**	10
Professional – **(P)**	13
Producer/Distributor – **(PD)**	7
Regulatory – **(R)**	7
TOTAL	**43**

PREFACE

Purpose and Application

This standard contains technical specifications (i.e., how to) for elements that are used in creating accessible functional spaces. For example, it specifies technical requirements for making doors, routes, seating and other elements accessible. These accessible elements are used for designing accessible functional spaces such as classrooms, hotel rooms, lobbies or offices.

This standard does not include scoping criteria (i.e., what, where and how many). Scoping provisions are contained in laws, ordinances or model building codes that reference this standard. This standard is for adoption by government agencies and by organizations setting model codes to achieve uniformity in the technical design criteria in building codes and other regulations. This standard is also used by nongovernmental entities as technical design guidelines or requirements to make buildings and facilities accessible to and usable by persons with physical disabilities.

Provisions of this standard are suitable for:

– the design and construction of new buildings and facilities, including both spaces and elements, site improvements and public walks.

– remodeling, alteration and rehabilitation of existing construction.

– permanent, temporary and emergency conditions.

Criteria are established for individual building spaces and elements. The intention is that these accessible spaces and elements combine to provide accessibility throughout a building and related site facilities. General criteria, such as the minimum width of an accessible route, can apply to different building or site elements, including sidewalks, corridors and aisles between library stacks. Other criteria are for specific elements such as drinking fountains, water closets, sinks and lavatories.

The principal purpose of the commentary is to provide a basic volume of knowledge and facts relating to building construction as it pertains to the regulations set forth in the ANSI A117.1.

In the chapters that follow, discussions focus on the full meaning and implications of the text. Guildelines suggest the most effective method of application, and the consequences of not adhering to the text. Illustrations are provided to aid understanding; they do not necessarily illustrate the only methods of achieving compliance.

The format of the commentary includes the full text of each section, table and figure in the standard, followed immediately by the commentary applicable to that text. At the time of printing, the commentary reflects the most up-to-date text of the 2003 ICC/ANSI A117.1. Each section's narrative includes a statement of its objective and intent and usually includes a discussion about why the requirement commands the conditions set forth. Standard text and commentary text are easily distinguished from each other. All standard text is shown as it appears in the ICC/ANSI A117.1 and all commentary is indented below the code text with the symbol ❖.

Readers should note that the commentary is to be used in conjunction with the ICC/ANSI A117.1 and not as a substitute for the standard. The commentary is advisory only; the code official alone possesses the authority and responsibility for interpreting the code and referenced standards.

Comments and recommendations are encouraged, for through you input, we can improve future editions. Please direct you comments to the Codes and Standards Development Department at the Chicago District Office.

Recommendations to Adopting Authorities

Administration

This standard does not establish which occupancy or building types are covered and the extent to which each type is covered. Such requirements for application of this standard must be specified by the adopting authority, including which and how many functional spaces and elements are to be made accessible within each building type.

The standard does not establish which or how many buildings, facilities and spaces or elements within these spaces must be made accessible. This standard correlates with the adoption of scoping provisions by the administrative authority. This is typically accomplished through the adoption of a model building code which references this standard. The adopted scoping provisions will establish where accessibility is required, and this standard will establish how those required elements and spaces are to be made accessible. A set of recommended scoping provisions was developed by the Board for the Coordination of the Model Codes of the Council of American Building Officials, and is reflected in the cur rent editions of the model building codes. The International Code Council (ICC) continues developing requirements through their public hearings and code development process.

By adopting this standard through the building code, enforcement can be accomplished at the state or local level. In contrast, the requirements of Titles II and III of the Americans with Disabilities Act (ADA) can be enforced only as a civil rights statute by the United States Department of Justice. Although many provisions in this standard are comparable to parallel requirements contained in the Americans with Disabilities Act Accessibility Guidelines (ADAAG), compliance with the ADA should be verified independently.

The ICC/ANSI A117.1 1998 and 2003 editions have been designated by the department of Housing and Urban Development (HUD) as 'safe harbor' documents for compliance with the technical provisions of the Fair Housing Act (FHA). However, scoping provisions for how many units must comply are contained in the FHA or the *International Building Code* (IBC®) 2003 or 2006 editions.

Number of Spaces and Elements

The administrative authority adopting this standard must specify the actual number of spaces and elements—or establish procedures for determining them—based on, but not limited to:

– population to be served.

– availability to occupants, employees, customers and visitors.

– distances and time required to use the accessible elements.

– provision of equal opportunity and treatment under the law.

The need for accessible spaces and elements can vary widely. For example, the number of parking spaces for some medical facilities may be significantly greater than for most commercial office buildings.

Remodeling

The specifications in this standard are based on the functional requirements of persons with physical disabilities. The administrative authority adopting this standard must specify the extent to which it is to cover remodeling, alteration or rehabilitation within its jurisdiction.

The administrative authority specifies the extent to which this standard applies to existing buildings, including buildings of historic significance. Accessibility in historic buildings and facilities that must be made accessible and usable by persons with disabilities should be accomplished in a manner that maintains the significant historic fabric and historic aspects of such buildings and facilities.

Historic aspects are the particular features of the historic site, building or facility that give it its historic significance. These may include historic background, noteworthy architecture, unique design, works of art, memorabilia and artifacts. Historic fabric consists of the original materials and portions of the building intact when exposed, or as they appeared and were used in the past. Historic buildings are buildings and facilities that are eligible for listing or are listed in the National Register of Historic Places, or such properties designated as historic under a statute of the appropriate state or local government body.

If the historic fabric or historic aspects are threatened or destroyed by strict compliance with the provisions of this standard, reasonably equivalent access and use may be accomplished by using these concepts. Reasonably equivalent access and use means that the entry to, and use of, a building or facility by persons with disabilities is achieved with standards or measures which are individually tailored to the historic building or facility.

Should the above still be deemed to destroy the historic fabric or historic aspect, additional consideration may be given to the following:

1. Deviations should be on an item-by-item or case-by-case basis.

2. Interpretive exhibits and/or equal services of significant historic aspects which do not comply with this standard are provided for the public in a location fully accessible to and usable by persons with disabilities, including people with hearing and sight impairments.

3. Services are provided in an accessible location equal to those services provided in the locations that do not comply with this standard.

4. The owner/designer has submitted written documentation stating the reasons for the consequent exemption. Such statements should include the opinions and/or comments of a representative local group of persons with disabilities and should be submitted to the administrative authority for approval.

Review Procedures

To promote effective compliance with the requirements of this standard, the administrative authority adopting it should establish a review and approval procedure for construction projects that come under its jurisdiction.

Where this standard is adopted by the administrative authority, a construction project that must comply with these provisions should be reviewed for compliance in the same manner the project is reviewed to determine compliance with other provisions of the building code.

Contents

List of Figures

Chapter 7. Communication Elements and Features 151

Chapter 8. Special Rooms and Spaces 177

Chapter 1. Application and Administration

❖ Chapter 1 provides for the general application of this document.

- Section 101 establishes the purpose of the standard.
- Section 102 establishes the basis for the technical requirements.
- Section 103 allows for alternative compliance.
- Section 104 establishes conventions used for the requirements.
- Section 105 provides a list of referenced standards.
- Section 106 includes definitions for the purpose of this document.

101 Purpose

The technical criteria in Chapters 3 through 9, and Sections 1002, 1003 and 1005 of this standard make sites, facilities, buildings and elements accessible to and usable by people with such physical disabilities as the inability to walk, difficulty walking, reliance on walking aids, blindness and visual impairment, deafness and hearing impairment, incoordination, reaching and manipulation disabilities, lack of stamina, difficulty interpreting and reacting to sensory information, and extremes of physical size. The intent of these sections is to allow a person with a physical disability to independently get to, enter, and use a site, facility, building, or element.

Section 1004 of this standard provides criteria for Type B units. These criteria are intended to be consistent with the intent of the criteria of the U.S. Department of Housing and Urban Development (HUD) Fair Housing Accessibility Guidelines. The Type B units are intended to supplement, not replace, Accessible units or Type A units as specified in this standard.

This standard is intended for adoption by government agencies and by organizations setting model codes to achieve uniformity in the technical design criteria in building codes and other regulations.

❖ Independence for persons with physical and sensory disabilities is a primary goal of this standard. It is essential that accessibility into and throughout buildings and facilities be part of the initial design process. ICC A117.1 provides details, dimensions and specifications to help building designers develop their plans so that the facility will offer unobstructed entry and ease of use to all users with disabilities.

The technical specifications in this standard are intended to create elements and spaces that can be used independently by persons with disabilities. The requirements are based on anthropometrics for an average adult male, and may not be appropriate for all applications. (See the commentary for Section 102.)

The intent is to serve as wide a spectrum of persons with disabilities as possible based on currently available knowledge and experience. Because needs and capabilities vary from individual to individual, it is not possible to set technical criteria that would permit independent use by all persons with disabilities. For example, not everyone is able to transfer from a wheelchair to a water closet, even though the clearances necessary for such a transfer satisfy this standard. Criteria contained in the standard are based on the best information and research available to the A117.1 Standard Review Committee during the process of review and update for the standard. The Committee welcomes results of recent research from all interested and affected parties.

For dwelling units and sleeping units, the Standard provides three distinct sets of criteria: Accessible units, Type A units and Type B units. The requirements in Section 1004 for Type B dwelling units and sleeping units are technical criteria that are consistent with the requirements of the Fair Housing Act. The criteria provide a lesser level of accessibility than Accessible units or Type A units. For additional information, see the commentary in Chapter 10.

Understanding and consistency in the application of the criteria throughout the country would be of immeasurable value to the person with a disability, as well as building regulators, designers and owners, and the community in general. Consistency would result in a greater level of comfort for a person with a disability in his or her daily activities. A person with a disability would know what to expect within a facility instead of finding new obstacles to overcome in each situation. There are many accessibility features that benefit not only people with disabilities, but are also a tangible benefit to people without disabilities.

101.1 Applicability. Sites, facilities, buildings, and elements required to be accessible shall comply with the applicable provisions of Chapters 3 through 9.

EXCEPTIONS:

1. Accessible units shall comply with Section 1002.

2. Type A units shall comply with Section 1003.

3. Type B units shall comply with Section 1004.

4. Dwelling units and sleeping units required to have accessible communication features shall comply with Section 1005.

❖ Criteria are established for individual building spaces and elements. These accessible spaces and elements are intended to combine to provide accessibility throughout a building and related site facilities. General criteria, such as the minimum width of an accessible route, can apply to different building or site elements, including sidewalks, corridors and aisles between library stacks. Other criteria are provided for specific elements such as drinking fountains, water closets, sinks and lavatories.

Specifics are provided for Accessible, Type A and Type B dwelling units and sleeping units in Chapter 10.

102 Anthropometric Provisions

The technical criteria in this standard are based on adult dimensions and anthropometrics. This standard also contains technical criteria based on children's dimensions and anthropometrics for drinking fountains, water closets, toilet compartments, lavatories and sinks, dining surfaces and work surfaces.

❖ Anthropometrics for an adult male who uses a wheelchair provided the technical basis for many of the requirements. For example, the 27-inch height for knees is used for the building block for the knee clearances, which in turn is referenced for the heights for drinking fountains, working surfaces and dining surfaces [see commentary Figure C102(a)].

Adult dimensions do not always work for children. Unique criteria for children have been provided for the listed elements. Designing for children is a choice, but once that choice has been made, the requirements for the element must be followed. For example, if a child-size bathroom is desired, all criteria for the child size toilet, sink and grab bar must be followed. (See commentary for the specific items listed for additional child size information.)

There are three basic types of devices that typically use the 'wheelchair' spaces.

Manual Chair: The manual chair category considers all wheelchair devices not powered by a motor. Attendant-driven devices (those wheelchairs that do not have a hand-held drive wheel) are also included in this category because they do not have a motor. The manual chair category spans the gamut from standard hospital chairs to light-weight sports chairs [see commentary Figure C102(b)].

Power Chair: This category includes motor-driven chairs that do not fall into the category of scooters. Power chairs are controlled primarily by a joystick and can use front, mid or rear drive wheels. Many power chairs come with therapeutic features such as the tilt-in-space feature that allows the owner to relieve pressure. Additionally, chairs in this category also use body positioning technology (such as head rests, pummels, adductor/abductor pads) that help keep one's body aligned [see commentary Figure C102(b)].

Scooter: This category is also motor-driven. The controls are typically on a tiller placed anterior to the individual. Overall, scooters tend to be the largest and take up the most space. Maneuvering a scooter can be difficult because of the tiller steering system (which allows for generally larger turning radii) [See commentary Figure C102(b)].

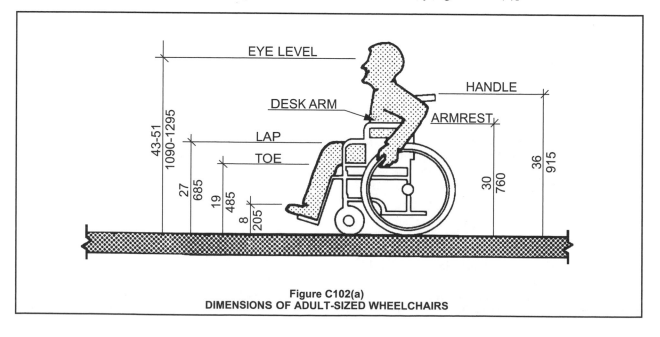

Figure C102(a)
DIMENSIONS OF ADULT-SIZED WHEELCHAIRS

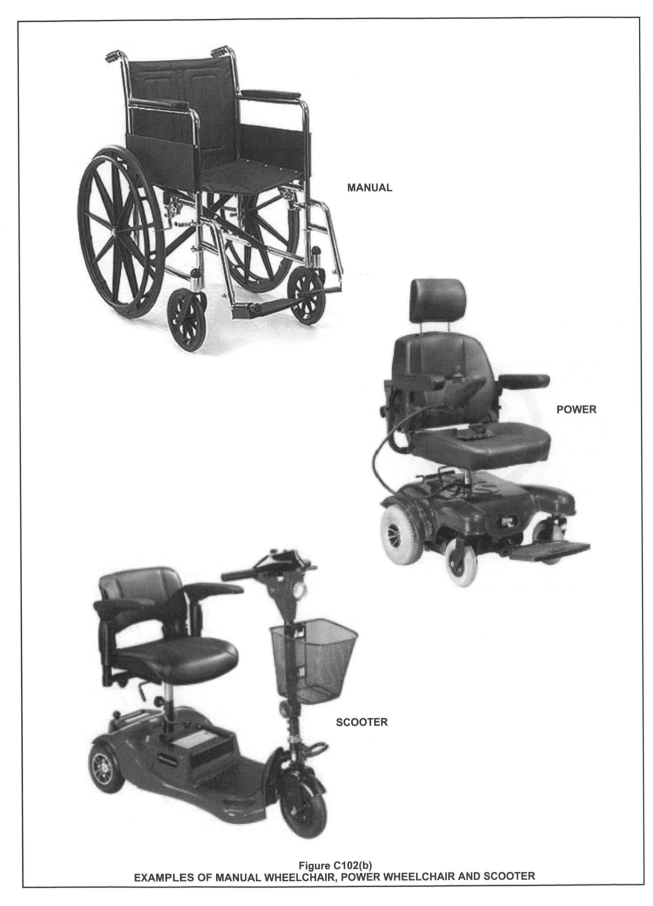

MANUAL

POWER

SCOOTER

Figure C102(b)
EXAMPLES OF MANUAL WHEELCHAIR, POWER WHEELCHAIR AND SCOOTER

103 Compliance Alternatives

Nothing in this standard is intended to prevent the use of designs, products, or technologies as alternatives to those prescribed by this standard, provided they result in equivalent or greater accessibility and such equivalency is approved by the administrative authority adopting this standard.

❖ The requirements in this standard are not intended to inhibit innovative ideas or technological advances. A comprehensive regulatory document cannot envision and then address all future innovations in the industry. The fact that a material, product or method of construction is not addressed is not an indication that prohibition of the material, product or method is intended. The building official is expected to apply sound technical judgment in accepting materials, systems or methods that, although not anticipated by the drafters of the current text, can be demonstrated to offer equivalent performance.

104 Conventions

104.1 General. Where specific criteria of this standard differ from the general criteria of this standard, the specific criteria shall apply.

❖ The standard contains various criteria for the same feature or element. As an example, the criteria for Type B dwelling units include specific provisions for a lavatory in a bathroom (Sections 1004.11.3.1.1 and 1004.11.3.2.1). These are specific for Type B units and take precedence over the general criteria for lavatories in Section 606.

104.2 Dimensions. Dimensions that are not stated as "maximum" or "minimum" are absolute. All dimensions are subject to conventional industry tolerances.

❖ Tolerances exist throughout the construction industry for many products and practices. Even though many dimensions in the standard are expressed as absolute or ranges, this is not intended to negate the existing tolerances.

The intent is to recognize conventional industry tolerances for field construction. This applies to the field work, not the design work. Information on specific tolerances may be available through industry or trade organizations and published references. A designer may choose to avoid specifying precisely the minimum and maximum where possible so that achieved dimensions fall within the requirements.

104.3 Figures. Unless specifically stated, figures included herein are provided for informational purposes only and are not considered part of the standard.

❖ The graphic conventions shown in Figure 104.3 are typical of those used in construction drawings. An effort has been made to set forth consistently those dimensions for which a tolerance has been set. Review the applicable text for the exact and full requirements.

104.4 Floor or Floor Surface. The terms floor or floor surface refer to the finish floor surface or ground surface, as applicable.

❖ Dimensions for clearances are measured from the finished floor to the underside of the surface above. The measurement should be from the finished floor surface, not the sub-floor. When elements are installed outdoors, this same measurement is made from the ground or pavement surface.

104.5 Referenced Sections. Unless specifically stated otherwise, a reference to another section or subsection within this standard includes all subsections of the referenced section or subsection.

❖ References include subsections. For example, a reference to Section 305 includes all the requirements in Section 305.1 through 305.7.2.

105 Referenced Standards

105.1 General. The standards listed in Section 105.2 shall be considered part of this standard to the prescribed extent of each such reference. Where criteria in this standard differ from those of these referenced standards, the criteria of this standard shall apply.

❖ A referenced standard or portion thereof is an enforceable extension of this standard as if the content of the standard were included in the body of this standard. For example, Section 407.1 references ASME A17.1 in its entirety for elevators. In those cases where the code references only portions of a standard, the use and application of the referenced standard is limited to those portions that are specifically identified. For example, Section 702.1 requires audible and visual alarms and notification appliances to be installed as required in NFPA 72. Section 702.1 cannot be construed to require compliance with NFPA 72 in its entirety. It is the intent of the standard to be in harmony with the referenced standards. If conflicts occur because of scope or purpose, the ICC A117.1 text governs.

105.2 Standards.

❖ Reference to existing standards reduces the probability of creating unnecessary conflicts and ensures that current technology is considered.

105.2.1 Manual on Uniform Traffic Control Devices: MUTCD - 2000 (The Federal Highway Administration, Office of Transportation Operations, Room 3408, 400 7th Street, S.W., Washington, DC 20590)

❖ This standard is referenced in Section 703.8, Pedestrian Signals.

Convention	Description
36 / 915	dimension showing English units (in inches unless otherwise specified) above the line and SI units (in millimeters unless otherwise specified) below the line
6 / 150	dimension for small measurements
33 - 36 / 840 - 915	dimension showing a range with minimum - maximum
min	minimum
max	maximum
>	greater than
≥	greater than or equal to
<	less than
≤	less than or equal to
 – – – – –	boundary of clear floor space or maneuvering clearance
 – · – · – ℄	centerline
 – · — · –	a permitted element or its extension
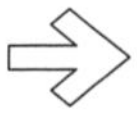 ⇒	direction of travel or approach
 ▬	a wall, floor, ceiling or other element cut in section or plan
 ▬	a highlighted element in elevation or plan
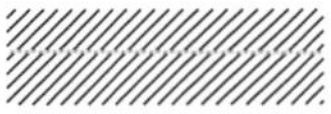 ▨	location zone of element, control or feature

Fig. 104.3
Graphic Convention for Figures

105.2.2 National Fire Alarm Code: NFPA 72-2002 (National Fire Protection Association, 1 Batterymarch Park, Quincy, MA 02269–9101)

❖ Past editions of the ICC A117.1 included audible and visible alarms requirements intended to be consistent with NFPA 72. Section 702, Alarms, now references NFPA for installation of audible and visible alarms and notification appliances. This standard is referenced for dwelling unit smoke detectors in Section 1005.2 and 1005.4.1.

105.2.3 Power Assist and Low Energy Power Operated Doors: ANSI/BHMA A156.19-1997 (Builders Hardware Manufacturers' Association, 355 Lexington Avenue, 17th Floor, New York, NY 10017)

❖ This standard is referenced in Sections 404.3, Automatic Doors, 408.3.1.2 for doors on limited-use/lim-

ited-application elevators and 409.3.1 for doors on private residence elevators.

105.2.4 Power Operated Pedestrian Doors: ANSI/BHMA A156.10-1999 (Builders Hardware Manufacturers' Association, 355 Lexington Avenue, 17th Floor, New York, NY 10017)

❖ This standard is referenced in Section 404.3 Automatic Doors.

105.2.5 Safety Code for Elevators and Escalators: ASME/ANSI A17.1-2000 and Addenda A17.1a-2002 (American Society of Mechanical Engineers International, Three Park Avenue, New York, NY 10016–5990)

❖ This standard is referenced in Sections 407.1, 407.4.3 and 407.4.10, Elevators; 408.1 and 408.4.3, Limited-use/limited-application elevators; 409.1, Private residence elevators; and 805.9, Escalators.

105.2.6 Safety Standard for Platform Lifts and Stairway Chairlifts: ASME/ANSI A18.1-1999, with Addenda A18.1a-2001 and A18.1b - 2001 (American Society of Mechanical Engineers International, Three Park Avenue, New York, NY 10016–5990)

❖ This standard is referenced in Section 410.1 for platform lifts.

106 Definitions

106.1 General. For the purpose of this standard, the terms listed in Section 106.5 have the indicated meaning.

❖ Terms that may have a specific meaning when used in the context of this standard are defined in Section 106.5.

106.2 Terms Defined in Referenced Standards. Terms specifically defined in a referenced standard, and not defined in this section, shall have the specified meaning from the referenced standard.

❖ Words and terms defined in the referenced standards in Section 105.2 are applicable for this standard unless defined otherwise in Section 106.5.

106.3 Undefined Terms. The meaning of terms not specifically defined in this standard or in a referenced standard shall be as defined by collegiate dictionaries in the sense that the context implies.

❖ Words or terms not defined within the ICC A117.1 are intended to be applied based on their "ordinarily accepted meanings." The intent is that a dictionary definition may suffice if it is in context. Oftentimes, terms used throughout the standard are not specifically defined in the standard or even in a dictionary. In such a case, the definitions contained in the referenced standards (see Section 105.2) and published textbooks on the subject in question are good resources.

106.4 Interchangeability. Words, terms, and phrases used in the singular include the plural, and those used in the plural include the singular.

❖ Although the definitions contained or referenced in Section 106 are to be taken literally, gender and tense are interchangeable.

106.5 Defined Terms.

❖ Terms defined in the standard are listed alphabetically in Section 106.5. Standards, by their very nature, are technical documents. Literally every word, term and punctuation mark can add to or change the meaning or the intended result. These terms often have multiple meanings depending on the context or discipline being used at the time. For these reasons, a consensus on the specific meaning of terms contained in the standard must be maintained. Section 106.5 performs this function by stating clearly what specific terms mean for the purpose of this standard.

accessible: Describes a site, building, facility, or portion thereof that complies with this standard.

❖ This general definition states that compliance with this standard will result in accessibility for the built environment. The definition does not attempt to prescribe any criteria for an accessible element. This is accomplished through the various requirements within the standard. (Refer to Section 1002 for requirements for Accessible dwelling and sleeping units.)

administrative authority: A jurisdictional body that adopts or enforces regulations and standards for the design, construction, or operation of buildings and facilities.

❖ Building codes are typically adopted at the state or local level. A city or county building department or a state building commission are examples of an administrative authority with code enforcement responsibility.

characters: Letters, numbers, punctuation marks, and typographic symbols.

❖ See the commentary for Section 703, Signs.

children's use: Spaces and elements specifically designed for use primarily by people 12 years old and younger.

❖ Specific provisions allowing for children's smaller size are stated for drinking fountains, water closets, toilet compartments, lavatories, sinks, dining surfaces and work surfaces.

circulation path: An exterior or interior way of passage from one place to another for pedestrians.

❖ A circulation path differs from an accessible route in that it can be used by most pedestrians, but not necessarily by those who use wheelchairs. Accessible stairs complying with Section 504 may be part of a circulation path, but not of an accessible route.

counter slope: Any slope opposing the running slope of a curb ramp.

❖ Slopes intersecting and opposite a running slope may create difficulty for persons using wheelchairs and persons with an ambulatory impairment. For example, the slope of a street from the center to the side creates a counter slope to the running slope of a curb ramp. Another example is the slope of a street gutter, which opposes the running slope of a curb ramp. See the commentary on Section 406.2 and Figure 406.2.

cross slope: The slope that is perpendicular to the direction of travel (see running slope).

❖ Cross slopes are a concern for persons with mobility impairments when they have to deal with a slope in two directions at the same time. See commentary on Section 405.3.

curb ramp: A short ramp cutting through a curb or built up to it.

❖ Curb ramps provide a means of access from a sidewalk to a street, parking lot or other vehicular way for a person using a wheelchair. The slope of a curb ramp also provides a cue to long-cane users that they have arrived at an intersection. See Section 406.

destination-oriented elevator system: An elevator system that provides lobby controls for the selection of destination floors, lobby indicators designating which elevator to board, and a car indicator designating the floors at which the car will stop.

❖ This type of elevator system has a unique call system. The intent is to allow for an efficient system of determining elevator car assignments and is an alternative to a zoned elevator system. Requirements are offered as exceptions to general elevator requirements in Section 407.

detectable warning: A standardized surface feature built in or applied to floor surfaces to warn of hazards on a circulation path.

❖ See commentary to Sections 406.12, 406.13, 406.14 and 705.

dwelling unit: A single unit providing complete, independent living facilities for one or more persons including permanent provisions for living, sleeping, eating, cooking and sanitation.

❖ A dwelling unit contains elements necessary for independent living, including provisions for living spaces (family rooms, living rooms, dens, etc.); sleeping quarters; food preparation and eating spaces; and personal hygiene, cleanliness and sanitation facilities. A dwelling unit is occupied in one of two ways, either through renting or by ownership. The standard requirements are applied consistently to all dwellings, regardless of the type of ownership. Both owner-occupied and rented or leased dwellings must comply with the requirements of the standard.

A dwelling unit can exist singularly as a one-family dwelling or in combination with other dwelling units. When two dwelling units are grouped together in the same structure, the structure is considered a two-family dwelling or duplex. Three or more dwelling units in the same structure are considered as a multiple-family dwelling or multiple single-family dwellings, such as an apartment building, condominiums or townhouses (see Chapter 10).

element: An architectural or mechanical component of a building, facility, space, or site.

❖ Examples of elements are telephones, curb ramps, doors, drinking fountains, seating and water closets.

elevator car call sequential step scanning: A technology used to enter a car call by means of an up or down floor selection button.

❖ See the commentary for Section 407.4.8.

facility: All or any portion of a building, structure, or area, including the site on which such building, structure, or area is located, wherein specific services are provided or activities are performed.

❖ An office, suite of offices, courtroom, condominium complex, strip mall and hospital are examples of a facility.

key surface: The surface or plane of any key or button that must be touched to activate or deactivate an operable part or a machine function or enter data.

❖ Key surface requirements for automatic teller machines and fare machines are discussed in Sections 707.6.1, 707.6.2, 707.9. Requirements for elevator call buttons and car controls do not use this term.

marked crossing: A crosswalk or other identified path intended for pedestrian use in crossing a vehicular way.

❖ Markings may be on the floor or ground, or signage may be used to mark a crossing. Regulations for color or pattern are often specified by state Departments of Transportation.

operable part: A component of an element used to insert or withdraw objects, or to activate, deactivate, or adjust the element.

❖ This term is used extensively, typically with a reference to Section 309. Examples of operable parts are telephone coin slots, push buttons, switches and handles. See Sections 309, 606.7, 1002.9, 1003.9 and 1004.9.

pictogram: A pictorial symbol that represents activities, facilities, or concepts.

❖ See the commentary for Section 703.5.

ramp: A walking surface that has a running slope steeper than 1:20.

❖ On an accessible route, ramps provide a means for independently going from one elevation to another by persons who cannot use stairs. See Section 405.

running slope: The slope that is parallel to the direction of travel (see cross slope).

❖ Running slope for a ramp is measured from landing to landing. See Sections 405.2 and 406.1.

sign: An architectural element composed of displayed textual, symbolic, tactile, or pictorial information.

❖ Uniformity of signage design and location at a facility provides for independent use by blind and sight-impaired persons. See Section 703.

Accessible elements can be identified using the International Symbols of Accessibility (see Figure 703.6.3.1).

site: A parcel of land bounded by a property line or a designated portion of a public right-of-way.

❖ This term is typically defined in model building codes. Accessibility requirements include the site, as well as the buildings within the site.

A site for purposes of accessibility requirements is the same as that considered in the application of other code requirements. The property within the boundaries of the site is under the control of the owner. The owner can be held responsible for code compliance of the site and all facilities on it.

sleeping unit: A room or space in which people sleep that can also include permanent provisions for living, sleeping, eating, and either sanitation or kitchen facilities but not both. Such rooms and spaces that are also part of a dwelling unit are not sleeping units.

❖ This definition is included to coordinate the *Fair Housing Act Guidelines* with the code. The definition for "sleeping unit" is needed to clarify the differences between sleeping units and dwelling units. Some examples would be a hotel guestroom, a dormitory, a boarding house, congregate residences, assisted living facilities, nursing homes, etc. Another example would be a studio apartment with a kitchenette (i.e., microwave, sink, refrigerator). Because the cooking arrangements are not permanent, this configuration would be considered a sleeping unit, not a dwelling unit. As already defined in this standard, a dwelling unit must contain permanent independent facilities for living, sleeping, eating, cooking and sanitation. (See Chapter 10.)

tactile: Describes an object that can be perceived using the sense of touch.

❖ Tactile requirements for signs are contained in Sections 703.3 and 703.4. This would include both raised letters and Braille.

TTY: An abbreviation for teletypewriter. Equipment that employs interactive, text-based communications through the transmission of coded signals across the standard telephone network. The term TTY also refers to devices known as text telephones and TDDs.

❖ TTYs include telecommunications display devices, telecommunication devices for deaf persons, text telephones and computers. See Sections 704.4 through 704.7.

vehicular way: A route provided for vehicular traffic.

❖ Examples are streets, driveways and parking lots.

walk: An exterior pathway with a prepared surface for pedestrian use.

❖ This includes general pedestrian areas such as sidewalks, plazas and courts.

Chapter 2. Scoping

❖ Chapter 2 is a general overview of the provisions within this technical standard.

- Section 201 covers the general principle for what makes something accessible.

- Section 202 introduces the special provisions for Accessible, Type A and Type B dwelling and sleeping units.

- Section 203 states that the administrative authority will administer this standard as an extension of their scoping requirements.

201 General

This standard provides technical criteria for making sites, facilities, buildings, and elements accessible. The administrative authority shall provide scoping provisions to specify the extent to which these technical criteria apply. These scoping provisions shall address the application of this standard to: each building and occupancy type; new construction, alterations, temporary facilities, and existing buildings; specific site and building elements; and to multiple elements or spaces provided within a site or building.

❖ The standard does not establish which or how many buildings, facilities and spaces or elements within these spaces must be made accessible. This standard correlates with the adoption of scoping provisions by the administrative authority. This is typically accomplished through the adoption of a model building code, which references this standard. The adopted scoping provisions will establish what, how many and where accessibility is required, and this standard will establish how those required elements and spaces are to be made accessible. A set of recommended scoping provisions was developed by the Board for the Coordination of the Model Codes of the Council of American Building Officials, and is reflected in the current editions of the model building codes published by the International Code Council® (ICC®).

By adopting this standard through the building code, enforcement can be accomplished at the state or local level. In contrast, the requirements of Title II of the Americans with Disabilities Act (ADA) can be enforced only as a civil rights statute by the United States Department of Justice. Although many provisions in this standard are comparable to parallel requirements contained in the Americans with Disabilities Act Accessibility Guidelines (ADAAG), compliance with the ADA should be verified independently. ICC continues to work with the federal government to coordinate requirements.

Scoping documents sometimes require elements, such as toilet facilities, and then specify which of those elements must be accessible. Scoping documents may require accessible elements only when those elements are provided, such as passenger drop offs. Certain elements covered in ICC A117.1 may not be scoped at all. For example, the ICC A117.1 provisions contain technical provisions for telephones in Section 704. If the scoping document does not specify accessible phones, the accessibility requirements in ICC A117.1 for phones are not a requirement, but a choice.

Certain items may be limited by the standard. For example, the scoping document may require accessible lavatories in accordance with Section 606. The enhanced reach ranges in Section 606.5, starting with "where … required" must be specifically scoped in order to be applicable. Section 606.5 is not generally applicable to all accessible lavatories.

202 Dwelling and Sleeping Units

Chapter 10 of this standard contains dwelling unit and sleeping unit criteria for Accessible units, Type A units, Type B units, and units with accessible communication features. The administrative authority shall specify, in separate scoping provisions, the extent to which these technical criteria apply. These scoping provisions shall address the types and numbers of units required to comply with each set of unit criteria.

❖ Chapter 10 covers technical provisions for dwelling and sleeping units. Please see the commentary for these defined terms in Section 106.5. The provisions for Accessible units and Type A units exceed Fair Housing Act requirements. The provisions for Type B units are intended to be consistent with the provisions in the Fair Housing Act. Accessible units are considered more accessible than Type A units. Type A units are considered more accessible than Type B units. Scoping provisions for all three types of units can be found in the model building code.

203 Administration

The administrative authority shall provide an appropriate review and approval process to ensure compliance with this standard.

❖ Where this standard is adopted by the administrative authority, a construction project that must comply with these provisions should be reviewed for compliance in the same manner the project is reviewed to determine compliance with other provisions of the applicable building code.

Chapter 3. Building Blocks

❖ Chapter 3 describes the core requirements that are referenced by other sections of this standard. The intent is to reduce duplication of requirements through the use of 'building blocks.' For example, knee and toe clearances are referenced for drinking fountains, working surfaces, dining surfaces and lavatories.

- Section 301 is a general statement indicating the 'building blocks' may be referenced directly from scoping provisions, or as part of requirements elsewhere in this standard.

- Section 302 contains requirements for floor and ground surfaces.

- Section 303 sets out criteria for changes in level, typically when floor surfaces change or at door thresholds.

- Section 304 provides technical criteria for turning.

- Section 305 contains criteria for a clear floor space for a wheelchair, including moving into a restricted area such as an alcove.

- Section 306 establishes the three dimensional space needed for clearances for knees and toes of a person using a wheelchair when they move under an element or counter.

- Section 307 contains criteria for objects that may protrude over a walking surface so the chances for injury for person with visual impairments are reduced.

- Section 308 provides guidance for the height of items so they can be reached by someone using a wheelchair. This includes reaching over obstructions such as a counter.

- Section 309 provides technical criteria for any operable parts, such as light switches, door hardware or controls on plumbing fixtures.

301 General

❖ This chapter is appropriately named "building blocks." The chapter provides the core requirements that are used to establish accessible items. These technical provisions and the limitations within them are used in the later chapters for the full range of elements and spaces that are included within the scope of the standard and eliminate the need for duplicating the provisions within numerous sections.

301.1 Scope. The provisions of Chapter 3 shall apply where required by the scoping provisions adopted by the administrative authority or by Chapters 4 through 10.

❖ Although the provisions of this chapter may, in general, improve the design and usability of all buildings, it is important to note that the section is qualified by the phrase "where required." This is intended to be consistent with the fact that scoping provisions are not included in this standard. See the commentary for Chapter 2.

302 Floor Surfaces

❖ Note that Section 104.4 states that the term "floor surface" refers as applicable to the finished floor or ground surface.

302.1 General. Floor surfaces shall be stable, firm, and slip resistant, and shall comply with Section 302. Changes in level in floor surfaces shall comply with Section 303.

❖ Ambulatory and semi-ambulatory people who have difficulty maintaining balance and those with restricted gaits are particularly sensitive to slipping and tripping hazards. For those people, a stable and regular surface is necessary to walk safely. Wheelchairs are propelled most easily on surfaces that are hard, stable and regular. Soft, loose surfaces such as shag carpet, loose sand, gravel, crushed stone or wet clay, and irregular surfaces such as cobblestone, significantly impede movement of a wheelchair.

A stable surface is one that remains unchanged by contaminants or applied force, so that when the contaminant or force is removed, the surface returns to its original condition. A firm surface resists deformation by either indentation or particles moving on its surface. It is not the intent of the standard to require only paved surfaces; however, any other types (e.g., wood chips, gravel) would need to be evaluated.

Slip resistance is based on the frictional force necessary to keep a shoe or crutch tip from slipping on a walking surface under the conditions of use likely for that surface. For example, outside surfaces or entryways may be wet from rain or snow, or bathroom floors may be wet and should be evaluated under those conditions; however, the tile on the upstairs hallway would typically not be influenced by outside weather and should be evaluated in a dry condition. Although it is known that the static coefficient of friction is one basis of slip resistance, there is not as yet a generally accepted method to evaluate the slip resistance of walking surfaces for all use conditions.

302.2 Carpet. Carpet or carpet tile shall be securely attached and shall have a firm cushion, pad, or backing or no cushion or pad. Carpet or carpet tile shall have a level loop, textured loop, level cut pile, or level cut/uncut pile texture. The pile shall be $^1/_2$ inch (13 mm) maximum in height. Exposed edges of carpet shall be fastened to the floor and shall have trim along the entire length of the exposed edge. Carpet edge trim shall comply with Section 303.

❖ Carpet can significantly increase the amount of force (roll resistance) needed to propel a wheelchair over a surface. The firmer the carpet and backing, the lower the roll resistance. Therefore, although no pad is preferred, if a pad is installed, it must be firm. The $^1/_2$-inch (13 mm) pile height is measured from the top of the carpet to the backing, cushion or pad. The edge of the carpet must be installed so as to avoid tripping hazards and allow for wheelchair movement over that edge.

Much more is to be done in developing both quantitative and qualitative criteria for carpeting. However, certain functional characteristics are well established. When both carpet and padding are used, it is desirable to have minimum movement (preferably none) between the floor and the pad and the pad and the carpet, which would allow the carpet to hump or warp. In heavily trafficked areas, a thick, soft (plush) pad or cushion, particularly in combination with long carpet

pile, makes it difficult for individuals in wheelchairs and those with other ambulatory disabilities to get about. Firm carpeting is achieved through proper selection and combination of pad and carpet, sometimes with the elimination of the pad or cushion, and with proper installation.

302.3 Openings. Openings in floor surfaces shall be of a size that does not permit the passage of a $^1/_2$ inch (13 mm) diameter sphere, except as allowed in Sections 407.4.3, 408.4.3, 409.4.3, 410.4, and 805.10. Elongated openings shall be placed so that the long dimension is perpendicular to the dominant direction of travel.

❖ These limitations are intended to eliminate openings of a size or orientation into which a crutch tip or the wheels of a chair could drop [see commentary Figure C302.3(a)]. If elongated openings are oriented perpendicular to the expected direction of travel, the casters of a wheelchair will roll over them without great difficulty because the openings will be no wider than $^1/_2$ inch (13 mm) in the direction of travel [see commentary Figure C302.3(b)].

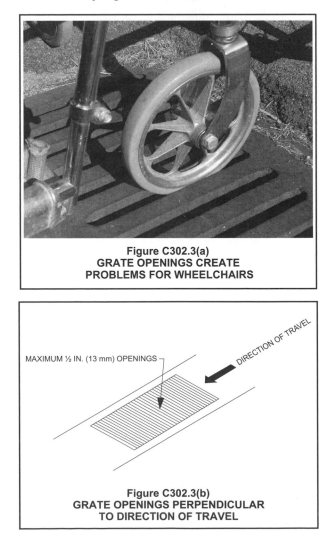

Figure C302.3(a)
GRATE OPENINGS CREATE
PROBLEMS FOR WHEELCHAIRS

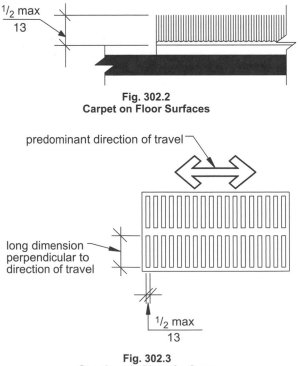

Fig. 302.2
Carpet on Floor Surfaces

Fig. 302.3
Openings in Floor Surfaces

Figure C302.3(b)
GRATE OPENINGS PERPENDICULAR
TO DIRECTION OF TRAVEL

303 Changes in Level

303.1 General. Changes in level in floor surfaces shall comply with Section 303.

❖ As used in the standard, a change in level is a change in the elevation of a walking surface. Typical examples would be a change in floor surface from tile to carpet or door thresholds.

303.2 Vertical. Changes in level of $1/4$ inch (6.4 mm) maximum in height shall be permitted to be vertical.

❖ Abrupt changes in elevation can create a significant barrier for a person using a wheelchair because of the small caster wheels on the wheelchair. Changes in elevation up to $1/4$ inch (6 mm) can be negotiated by a person using a wheelchair with minimal difficulty and do not present an unreasonable tripping hazard. The standard permits a vertical edge at the level change and does not require a beveled or special edge treatment.

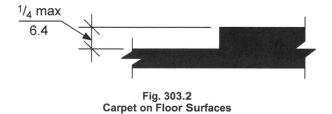

Fig. 303.2
Carpet on Floor Surfaces

303.3 Beveled. Changes in level greater than $1/4$ inch (6.4 mm) in height and not more than $1/2$ inch (13 mm) maximum in height shall be beveled with a slope not steeper than 1:2.

Changes in level greater than $1/2$ inch (13 mm) in height shall be ramped and shall comply with Section 405 or 406.

❖ Changes in elevation between $1/4$ inch and $1/2$ inch (6 mm and 13 mm) cannot be as easily negotiated by a wheelchair. They create edges on the accessible route surface that can "catch" the small caster wheels on a wheelchair. Additionally, they present a greater potential tripping hazard because of the increased likelihood of a crutch tip or toe of a shoe catching the edge. For changes in elevation in this range, it is preferable that the entire edge be beveled as shown in Figure 303.3(b) of the standard. However, by combining the provisions of Section 303.2 and 303.3 it could be acceptable to bevel only the portion that is over $1/4$ inch in height. See Fig. 303.3(a). This permits the bottom $1/4$ inch (6 mm) of the edge created by the elevation change to be an abrupt vertical change and requires the remainder of the edge between $1/4$ inch (6 mm) and $1/2$ inch (13 mm) to be sloped or beveled at a slope no steeper than 1 unit vertical to 2 units horizontal (50-percent slope). This is significantly steeper than is allowed for a ramp but is adequate for the limited rise. However, in no case may the combined changes in level exceed $1/2$ inch (13 mm).

Changes in level exceeding $1/2$ inch (13 mm) must comply with ramps, curb ramps or sloped walks.

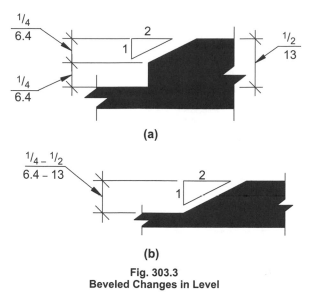

(a)

(b)
Fig. 303.3
Beveled Changes in Level

304 Turning Space

304.1 General. A turning space shall comply with Section 304.

❖ This section provides the requirements for a space that will permit a person using a wheelchair, scooter or other walking aids to turn and change directions along their route of travel. The standard specifies where the turning space is actually required (see Sections 603.2.1, 803.2, 1002.3.2 and 1003.3.2).

304.2 Floor Surface. Floor surfaces of a turning space shall have a slope not steeper than 1:48 and shall comply with Section 302.

❖ Any type of cross slope steeper than 1:48 on the surface of a turning space can cause considerable difficulty in maneuvering or propelling a wheelchair in a straight line. The 1:48 slope is for allowances to slope surfaces to drain or for material tolerances. For ease of use, abrupt changes in elevation (e.g., such as a change in flooring or a threshold) within the turning space should be avoided; however, if they are present, they must be limited to $1/2$ inch (13 mm) or less in accordance with Section 303. This is not intended to prohibit tile grout lines or rounded edges on wood deck boards. The reference to Section 302 would require the turning space to have a stable and firm surface.

304.3 Size. Turning spaces shall comply with Section 304.3.1 or 304.3.2.

❖ This section simply refers to both the circular space and the T-shaped space as acceptable methods for providing a turning space. The specific requirements for these two methods are found in Sections 304.3.1 and 304.3.2.

The user and wheelchair shown in commentary Figure C102(a) represent typical dimensions for a large adult male. The space requirements in this standard are based on maneuvering clearances that accommodate most manual wheelchairs. Commentary Figure C102(a) provides a uniform reference for design not covered by this standard. Sport or other special wheelchairs do not necessarily fall within the dimensions contained within this section.

(a) Circular

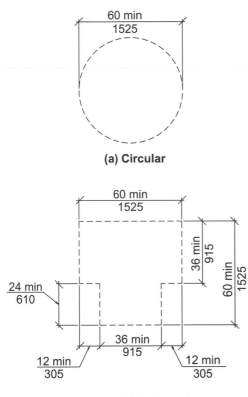

(b) T-shaped

Fig. 304.3
Size of Turning Space

304.3.1 Circular Space. The turning space shall be a circular space with a 60-inch (1525 mm) minimum diameter. The turning space shall be permitted to include knee and toe clearance complying with Section 306.

❖ This section specifies a minimum space of 60 inches (1525 mm) diameter for a pivoting 180-degree (3.14 rad) turn of a wheelchair. This space is adequate for turning around, but many people are not able to turn without repeated tries and bumping into surrounding objects [see commentary Figure C304.3.1(a)].

To make a turn, both wheels are simultaneously turned in opposing directions within a 60-inch diameter. For electrically powered wheelchairs, coordination of this opposing wheel rotation, coupled with the longer wheel base typical of powered chairs, makes the

full turning space even more critical compared to a smaller, manually operated wheelchair.

The standard does permit objects such as lavatories, drinking fountains or any other item to encroach into the 60-inch diameter circle provided the knee and toe clearances beneath such objects comply with Section 306 of the standard. See Section 306 for additional details and discussion. This will mean that when properly located, the space under an element may be usable when making a turn [see commentary Figure C304.3.1(b)].

304.3.2 T-Shaped Space. The turning space shall be a T-shaped space within a 60-inch (1525 mm) minimum square, with arms and base 36 inches (915 mm) minimum in width. Each arm of the T shall be clear of obstructions 12 inches (305 mm) minimum in each direction, and the base shall be clear of obstructions 24 inches (610 mm) minimum. The turning space shall be permitted to include knee and toe clearance complying with Section 306 only at the end of either the base or one arm.

❖ The T-shaped space permits the user to approach and turn within the space. The T-shaped space is every bit as acceptable as the circular space listed in Section 304.3.1. The layout of the T and the approach to it may be made from either direction on the arm or from the base. This type of turning space is commonly used at intersections of accessible routes or within rooms or areas where cabinets or counters may be located in the spaces adjacent to the T [see commentary Figure C304.3.2(a)]. As discussed in the commentary with Section 304.3.1, the T-shaped space may include knee and toe clearances beneath an object as long as it is in compliance with Section 306. See Section 306 for additional details and discussion [see commentary Figure C304.3.2(b)].

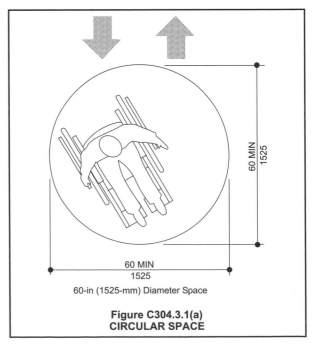

60-in (1525-mm) Diameter Space

Figure C304.3.1(a)
CIRCULAR SPACE

304.4 Door Swing. Unless otherwise specified, doors shall be permitted to swing into turning spaces.

❖ A door swinging through the turning circle will generally not create a problem because Section 404.2.4 requires maneuvering clearances around the door. This permits the user to operate the door and then, once it is closed or out of the turning space, they are able to make their turn.

305 Clear Floor Space

❖ Note that Section 104.4 states that the term floor surface refers to the finished floor or ground surface as applicable.

305.1 General. A clear floor space shall comply with Section 305.

❖ This section assures that a properly sized space is available for people to be able to position themselves to use accessible fixtures and facilities. The user and wheelchair shown in commentary Figure C102(a) represent typical dimensions for a large adult male. The space requirements in this standard are based on maneuvering clearances that accommodate most manual wheelchairs. Commentary Figure C102(a) provides a uniform reference for design not covered by this standard. Sport or other special wheelchairs do not necessarily fall within the dimensions contained within this section.

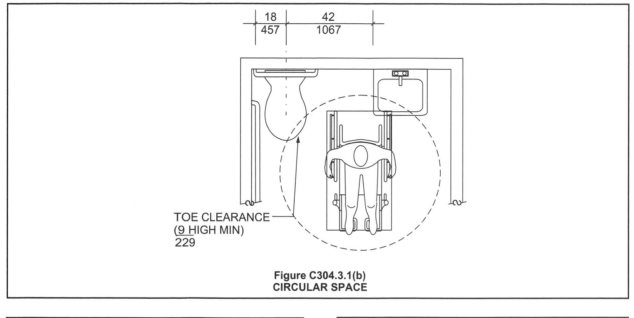

Figure C304.3.1(b)
CIRCULAR SPACE

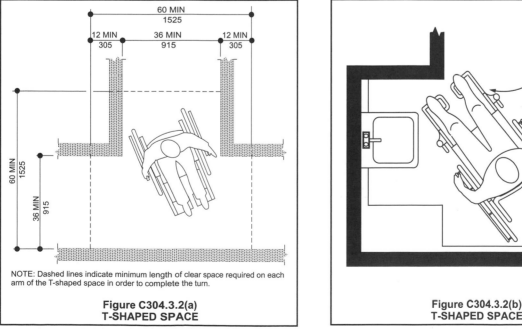

NOTE: Dashed lines indicate minimum length of clear space required on each arm of the T-shaped space in order to complete the turn.

Figure C304.3.2(a)
T-SHAPED SPACE

Figure C304.3.2(b)
T-SHAPED SPACE

305.2 Floor Surfaces. Floor surfaces of a clear floor space shall have a slope not steeper than 1:48 and shall comply with Section 302.

❖ Cross slopes steeper than 1:48 on walks and ground or floor surfaces cause considerable difficulty in propelling a wheelchair in a straight line or when moving into a position to use an accessible item. Steeper slopes can also create an unstable situation where users may be more likely to tip or simply feel off balance. See also the commentary at Section 302. Section 302 addresses the general characteristics of floor and ground surfaces, including such things as slip resistance and surface texture. These provisions are equally necessary for the designated clear floor space anticipated to be occupied by a person using a wheelchair; therefore, compliance with Section 302 is required.

305.3 Size. The clear floor space shall be 48 inches (1220 mm) minimum in length and 30 inches (760 mm) minimum in width.

❖ The minimum clear floor space specified in the standard is consistent with the typical dimensions of an average adult male, discussed in the commentary for Sections 102 and 305.1. An additional 2 inches (51 mm) of clear width on each side is included to anticipate hand and forearm clearance beyond the chair. This fundamental dimension is the basis for many of the provisions throughout this standard for maneuvering clearances and spaces anticipated to be occupied by a wheelchair.

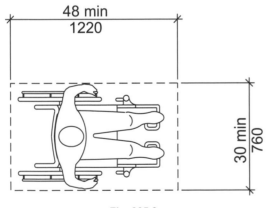

Fig. 305.3
Size of Clear Floor Space

305.4 Knee and Toe Clearance. Unless otherwise specified, clear floor space shall be permitted to include knee and toe clearance complying with Section 306.

❖ Section 306 contains the dimensional criteria for knee and toe clearances that permit a person using a wheelchair access to an element or fixture while their knees or toes extend beneath it. For example, a forward approach to a countertop work surface, lavatory or a drinking fountain necessitates the feet and legs extending under that element. The provisions of Section

305.4 simply establish that, as a general rule, the knee and toe clearances may be used at the front end of the clear floor space which serves the fixture. In many cases, such as Sections 606.2, 902.2 and 1003.12.3.1, the standard specifically requires the clear floor area to include knee and toe clearances below an element (see commentary Figure C305.4).

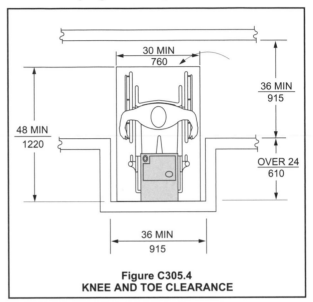

Figure C305.4
KNEE AND TOE CLEARANCE

305.5 Position. Unless otherwise specified, the clear floor space shall be positioned for either forward or parallel approach to an element.

❖ To use an element or device such as a plumbing fixture, telephone or light switch, or to occupy a space such as a viewing location in an assembly occupancy or the access aisle adjacent to a parking space, a person using a wheelchair must approach the element and subsequently position the chair in preparation for use of the element. Assuming an unlimited amount of space around a given point, a person in a wheelchair could approach that point from an infinite number of angles. Where an accessible element or fixture is located on or at a wall surface, the person using a wheelchair could approach the element from any one of 180 degrees of angle, assuming there are no obstructions to the clear floor space.

This provision would result in the greatest degree of accessibility by affording the full range of possible approach angles. However, this also requires a larger clear floor space around accessible elements, which could place unnecessary constraints on floor layout and design, spacing of a battery of accessible elements, corridor and passageway widths, and similar building features. To balance such design impacts with an acceptable degree of accessibility, the standard requires that the approach to accessible elements need be provided based on either (not both) a parallel approach or a forward approach to the element.

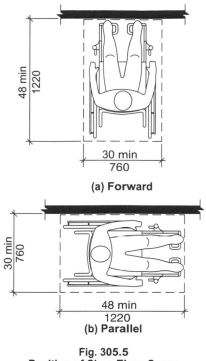

(a) Forward

(b) Parallel

Fig. 305.5
Position of Clear Floor Space

305.6 Approach. One full, unobstructed side of the clear floor space shall adjoin or overlap an accessible route or adjoin another clear floor space.

❖ The requirement that one full side of the wheelchair clear floor space adjoin an accessible route ensures that the clear floor space at the accessible element is reachable from the accessible route that leads to the accessible element. This can be the either the 30 inch (760 mm) side or the 48 inch (1220 mm) side. Clearly, any clear floor space at an element or fixture is of no value if it cannot be reached from an accessible route.

305.7 Alcoves. If a clear floor space is in an alcove or otherwise confined on all or part of three sides, additional maneuvering clearances complying with Sections 305.7.1 and 305.7.2 shall be provided, as applicable.

❖ The provisions for alcoves require additional width for a forward approach or additional length for a parallel approach when the alcove or other obstruction exceeds the depths specified in Section 305.7.1 or 305.7.2. This additional size is intended to ensure that sufficient space is provided to maneuver the wheelchair into position for using the element located within the alcove (see Figure 305.7).

305.7.1 Parallel Approach. Where the clear floor space is positioned for a parallel approach, the alcove shall be 60 inches (1525 mm) minimum in width where the depth exceeds 15 inches (380 mm).

❖ Similar to the parallel parking of a car, maneuvering clearances are needed to permit a person using a wheel-

chair to perform a parallel approach and then transition into the clear floor space that is located within an area where three sides are confined. Looking at commentary Figure C102(a), the length of the chair and the users feet are at the 48 inch (1220 mm) limit which is normally required for the clear floor space. Therefore, the increased length of 60 inches (1525 mm) is needed when the clear floor space is located within an alcove.

305.7.2 Forward Approach. Where the clear floor space is positioned for a forward approach, the alcove shall be 36 inches (915 mm) minimum in width where the depth exceeds 24 inches (610 mm).

❖ The normal 30 inch (760 mm) width of a clear floor space must be increased to 36 inches (915 mm) when any type of obstruction occurs on all or part of three sides and the clear floor space extends more than 24 inches (610 mm) into the confined area. A drinking fountain located within a deep alcove or a countertop work area with adjacent base cabinets below would be examples where this provision could be applicable. It is important to consider how far the required clear floor space extends into the alcove, not just the actual depth of the alcove (see commentary Figure C305.4).

As an example, if a counter top work area had 31 inches (790 mm) of clear floor space located out in a circulation aisle and had the remaining 17 inches (430 mm) of length as the minimum size knee and toe clearance beneath the counter, it would not matter that the actual depth of the area beneath the counter where the knee and toe clearance was located extended to a greater depth of 28 inches (710 mm). In such a situation, the width would remain as a minimum of 30 inches (760 mm) for the clear floor space.

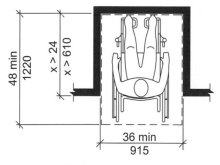

(a) Forward Approach

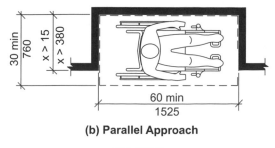

(b) Parallel Approach

Fig. 305.7
Maneuvering Clearance in an Alcove

306 Knee and Toe Clearance

306.1 General. Where space beneath an element is included as part of clear floor space at an element, clearance at an element, or a turning space, the space shall comply with Section 306. Additional space beyond knee and toe clearance shall be permitted beneath elements.

❖ Minimum dimensions for knee and toe clearances are specified to provide design criteria when access to an accessible element or fixture involves using the space underneath an element or fixture. For example, a forward approach to a counter top or work surface necessitates the feet and legs extending under the counter top or work surface [see commentary Figure C306.1(a)]. The knee and toe clearance dimensions establish the required unobstructed space that must be provided to afford access to the element. Where knee and toe clearance is required, such as beneath a lavatory or drinking fountain, those provisions will reference Section 306.

Knee and toe clearances are often a 'package deal.' Provisions for minimums and maximums for both knee and toes clearances must be addressed when looking for adequate clearance under an object [see commentary Figures C306.1(b) and C306.1(c) and Sections 306.2 and 306.3].

Clearances are measured in relation to the usable clear floor space, not necessarily the vertical support for an element. When determining clearance under an element, care should be taken to ensure the space is clear of any obstructions that would reduce the effective knee and toe clearances.

306.2 Toe Clearance.

❖ The subsections of Section 306.2 contain all the technical provisions for toe clearance. Figure 306.2 shows some of the requirements for the toe space. While knee and toe clearances have separate technical requirements, they are often required as a package. See the commentary for Section 306.1 for related discussion.

306.2.1 General. Space beneath an element between the floor and 9 inches (230 mm) above the floor shall be considered toe clearance and shall comply with Section 306.2.

❖ The 9 inches (230 mm) for toe clearance is based on the typical height of the kick plates on the front of a wheelchair. For example, although not required, the kickplates on cabinets may be raised to over 9 inches (230 mm) to facilitate moving closer to a counter over a cabinet when a front approach is provided. Another example would be the allowances for tighter toilet stalls when the partitions are raised 9 inches (230 mm) or more so that the footplates can extend underneath during maneuvering (Section 604.8.5).

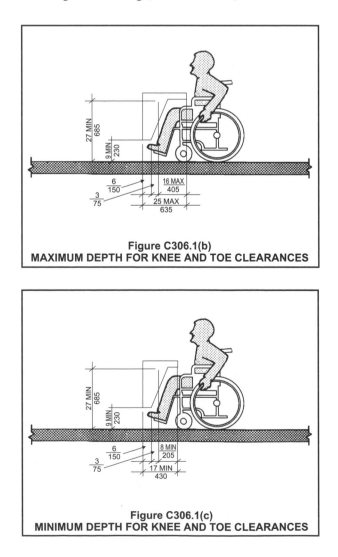

Figure C306.1(b)
MAXIMUM DEPTH FOR KNEE AND TOE CLEARANCES

Figure C306.1(a)
KNEE AND TOE CLEARANCE UNDER WORK SURFACES

Figure C306.1(c)
MINIMUM DEPTH FOR KNEE AND TOE CLEARANCES

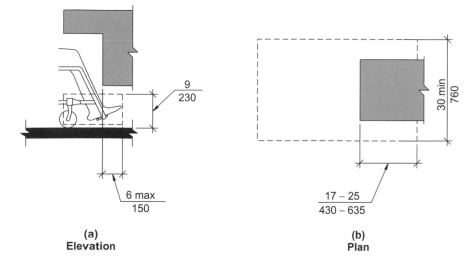

(a)
Elevation

(b)
Plan

Fig. 306.2
Toe Clearance

306.2.2 Maximum Depth. Toe clearance shall be permitted to extend 25 inches (635 mm) maximum under an element.

❖ This depth limit is based on the size of the typical user and wheelchair. The 25 inch (635 mm) maximum depth includes both the knee and toe clearances and limits how much of the required clear floor space may extend underneath an element. The location of the upper body and/or arms of the wheelchair, would not allow a person to slide farther under the counter or fixture [see commentary Figure C306.1(b)]. The actual area beneath the element may extend beyond the 25 inch (635 mm) limit, but that space is not considered part of the toe or knee space or the area designated as being the clear floor space. The maximum dimension does not require any area beyond the 25 inch (635 mm) length to be blocked off even though the space extends beyond that depth. See also commentary for Section 306.3.2.

306.2.3 Minimum Depth. Where toe clearance is required at an element as part of a clear floor space, the toe clearance shall extend 17 inches (430 mm) minimum beneath the element.

❖ This minimum depth is established to assure that a user may get positioned under the element and have items be within their reach range. See Figures 308.2.1 and 308.2.2 of the standard for examples of how the position of the clear floor space, and therefore, where the person using a wheelchair is located affects the use of a fixture or element. Note that this is when toe spaces is required under an element [see commentary Figure C306.1(c) and commentary for Section 306.3.3].

306.2.4 Additional Clearance. Space extending greater than 6 inches (150 mm) beyond the available knee clearance at 9 inches (230 mm) above the floor shall not be considered toe clearance.

❖ If there is a barrier or wall blocking the knee clearance under a counter or fixture (e.g., pipe protection under a lavatory), the toe clearance cannot extend more than 6 inches (150 mm) past the provided knee clearance [see commentary Figure C306.1(b)]. Space may be available beyond this required limit, but because it would not be useable as toe clearance, the additional space cannot be considered as being a part of the required knee and toe space or the area designated as being the clear floor space. As discussed with the commentary to Section 306.2.2, the additional space need not be blocked off in any manner.

306.2.5 Width. Toe clearance shall be 30 inches (760 mm) minimum in width.

❖ This requirement coordinates with the minimum required width for a clear floor space and permits persons using wheelchairs to fit their toes and the chair beneath the obstruction. If this space is under a counter and is used as part of a T-turn, the width would have to be 36 inches (915 mm) in accordance with Section 304.3.2 [See Figure 305.3, Figure 304.3(b) and commentary Figure C305.4].

306.3 Knee Clearance.

❖ The subsections of Section 306.3 contain all the technical provisions for knee clearance. Figure 306.3 shows some of the requirements for the knee space. Even though knee and toe clearances have separate technical requirements, they are often required as a package. See the commentary for Section 306.1 for related discussion.

306.3.1 General. Space beneath an element between 9 inches (230 mm) and 27 inches (685 mm) above the floor shall be considered knee clearance and shall comply with Section 306.3.

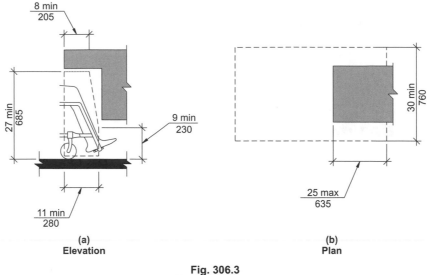

Fig. 306.3
Knee Clearance

❖ Space below 9 inches (230 mm) is considered toe clearance. Space between 9 inches and 27 inches (685 mm) is considered knee clearance. See the commentary to Section 306.2.

306.3.2 Maximum Depth. Knee clearance shall be permitted to extend 25 inches (635 mm) maximum under an element at 9 inches (230 mm) above the floor.

❖ This depth limit is based on the size of the typical user and wheelchair. The 25 inch (635 mm) maximum depth includes both the knee and toe clearances and limits how much of the required clear floor space may extend underneath an element. The location of the upper body and/or arms of the wheelchair would not allow a person to slide farther under the counter or fixture [see commentary Figure C306.1(b)]. The actual area beneath the element may extend beyond the 25 inch (635 mm) limit, but that space is not considered part of the toe or knee space or the area designated as being the clear floor space. The maximum dimension does not require any area beyond the 25 inch (635 mm) length to be blocked off even though the space extends beyond that depth.

Combined with the requirements of Section 306.2.2, the actual maximum depth of the knee clearance is 19 inches (480 mm) maximum (i.e., 25 inch depth - 6 inch toe clearance = 19 inches) at the bottom of the knee space, and 16 inches (i.e., 25 inch depth - 6 inch toe clearance - 3 inch slope allowance = 16 inches) at the top of the knee space. [see commentary Figure C306.1(b)].

306.3.3 Minimum Depth. Where knee clearance is required beneath an element as part of a clear floor space, the knee clearance shall be 11 inches (280 mm) minimum in depth at 9 inches (230 mm) above the floor, and 8 inches (205 mm) minimum in depth at 27 inches (685 mm) above the floor.

❖ Minimum dimensions for knee and toe clearances are specified to provide design criteria when access to an accessible element or fixture involves using the space underneath an element or fixture. For example, a forward approach to a counter top or work surface necessitates the feet and legs extending under the counter top or work surface as shown in commentary Figure C306.1(c). The knee and toe clearance dimensions establish the required unobstructed space that must be provided to afford access to the element. Where knee and toe clearance is required, such as beneath a lavatory or drinking fountain as specified in Section 602.2 or 606.2, these minimum dimensions are required.

As shown in Figure 306.3 the area represented by the dashed lines shows how the knee clearance may be less deep at the top and then increased as it approaches the toe clearance level. The increase of the depth of the knee clearance, starting at 8 inches (205 mm) at the top and increasing to 11 inches (280 mm) at the bottom, is in recognition of the alignment of the legs of a person sitting in a wheelchair.

Combined with the requirements of Section 306.2.3, the actual minimum depth of the knee clearance results in a total of 17 inches (430 mm) for knee and toe clearances under a counter or fixture [see commentary Figure C306.1(c)].

306.3.4 Clearance Reduction. Between 9 inches (230 mm) and 27 inches (685 mm) above the floor, the knee clearance shall be permitted to be reduced at a rate of 1 inch (25 mm) for each 6 inches (150 mm) in height.

❖ The minimum depth requirements for knee clearance are established in Section 306.3.3. If additional knee space is provided, the clearance reductions is intended to be consistent with the allowance for the alignment of a person's legs for all knee clearances [see commentary Figures C306.1(b) and C306.1(c)].

306.3.5 Width. Knee clearance shall be 30 inches (760 mm) minimum in width.

❖ This requirement coordinates with the minimum required width for a clear floor space and will permit a person using a wheelchair to fit his legs and the chair beneath the obstruction. If this space is under a counter and is used as part of a T-turn, the width would be required to be 36 inches (915 mm) in accordance with Section 304.3.2 [see Figures 305.3, 304.3(b) and 306.3(b) and commentary Figure C305.4].

307 Protruding Objects

❖ Many items along the path of travel can be protruding objects for persons with visual impairments, or persons who may be momentarily distracted. There are additional concerns during emergency events where smoke may obscure objects and people are hurrying to escape. The following section addresses criteria for a variety of protruding objects (see commentary Figure C307).

307.1 General. Protruding objects on circulation paths shall comply with Section 307.

❖ This section addresses items which extend into the circulation path that people may bump into. Guide dogs are trained to recognize and assist their handlers to avoid hazards. However, people with severe impairments of vision may use the long cane as an aid to mobility. With the customary cane technique, the cane is moved in arcs from side to side to touch points outside both shoulders of the user [see commentary Figures C307.1(a) and C307.1(b)].

Potentially hazardous objects may be detected by long-cane users if they fall within the detection range of canes. This gives a person sufficient time to detect the element with the cane before there is body contact. People with visual impairments walking toward an object can detect an overhang if its lowest surface is no higher than 27 inches (685 mm) [see commentary Figure C307.1(c)]. Because of imperfect forward protection provided by the long cane and individual vari-

Figure C307
EXAMPLES OF PROTRUDING OBJECTS

ations in how people use their canes, detection of protruding objects is not assured. Individuals with low vision may have poor acuity or depth perception and cannot reliably see low-lying protruding objects.

It is also important to check all portions of the projection and not just the lowest part. For example, a bowl type drinking fountain may be mounted on an arm or pedestal which is at the 27 inch (685 mm) height, but because the bowl above it sticks out farther and is at a higher level, the projection must also be considered. Therefore, check both the height and the overall projection of all elements that protrude into the circulation path.

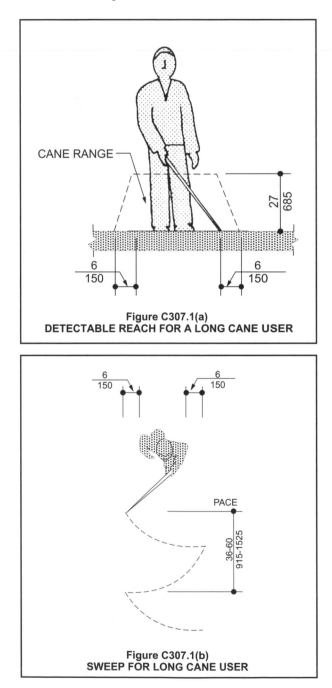

Figure C307.1(a)
DETECTABLE REACH FOR A LONG CANE USER

Elements with knee and toe space provided below, such as drinking fountains, may need barriers (e.g., placement in an alcove, wing walls) if their leading edges are located more than 27 inches (685 mm) above the floor. Because knee space, if provided, must be at least 27 inches (685 mm) above the floor, it is almost impossible to install drinking fountains with edges at precisely 27 inches (685 mm) that provide knee space without having to provide a barrier. To be detectable with a long cane, the leading edge of the projection or of the guard must be located no more than 27 inches (685 mm) above the floor [see commentary Figures C307 and C307.1(c)].

It should be noted that these requirements would also apply to operable elements. Items that are retractable, such as casement windows or awnings and their supports, must meet protruding object requirements when fully extended.

It should be noted that although acceptable by the standard, the 27 inch (685 mm) height is generally considered as too tall for many cane users. This is because that height is based on the average male user. Because the "average" user is smaller than the average male user and the unlikelihood that the drinking fountain is exactly at the 27 inch (685 mm) height so that both the knee and toe clearance, as well as the protruding object limits are met, most drinking fountains should be located in an alcove or in a corner so they do not protrude into the circulation path.

307.2 Protrusion Limits. Objects with leading edges more than 27 inches (685 mm) and not more than 80 inches (2030 mm) above the floor shall protrude 4 inches (100 mm) maximum horizontally into the circulation path.

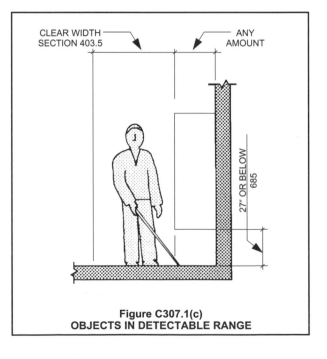

Figure C307.1(c)
OBJECTS IN DETECTABLE RANGE

Figure C307.1(b)
SWEEP FOR LONG CANE USER

EXCEPTIONS:

1. Handrails shall be permitted to protrude 4¹/₂ inches (115 mm) maximum.

2. Door closers and door stops shall be permitted to be 78 inches (1980 mm) minimum above the floor.

❖ The overall height limitation of 80 inches (2030 mm) is important. One of the more common injuries for person with sight impairments is striking their heads on overhanging objects, such as overhead signage or sconces.

Objects such as drinking fountains with a leading edge that is 27 inches (685 mm) above a surface, allow a person using a wheelchair to make a forward approach and use the space below as knee and toe space. It is also the highest point at which a long-cane user can detect the object [see commentary Figure C307.1(a)]. As such, any protrusion above 27 inches (685 mm) will not be readily detectable. The user could unexpectedly impact the protrusion and could sustain an injury. An object with the leading edge at or below 27 inches (685 mm) above the floor can protrude any amount because the protrusion is considered detectable and avoidable.

The allowable protrusion of 4 inches (100 mm) recognizes that avoidance of all protrusions is unrealistic, and limits them to an extent that minimizes the likelihood of inadvertent contact. Protrusions higher than 80 inches (2030 mm) above the floor are not limited because they are assumed to be overhead and not subject to accidental impact (see Figure 307.2). Eighty inches (2030 mm) is consistent with the required headroom clearances specified in the model building codes. These limitations on protruding objects serve to protect all people, not just those with a vision impairment, from unintended contact and potential injury.

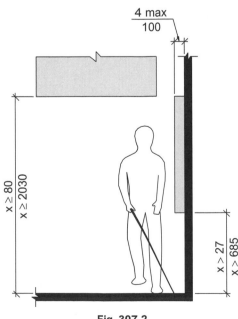

Fig. 307.2
Limits of Protruding Objects

It is important to look at the entire object which is protruding and determine what the appropriate requirements would be. For example, part of the object may be located so that it is below the 27 inch (685 mm) limitation even though other portions may be located at a higher level or extend beyond the lower projection. In these circumstances it is important to determine the lowest, the highest and the farthest projections of that object to determine exactly how the protrusion must be protected and how far it may extend.

The exception for handrails is based on the fact that handrails are typically installed on stairs and ramps and the level changes would help to provide the user with an awareness of the handrail. The 4¹/₂ inch (115 mm) dimension coordinates with the projection depth for handrails in the *International Building Code®* (IBC®). Although this exceeds the normal depth permitted for a protruding object, the limited location and the fact that handrails must be mounted within a height of 34 to 38 inches (864 to 965 mm) above the walking surfaces help to make this situation acceptable. (See Section 505.4.) This exception is limited to the run of the stair or ramp. End projections must be detectable.

The second exception is to allow for a minimal reduction in clearance for door closers. With an 80-inch (2030 mm) minimum height required for door openings, the door closer must protrude below the frame to attach to and retract the door.

307.3 Post-Mounted Objects. Objects on posts or pylons shall be permitted to overhang 4 inches (100 mm) maximum where more than 27 inches (685 mm) and not more than 80 inches (2030 mm) above the floor. Objects on multiple posts or pylons where the clear distance between the posts or pylons is greater than 12 inches (305 mm) shall have the lowest edge of such object either 27 inches (685 mm) maximum or 80 inches (2030 mm) minimum above the floor.

❖ Similar to wall- and ceiling-mounted protrusions discussed in the commentary for Section 307.2, the intent of these provisions is to specify dimensional criteria that limit protrusions within various ranges that may not be readily detectable and avoidable. These limitations benefit all people, not just those with a visual impairment.

The criteria for objects mounted between posts or pylons apply when the pylons are more than 12 inches (305 mm) apart (see Figure 307.3). In this circumstance, it is possible that a person using a long cane could directly approach the pylons but not detect them with the sweep pattern of the cane. Therefore, the standard requires that the bottom edge of the obstruction between the pylons be either 27 inches (685 mm) maximum above the floor, so that the cane will detect the object before the person bumps into it, or it must be at least 80 inches (2030 mm) above the floor.

To be consistent with the protruding object provisions in Section 307.2, the outside edge of the sign on multiple posts, or items mounted on single posts (e.g., accessible parking signs, outdoor telephones) may not protrude more than 4 inches (100 mm) from the support.

These provisions are for objects along flat walking surfaces and are not intended to be applied to the sloped portion of handrails along a stair or ramp (excluding end projections) or signs located over grass areas

307.4 Reduced Vertical Clearance. Guardrails or other barriers shall be provided where object protrusion is beyond the limits allowed by Sections 307.2 and 307.3, and where the vertical clearance is less than 80 inches (2030 mm) above the floor. The leading edge of such guardrail or barrier shall be 27 inches (685 mm) maximum above the floor.

❖ For safety reasons, generally the means of egress requirements in model building codes do not permit headroom clearances of less than 80 inches (2030 mm) above a walking surface. However, there are circumstances, such as the space beneath a stairway, where it is possible for a person with a visual impairment to approach that area and bump into the portion that occurs below the headroom clearance height of 80 inches (2030 mm). The purpose of this provision is to require that a guard or other type of barrier be installed so that it can be detected

before a person bumps into the overhead protrusion. Figure 307.4 illustrates this requirement.

Note that whatever barrier is chosen, it must be detectable by a long cane. This could be a full height wall, a low rail, a planter, etc (see commentary Figure C307.4). A single rail at guard or handrail height might stop someone from walking under the stairway, but would not meet this requirements. A person using a long cane could walk into the rail before they detected it.

At the same time, a platform or curb under the stair would be detectable, but if it could be perceived by a person with low vision as a step up, rather than a barrier, it would not meet the intent of this provision.

307.5 Required Clear Width. Protruding objects shall not reduce the clear width required for accessible routes.

❖ The provisions in Sections 307.2 through 307.4 establish allowable protrusions into an accessible route. Under no circumstances is a protrusion permitted to reduce the minimum required clear width of an accessible route, even if the protrusion complies with one of the previous sections. This would otherwise defeat the purpose of providing an accessible route because the protrusion would effectively render the route inaccessible (see commentary Figure C307.5). This re-

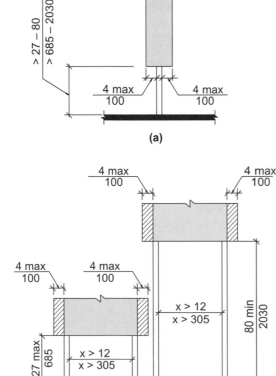

(a)

(b)

Fig. 307.3
Post-Mounted Protruding Objects

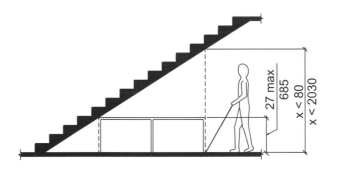

Fig. 307.4
Reduced Vertical Clearance

Figure C307.4
BARRIER UNDER STAIRWAY

quirement can be viewed as being comparable to the provisions for accessible routes in Section 403.5 and shown in Figure 403.5 of the standard.

308 Reach Ranges

308.1 General. Reach ranges shall comply with Section 308.

❖ These provisions identify the reach range that is understood to be achievable by the person using a wheelchair. From a sitting position, one can reach up or down, to either the front or the side only to a limited point. These dimensions determine the vertical dimensions within which an element must be located to be accessible. Anything located outside these ranges may not be reachable, and therefore, not accessible. These ranges also benefit persons who are short of stature. See commentary, Section 308.3.

It should also be noted that the standard currently addresses the reach restrictions for depth of adults with dwarfism and others of short stature to a limited extent with Sections 606.5 and 606.7.

The U.S. Access Board has reviewed provisions for children. Commentary Table C308.1 is based on that research and provides guidance on unobstructed reach ranges for children according to age where building elements such as coat hooks, lockers, or operable parts are designed for use primarily by children. This table is for information only and is not intended to provide requirements. The dimensions

apply to either forward or side reaches. Accessible elements and operable parts designed for adult use or children over age 12 are addressed by Section 308.

308.2 Forward Reach.

❖ Technical requirements for a forward reach when persons using a wheelchair can locate themselves directly in front of an object (unobstructed) or when they must reach over a counter, table or other object (obstructed) are indicated in this section. It is difficult for persons using a wheelchair to reach past their toes. Reach ranges are typically referenced for access to controls (e.g., lights, heating/air conditioning, appliance controls, plumbing controls).

308.2.1 Unobstructed. Where a forward reach is unobstructed, the high forward reach shall be 48 inches (1220 mm) maximum and the low forward reach shall be 15 inches (380 mm) minimum above the floor.

❖ The forward reach to an element is considered unobstructed when the wheelchair can be moved as close as possible to the element, typically a switch or control on a wall as shown in Figure 308.2.1. This position allows the greatest possible forward reach from a sitting position.

It is not the intent of this section to consider types of wall finishes or standard trim, such as baseboards or chair rails as obstructions. Although a specific limit for the depth is not indicated, the concern is whether the

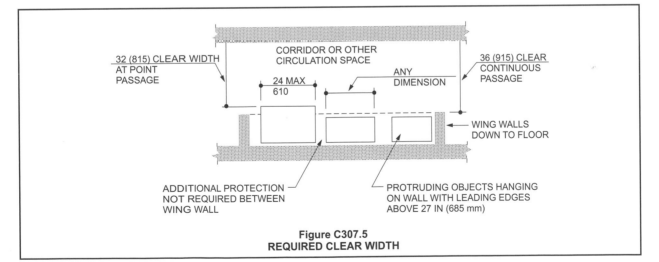

Figure C307.5
REQUIRED CLEAR WIDTH

Table C308.1
UNOBSTRUCTED CHILDREN'S REACH RANGES

UNOBSTRUCTED CHILDREN'S REACH RANGES			
Forward or Side Reach	Ages 3 and 4	Ages 5 through 8	Ages 9 through 12
High (maximum)	36 in. (915 mm)	40 in. (1015 mm)	44 in. (1120 mm)
Low (minimum)	20 in. (510 mm)	15 in. (455 mm)	16 in. (405 mm)

wall finish or trim stopped the person using the wheelchair from moving forward to the maximum extent possible. A common error is the 40 inches (1015 mm) being measured to the center of the electrical box instead of the control, for example on some styles of thermostats.

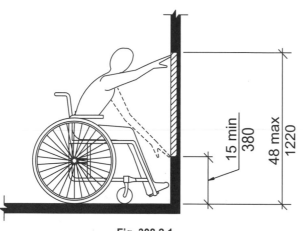

Fig. 308.2.1
Unobstructed Forward Reach

308.2.2 Obstructed High Reach. Where a high forward reach is over an obstruction, the clear floor space shall extend beneath the element for a distance not less than the required reach depth over the obstruction. The high forward reach shall be 48 inches (1220 mm) maximum where the reach depth is 20 inches (510 mm) maximum. Where the reach depth exceeds 20 inches (510 mm), the high forward reach shall be 44 inches (1120 mm) maximum, and the reach depth shall be 25 inches (635 mm) maximum.

❖ This section establishes the reach height limitation based on the horizontal reach depth over an obstruction, such as a counter. The forward reach to an element is considered obstructed when an architectural feature such as a countertop prevents the person using a wheelchair from moving as close as possible to the element. In such cases, the effective reach height is reduced. The effective reach height is a function of the depth of the obstruction and how close the obstruction allows the user to go to the element. The farther from the element, the lower the reachable distance above the element. The closer to the element, the higher the reachable distance.

In a lot of situations, the knee and toe clearances available under the counter are the same depth as the counter. If there is something under the counter that would stop someone from moving fully under the counter (e.g., pipe protection, privacy shield, cable tray), the obstruction under the counter could effectively control the possible reach over the counter. Therefore, the requirement for "shall extend beneath the element for a distance not less that the required reach depth" would require a designer to look at the depth someone could

move under a counter, as well as the reach over the counter to determine the appropriate height of the switch or control located on the wall. Such under-counter protrusion could be interpreted to be allowed in the space in front of the knee and toe clearance [see commentary Figures C306.1(b) and C306.1(c)].

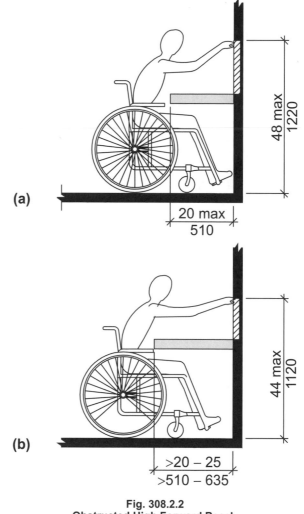

(a)

(b)

Fig. 308.2.2
Obstructed High Forward Reach

308.3 Side Reach.

❖ Research with persons using wheelchairs has shown that the reach height from the side of a wheelchair (parallel approach – 9 inches to 54 inches) varies from that for a forward reach (forward approach –15 inches to 48 inches). This occurs because the parallel approach brings the person closer to the element and also because of the body's range of motion. Any obstructions that limit the proximity of the wheelchair to the element will reduce the reach range.

The A117.1 development committee revised the side reach ranges in the 1998 edition of the standard. This revision was based on information provided by an organization called Little People of America. They were able to provide statistical information based on the limited reach of some of their members that demonstrated the need for the 48 inch (1220 mm) maximum reach.

308.3.1 Unobstructed. Where a clear floor space allows a parallel approach to an element and the side reach is unobstructed, the high side reach shall be 48 inches (1220 mm) maximum and the low side reach shall be 15 inches (380 mm) minimum above the floor.

EXCEPTION: Existing elements shall be permitted at 54 inches (1370 mm) maximum above the floor.

❖ This section includes the effective reach range assumed to be achievable by a person using a wheelchair when there arc no obstructions that limit how close the chair can be positioned relative to the element. Side reach is considered unobstructed when something below an operable part is both less than 10 inches (255 mm) deep and 34 inches (865 mm) high (see commentary to Section 308.3.2). This allowance would permit side approaches to be considered unobstructed when a person would need to reach over low projections, such as heating controls over baseboard heaters, or the hardware on the door that is immediately adjacent to the light switch.

Although many persons using wheelchairs can reach lower, the 15-inch (380 mm) criterion serves persons with arthritis, back problems, severely limited reach and limited finger dexterity.

The exception recognizes that earlier editions of the standard permitted a high side reach range of 54 inches (1370 mm). Therefore, in facilities constructed using the earlier standard, some elements may be located at this higher level.

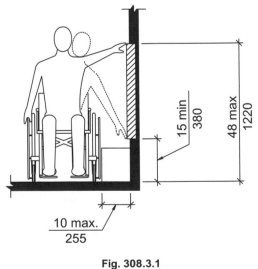

Fig. 308.3.1
Unobstructed Side Reach

308.3.2 Obstructed High Reach. Where a clear floor space allows a parallel approach to an object

and the high side reach is over an obstruction, the height of the obstruction shall be 34 inches (865 mm) maximum and the depth of the obstruction shall be 24 inches (610 mm) maximum. The high side reach shall be 48 inches (1220 mm) maximum for a reach depth of 10 inches (255 mm) maximum. Where the reach depth exceeds 10 inches (255 mm), the high side reach shall be 46 inches (1170 mm) maximum for a reach depth of 24 inches (610 mm) maximum.

❖ The maximum reach range is reduced when an obstruction prevents the person using a wheelchair from moving within 10 inches (255 mm) of the element. Note that the maximum projection of the obstruction is indicated as 24 inches (610 mm). This effectively means that if the wheelchair cannot move to within at least 24 inches (610 mm) of the element, the element would not be considered reachable, and therefore, not accessible. See Figure 308.3.2 of the standard for details of this requirement.

The height of the obstruction is also limited. An obstruction that is higher would not permit the user to reach beyond that obstruction with his arm fully extended to the side. Because of this height limitation, most electrical receptacles and switches located on the wall behind and above kitchen counters [which are typically higher than 34 inches (865 mm)] would not be accessible. Options would be to locate the outlets or switches on the front surface of the cabinets, locate the outlets and switches over thc acccssible work surface or accessible sink location, or locate the switches on a wall that is not over the counter. See Section 309 for additional discussions.

309 Operable Parts

❖ For buildings and spaces to be usable by all people, all of the components possible are required to be accessible. This includes the controls and operable parts of equipment and appliances intended for operation by the occupants in a space. If a standard control would be out of the reach range (e.g., exhaust hood over a cooktop, ceiling fan), a solution would be redundant controls at an accessible location.

309.1 General. Operable parts required to be accessible shall comply with Section 309.

❖ To make sure that the elements truly are accessible, other sections of the standard such as those for drinking fountains (Section 602.3), water closet flush controls (Section 604.6), lavatories and sinks (Section 606.4), and kitchen appliances (Section 804.6.2) will direct the user back to and require compliance with this section. Other examples of operable parts that are within the scope of this provision include light switches, dispenser controls, electrical appliance controls, electrical receptacles and communications system receptacles.

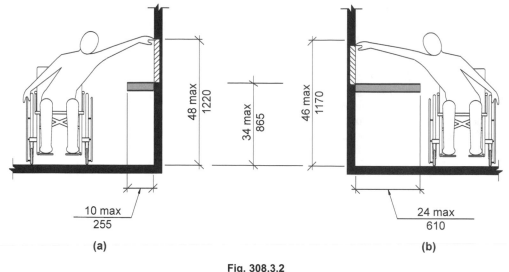

48 max / 1220

34 max / 865

46 max / 1170

10 max / 255

24 max / 610

(a)

(b)

Fig. 308.3.2
Obstructed High Side Reach

309.2 Clear Floor Space. A clear floor space complying with Section 305 shall be provided.

❖ Providing a place for persons using a wheelchair to position their chair in close proximity to controls is especially important for operable parts of equipment and appliances. Walls fixtures or equipment that create an alcove situation must also be considered.

309.3 Height. Operable parts shall be placed within one or more of the reach ranges specified in Section 308.

❖ All of a control, receptacle or other operable part are to be within the specified reach ranges. Electrical and communications receptacles on walls are required by Sections 308.2 and 308.3 to be at least 15 inches (380 mm) above the floor.

Specific requirements and/or exceptions in other part of the standard, or scoping requirements from the model codes, may limit this requirement. For example, model codes exempt spaces that are accessed only by maintenance and service personnel; therefore, special equipment with operational needs that preclude installation within reach ranges may be exempted. An example is the controls on a furnace or boiler located in a basement furnace room for an office building.

A second example would be applicable to dedicated outlets such as the one for a refrigerator that is located behind the appliance. Requirements in kitchens are for access to appliance controls. The refrigerator would have to be moved to have access to that outlet; therefore, the outlet for the refrigerator would not need to be within the normal reach ranges.

309.4 Operation. Operable parts shall be operable with one hand and shall not require tight grasping, pinching, or twisting of the wrist. The force required to activate operable parts shall be 5.0 pounds (22.2 N) maximum.

EXCEPTION: Gas pump nozzles shall not be required to provide operable parts that have an activating force of 5.0 pounds (22.2 N) maximum.

❖ As with all types of hardware and other operating controls, limited hand dexterity must be considered in making spaces, facilities, equipment, appliances and other features accessible and usable. Controls and hardware that require grasping, pinching or twisting of the wrist, or that require excessive force can make a feature of the building unusable.

The exception for gas pump nozzles results from the concern that safety requirements to prevent the gas nozzles from spilling would not allow the nozzles to meet the 5-pounds-force requirements. The gas nozzle could still need to comply with the requirements for no tight grasping, pinching or twisting of the wrist to operate. The other operable parts for a gas pump must still comply with all requirements, including reach range (see commentary Figure C309.4).

Figure C309.4
GAS PUMPS

Chapter 4. Accessible Routes

❖ Chapter 4 provides the technical requirements for accessible routes, both outside and inside of a building. Accessible routes connect accessible elements.

- Section 401 is a general statement about the Chapter 4 criteria being applicable for accessible routes where required by the authority having jurisdiction.
- Section 402 lists what elements are considered part of an accessible route, as well as stating that revolving doors, gates and turnstiles cannot be part of an accessible route.
- Section 403 deals with walking surface requirements.
- Section 404 contains criteria for all types of doors – manual swinging and sliding doors, door openings and automatic doors, including power-assisted, low-energy and fully powered.
- Section 405 and 406 overlap with criteria for ramps and curb ramps.
- Sections 407, 408 and 409 address requirements for different types of passenger elevators – passenger, limited-use/limited access and private residence. Unique criteria for destination-oriented and existing elevators are dispersed throughout where applicable. Where each type of passenger elevator can be used is limited by the referenced standard, ASME A17.1.
- Section 410 is concerned with platform lift criteria.

401 General

401.1 Scope. Accessible routes required by the scoping provisions adopted by the administrative authority shall comply with the applicable provisions of Chapter 4.

❖ A route must comply with all of the applicable pieces of Chapter 4 to be considered as an acceptable accessible route. This section further clarifies that all of the individual components of an accessible route, such as width, passing space, surface texture, slope and the other features, must comply with the applicable provisions. The sum total of all components of an accessible route is that which accomplishes the intent of this standard to provide access to required elements of buildings and facilities.

Note that these provisions apply to the accessible routes required by the scoping provisions, not all routes (see Section 201).

402 Accessible Routes

❖ The accessible route allows a person with a disability to approach, enter and use a building or facility. Interior ac-

cessible routes may include doors, floors, ramps, elevators, platform lifts and clear floor space at fixtures. Exterior accessible routes may include parking, access aisles, walks, ramps and curb ramps. The extent to which accessible elements and spaces must be connected by an accessible route is established in scoping provisions.

402.1 General. Accessible routes shall comply with Section 402.

❖ Accessible routes must comply with all of the provisions of Section 402 to provide an acceptable degree of accessibility to the elements they serve. See the requirements in Section 402.2 for components that make up accessible routes.

402.2 Components. Accessible routes shall consist of one or more of the following components: Walking surfaces with a slope not steeper than 1:20, doors and doorways, ramps, curb ramps excluding the flared sides, elevators, and platform lifts. All components of an accessible route shall comply with the applicable portions of this standard.

❖ This section identifies the various types of architectural elements that contribute to an accessible route. In effect, any surface that a person can travel using a wheelchair to reach an accessible element can be a part of an accessible route if it complies with the provisions of Chapter 4. Chapter 4 includes provisions for the elements listed as part of the accessible route (see commentary Figure C402.2).

By the definition for ramps in Section 106.5, any walking surface that slopes at 1:20 (1 inch rise to 20 inches of run) or less is considered a sloped walkway. Walking surfaces that slope from 1:20 up to 1:12 (1 inch rise to 12 inches of run) are considered to be accessible ramps (Section 405) or curb ramps (Section 406).

Although stairways may have elements that could be a concern for persons with mobility impairments, they are not considered part of an accessible route.

402.3 Revolving Doors, Revolving Gates, and Turnstiles. Revolving doors, revolving gates, and turnstiles shall not be part of an accessible route.

❖ This section states that manually operated revolving doors, revolving gates and turnstiles are not to be used within an accessible route for ingress or egress; however, under certain circumstances the model building codes allow the use of revolving doors, revolving gates and turnstiles as part of a means of egress.

Even when allowed in a means of egress, there must be a side swinging door adjacent to the revolving door or gate. When they are permitted they could create problems for accessibility.

(a) Walks

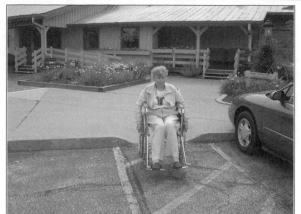

(d) Curb ramps

(b) Entrances

(e) Elevators

(c) Ramps

(f) Platform Lifts

Figure C402.2
ACCESSIBLE ROUTE COMPONENTS

A route through a hinged or sliding door differs remarkably from that provided through a revolving door. For a revolving door, the route includes a turn into the doorway, an arcing path of travel as the door revolves, followed by a change of direction when leaving the door. Items that may cause difficulty for anyone with mobility impairments could involve the overall doorway diameter, the number of leaves and their relative angle, and the configuration of the return walls surrounding the revolving door. Additionally, the speed of the door movement if motorized, or the force required for movement if not motorized, would be a concern for anyone who needed to keep both hands on their device to move forward (e.g., walker or wheelchair).

Automatic revolving doors, if large enough, may be usable by many people who use wheelchairs. However, the intent of this section is that these types of doors not be the only means of passage at an entrance or exit. An alternate door in full compliance with this section is considered necessary because some people with disabilities may be uncertain of the usability, or may not have enough strength or speed to use them. Although manufacturers have developed safety criteria, certain questions remain, such as the appropriate maximum and minimum speeds.

It is important to remember that application of this section is limited because it is part of Section 404.2 rather than Section 404.3 and because it applies only to revolving doors, revolving gates and turnstiles. Therefore, it is possible that automatic items such as fare gates which may be considered being included in the generic phrase "turnstiles" by some people could be found on an accessible route. An appropriate fare gate would be permitted because they are not included in the prohibition of this section and because they are permitted by other sections of the standard.

403 Walking Surfaces

403.1 General. Walking surfaces that are a part of an accessible route shall comply with Section 403.

❖ This section regulates the various characteristics of the floor surface to ensure that the route is stable, usable and does not contain obstructions that would prevent its use in reaching an accessible element.

403.2 Floor Surface. Floor surfaces shall comply with Section 302.

❖ The suitability of an accessible route depends on certain characteristics of the surface itself. This section requires compliance with the general provisions of Section 302, which addresses characteristics that relate to both safety (slip resistance) and usability (stable and firm).

Section 104.4 states that the term floor surface refers to the finished floor or ground surface as applicable.

Ambulatory and semi-ambulatory people who have difficulty maintaining balance and those with restricted gaits are particularly sensitive to slipping and tripping hazards. For those people, a stable and regular surface is necessary to walk safely. Wheelchairs are propelled most easily on surfaces that are hard, stable and regular. Soft, loose surfaces such as shag carpet, loose sand, gravel, crushed stone or wet clay, and irregular surfaces such as cobblestone, significantly impede movement of a wheelchair.

A stable surface is one that remains unchanged by contaminants or applied force, so that when the contaminant or force is removed, the surface returns to its original condition. A firm surface resists deformation by either indentation or particles moving on its surface. It is not the intent of the standard to require only paved surfaces, however, any other types (e.g., wood chips, gravel) would need to be evaluated.

Slip resistance is based on the frictional force necessary to keep a shoe or crutch tip from slipping on a walking surface under the conditions of use likely to be found on the surface. For example, outside surfaces or entryways may be wet from rain or snow, or bathroom floors may be wet and should be evaluated under those conditions. The tile on the upstairs hallway would typically not be influenced by outside weather and should be evaluated in a dry condition. Although it is known that the static coefficient of friction is one basis of slip resistance, there is not as yet a generally accepted method to evaluate the slip resistance of walking surfaces for all uses.

403.3 Slope. The running slope of walking surfaces shall not be steeper than 1:20. The cross slope of a walking surface shall not be steeper than 1:48.

❖ The slope of an accessible route is an important factor that affects the usability of such routes by people with mobility impairments. This section correlates with Section 405 by limiting the slope of a "walking surface" to a maximum slope of 1:20. Therefore, any portion of an accessible route with a slope steeper than 1:20 is considered a ramp that must comply with the provisions of Section 405 for ramps.

Controlling the cross slope of an accessible route is important to provide a reasonably level surface across one's direction of travel. Excessive cross slope could affect the balance of a person who uses a walking aid while traveling on the accessible route and also cause considerable difficulty in a straight line motion. In worst cases, extreme cross slopes are hazardous and unsafe. They can cause the person using a wheelchair to lose control and veer to the side.

403.4 Changes in Level. Changes in level shall comply with Section 303.

❖ Change in level means a change in elevation between horizontal planes in the direction of travel along an accessible route. These provisions are covered in Section 303, which is generally applicable to all floor surfaces of accessible routes. See commentary for Section 303.

403.5 Clear Width. Clear width of an accessible route shall comply with Table 403.5.

❖ Most persons using a wheelchair need a 30-inch (765 mm) clear opening width for doorways, gates and other openings when the passage through the opening is straight on. Greater clear widths are needed if the person using a wheelchair is making a turn, is unfamiliar with a building, if competing traffic is heavy, if sudden or frequent movements are needed, a difficult threshold, is encountered etc. For most situations, the addition of an inch (25 mm) of leeway on either side is sufficient to address these difficulties. Thus, a minimum clear width of 32 inches (815 mm) provides adequate clearance. However, if an opening or another type of restriction in a passageway is more than 24 inches (610 mm) in depth, it is essentially a passageway and must be a minimum of 36 inches (915 mm) wide (see

commentary Figure C403.5). This allows for doors, framed openings, pilasters or other minimal protrusions along the accessible route.

Although people who use walking aids do maneuver through clear width openings of 32 inches (815 mm), they need passageways and walks that are 36 inches (915 mm) wide. Crutch tips, often extending down at a wide angle, are a hazard in narrow passageways where they are not seen by other pedestrians.

Able-bodied people in winter clothing, walking straight ahead with arms swinging, need 32 inches (815 mm) of width, which includes 2 inches (51 mm) on either side for sway, and another 1-inch (25 mm) toler-

Table 403.5—Clear Width of an Accessible Route

Segment Length	Minimum Segment Width
≤ 24 inches (610 mm)	32 inches (815 mm)[1]
> 24 inches (610 mm)	36 inches (915 mm)

[1]Consecutive segments of 32 inches (815 mm) in width must be separated by a route segment 48 inches (1220 m) minimum in length and 36 inches (915 mm) minimum in width.

❖ As indicated in the commentary for Section 403.5, the minimum width for an accessible route is 36 inches (915 mm) in general, but when the reduction or obstruction is for only a short distance [24 inches (610 mm) or less], the minimum width may be reduced to 32 inches (815 mm). The footnote to this table is important to establish that any narrow portions of the route be separated a minimum of 48 inches (1220 mm) from the next portion which is of a reduced width. See Figure 403.5 for an illustration of this requirement. With a minimum of a 'wheelchair clear floor space' this allows a person to address one narrowing at a time.

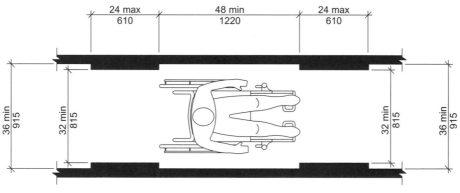

Fig. 403.5
Clear Width of an Accessible Route

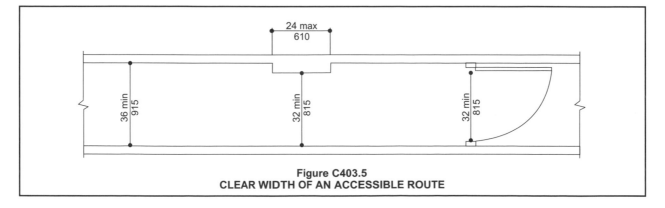

Figure C403.5
CLEAR WIDTH OF AN ACCESSIBLE ROUTE

ance on either side for clearing nearby objects or other pedestrians. Almost all persons using a wheelchair and those who use walking aids also manage within this 32-inch (815 mm) width for short distances.

403.5.1 Clear Width at Turn. Where an accessible route makes a 180 degree turn around an object that is less than 48 inches (1220 mm) in width, clear widths shall be 42 inches (1065 mm) minimum approaching the turn, 48 inches (1220 mm) minimum during the turn, and 42 inches (1065 mm) minimum leaving the turn.

> **EXCEPTION:** Section 403.5.1 shall not apply where the clear width at the turn is 60 inches (1525 mm) minimum.

❖ The requirements for clear width at turns is for level surfaces, not ramps. For ramp landing requirements see Section 405.7.

It is much more difficult for a person using a wheelchair to negotiate a U-turn (half-circle turn) around a narrow obstacle than to make two right-angle turns separated by a distance of 48 inches (1220 mm) minimum. The accessible route, therefore, must be wider if the person using a wheelchair has to negotiate a turn around a narrow obstacle. Figure 403.5.1(a) of the standard illustrates this requirement. The standard does not specify how far back into the approaching path the 42-inch (1065 mm) increased width must extend. Therefore the administrative authority adopting this standard would need to make such a determination if the approaching path was being widened to the 42 inch (1065 mm) width only as it neared the turn.

Another alternative would be to maintain the 36-inch (915 mm) wide path but then provide a 60-inch (1525 mm) turning space in accordance with the exception at the turn where the obstruction is less than 48 inches (1220 mm) wide. See Figure 403.5.1(b) for an illustration of this option.

When the obstruction is 48 inches (1220 mm) or more, it will essentially result in the person using a wheelchair making two right-angle turns and therefore the route may remain at 36 inches (915 mm) minimum width through the entire path. Commentary Figure C403.5.1 illustrates this provision.

403.5.2 Passing Space. An accessible route with a clear width less than 60 inches (1525 mm) shall provide passing spaces at intervals of 200 feet (61 m) maximum. Passing spaces shall be either a 60 inch (1525 mm) minimum by 60 inch (1525 mm) minimum space, or an intersection of two walking surfaces that provide a T-shaped turning space complying with Section 304.3.2, provided the base and arms of the T-shaped space extend 48 inches (1220 mm) minimum beyond the intersection.

❖ This provision ensures that passing spaces are available at reasonable intervals along a long, narrow accessible route, anticipating the possibility of wheelchair traffic approaching from opposite directions along such a path. A person using a wheelchair and an another adult walking together take up a width of about 48 inches (1220 mm). Two persons using wheelchairs need a minimum of 60 inches (1525 mm) in width [see commentary Figure C403.5.2(a)].

Passing spaces at the specified interval minimize the need for either person to have to back up excessive distances to reach a point at which they can pass one another. One person can also see the other approach-

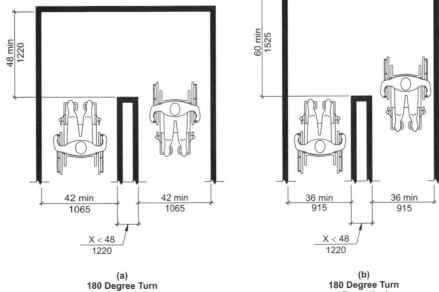

(a)
180 Degree Turn

(b)
**180 Degree Turn
(Exception)**

Fig. 403.5.1
Clear Width at Turn

ing and wait at a passing space until the other user passes. This concept is a compromise that minimizes the impact on space design and layout. It would be unduly restrictive to require that the full length of all accessible routes be 60 inches (1525 mm) wide to allow passage of two wheelchairs at all points. The intersections of two walks, paths or corridors are considered passing spaces. When the accessible route is widened to provide the 60 inch by 60 inch (1525 by 1525 mm) space as shown in commentary Figure C403.5.2(b), it essentially is creating a parallel approach maneuvering clearance in an alcove similar to that shown in Figure 305.7(b) of the standard. A T-turn at an intersection of corridors is another option for providing a passing space. For this option to work effectively, both parties must be able to maneuver out of the path of the other [See commentary Figure C403.5.2(c)].

The nature of building design would make for passing spaces in a number of locations, but a path outside may require a wider area at intervals [See commentary Figure C403.5.2(d)].

403.6 Handrails. Where handrails are required at the side of a corridor they shall comply with Sections 505.4 through 505.9.

❖ Handrails are sometimes provided along hallways for persons with mobility impairments. This is most commonly seen in nursing homes. The limitations to the handrails requirements in Section 505 is based on this type of use and only when handrails are required by the scoping documents. This section is not intended to include handrails within elevators or platform lifts.

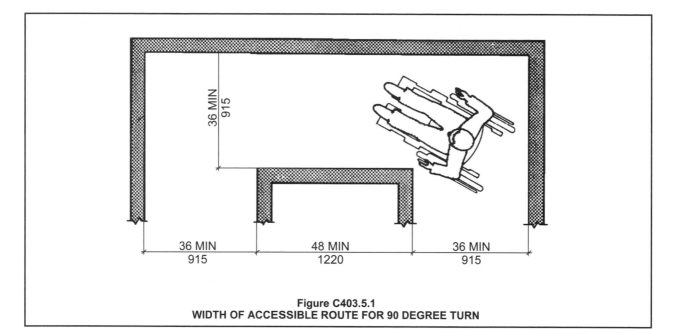

Figure C403.5.1
WIDTH OF ACCESSIBLE ROUTE FOR 90 DEGREE TURN

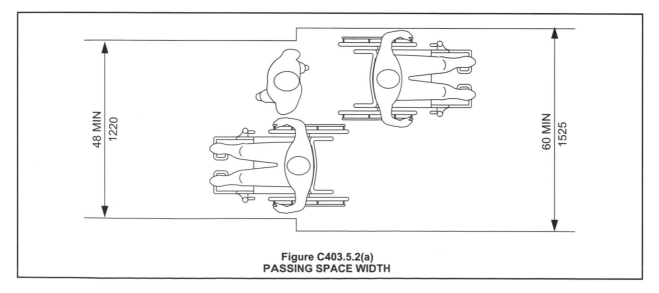

Figure C403.5.2(a)
PASSING SPACE WIDTH

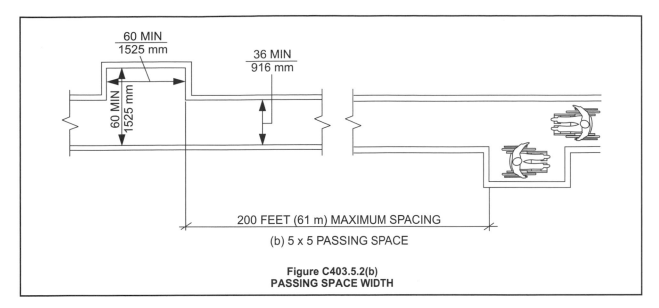

Figure C403.5.2(b)
PASSING SPACE WIDTH

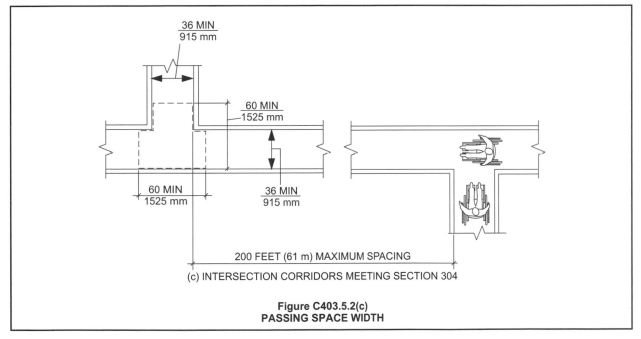

Figure C403.5.2(c)
PASSING SPACE WIDTH

404 Doors and Doorways

404.1 General. Doors and doorways that are part of an accessible route shall comply with Section 404.

❖ The provisions for doors and doorways are applicable only for doors that are part of an accessible route. Doors that are not part of an accessible route need not comply with these provisions.

Because both doors and doorways may create obstructions that would interfere with movement along an accessible route, the standard requires that they comply with the provisions found within this section. The section is divided into two sections which deal with manual doors (Section 404.2) and automatic doors (Section 404.3).

Requirements for approaches, thresholds, hardware, closers and opening force are stated in this section. Care should be exercised in considering any or all doors, and the maneuvering space necessary to make them accessible. When using a combination of forward reach and side reach and the minimum approach clearances, an inadvertent reversal of the latch side to the hinge side may render the door inaccessible to an individual in a wheelchair. Therefore, each door should be reviewed not only during the design stage of a project but also once the installation is completed to assure that the installation complies with the standard.

Figure C403.5.2(d)
EXAMPLE OF EXTERIOR PASSING SPACE

404.2 Manual Doors. Manual doors and doorways, and manual gates, including ticket gates, shall comply with the requirements of Section 404.2.

> **EXCEPTION:** Doors, doorways, and gates designed to be operated only by security personnel shall not be required to comply with Sections 404.2.6, 404.2.7, and 404.2.8.

❖ When a door must be manually operated by the user, it must comply with all of the applicable provisions of this section. This includes the width, maneuvering clearances, arrangement, hardware and other items that affect the usability of the door. This section simply provides a reminder to users of the standard of all of the potential requirements.

Doors that are operated only by security personnel should meet accessible door requirements with the exception of door hardware, closing speed and door opening force. Examples of security personnel are guards in jails, bailiffs in courthouses, guards at security gates. The intent is not to exempt all the doors that these people access, but to exempt doors that these people are responsible for opening, closing and/or locking for security reasons. An example would be the door at the cells and between the courtroom and cells in a courthouse. Security personnel should have sole control of the doors. It is not acceptable for security personnel to operate the doors for people with disabilities and allow others independent access.

404.2.1 Double-Leaf Doors and Gates. At least one of the active leaves of doorways with two leaves shall comply with Sections 404.2.2 and 404.2.3.

❖ Typically, the exterior entrance to a building consists of a pair of doors without a center mullion. These double-leaf doorways can be a barrier unless the clear width and maneuvering clearances established in Sections 404.2.3 and 404.2.4 are provided for at least one of the active leaves. Automatic doors can be used to provide access for double-leaf door narrow leaves or doors that do not have the proper maneuvering clearances.

404.2.2 Clear Width. Doorways shall have a clear opening width of 32 inches (815 mm) minimum. Clear opening width of doorways with swinging doors shall be measured between the face of door and stop, with the door open 90 degrees. Openings, doors and doorways without doors more than 24 inches (610 mm) in depth shall provide a clear opening width of 36 inches (915 mm) minimum. There shall be no projections into the clear opening width lower than 34 inches (865 mm) above the floor. Projections into the clear opening width between 34 inches (865 mm) and 80 inches (2030 mm) above the floor shall not exceed 4 inches (100 mm).

EXCEPTIONS:

1. Door closers and door stops shall be permitted to be 78 inches (1980 mm) minimum above the floor.

2. In alterations, a projection of $^5/_8$ inch (16 mm) maximum into the required clear opening width shall be permitted for the latch side stop.

❖ A person using a wheelchair must, in many cases, approach a doorway at an angle rather than perpendicular to the opening. Thresholds, angled approaches and some surfaces create a condition that necessitates a doorway having a clear opening of at least 32 inches (815 mm). A 34-inch (865 mm) wide, 1³/₄ inch (46 mm) thick door does not generally provide the required clear opening after the door thickness and the door stop have been subtracted. It is also important to note that the standard requires that this measurement be made when the door is opened 90 degrees (1.6 rad). Some building codes have permitted the clear width at doors to be measured when the door is "fully opened." However, when the issue is accessibility, the 90 degree (1.6 rad) requirement from the standard must be used for determining the clear width.

If the wall in which the doorway is installed or the jambs of the doorway itself are more than 24 inches (610 mm) deep, the clear width of the opening must be increased from 32 inches (815 mm) to 36 inches (915 mm). This increased width coincides with the accessible route requirements of Section 403.5 for segments over 24 inches (610 mm) long.

Although the standard does not specifically mention door hardware, that is the intent of the requirements related to projections. If a cylinder that is the size of the height and width requirements could be maneuvered through the doorway without coming into contact with the door hardware, accessibility is achieved [see commentary Figure C404.2.2(a)]. This would be of most concern when a door is equipped with panic hardware that extends the full width of the door. Commentary Figure C404.2.2(b) Illustrates this requirement. Door hardware which is located above the 34 inch (865 mm) height is regulated as a protruding object and is consistent with the maximum projection found in Section 307.2. Based on the projections, it is important to realize that the "clear width" at the door may be different for accessibility purposes than what it is for general egress purposes.

Some of the rationale used in establishing minimum widths for person using a wheelchairs and persons using walking aids is found in the commentary to Section 403.5.

A reduction of the minimum height requirement is provided for door closers and stops. For the door closer to operate, the operator must extend below the door frame.

The second exception is an allowance for the latch side stop on existing doors.

404.2.3 Maneuvering Clearances at Doors.
Minimum maneuvering clearances at doors shall comply with Section 404.2.3 and shall include the full clear opening width of the doorway.

❖ The ability of an individual not only to approach a door but also to get the necessary leverage to open the door is the basis for the clearances established in this section [see commentary Figure C404.2.3(a), (b), (c) and (d)]. Many combinations of conditions may confront a disabled person: approaching from the pull, push, hinge or latch side; whether the door is equipped with a closer; a parallel or perpendicular approach; and so forth. The front approach is similar to the forward reach (see Section 308.2.1) and the hinge or latch side approach is similar to the side reach (see Section 308.3.1).

Although doors are listed as part of the accessible route components in Section 402.2, the scoping provisions may not require every possible route to be accessible. When doors may be approached from more than one direction (e.g., a door along a hallway) even though providing for more than one clearance at the

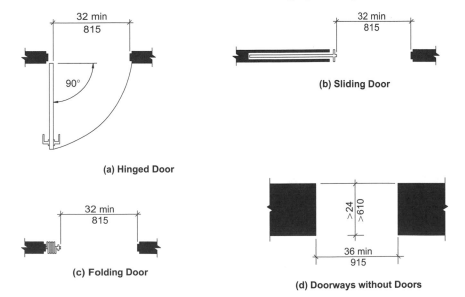

(a) Hinged Door

(b) Sliding Door

(c) Folding Door

(d) Doorways without Doors

**Fig. 404.2.2
Clear Width of Doorways**

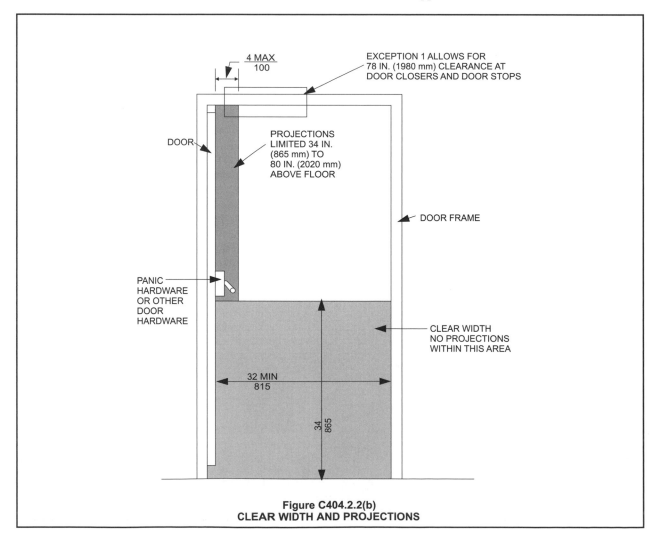

Figure C404.2.2(a)
TYPICAL DOOR OPENING CLEARANCE

doors along the normal routes of travel may be the better design, the literal requirement is only to provide one maneuvering clearance at each door. Some configurations may require a person to move past the door, turn around and come back from another direction to have maneuvering clearance to open the door. At the same time, there is no prohibition from having maneuvering clearances at adjacent doors or doors across the hall overlap. A person is expected to move through the door, not sit there like at a plumbing fixture.

Maneuvering clearances at doors permit the user passage and approach. The standard does not require maneuvering clearances that would permit the user to make a turn and pull or push the door closed after passing through the doorway. If such maneuvering space is provided near, but not adjacent to, the door, then the user must make a 180-degree (3 rad) turn where space is provided, retrace the path, close the door and move away from the door backward. Consideration should be given to providing sufficient maneuvering space for both the closing and opening of, as well as approach to and retreat from, doors.

Figure C404.2.2(b)
CLEAR WIDTH AND PROJECTIONS

404.2.3.1 Swinging Doors. Swinging doors shall have maneuvering clearances complying with Table 404.2.3.1.

❖ This section provides the reference to Table 404.2.3.1, which establishes the minimum clearances for maneuvering clearances adjacent to manual swinging doors. The table establishes the actual requirements that are then illustrated in Figures 404.2.3.1(a) through (g). Figure C404.2.3.1 helps to illustrate how a person using a wheelchair would need to operate a door and therefore how and why the maneuvering clearances are established. See the commentary to Section 404.2.3.

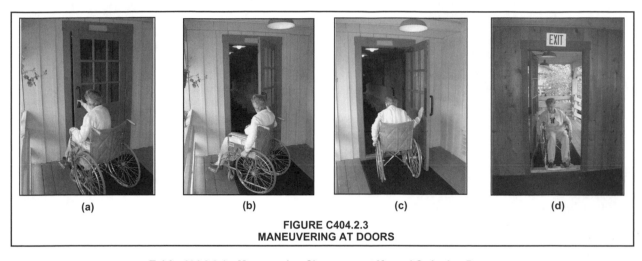

(a) (b) (c) (d)

FIGURE C404.2.3
MANEUVERING AT DOORS

Table 404.2.3.1—Maneuvering Clearances at Manual Swinging Doors

TYPE OF USE		MINIMUM MANEUVERING CLEARANCES	
Approach Direction	Door Side	Perpendicular	Parallel to Doorway (beyond latch unless noted)
From front	Pull	60 inches (1525 mm)	18 inches (455 mm)
From front	Push	48 inches (1220 mm)	0 inches (0 mm)[3]
From hinge side	Pull	60 inches (1525 mm)	36 inches (915 mm)
From hinge side	Pull	54 inches (1370 mm)	42 inches (1065 mm)
From hinge side	Push	42 inches (1065 mm)[1]	22 inches (560 mm)[3 & 4]
From latch side	Pull	48 inches (1220 mm)[2]	24 inches (610 mm)
From latch side	Push	42 inches (1065 mm)[2]	24 inches (610 mm)

[1]Add 6 inches (150 mm) if closer and latch provided.
[2]Add 6 inches (150 mm) if closer provided.
[3]Add 12 inches (305 mm) beyond latch if closer and latch provided.
[4]Beyond hinge side.

❖ Figures 404.2.4.1(a) through (g) are diagrams for the information in Table 404.2.3.1. The direction of the arrow is the anticipated approach toward the door. It is important to pay attention to notes for the table (indicated as asterisks in the figures). When closers and/or latches are installed, the doors may be more difficult to operate; therefore, additional clearances will be required. Overall sizes are not indicated because door sizes may vary.

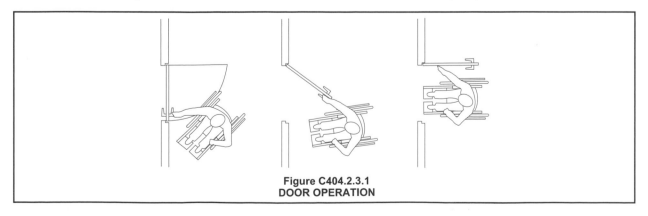

Figure C404.2.3.1
DOOR OPERATION

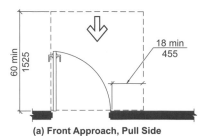

Fig. 404.2.3.1(a)
Maneuvering Clearance at Manual Swinging Doors

❖ The front approach to the pull side of a door requires an 18-inch (455 mm) clear space adjacent to the latch side of the door. This space may be used to position a wheelchair, crutches or other walking aid to gain the leverage necessary to open the door. This space also enables the user to be outside the swing of the door as it begins to open. By pulling at an angle to the axis of the wheelchair without the required clearances, there is a possibility of interference between the edge of the door and the footrest on the wheelchair, which would render the door inaccessible to the person using a wheelchair.

The dimension perpendicular to the door of 60 inches (1525 mm) accommodates the wheelchair in the clear floor space dimension of 48 inches (1220 mm) at an angle [see Figure 404.2.3.1(a)].

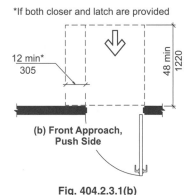

Fig. 404.2.3.1(b)
Maneuvering Clearance at Manual Swinging Doors

❖ The front approach to the push side of a door that has a latch and closer requires a smaller clear space to the side because it is easier to push and follow than to pull and maneuver through the opening. For the same reason, the dimension perpendicular needs to be only 48 inches (1220 mm) instead of the 60 inches (1525 mm) because the smaller dimension is the same as found in Section 305.

Doors equipped with only a closer or a latch (but not both) are not required to have the 12-inch (305 mm) maneuvering space. The additional maneuvering space requirement is based on the fact that the user needs to exert more force and perform a combination of movements to open doors that have both a latch and a closer. A door that has a latch but no closer can be opened by disengaging the latching mechanism and pushing with the hand, with the door remaining open

during passage. A door that has a closer but no latch can be pushed open by the momentum of the user without requiring additional hand or arm movement. Typically, this is accomplished by pushing the door open with the feet and footrest. For a door that has both a latch and a closer, the user must perform all of these movements simultaneously, which requires additional maneuvering space. Figure 404.2.3.1(b) illustrates the requirements for this type of door use.

The front approach to the push side of a door that does not have both a latch and a closer requires less maneuvering and effort to open; therefore, less space is required. Clear space is not required on the side adjacent to the door opening because the approach would be directly in line with the 32-inch (1815 mm) minimum required doorway. The dimension, perpendicular, is the same as found in Section 305 and is required in most cases when a front approach is used and no additional maneuvers are needed, such as to water fountains in an alcove.

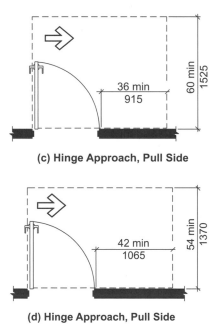

(c) Hinge Approach, Pull Side

(d) Hinge Approach, Pull Side

Fig. 404.2.3.1(c) and (d)
Maneuvering Clearance at Manual Swinging Doors

❖ Of the various configurations and approaches, this is probably the most difficult and requires the largest clear floor space. A space of approximately 15 square feet (1.4 m^2) is required to the side of the door because of the need to unlatch, reverse direction while opening the door, maneuver around the door, and then turn and pass through. These dimensions are required regardless of the existence of a latch or a closer on the door.

The dimensions of the maneuvering space depend on the configuration of the walls surrounding the door. If the dimension adjacent to the latch is between 36 inches (915 mm) and 42 inches (1065 mm), the dimension perpendicular to the door in the closed position must be no less than 60 inches (1525 mm). When the length of the adjacent wall is 42 inches (1065 mm) or more, the other dimension need be only 54 inches (1370 mm). Figures 404.2.3.1(c) and (d) show these two situations.

The designer has a number of options available to reduce the space required. Changing from a left-hand to a right-hand door, reversing the swing and placing a sliding or folding door in the opening can often reduce the required clearance.

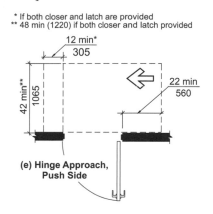

* If both closer and latch are provided
** 48 min (1220) if both closer and latch provided

(e) Hinge Approach, Push Side

Fig. 404.2.3.1(e)
Maneuvering Clearance at Manual Swinging Doors

❖ Without both a latch and a closer, a parallel approach to the hinge side of a door that swings in the direction of travel requires a maneuvering clear space width of 22 inches (560 mm) measured from the hinge side of the door and a perpendicular distance of 42 inches (1065 mm). This requirement is shown in Figure 404.2.3.1(e).

When the door is equipped with both a latch and a closer, this arrangement requires a perpendicular dimension of 48 inches (1220 mm) instead of the previously stated 42 inches (1065 mm) and an additional 12 inches (305 mm) measured from the latch side. Assuming a 32 inch (845 mm) clear width door, the total width would be 66 inches (1675 mm) total width. This additional maneuvering space is required to allow the user enough maneuvering space to get the

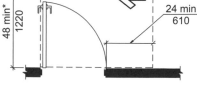

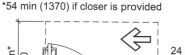

*54 min (1370) if closer is provided

(f) Latch Approach, Pull Side

Fig. 404.2.3.1(f)
Maneuvering Clearance at Manual Swinging Doors

❖ When approaching the latch-side of a door without a closer that swings against the direction of travel, ma-

neuvering space must be provided along the wall adjacent to the latch side. This dimension shall be at least 24 inches (610 mm). The dimension perpendicular to this wall must be at least 48 inches (1220 mm). Figure 404.2.3.1(f) provides the detail of this provision. Because this condition assumes a parallel approach, these dimensions differ from the front approach shown in Figure 404.2.3.1(a).

If the door has a closer, an additional 6 inches (150 mm) [for a total of 54 inches (1370 mm)] is needed perpendicular to the doorway. This additional 6 inches (150 mm) is required to allow the user enough maneuvering space to overcome the closer.

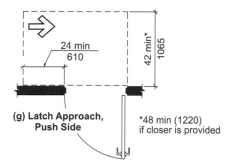

(g) Latch Approach, Push Side

*48 min (1220) if closer is provided

Fig. 404.2.3.1(g)
Maneuvering Clearance at Manual Swinging Doors

❖ When approaching the latch-side of a door that swings in the direction of travel and the door is not equipped with a closer, 24 inches (610 mm) of maneuvering space must be provided along the wall adjacent to the latch side. This is the same dimension that is required for the same approach, but from the pull side of the door. See commentary to Figure 404.2.3.1(f). The dimension perpendicular to the doorway must be not less than 42 inches (1065 mm). The resulting space, at least 56 inches (1420 mm) [24 inches plus 32 inches] by 42 inches (1065 mm), is required to complete the turn.

Similar to the latch approach from the pull side [Figure 404.2.3.1(f)] an additional space of 6 inches (150 mm) is needed perpendicular to the doorway if the door has a closer. This 6 inch (150 mm) increase in both Figures 404.2.3.1(f) and (g) is based solely on the installation of a closer and is not like the requirements shown in Figures 404.2.3.1(b) and (e) that require an increase when both a closer and a latch are installed.

404.2.3.2 Sliding and Folding Doors. Sliding doors and folding doors shall have maneuvering clearances complying with Table 404.2.3.2.

❖ This section provides the reference to Table 404.2.3.2, which establishes the minimum maneuvering clear-ances adjacent to manual sliding and folding doors. The table establishes the actual requirements which are then illustrated in Figures 404.2.3.2(a) through (c). See the commentary to Section 404.2.3.

Table 404.2.3.2—Maneuvering Clearances at Sliding and Folding Doors

Approach Direction	MINIMUM MANEUVERING CLEARANCES	
	Perpendicular to Doorway	Parallel to Doorway (beyond stop or latch side unless noted)
From front	48 inches (1220 mm)	0 inches (0 mm)
From nonlatch side	42 inches (1065 mm)	22 inches (560 mm)[1]
From latch side	42 inches (1065 mm)	24 inches (610 mm)

[1]Beyond pocket or hinge side.

❖ Figures 404.2.3.2(a) through (c) are diagrams showing the information in Table 404.2.3.2. The direction of the arrow is the anticipated approach toward the door. Overall sizes are not shown because door sizes may vary.

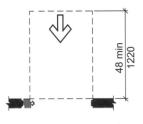

(a) Front Approach

**Fig 404.2.3.2(a)
Maneuvering Clearance at Sliding and Folding Doors**

❖ A front approach to a sliding or folding door demands the least maneuvering space of all door conditions–48 inches (1220 mm) perpendicular to the doorway with the minimum width of 32 inches (815 mm) as found in Section 404.2.2. These dimensions are also consistent with the forward reach concepts. The person approaching the door has sufficient leverage based on the position of the door relative to the user.

Consideration should be given to the fact that many who use wheelchairs are unable to extend their arms and hands beyond their toes. Therefore, the hardware required to operate the door that is located on the door may not be reachable if a person using a wheelchair is perpendicular to it. Space provided in front of the door that is wider than the door opening would allow the user to become parallel with the door to pull or push it open.

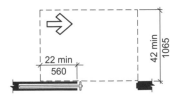

(b) Pocket or Hinge Approach

**Fig 404.2.3.2(b)
Maneuvering Clearance at Sliding and Folding Doors**

❖ When a sliding or folding door is approached from a parallel position, a minimum of 42 inches (1065 mm)

perpendicular to the doorway enables the user to operate the hardware and then move forward or backward as required to either push or pull the door. This dimension applies to both a sliding-side and latch-side approach as shown in Figures 404.2.3.2(b) and (c).

When the user is approaching the side where the door rests in the open position (the slide-side), the other dimension of the maneuvering space must be measured parallel to the door a distance of at least 22 inches (560 mm) from the stop side plus the width of the door [i.e., 54 inches (1370 mm) total with a 32 inch (815 mm) clear width door] from the latch side toward the approach position. This requirement is found in Table 404.2.3.2 and footnote 1 to the table. Figure 404.2.3.2(b) depicts this requirement.

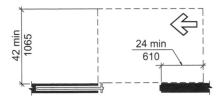

(c) Stop or Latch Approach

**Fig 404.2.3.2(c)
Maneuvering Clearance at Sliding and Folding Doors**

❖ See commentary for Figure 404.2.3.2(b) regarding the dimension perpendicular to the doorway.

For the dimension parallel to the doorway, the maneuvering space must begin at the edge of the opening when the door is in the fully opened position, and extend past the latch side toward the approach position a minimum of 24 inches [i.e., 56 inches (1425 mm) total with a 32 inch (815 mm) clear width door]. For a side reach to be completed, the user needs this additional space along the wall to engage the hardware and advance in the direction of travel.

404.2.3.3 Doorways without Doors. Doorways without doors that are less than 36 inches (915 mm) in width shall have maneuvering clearances complying with Table 404.2.3.3

❖ This section refers to Table 404.2.3.3, which establishes the minimum maneuvering clearances adjacent to doorways which do not have a door installed in them. This is essentially dealing with cased openings. The table establishes the actual requirements which are fairly simple to comply with. See the commentary to Section 404.2.3

Table 404.2.3.3—Maneuvering Clearances for Doorways without Doors

Approach Direction	MINIMUM MANEUVERING CLEARANCES Perpendicular to doorway
From Front	48 inches (1220 mm)
From side	42 inches (1065 mm)

❖ Figures 404.2.3.3(a) and (b) are diagrams showing the information in Table 404.2.3.3. The direction of the arrow is the anticipated approach toward the doorway. Overall sizes are not shown because doorway sizes may vary.

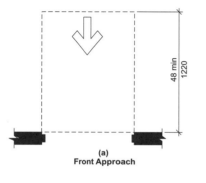

(a)
Front Approach

Figure 404.2.3.3(a)
Maneuvering Clearance at Doorways with Doors

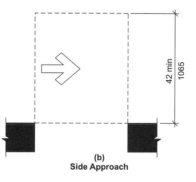

(b)
Side Approach

Figure 404.2.3.3(b)
Maneuvering Clearance at Doorways with Doors

❖ When the approach is from the front (forward approach) a clear space of 48 inches (1220 mm) is required perpendicular to the doorway. This essentially creates a space very similar to the clear floor space shown in Figure 305.5(a) of the standard. The only difference is that the space must be slightly wider. The clear floor space must be the full width of the doorway and would be a minimum of 32 inches (815 mm) wide to comply with Sections 403.5 and 404.2.2.

❖ When the approach is from the side, a 42 inch (1065 mm) distance perpendicular to the doorway is required. This is similar to the dimension required and shown in Figures 404.2.3.2(b) and (c) for sliding and folding doors. However, this section does not specify any additional dimension beyond the full width of the door. The general accessible route requirements will adequately provide any additionally needed maneuvering space near the doorway, and because the user does not have to operate any door hardware or push and pull a door, a turn is the only maneuver which the user may need to make.

404.2.3.4 Recessed Doors. Where any obstruction within 18 inches (455 mm) of the latch side of a doorway projects more than 8 inches (205 mm) beyond the face of the door, measured perpendicular to the face of the door, maneuvering clearances for a forward approach shall be provided.

❖ A door can be recessed because of wall thickness or because of the placement of the trim or other fixed elements adjacent to the door. Doors may also be recessed in an alcove to meet means of egress requirements for minimum clearances in exit access corridors. This section addresses situations in which a door is recessed for any of these reasons. The provisions are intended to address configurations similar to those shown in Figures 404.2.3.1(a) and (b). Because these doors are recessed from the general circulation route the standard requires an arrangement that permits a front approach. Depending on the type of door involved, manual swinging or sliding and folding doors, Sections 404.2.3.1 and 404.2.3.2 would specify the required clearances. These spaces must be provided so that the door is approachable and usable. Consideration also must be given to the maneuvering space on the other side of the door.

The provisions of this section apply when the door is recessed more than 8 inches (200 mm) from the plane of the wall adjacent to the general accessible route. The clear width requirements of Section 403.5 should also be considered for these doors. When the alcove is over 24 inches (610 mm) deep, the minimum required clear width of the alcove will be increased from 32 inches to 36 inches (815 to 915 mm). The clear width of the doorway may still be 32 inches (815 mm) even when the alcove depth is over 24 inches (610 mm). See the commentary to Section 404.2.3.

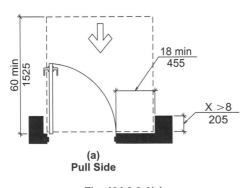
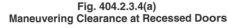

(a)
Pull Side

Fig. 404.2.3.4(a)
Maneuvering Clearance at Recessed Doors

❖ See the commentary for Figure 404.2.3.1(a).

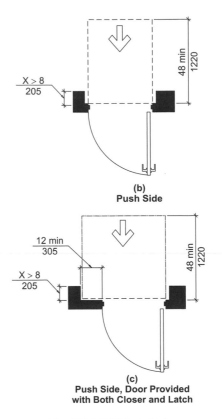

(b)
Push Side

(c)
Push Side, Door Provided
with Both Closer and Latch

Fig. 404.2.3.4(b) and (c)
Maneuvering Clearance at Recessed Doors

❖ See the commentary for Figure 404.2.3.1(b). Note the difference in maneuvering clearances when a closer and latch is provided.

404.2.3.5 Floor Surface. Floor surface within the maneuvering clearances shall have a slope not steeper than 1:48 and shall comply with Section 302.

❖ A sloped surface would make it difficult for a person using a wheelchair or a person using walking aids to remain stationary while at the same time trying to unlatch and open a door. Thus, the slope of these floor surfaces is limited to the same slope allowed for the cross-slope of accessible routes in general. The slope in any direction shall not be steeper than 1:48.

404.2.4 Thresholds at Doorways. If provided, thresholds at doorways shall be $\frac{1}{2}$ inch (13 mm) maximum in height. Raised thresholds and changes in level at doorways shall comply with Sections 302 and 303.

EXCEPTION: Section 404.2.4 shall not apply to existing thresholds or altered thresholds $\frac{3}{4}$ inch (19 mm) maximum in height that have a beveled edge on each side with a maximum slope of 1:2 for the height exceeding $\frac{1}{4}$ inch (6.4 mm).

❖ Thresholds and changes in the surface height at doorways are particularly inconvenient for person using a wheelchairs who also may have low stamina or restrictions in arm movement because complex maneuvering is required to get over the level change while operating the door.

The model building codes typically establish $\frac{1}{2}$ inch (13 mm) as the maximum change in elevation at a doorway where access for a person with a disability is required and a different amount at other doorways. Section 303 requires that where a threshold is over $\frac{1}{4}$ inch (6 mm) high, at least half of the height of the threshold should be beveled (see commentary Figure C404.2.4).

The exception is in recognition of the difficulties with existing buildings and changes in flooring materials and elevations at doors and doorways.

404.2.5 Two Doors in Series. Distance between two hinged or pivoted doors in series shall be 48 inches (1220 mm) minimum plus the width of any door swinging into the space. The space between the doors shall provide a turning space complying with Section 304.

❖ Typically, the doors-in-series condition occurs in entry vestibules that are used to reduce the infiltration of outside air. It is important to realize that this requirement applies only when the user must pass through two doors in succession. The requirement would not be applicable if, instead of a vestibule, the situation was a corridor and the two doors were into offices located on opposite sides of the corridor. A storm or screen door immediately in front of an entrance door or communicating doors in between two hotel rooms are not considered doors in a series.

Swinging doors in a series placed too closely together can create a condition where a person using a wheelchair may pass through one door, and still have to hold that door open while trying to open the second door. To resolve this condition, a minimum distance of 48 inches (1220 mm) is required between the doors if the doors swing away from each other or 48 inches (1220 mm) plus the width of any door swinging into the space is required [see Figure 404.2.5 and commentary Figure C404.2.5(a)].

Doors in a series are not always in a straight line. Doors may be offset, or located on adjacent walls rather than opposite walls. The intent is that a clear floor space for a wheelchair [i.e., 30 inches by 48 inches (765 by 1220 mm)] is available past the swing of the first door so the person entering can let one door close before the start to open the second door [see commentary Figure C404.2.5(b) and C404.2.5(c)].

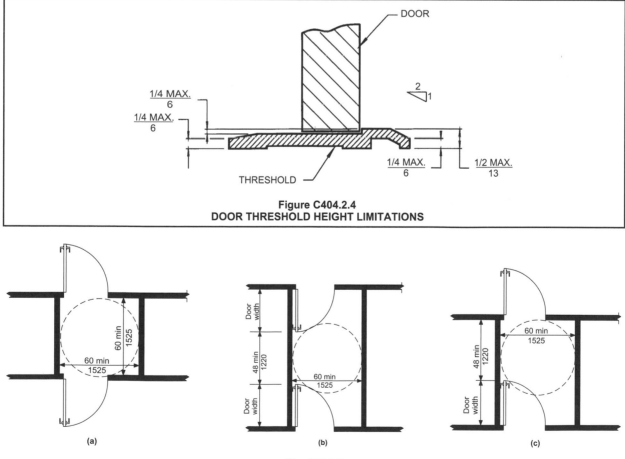

Figure C404.2.4
DOOR THRESHOLD HEIGHT LIMITATIONS

(a)   (b)   (c)

Fig. 404.2.5
Two Doors in a Series

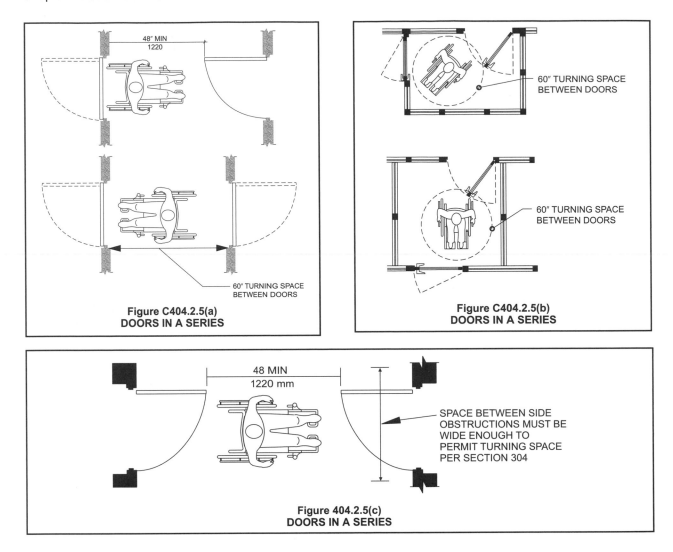

Figure C404.2.5(a)
DOORS IN A SERIES

Figure C404.2.5(b)
DOORS IN A SERIES

Figure 404.2.5(c)
DOORS IN A SERIES

The requirement for 5 pounds (22 N) maximum opening force in Section 404.2.8 is not applicable to outside doors; thus, sometimes outside doors are difficult for persons with limited mobility to open. In addition, the second door in a series could be locked. A turning space is required between the doors to avoid entrapment in this area. The turning space can overlap the swing of the doors and the door maneuvering clearances.

404.2.6 Door Hardware. Handles, pulls, latches, locks, and other operable parts on accessible doors shall have a shape that is easy to grasp with one hand and does not require tight grasping, pinching, or twisting of the wrist to operate. Operable parts of such hardware shall be 34 inches (865 mm) minimum and 48 inches (1220 mm) maximum above the floor. Where sliding doors are in the fully open position, operating hardware shall be exposed and usable from both sides.

> **EXCEPTION:** Locks used only for security purposes and not used for normal operation are permitted in any location.

❖ Some people with disabilities are unable to grasp objects with their hands or twist their wrists. Such people are unable to operate, or have great difficulty in operating, door hardware other than lever-operated mechanisms, push-type mechanisms and U-shaped handles. Door hardware that can be operated with a closed fist or a loose grip accommodates the greatest range of users. Hardware that requires simultaneous hand and finger movement requires greater dexterity and coordination and should be avoided for doors along an accessible route (see commentary Figure C404.2.6).

This section also assures that the hardware falls within the reach ranges specified in Section 308. The exception would accept a situation such as an unframed glass door at the entry to a building where the door lock is located at the very bottom of the door. Note that the security lock should not conflict with the door surface on the push side per Section 404.2.9.

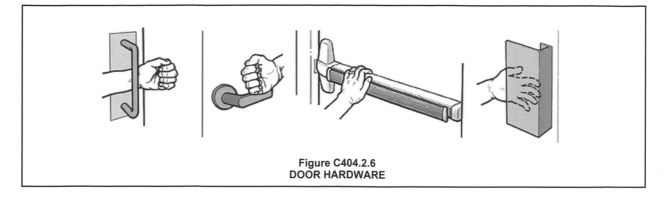

Figure C404.2.6
DOOR HARDWARE

404.2.7 Closing Speed.

404.2.7.1 Door Closers. Door closers shall be adjusted so that from an open position of 90 degrees, the time required to move the door to an open position of 12 degrees shall be 5 seconds minimum.

❖ Closers with delayed action features give a person more time to maneuver through doorways. They are particularly useful on frequently used interior doors. When used on fire doors, the closer should be adjusted so that the delay does not exceed requirements established by the administrative authority. This requirement also provides sufficient time for persons using walking aids, such as walkers and crutches, to maneuver through the door without the added burden of working against the door and closer.

404.2.7.2 Spring Hinges. Door spring hinges shall be adjusted so that from the open position of 70 degrees, the door shall move to the closed position in 1.5 seconds minimum.

❖ Although not considered as a "door closer" in the general sense, spring hinges create the same difficulty for people trying to open and then maneuver through the door. Therefore, for the same reasons that are mentioned in the commentary for Section 404.2.7.1 the standard establishes a minimum length of time for the door to close.

404.2.8 Door-Opening Force. Fire doors shall have the minimum opening force allowable by the appropriate administrative authority. The force for pushing or pulling open doors other than fire doors shall be as follows:

1. Interior hinged door: 5.0 pounds (22.2 N) maximum

2. Sliding or folding door: 5.0 pounds (22.2 N) maximum

These forces do not apply to the force required to retract latch bolts or disengage other devices that hold the door in a closed position.

❖ The maximum force pertains to the continuous application of force necessary to fully open a door, not the initial force needed to overcome the inertia of the door. It does not apply to the force required to retract bolts or to disengage other devices used to keep the door in a closed position.

Although some people with disabilities are unable to exert the maximum allowable force to open the door as given in this subsection, these forces are the minimum practical forces to permit the door closers to function. Door closers have certain minimum closing forces to close doors satisfactorily. Opening forces are measured with a spring scale as follows:

1. Hinged Doors. Apply force perpendicular to the door at the actuating device or 30 inches from the hinged side, whichever is the farthest from the hinge.

2. Sliding or Folding Doors. Apply force parallel to the door at the door pull or latch.

3. Application of the Force. Apply force gradually so that the applied force does not exceed the resistance of the door. Air-pressure differentials, especially in high-rise buildings, have an adverse effect on door-opening force. Accessible openings located in these areas sometimes require modification or possibly the use of automatic or power-assisted doors to comply with the allowable forces given.

Forces to operate a door involve more than a simple, single operation. For example, doors that are latched are unlatched by a force that consists of depressing a lever or applying a direct force. The additional force to overcome the inertia of a door exceeds that required to maintain movement of the door. In general, only a momentary auxiliary force is needed to exceed the force given in Section 404.2.8. It is important to notice that this section does not apply to "fire doors." This exclusion should not be considered as allowing an unlimited amount of force but is instead simply recognizing that for the door to be able to close against the force (pressures) generated by a fire, the door closer may need to exceed the 5.0 pound (22 N) limitation. The administrative authority should make sure that the closer on a fire door has the capacity to close against the forces generated by the fire, but the actual force should be kept as low as possible. Doing this will help to assure that the fire door can perform as intended but also still permit use of the door by people who may have strength and mobility limitations.

404.2.9 Door Surface. Door surfaces within 10 inches (255 mm) of the floor, measured vertically, shall be a smooth surface on the push side extending the full width of the door. Parts creating horizontal or vertical joints in such surface shall be within $1/16$ inch (1.6 mm) of the same plane as the other. Cavities created by added kick plates shall be capped.

EXCEPTIONS:

1. Sliding doors.

2. Tempered glass doors without stiles and having a bottom rail or shoe with the top leading edge tapered at no less than 60 degrees from the horizontal shall not be required to meet the 10 inch (255 mm) bottom rail height requirement.

3. Doors that do not extend to within 10 inches (255 mm) of the floor.

❖ This provision is intended to assist people who will be attempting to open a door from the "push" side of the door. Some persons with disabilities push against doors with their chairs or walkers to open them. Applied kick plates on doors with closers reduce the required maintenance by withstanding abuse from wheelchairs and canes. By providing a smooth surface (one with no more than $1/16$ inch (1.6 mm) variation), a user can be assured that the door will slide

along the leg rest of a wheelchair, their foot or the bottom of a walker or crutch that is being pushed against the door without catching. A vertical bar or rod on the latch side of a door is likely to interfere with the opening of a door when the feet or footrest are pressed against a door to open it [see commentary Figure C404.2.9(a)]. To be effective, a kick plate must cover the door width, less approximately 2 inches (50 mm), up to a height of 10 inches (255 mm) from the floor [see commentary Figure C404.2.9 (b)]. This range will allow for the most common height settings for wheelchair foot plates.

The sentence requiring that cavities be capped will typically be applied when the kick plate is added onto a glass or panel door and the bottom rail of the door is less than 10 inches (255 mm) in height.

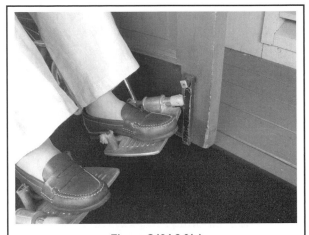

Figure C404.2.9(a)
DOOR SURFACE OBSTRUCTION

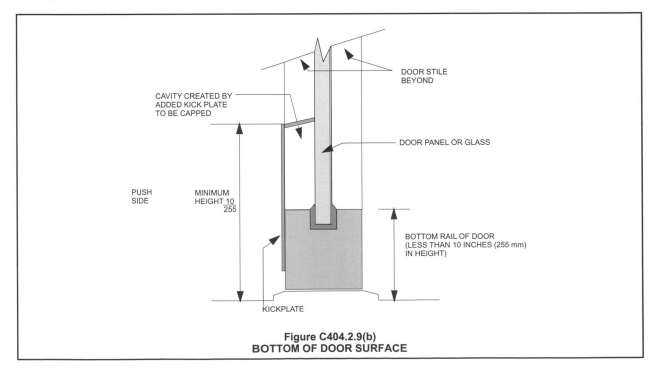

Figure C404.2.9(b)
BOTTOM OF DOOR SURFACE

404.2.10 Vision Lites. Doors and sidelites adjacent to doors containing one or more glazing panels that permit viewing through the panels shall have the bottom of at least one panel on either the door or an adjacent sidelite 43 inches (1090 mm) maximum above the floor.

EXCEPTION: Vision lites with the lowest part more than 66 inches (1675 mm) above the floor are not required to comply with Section 404.2.10.

❖ If either a door with glazing or a sidelite located adjacent to the door would permit viewing from one side of the door to the other, at least one portion of the glazing must be located at a maximum height of 43 inches (1090 mm) above the floor. There are two important aspects of this requirement to be aware of. The first is that the provision does not require a vision panel. It simply states that when one is installed which permits viewing, that one must be installed at the maximum height (see commentary Figure C404.2.10). Secondly, it is important to note that only one glazed panel is required to meet this height limitation. Therefore, if a door has a glazed portion located with the bottom edge 60 inches (1525 mm) above the floor and a sidelite is also installed, having the sidelite meet the 43 inch (1090 mm) maximum height limitation and not require a lower glazing height on the door itself would be acceptable. This 43 inch (1090 mm) height was established to provide a person using a wheelchair a view through the glazing at a height that is as low as possible without interfering with the typical door hardware installation height. See Figure C102(a) to see how this height coordinates with the view of the typical person using a wheelchair.

The intent of the exemption is only to regulate vision lites that are located at a height where the typical person could see through. If glazing such as a transom window above a door is installed, this section should not be viewed as requiring the low level viewing panel. The exception allows glazing that has a bottom edge above a height 66 inches (1675 mm) or higher above the floor. This is typically a fire door.

404.3 Automatic Doors. Automatic doors and automatic gates shall comply with Section 404.3. Full powered automatic doors shall comply with ANSI/BHMA A156.10 listed in Section 105.2.4. Power-assist and low-energy doors shall comply with ANSI/BHMA A156.19 listed in Section 105.2.3.

EXCEPTION: Doors, doorways, and gates designed to be operated only by security personnel shall not be required to comply with Sections 404.3.2, 404.3.4, and 404.3.5.

❖ Besides requiring compliance with the applicable standard, this section provides a reminder to the requirements found within the subsections, which address the clear opening width and other issues related to these doors. The building hardware industry has developed two separate consensus standards for automatic doors. Issues such as safety, durability, usability, operation and installation are covered. The standards are available from the American National Standards Institute, 25 West 43rd Street, Fourth Floor, New York, New York 10036.

The model building codes also have requirements with which power-operated and power assisted door must comply to ensure the usability of these doors when they are part of required means of egress. The term "automatic doors" is actually more of a generic term which includes both the "full powered" doors which open on their own and the "low-energy"/"power-assisted" doors which typically will not open automatically but will in-

Figure C404.2.10
VISION LITES

stead open with the opening forces at a very minimal level. The key distinctions between the "power-operated" and "power-assisted" doors are found within the two distinct standards. A different industry standard applies to power-assisted doors because of the differences in the method of initiating the opening of the door. See the definition and commentary for "power-assisted door" in Section 106.5.

Automatic doors, in general, are favored by people with disabilities because of the ease of use. These doors can be used by individuals with disabilities who are unable to use manually operated doors.

Doors that are operated only be security personnel should meet accessible requirements for automatic doors with the exception of maneuvering clearance, doors in series and control switches. Examples of security personnel are guards in jails, bailiffs in courtrooms, guards at security gates. The intent is not to exempt all the doors that these people access, but to exempt doors that these people are responsible for opening, closing and/or locking for security reasons. An example would be the door at the cells and between the courtroom and cells in a courthouse. Security personnel should have sole control of the doors. It is not acceptable for security personnel to operate the doors for people with disabilities and allow others to have independent access.

404.3.1 Clear Opening Width. Doorways shall have a clear opening width of 32 inches (815 mm) in power-on and power-off mode. The minimum clear opening width for automatic door systems shall be based on the clear opening width provided with all leafs in the open position.

❖ This provision assures that the 32 inch clear width required by the accessible route provisions of Section 403.5 is maintained at the door. This also matches the width found in Section 404.2.2 for manual doors. This clear width is required whether the door is on and operating or is not turned on. The second portion of this section is an important distinction between automatic doors and manual doors. Under this provision, if an automatic door uses two leaves to meet the 32 inch (815 mm) clear width that is acceptable. Manual doors are limited by Section 404.2.1 to having at least one leaf that meets this clear width requirement. Because of this, an automatic door which has two 30 inch (765 mm) leaves which both open together would be acceptable in meeting the clear width requirement.

404.3.2 Maneuvering Clearances. Maneuvering clearances at power-assisted doors shall comply with Section 404.2.3.

❖ Instead of duplicating the requirements, a reference to the provisions for manual doors is used. See the commentary in Section 404.2.3. Maneuvering clearances at doors permit the user passage and approach whether the door is manual or power-assisted.

Fully automatic doors do not need maneuvering clearances except the straight on approach of any ac-

cessible route because the door is opening for the user without any application of force except perhaps at a remote button/switch. One of the advantages of using automatic doors is that they work where the maneuvering space is not available. This is especially true for rehabilitation of existing buildings.

404.3.3 Thresholds. Thresholds and changes in level at doorways shall comply with Section 404.2.4.

❖ Instead of duplicating the requirements, a reference to the provisions for manual doors is used. See the commentary in Section 404.2.4. Thresholds and other changes in level at doors could affect access whether the door is manual or automatic.

404.3.4 Two Doors in Series. Doors in series shall comply with Section 404.2.5.

❖ Instead of duplicating the requirements, a reference to the provisions for manual doors is used. See the commentary in Section 404.2.5. Doors placed too close together can affect access whether the door is manual or automatic.

404.3.5 Control Switches. Manually operated control switches shall comply with Section 309. The clear floor space adjacent to the control switch shall be located beyond the arc of the door swing.

❖ See the commentary in Section 309. By referring to Section 309 any control switches that must be operated by the user must be provided with a clear floor space near the device, be located at a height that is within the reach ranges and be easily operated. An example of items affected by this provision would be the push button that is often used with automatic doors. A person operating the button to initiate the opening of the automatic door must be located so that when the door opens, it will not bump into the person who pushed the button (see commentary Figure C404.3.5).

Exception 2 of Section 309.3 exempts controls that are not intended for general use by the building occupants. An example of this is some power-operated doors

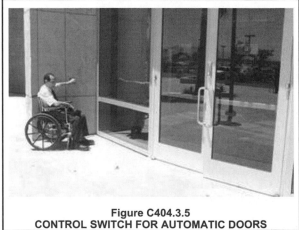

Figure C404.3.5
CONTROL SWITCH FOR AUTOMATIC DOORS

having a switch located near the top of the door that can be used to either turn off power to the door or to an occupant sensing device. These switches are not used in the normal door operation by the building occupants.

405 Ramps

❖ The intent of this section is to address ramps that are part of an accessible route. Ramps that are not part of an accessible route, such as those in portions of assembly seating that are not required to be accessible, may have steeper slopes where permitted by the model codes adopted by the authority having jurisdiction and are not required to comply with the provisions for accessible ramps in this standard.

The model codes also include provisions for guards at drop offs as an issue of safety. These would be applicable to all ramps, including accessible ramps. Although this section does include requirements for edge protection and handrails, this section does not include information on guards. See commentary Figure C405 for an example of a ramp with a required guard.

405.1 General. Ramps along accessible routes shall comply with Section 405.

❖ According to the definition for ramps in Section 106.5, a sloped walking surface with a rise of more than 1 inch per 20 inches (1:20) of run is considered a ramp. If elevators or platform lifts are not available to connect different levels, ramps are essential for a person using a wheelchair or scooter.

A gradual slope of 1:20 or less is treated as essentially level. However, many persons who use wheelchairs cannot travel long distances on such a slope. Therefore, even if the sloped walking surface does not qualify as a ramp, level areas should be provided in a path of travel at intervals of not more than 200 feet (61 mm) to provide rest areas (see Section 403.5.2, Passing Space).

405.2 Slope. Ramp runs shall have a running slope not steeper than 1:12.

EXCEPTION: In existing buildings or facilities, ramps shall be permitted to have slopes steeper than 1:12 complying with Table 405.2 where such slopes are necessary due to space limitations.

❖ The ability to manage an incline is related to both its slope and its length. Persons using wheelchairs with disabilities affecting arms or with low stamina have serious difficulty using inclines. Most ambulatory people and most people who use wheelchairs can more easily manage a slope of 1:16 and runs of 20 feet (6100 mm). Many people have difficulty managing a slope of 1:12 for 30 feet (9150 mm). Ramps should be straight, not curved, unless engineering analysis has been performed to ensure that the slope of the curved ramp is not steeper than 1:12 anywhere along the line of travel and the maximum cross slope in Section 405.3 is not exceeded. All four wheels of a wheelchair must remain in contact with the ramp surface at all times.

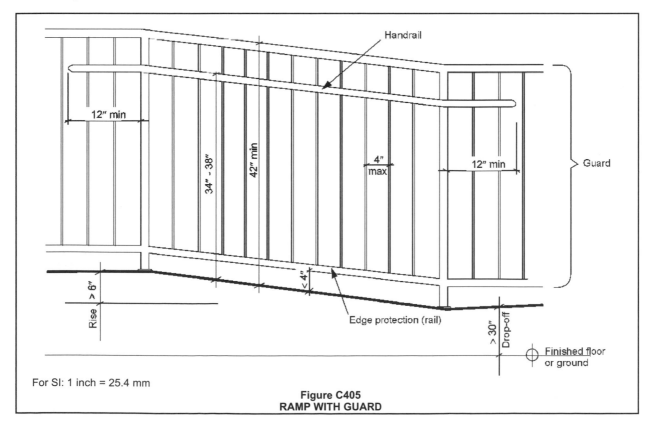

For SI: 1 inch = 25.4 mm

Figure C405
RAMP WITH GUARD

**Table 405.2—Allowable Ramp Dimensions for Construction in
Existing Sites, Buildings, and Facilities**

Slope[1]	Maximum Rise
Steeper than 1:10 but not steeper than 1:8	3 inches (75 mm)
Steeper than 1:12 but not steeper than 1:10	6 inches (150 mm)

[1]A slope steeper than 1:8 shall not be permitted.

The steeper slopes permitted for existing facilities are severely limited in rise and length to ensure that all four wheels of a wheelchair will not be on the sloped surface at the same time.

405.3 Cross Slope. Cross slope of ramp runs shall not be steeper than 1:48.

❖ The slope of a ramp in the direction perpendicular to the path of travel can greatly affect the use of a ramp. Where the "cross slope" of the ramp is too great, it can make moving on the ramp in a straight direction very difficult. If severe enough, it may create situations in which a chair user is concerned with tipping or could prevent a chair user or a person using a walker from being adequately supported. A larger cross slope can also affect pedestrians by causing their feet and ankles to tip to uncomfortable angles.

The cross slope of a curved ramp should be carefully designed and checked. A curved ramp is likely to have a difference in elevation from the inside to the outside of the curve, which creates a cross slope steeper than 1:48 and a curved surface on which only three of the four wheels of a wheelchair rest at any one time. Dangerous handling problems are therefore created for the person using a wheelchair. It is not possible to maneuver a wheelchair to precisely follow the curvature of the ramp. A curved ramp is negotiated by a series of rectilinear movements, with intermittent "corrections" to compensate for the curvature of the ramp. All portions of the curved ramp must also comply with the general slope provisions of Section 405.2.

405.4 Floor Surfaces. Floor surfaces of ramp runs shall comply with Section 302.

❖ Because the movement on a ramp is difficult enough, it is important that the surface of both the ramp and landings comply with the provisions of Section 302. This will assure that the surface provides a firm base of support without excessive cushioning, changes of level or openings.

405.5 Clear Width. The clear width of a ramp run shall be 36 inches (915 mm) minimum. Where handrails are provided on the ramp run, the clear width shall be measured between the handrails.

❖ The required ramp width corresponds to the minimum width for a passageway longer than 24 inches (610 mm). See Section 403.5. Based on the effort and types of movement needed to maneuver on the ramp, the 36-inch (915 mm) width makes the ramp easier to use

for persons in a chair or using a walker or cane/crutches. Although handrails are permitted to protrude from the walls along an accessible route (see Section 307.2, Exception 1), in order for the handrails to not be an obstruction, the clear width should be measured between the handrails and also be available between any post supports for the handrail (see commentary Figure C405.5).

**Figure C405.5
MINIMUM CLEAR WIDTH**

405.6 Rise. The rise for any ramp run shall be 30 inches (760 mm) maximum.

❖ The ability to manage an incline is related to both its slope and its length. A person using a wheelchair with disabilities affecting arms or with low stamina has serious difficulty using inclines. Therefore, the code establishes a maximum rise of 30 inches (765 mm) for any ramp between landings or floor levels. Though accepted by the standard, some people may have difficulty managing a slope of 1:12 for 30 feet (9 m). Therefore, a smaller rise and lower slope would generally improve access. Most ambulatory people and most people who use wheelchairs can more easily manage a slope of 1:16 and runs of 20 feet (6 m) versus the permitted 1:12 slope and a 30 inch (765 mm) rise that would be obtained over a 30 foot (9 m) run.

405.7 Landings. Ramps shall have landings at bottom and top of each ramp run. Landings shall comply with Section 405.7.

❖ Landings provide an area for resting, turning or passing another wheelchair. They are, therefore, an important part of creating accessible ramps that permit the transition from one level to another along an accessible route. The individual features of slope, width, length, change in direction and doorways are addressed by the referenced subsections (see Figure 405.7 and commentary Figure C405.7.4).

405.7.1 Slope. Landings shall have a slope not steeper than 1:48 and shall comply with Section 302.

❖ The general intent of this provision is to require that landings be level or have only a very low slope. The 1:48 slope is intended to match the cross slope provisions found in Sections 403.3 and 405.3. Providing a level landing where a ramp changes direction precludes the creation of a cross slope greater than 1:48, which could otherwise result from the simultaneous sloping and turning plane of the ramp surface. The 1:48 maximum slope will also permit sloping an exterior landing enough for drainage and yet still have it flat enough to be usable as an accessible route.

405.7.2 Width. Clear width of landings shall be at least as wide as the widest ramp run leading to the landing.

❖ This provision simply assures that the landing is at least as wide as any ramp that it serves and therefore does not narrow or reduce the available route of travel. If the ramp is wider than the minimum width required by Section 405.5, the landing width must also be increased even though the ramp is in excess of the minimum required width. This provision does not deal with the "required" width but is instead tied to the actual width of the ramp that the landing serves. The width of the landing may need to be increased from that specified by this section if the landing is being used to change the direction of travel. See Section 405.7.4.

405.7.3 Length. Landings shall have a clear length of 60 inches (1525 mm) minimum.

❖ A length of 60 inches provides a stopping distance, which is greater than the length of the wheelchair. This will also provide additional space to allow a chair user to maneuver before approaching another ramp, door or other object because the landing is longer than the wheelchair.

405.7.4 Change in Direction. Ramps that change direction at ramp landings shall be sized to provide a turning space complying with Section 304.3.

❖ The minimum landing where a ramp changes direction provides maneuvering space for the person using a wheelchair (see commentary Figure C405.7.4). The 60-inch (1525 mm) turning space may result in a landing that is larger than the width which is required by Section 405.7.2. This size landing can provide for a turning space in compliance with Section 304.3 or can allow passage of two chair users at the landing similar to the requirements of Section 403.5.2.

Providing a landing where a ramp changes direction precludes the creation of a cross slope greater than 1:48, which could otherwise result from the simultaneous sloping and turning plane of the ramp surface. See Sections 405.3 and 405.7.1.

405.7.5 Doorways. Where doorways are adjacent to a ramp landing, maneuvering clearances required by Sections 404.2.3 and 404.3.2 shall be permitted to overlap the landing area. Where doors that are subject to locking are adjacent to a ramp landing, landings shall be sized to provide a turning space complying with Section 304.3.

❖ This section serves to remind designers that the landing may be used for the dual purpose of also providing the

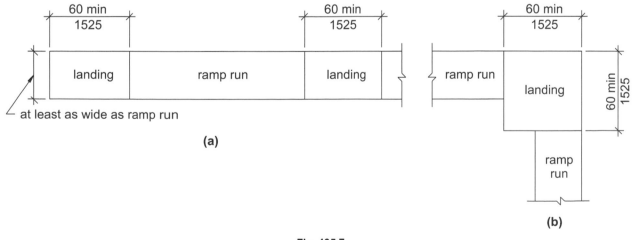

**Fig. 405.7
Ramp Landings**

maneuvering space adjacent to a doorway [see commentary Figure C405.7.5(a)]. One aspect of this section that is important to note, but is very subtle, is the fact that the doors are permitted only adjacent to the ramp landing and not adjacent or on the ramp itself. This wording about "adjacent to a ramp landing" can also be considered as supporting or reinforcing the provision of Section 404.2.4.5 that requires a level landing.

It is not possible for a person in a wheelchair to travel backwards down a ramp and maintain adequate control. If the door at the top or bottom landing of a ramp could be locked, a turning space must be provided at that top or bottom landing to allow the person to turn around and go back along the ramp if they cannot get in [see commentary Figure C405.7.5(b)].

405.8 Handrails. Ramp runs with a rise greater than 6 inches (150 mm) shall have handrails complying with Section 505.

❖ Handrails on ramps provide a graspable object for guidance and support while negotiating a ramp. Although handrails on ramps serve many of the same functions as those on stairs, the need for a handrail on a stairway is recognizably more critical because of the greater degree of difficulty involved in traversing a stairway as compared to a ramp. Handrails are nonetheless necessary for ramps because the ramp is not a flat, level surface and the user must exercise caution to avoid a slip or fall. The handrail provides a solid, stable element to grasp that can help arrest a fall. This is especially important for individuals with varying

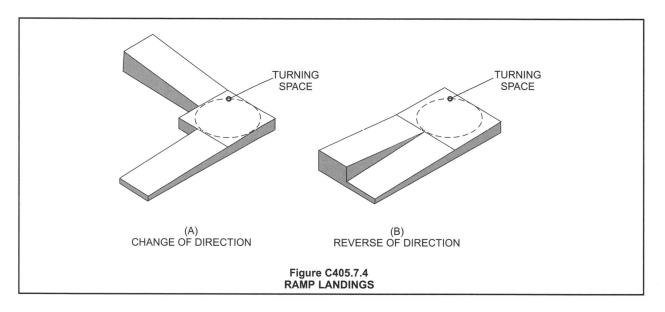

(A)
CHANGE OF DIRECTION

(B)
REVERSE OF DIRECTION

Figure C405.7.4
RAMP LANDINGS

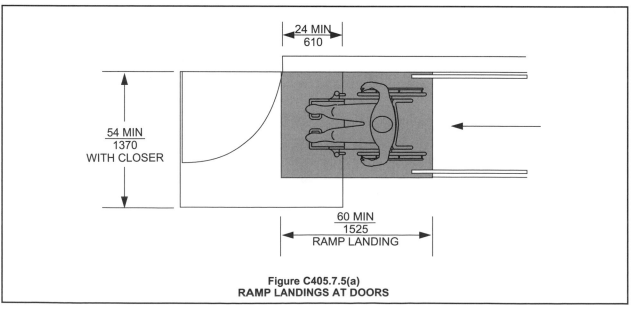

Figure C405.7.5(a)
RAMP LANDINGS AT DOORS

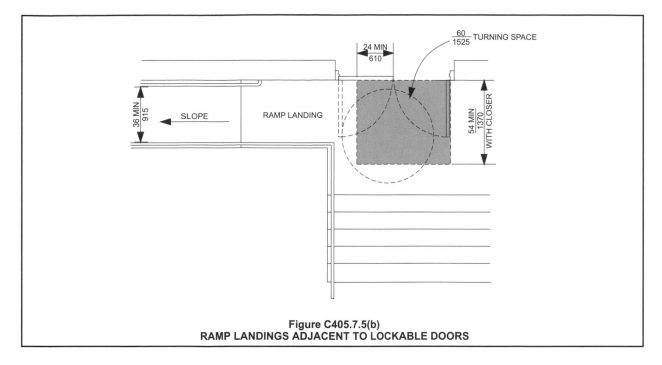

Figure C405.7.5(b)
RAMP LANDINGS ADJACENT TO LOCKABLE DOORS

degrees of mobility impairments. A handrail can also be used to propel a wheelchair forward, to control forward descent and to control backward descent. The exclusion for ramps with a rise of 6 inches (150 mm) or less recognizes that most users would be able to easily manage a climb or descent of such heights and lengths.

Handrails may protrude over an accessible route, but along the ramp they must not reduce the clear width of the ramp to less than 36 inches (915 mm) between the handrails (see Section 405.5).

405.9 Edge Protection. Edge protection complying with Section 405.9.1 or 405.9.2 shall be provided on each side of ramp runs and at each side of ramp landings.

EXCEPTIONS:

1. Ramps not required to have handrails where curb ramp flares complying with Section 406.3 are provided.

2. Sides of ramp landings serving an adjoining ramp run or stairway.

3. Sides of ramp landings having a vertical drop-off of $1/2$ inch (13 mm) maximum within 10 inches (255 mm) horizontally of the minimum landing area.

❖ Handrails, curbs, walls and extended edges serve to prevent wheels of wheelchairs from dropping off the edge of a ramp and stranding or injuring the user. They also serve a similar purpose for persons using other walking aids. Handrails and walls are also used by some person using a wheelchairs to slow their rate of descent if necessary. This section provides the reference to the two sections which provide the specific details of how edge protection is to be obtained. Figures 405.9(a) and (b) from the standard illustrate the options found in the two subsections. Commentary Figure C405.9 provides examples of alternate options and different views.

The three exceptions address situations where either the ramp or landings are not required to have edge pro-

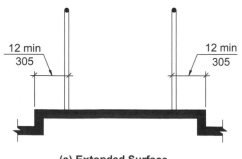

(a) Extended Surface

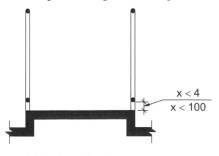

(b) Curb or Barrier

Fig. 405.9
Ramp Edge Protection

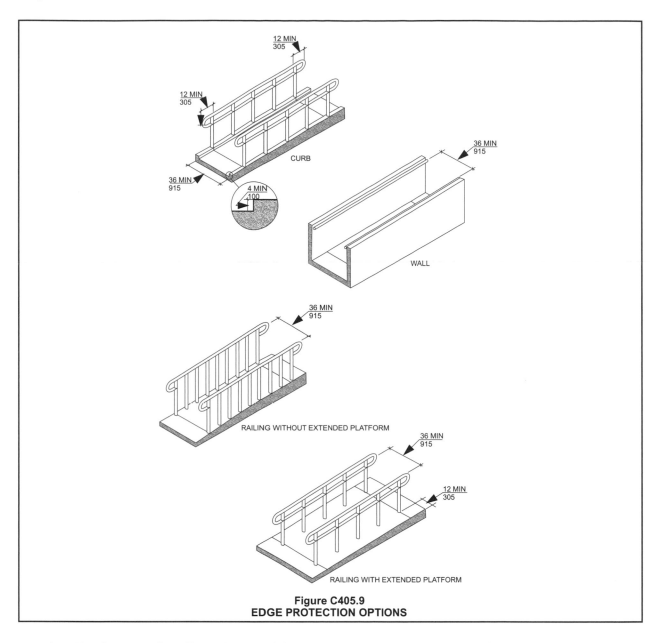

Figure C405.9
EDGE PROTECTION OPTIONS

tection. The first exception allows the use of flared sides adjacent to the ramp similar to those used for curb ramps. The second exception addresses a case that should really be self-evident, but will assure that a curb or other type of edge protection is not placed between the ramp and the landing. The last exception recognizes that when the ramp and landing are essentially at the same level as the adjacent ground or floor level that there is no danger of the user dropping off of the edge.

405.9.1 Extended Floor Surface. The floor surface of the ramp run or ramp landing shall extend 12 inches (305 mm) minimum beyond the inside face of a railing complying with Section 505.

❖ See commentary for Section 405.9, Figure 405.9(a) or the "extended platform" shown in commentary Figure C405.9. By extending the surface of the ramp or

landing beyond the railing or by being at the same level as the floor or ground surface, a person using a wheelchair will be less likely to get near any edge where a wheel could drop over. This is also beneficial for persons using walkers, canes or crutches.

405.9.2 Curb or Barrier. A curb or barrier shall be provided that prevents the passage of a 4-inch (100 mm) diameter sphere where any portion of the sphere is within 4 inches (100 mm) of the floor.

❖ Any type of curb or barrier that can prevent the passage of a 4 inch (100 mm) diameter sphere at this low height will be adequate to keep the wheels of a chair from getting to the edge of the ramp or landing. Figure 405.9(b) shows how a bar which is elevated no more than 4 inches (100 mm) above the ramp or landing surface may provide this protection. The "curb" and "wall" figures shown in Figure C405.9 provide two other acceptable alternates. The "railing without extended platform" detail which is shown in Figure C405.9 could also be accepted if the spacing of the vertical balusters in the railing are located less than 4 inches (100 mm) apart. If the vertical balusters are spaced farther than 4 inches (100 mm) apart, then a curb, a horizontal rail or extended floor surface would be needed. If a curb is chosen, the curb must be a minimum of 4 inches (100 mm) high.

405.10 Wet Conditions. Landings subject to wet conditions shall be designed to prevent the accumulation of water.

❖ This is a universally sound design principle that has many benefits beyond the accessibility perspective. The concern of this standard is the potential safety hazard that would exist. Standing water can render a ground surface significantly more slippery for both foot traffic and crutch tips. In freezing climates, water that accumulates can freeze, creating an extremely dangerous condition for all pedestrians, including people in wheelchairs. Standing water at building entrances can be tracked inside the building, increasing the slipperiness of interior floor surfaces such as tile and terrazzo. Under most circumstances, the allowable slope of 1:48 will be sufficient for drainage. Care should also be taken to avoid drainage from overhead surfaces discharging onto ramp surfaces and approaches. In situations where gutters may freeze and overflow, it may be prudent to locate ramps so that they are not under gutters so that ice will not accumulate on the ramped surface. Wet conditions may also be found in some indoor spaces, such as adjacent to pool areas.

406 Curb Ramps

406.1 General. Curb ramps on accessible routes shall comply with Sections 406, 405.2, 405.3, and 405.10.

❖ Curb ramps are a unique type of ramp construction suited for use at curbs between sidewalks and vehicular ways or any other similar location wherein a change in level occurs along an accessible path. Curb ramp construction can comply with some of the provisions of Section 405 for ramps and be functional. For example, it would be impractical to require handrails (Section 405.8) or guards or other edge protection (Section 405.9) because of the obstructions such features would present to the surrounding areas, which are typically a circulation path or public way. The attributes that are unique to curb ramps make them suitable for their purpose primarily because of the limited rise (curb height) that they serve.

By the references to Sections 405.2 and 405.3, the primary sloped segment of a curb ramp is required to have a slope of 1:12 maximum and a cross slope of 1:48 maximum, the same as that for all other ramps. This is appropriate to provide a slope that can be negotiated by a wheelchair without great difficulty and is also consistent with Section 303.4, which effectively establishes that the slope of the transition between changes in level greater than $1/2$ inch (13 mm) is a critical consideration.

Because curb ramps are most often located outside, they should be constructed so water does not accumulate at the approach to or along the curb ramp. Water on the surfaces could cause slick conditions, so these surfaces should be sloped to drain (see Section 405.10).

406.2 Counter Slope. Counter slopes of adjoining gutters and road surfaces immediately adjacent to the curb ramp shall not be steeper than 1:20. The adjacent surfaces at transitions at curb ramps to walks, gutters and streets shall be at the same level.

❖ In general, this provision results in a transition across a curb that is reasonably and smoothly usable by a wheelchair while minimizing the impact of its presence on other pedestrian traffic. Counter slopes typically occur at the bottom of curb ramps because of the beveling of gutter sides or the crown of the road surface. Counter slopes steeper than 1:20 pose a risk that the footrest of the wheelchair could catch on the ascending slope of the gutter or road crown, ultimately tipping the person out of the wheelchair.

406.3 Sides of Curb Ramps. Where provided, curb ramp flares shall not be steeper than 1:10.

❖ One of the aspects of curb ramp placement that should be given careful consideration is their location relative to cross-pedestrian traffic. It would be preferable to locate curb ramps so that they do not extend perpendicular into a primary path of pedestrian travel. If they are not located out of the main circulation path, pedestrians are then faced with traveling across a portion of the curb ramp and stepping onto the flared side or the

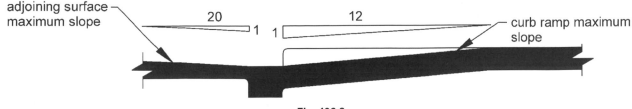

Fig. 406.2
Counter Slope of Surfaces Adjacent to Curb Ramps

sloped portion of the curb ramp. Where this does occur, Section 406.7 provides specific provisions to account for that condition [see commentary Figure C406.3(a)].

The standard does not require a curb ramp to have flared sides if the expected traffic pattern would not involve pedestrians crossing the curb ramp. The curb ramp could cut through a parkway [see commentary Figure C406.3(b)].

Where flared sides are used, whether or not they are required, the flared sides are limited in slope to 1:10 to minimize the potential hazard for pedestrians. Locating curb ramps where they will not extend into expected pedestrian cross-traffic paths is preferable, but this is not always feasible. Rather than leaving the transition from the sides of curb ramps to adjoining surfaces abrupt, flared sides are provided as a safety feature for all pedestrians.

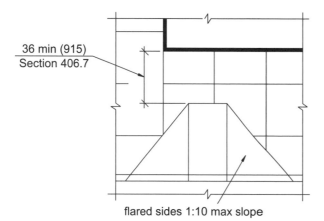

36 min (915)
Section 406.7

flared sides 1:10 max slope

**Fig. 406.3
Sides of Curb Ramps**

406.4 Width. Curb ramps shall be 36 inches (915 mm) minimum in width, exclusive of flared sides.

❖ The required width of the curb ramp corresponds to the standard wheelchair passage width for a passageway longer than 24 inches (610 mm). See Section 403.5. While the sides of a curb ramp are seldom enclosed by construction such as walls, the required 36-inch (915 mm) width represents an appropriate, functional minimum for the construction of curb ramps [see commentary Figures C406.3(a), C406.3(b), C406.7(a) and C406.7(b)].

406.5 Floor Surface. Floor surfaces of curb ramps shall comply with Section 302.

❖ The surface features of curb ramps are just as critical as other floor or ramp surfaces required to comply with Section 302.

As noted in Section 406.13, the standard does not require detectable warnings on the curb ramps.

406.6 Location. Curb ramps and the flared sides of curb ramps shall be located so they do not project into vehicular traffic lanes, parking spaces, or parking access aisles. Curb ramps at marked crossings shall be wholly contained within the markings, excluding any flared sides.

❖ This provision ensures the curb ramps remain usable and are not blocked or damaged by vehicles, as well as protecting persons using wheelchairs from moving vehicles. Also see Section 406.8.

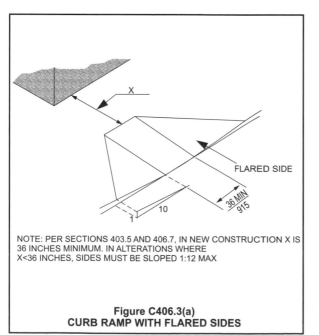

FLARED SIDE

36 MIN
915

10

1

NOTE: PER SECTIONS 403.5 AND 406.7, IN NEW CONSTRUCTION X IS 36 INCHES MINIMUM. IN ALTERATIONS WHERE X<36 INCHES, SIDES MUST BE SLOPED 1:12 MAX

**Figure C406.3(a)
CURB RAMP WITH FLARED SIDES**

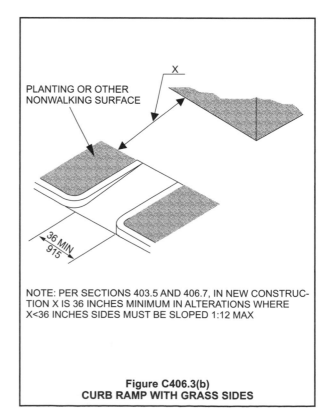

X

PLANTING OR OTHER NONWALKING SURFACE

36 MIN
915

NOTE: PER SECTIONS 403.5 AND 406.7, IN NEW CONSTRUCTION X IS 36 INCHES MINIMUM IN ALTERATIONS WHERE X<36 INCHES SIDES MUST BE SLOPED 1:12 MAX

**Figure C406.3(b)
CURB RAMP WITH GRASS SIDES**

Previously these provisions applied only to "built-up" curb ramps. Depending on the specific design, the problems addressed by this section could affect either a depressed or built-up curb ramp. Built-up curb ramps can be an effective solution where space limitations, such as narrow sidewalks, preclude the use of a depressed curb ramp. Flares of built-up curb ramps that extend to front doors of cars and adjacent to side-mounted wheelchair lifts create uneven, dangerous sloping surfaces that make maneuvering for boarding vehicles difficult, if not impossible, for many persons using wheelchairs and persons with mobility impairments. Further, the extreme hazard to the user that would be created if the ramp extended into vehicular lanes makes it clearly unacceptable and an arrangement to be avoided. Figure C406.7(b) helps to show how a built-up curb ramp may create problems if it does protrude into the listed locations.

This provision ensures that the designed traffic pattern for persons using wheelchairs occurs within the same designed traffic pattern for all pedestrians. There is a certain degree of protection from vehicular traffic that is afforded by the marking of pedestrian crosswalks. It would be inappropriate to locate the curb ramp where the person using a wheelchair would have to leave the marked crossing while still in the vehicular way, and thus be exposed to a greater level of danger than other pedestrians. The exclusion for the flared sides is important because they can occur either partially or wholly outside of the marked crossing (see commentary Figure C406.6).

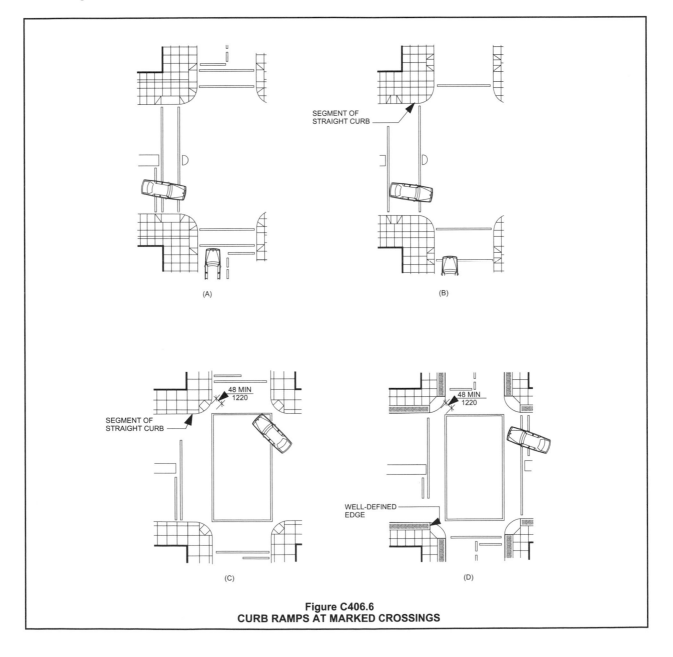

Figure C406.6
CURB RAMPS AT MARKED CROSSINGS

406.7 Landings. Landings shall be provided at the tops of curb ramps. The clear length of the landing shall be 36 inches (915 mm) minimum. The clear width of the landing shall be at least as wide as the curb ramp, excluding flared sides, leading to the landing.

> **EXCEPTION:** In alterations, where there is no landing at the top of curb ramps, curb ramp flares shall be provided and shall not be steeper than 1:12.

❖ Persons using the sidewalk perpendicular to the curb ramp have a difficult time with the changes in slopes if they have to move across the curb ramp. Therefore, in new construction, a minimum of a 36 inch (915 mm) wide path must be available across the top the curb ramp to allow for a flat perpendicular route [see commentary Figures C406.3(a) and C406.3(b)]. If there is not enough space to allow for this configuration, an alternative would be to lower a portion of the sidewalk to be level with the parking or road surface, with a straight curb ramp at both ends. For an illustration of this option, see commentary Figure C406.7(a).

Built-up curb ramps are another alternative [see commentary Figure C406.7(b)]. However, if built-up ramps are chosen they must not protrude into the aisle accessway for parking spaces or passenger loading zones. Those areas are required to be level.

In alterations, when it is necessary to locate a curb ramp where the width of the walking surface adjacent to the top of the curb ramp is less than 36 inches (915 mm), the flared sides become part of the accessible route that the person using a wheelchair must traverse. The slope of the flared sides is then limited to 1:12 to provide a gentler slope. Technically, 1:12 is correlated with the maximum permitted ramp slope (Section 405.2). This benefits all pedestrians, including wheelchair and other mobility aid users [see commentary Figure C406.3(a)].

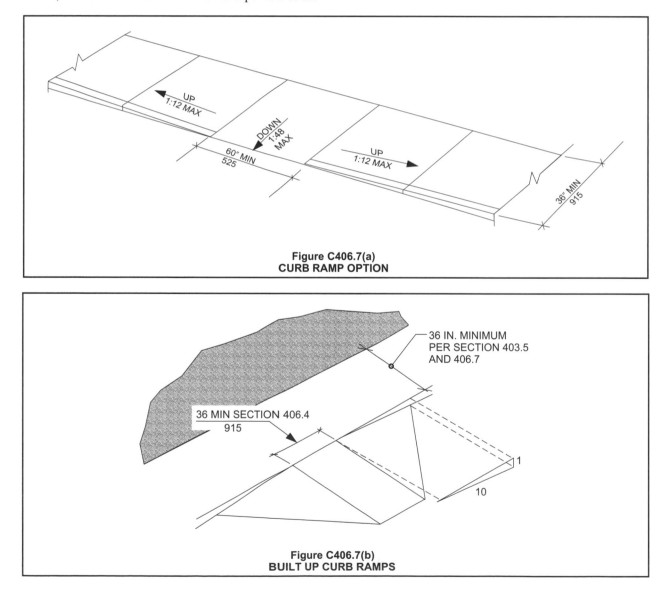

Figure C406.7(a)
CURB RAMP OPTION

Figure C406.7(b)
BUILT UP CURB RAMPS

406.8 Obstructions. Curb ramps shall be located or protected to prevent their obstruction by parked vehicles.

❖ Clearly, a curb ramp is unusable when it is obstructed by a parked vehicle. Many times, curb ramps will occur at corners and at pedestrian crossings where parking is typically prohibited and policed by local authorities. However, at any location where a parked vehicle blocks a curb ramp, some type of design modification such as moving the ramp location, installing a vehicle barrier or posting of signs is required.

406.9 Handrails. Handrails are not required on curb ramps.

❖ Handrails are not necessary at curb ramps because of the limited rise and run of the curb ramp. They present an unnecessary and undesirable obstruction to pedestrian cross-traffic. Unlike ramps (Section 405.8), this is true even when the curb ramp has a rise of more than 6 inches (150 mm).

406.10 Diagonal Curb Ramps. Diagonal or corner-type curb ramps with returned curbs or other well-defined edges shall have the edges parallel to the direction of pedestrian flow. The bottoms of diagonal curb ramps shall have 48 inches (1220 mm) minimum clear space outside active traffic lanes of the roadway. Diagonal curb ramps provided at marked crossings shall provide the 48 inches (1220 mm) minimum clear space within the markings. Diagonal curb ramps with flared sides shall have a segment of curb 24 inches (610 mm) minimum in length on each side of the curb ramp and within the marked crossing.

❖ These requirements are intended to accomplish much the same purpose as described in the commentary for other sections under Section 406, namely a smooth transition over a curb in a manner that keeps the person using a wheelchair within the marked pedestrian crossing area and does not present an undue obstruction or difficulty for other pedestrian traffic. Commentary Figures C406.6(c) and (d) as well as Figure 406.10 from the standard illustrate these requirements.

406.11 Islands. Raised islands in crossings shall be a cut-through level with the street or have curb ramps at both sides. Each curb ramp shall have a level area 48 inches (1220 mm) minimum in length and 36 inches (915 mm) minimum in width at the top of the curb ramp in the part of the island intersected by the crossings. Each 48-inch (1220 mm) by 36-inch (915 mm) area shall be oriented so the 48-inch (1220 mm) length is in the direction of the running slope of the curb ramp it serves. The 48-inch (1220 mm) by 36-inch (915 mm) areas and the accessible route shall be permitted to overlap.

❖ Islands that occur within a vehicular way, such as at boulevards or within some parking lots, must be constructed to accommodate persons using a wheelchair. This can be accomplished with a wheelchair passageway that cuts through the island, so the wheelchair never rises up to the level of the island.

Alternatively, curb ramps must be used to reach the level of the island and sufficient level space must be provided on the island for one wheelchair. The intent is to avoid having a person using a wheelchair either go around the island or wait in the vehicular traffic lane before proceeding across the remainder of the street. See commentary Figure C406.11 and Figure 406.11.

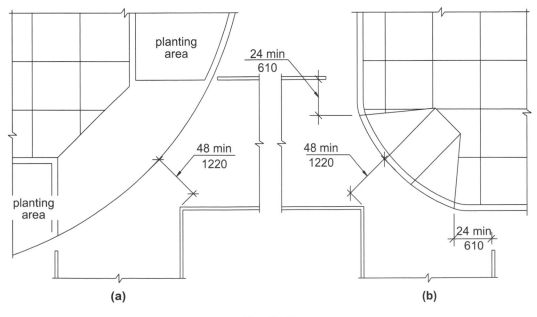

Fig. 406.10
Diagonal Curb Ramps

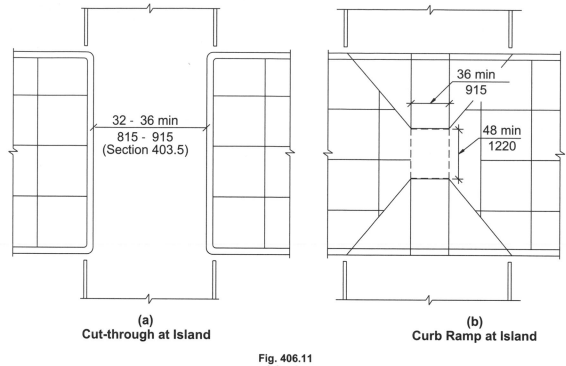

(a)
Cut-through at Island

(b)
Curb Ramp at Island

Fig. 406.11
Islands

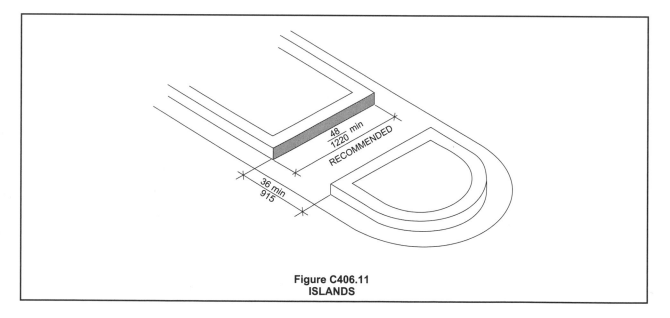

Figure C406.11
ISLANDS

406.12 Detectable Warnings at Raised Marked Crossings. Marked crossings that are raised to the same level as the adjoining sidewalk shall be preceded by a 24-inch (610 mm) deep detectable warning complying with Section 705, extending the full width of the marked crossing.

❖ A curb or the sloped surface of the curb ramp is a clue for persons with visual impairments as they are enter an area where vehicles could be present. When the cross-walk is raised to the elevation of the sidewalk, neither of these clues is provided; therefore, a detect-

able warning must be provided for the full length of the crossing.

406.13 Detectable Warnings at Curb Ramps. Where detectable warnings are provided on curb ramps, they shall comply with Sections 406.13 and 705.

❖ This standard does not require detectable warnings at curb ramps; however, when they are provided they must meet the provision for coverage and location in the following subsections and comply with the contrast, resilience/sound-on-cane and truncated dome requirements in Section 705. Detectable warnings should be standardized throughout a building, facility, site or group of buildings, so persons with visual impairments can more easily recognize the warnings.

406.13.1 Area Covered. Detectable warnings shall be 24 inches (610 mm) minimum in the direction of travel and extend the full width of the curb ramp or flush surface.

❖ Detectable warnings must extend across the full width of the curb ramp in a strip along the edge of the curb ramp closest to the vehicular routes. The strip must be a minimum of 24 inches (610 mm) deep so it is detectable by the sweep of a long cane and allows time for people to stop.

406.13.2 Location. The detectable warning shall be located so the edge nearest the curb line is 6 inches (150 mm) to 8 inches (205 mm) from the curb line.

❖ This section gives a range for the edge of the 24 inch (610 mm) wide strip of detectable warnings required by Section 406.13.1. The requirements assume a standard cut-in curb ramp. Being a clue for entering the areas where vehicles are present, alternatives such as the built-up or depressed-entry curb ramps have to follow the intent of the detectable warnings. As a reminder, Section 406.6 prohibits curb ramps from protruding into the vehicular way (see commentary Figure C406.13.2).

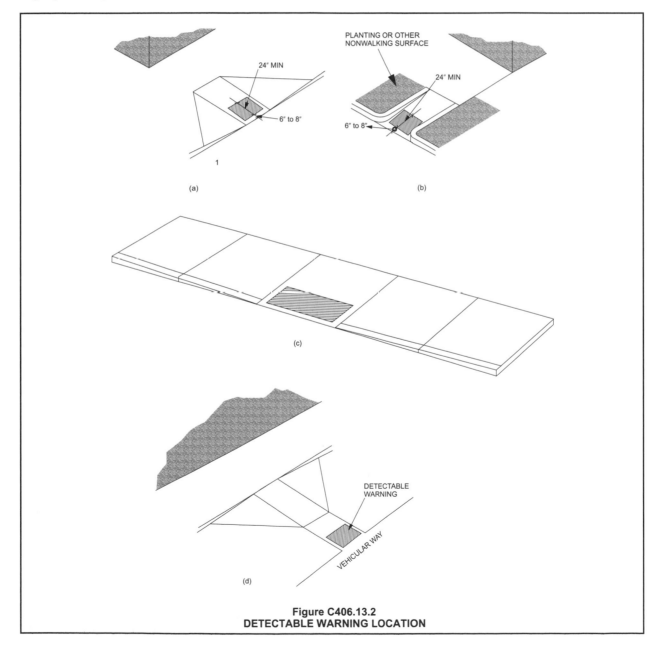

Figure C406.13.2
DETECTABLE WARNING LOCATION

406.14 Detectable Warnings at Islands or Cut-through Medians. Where detectable warnings are provided on curb ramps or at raised marked crossings leading to islands or cut-through medians, the island or cut-through median shall also be provided with detectable warnings complying with Section 705, are 24 inches (610 mm) in depth, and extend the full width of the pedestrian route or cut-through. Where such island or cut-through median is less than 48 inches (1220 mm) in depth, the entire width and depth of the pedestrian route or cut-through shall have detectable warnings.

❖ The intent of this provision is to provide consistent information regarding when a person with visual impairments crosses a street. When detectable warnings are provided on the curb cuts and there is an intermediate island, detectable warnings should also be located on the island. This way, persons would know when they were in a safe location and when they were on the street and possibly within a vehicle's path [see commentary Figures C406.14(a) and C406.14(b)].

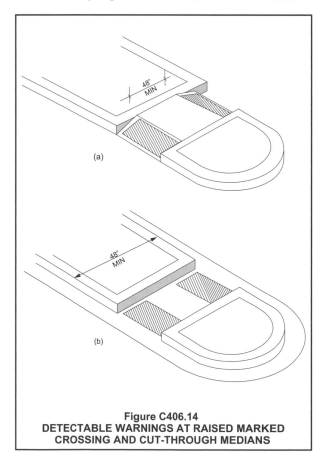

(a)

(b)

Figure C406.14
DETECTABLE WARNINGS AT RAISED MARKED CROSSING AND CUT-THROUGH MEDIANS

407 Elevators

❖ The origin of many of the elevator provisions in Section 407 are described in the book by Edward A. Donoghue, *ADA and Building Transportation*, available from Elevator World, P. O. Box 6507, Mobile, AL 36660 or http://www.elevator-world.com. *ADA and Building Transportation* served as the basis for much of the commentary in Section 407.

407.1 General. Elevators shall comply with Section 407 and ASME A17.1 listed in Section 105.2.5. Elevators shall be passenger elevators as classified by ASME A17.1. Elevator operation shall be automatic.

❖ During the development of the 2003 edition of ICC A117.1, the elevator requirements were editorially reformatted to harmonize with the April 2002 draft of the *ADA/ABA Accessibility Guidelines*. Provisions for destination-oriented elevators and existing elevators have been incorporated into the relevant sections in Section 407. Limited-access/limited-use elevator technical provisions are in Section 408. Private residence elevator requirements were moved from Chapter 10 to Section 409. All types of elevators listed in these sections are considered passenger elevators and are permitted to serve as part of an accessible route. Where each type can be used is limited by the referenced standard, ASME A17.1. For example, ASME A17.1 limits the use of private residence elevators to installations either within individual dwelling units or to serve single dwelling units (ASME A17.1, Sections 5.3 and 5.4) provided the elevator is not accessible to the general public. Private residence elevators are small and cannot conform to Section 407.4.1. Provisions for passenger elevators in this section are divided into elevator landing requirements (Section 407.2), elevator door requirements (Section 407.3) and elevator car requirements (Section 407.4) (see commentary Figure C407.1).

Elevators are used as the primary means to provide wheelchair access to upper and lower floors in multistory buildings. Typically, the scoping provisions

Figure C407.1
ELEVATORS

in the model building codes do not specifically mandate that an elevator be provided for access from the ground floor. The designer is given the option of providing access to other floors by any approved means, such as a ramp. Elevators remain the most commonly used method.

For accessibility, elevators that are attendant operated are not considered acceptable because of the potential for the attendant to not be readily available. Also, elevator controls that require continuous pressure for operation are not acceptable because they are not suitable for people who have limited use of their hands.

ASME A17.1 does not recognize "combination passenger and freight elevators." Rather, it allows passenger elevators to carry freight, and under very strict limitations, freight elevators to carry passengers. In the latter instance, the elevator must not be accessible to the general public, the elevator capacity must meet the minimum rated load for passenger use and be capable of withstanding a passenger overload, and the elevator entrance must be approved for passenger use (ASME A17.1, Sections 2.11 and 2.16.4). Typical passenger elevator entrances are the horizontally sliding type. However, some vertically sliding type entrances, normally associated with freight elevators, are also approved for passenger elevator applications. In short, most elevators installed and used exclusively for carrying freight will not be classified as a passenger elevator and cannot be considered accessible.

Destination-oriented elevators – Destination-oriented elevators are an alternative to conventional elevators where floor selection is made by passengers after they enter the elevator car. This system provides lobby controls enabling passengers to select floor stops when they enter the elevator lobby instead of inside the elevator car itself. Responding cars are programmed for maximum efficiency by reducing the number of stops to deliver passengers that the elevator will be making on each trip. Lobby indicators let the passengers know which elevator is responding to their floor request. Indicators inside the car let passengers know which floors that particular car will be stopping at.

Existing Elevators – Scoping provisions in the model building codes can require that accessibility be upgraded in existing buildings that undergo renovations, alterations and changes of occupancy. It would be overly restrictive and impractical to mandate that existing elevators be retrofitted to fully comply with all of the requirements for accessibility that are applicable to new elevators. However, certain upgrades are reasonable and appropriate to improve accessibility, particularly where a building is not currently accessible. The applicable provisions in Section 407 represent the baseline minimum expectations for an existing elevator to be considered as providing a reasonable degree of accessibility – watch the exceptions for allowances. Certain provisions for new elevators

in this standard are intended to be retroactively applicable to existing elevators.

Determining the extent that existing elements are required to conform to the requirements for new elements cannot be done arbitrarily and without consideration of the impact. A general principle in construction code enforcement holds that existing construction, which complies with the codes and standards applicable at the time of original construction has a right to exist without change unless one of the three following situations occurs:

1. The existing construction, in this case an elevator, is unsafe;

2. Retroactive provisions are established requiring upgrading of the existing elevator, or

3. The owner, on his own initiative, decides to upgrade his elevator.

There is precedent in code enforcement law that supports the validity of applying reasonable and justified regulations retroactively. The model building codes and Safety Code for Existing Elevators and Escalators, ASME A17.3, adequately address retroactive safety provisions. This standard deals with retrospective provisions that are deemed reasonable and justified for accessibility.

The specific provisions for new construction identified in this subsection as applicable to existing accessible elevators were chosen based on either their necessity to provide absolute minimum acceptable accessibility, or the ease with which compliance can be achieved, or both. Ease of compliance can be considered based on physical and economic practicality. Some degree of physical and economic impact will likely occur, but is justified in view of the benefit gained in the increased accessibility of the facility.

Many existing elevator arrangements will have multiple elevator cars programmed to respond to the same call button, but not all of the elevator cars will be in compliance with the requirements for existing elevators. This section requires one of two things to occur: either the call buttons and programming must be rearranged so only the elevator(s) that comply will respond to a call button specifically intended to call for an accessible elevator, or all of the elevators that respond to the call button must comply with these provisions. The intent is to avoid the situation in which a disabled person calls for an elevator, but is left to chance as to whether an accessible elevator responds to the call. Several repeated calls may then be necessary before that person can use an elevator.

If an elevator is upgraded to comply with existing elevator requirements, the reader is cautioned that the alteration provisions in ASME A17.1, Section 8.7 may require additional safety modifications. Compliance with the Safety Code for Existing Elevators and Escalators, ASME A17.3, may also be required.

407.2 Elevator Landing Requirements. Elevator landings shall comply with Section 407.2.

❖ This section provides technical requirements for elevator landings including call controls, hall signals, hoistway signs and destination signs.

407.2.1 Call Controls. Where elevator call buttons or keypads are provided, they shall comply with Sections 407.2.1 and 309.4. Call buttons shall be raised or flush. Objects beneath hall call buttons shall protrude 1 inch (25 mm) maximum.

EXCEPTIONS:

1. Existing elevators shall be permitted to have recessed call buttons.

2. The restriction on objects beneath call buttons shall not apply to existing call buttons.

❖ Several locations are usually provided in the lobby or approach to the lobby to call the elevator. All locations must be accessible. The reference to Section 407.2.1 picks up subsections 407.2.1.1 through 407.2.1.7; the reference to Section 309.4 picks up the operational requirements under operable parts.

For standard call buttons, the requirement for the buttons to be raised or flush (not recessed) ensures that the buttons are suitable for people who have limited use of their hands. With destination-oriented elevators, a keypad is used in place of elevator call buttons. The desired floor is selected prior to boarding the elevator. Projections beneath the buttons are restricted to eliminate hazards for the visually impaired who may need to feel for the buttons and to allow unrestricted access for persons with short stature and persons using wheelchairs and scooters.

407.2.1.1 Height. Call buttons and keypads shall be located within one of the reach ranges specified in Section 308, measured to the centerline of the highest operable part.

EXCEPTION: Existing call buttons and existing keypads shall be permitted to be located 54 inches (1370 mm) maximum above the floor, measured to the centerline of the highest operable part.

❖ The maximum button or keypad height is equal to the maximum high forward and side reach range specified in Sections 308.2 and 308.3. This height requirement was new to the 1998 edition of ICC A117.1. Prior editions specified that call buttons in elevator lobbies be centered at 42 inches (1065 mm). This was based on a continued use of the former industry standards established by National Elevator Industry, Inc. (NEII) in the mid-1970s. Although a lower end dimension different from the reach ranges [(i.e., 15 inches (386 mm)] is not specified, call buttons and keypads below 35 inches (890 mm) may be too low for proper access for taller persons.

The exception for existing elevators is based on the earlier editions of ICC A117.1 and the 1994 ADAAG allowing 54 inches (1370 mm) maximum height for a side reach range.

407.2.1.2 Size. Call buttons shall be $^{3}/_{4}$ inch (19 mm) minimum in the smallest dimension.

EXCEPTION: Existing elevator call buttons shall not be required to comply with Section 407.2.1.2.

❖ Minimum dimensions for the buttons ensure that the buttons are suitable for people who have limited use of their hands. See also Section 407.2.1.6.

407.2.1.3 Clear Floor Space. A clear floor space complying with Section 305 shall be provided at call controls.

❖ Requirements for the 30 inch by 48 inch (765 by 1220 mm) wheelchair space in front of the call controls allow for easy access. Although either a side or front approach is permitted, note that the specific protrusions limits under Section 407.2.1 would not allow for reaches over an obstruction greater than 1 inch (25 mm). If the location of the call buttons is confined on three sides in some manner the alcove provisions in Section 305.7 must also be observed.

407.2.1.4 Location. The call button that designates the up direction shall be located above the call button that designates the down direction.

EXCEPTION: Destination-oriented elevators shall not be required to comply with Section 407.2.1.4.

❖ Consistency in the location of the up and down buttons rather than the centerline of the fixture is important to

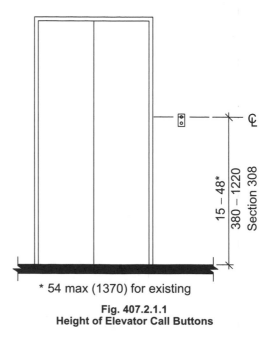

15 – 48*
380 – 1220
Section 308

* 54 max (1370) for existing

**Fig. 407.2.1.1
Height of Elevator Call Buttons**

people with visual impairments who may not be able to distinguish the marking on the buttons. Destination-oriented elevators are not required to comply with this provision because the call buttons operate differently (see Section 407.2.1.6 and 407.2.1.7).

407.2.1.5 Signals. Call buttons shall have visible signals to indicate when each call is registered and when each call is answered.

EXCEPTIONS:

1. Destination-oriented elevators shall not be required to comply with Section 407.2.1.5, provided visible and audible signals complying with Section 407.2.1.7 are provided.

2. Existing elevators shall not be required to comply with Section 407.2.1.5.

❖ Visual indications are required to let the user know that a call has been registered and when it is answered, to aid users with hearing impairments. The different approach for notification for destination-oriented elevators is recognized in Exception 1.

407.2.1.6 Keypads. Where keypads are provided, keypads shall be in a standard telephone keypad arrangement and shall comply with Section 407.4.7.2.

❖ For destination-oriented elevators call buttons in the lobby and halls approaching the lobby are generally in the form of a large keypad. The keypad assembly has several associated items; a visual display located above the keypad, a bar key located below the keypad and a speaker located within the keypad enclosure. Keypads are in standard telephone format and have $^3/_4$ inch (20 mm) minimum buttons with $^5/_8$ inch (16 mm) visual numbers. For tactile information that the standard telephone arrangement is used, there is a tactile dot on the number "5" key. For consistency the star appearing on the lower left key will be visually the

same as the 5 pointed star in Table 407.4.7.1.3 and when pushed will enter a call to the "Main" floor designated for the elevator. Entering the "Main" floor number will do the same. The "Pound" key position in the lower right hand position is used to enter minus "-" floors (floors below the "Main" floor) such as levels or parking. The "Pound" key position and then a number in succession will enter the appropriate calls to these floors. To enter floor calls above the "Main" floor such as floor 15, it is only necessary to push "1" and then "5" in succession.

407.2.1.7 Destination-oriented Elevator Signals. Destination-oriented elevators shall be provided with visible and audible signals to indicate which car is responding to a call. The audible signal shall be activated by pressing a function button. The function button shall be identified by the International Symbol for Accessibility and tactile indication. The International Symbol for Accessibility, complying with Section 703.6.3.1, shall be $^5/_8$ inch (16 mm) in height and be a visual character complying with Section 703.2. The tactile indication shall be three raised dots, spaced $^1/_4$ inch (6.4 mm) at base diameter, in the form of an equilateral triangle. The function button shall be located immediately below the keypad arrangement or floor buttons.

❖ For destination-oriented elevators, the visual display above the keypad provides two pieces of information: 1) the car's designation (e.g., "A", "B") and 2) the direction of the car (e.g., left, right).

The audible hall signals are normally inactive unless turned on at the control keypad. Usually a bar key located just below the keypad serves this purpose. The format is similar to a button used to activate the in car audible floor signal. The bar key also turns on several other accessibility features not required but usually provided; such as more time to push successive keypad numbers, more time to reach the car, a larger

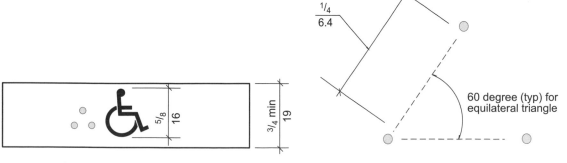

Visual and tactile information

Tactile information

60 degree (typ) for equilateral triangle

Fig. 407.2.1.7
Destination-oriented Elevator Indication

allocation of car space where possible, (e.g., fewer passengers assigned to use designated car) and optional visual and audible enhancements. See also the commentary to Section 407.2.2.1.

407.2.2 Hall Signals. Hall signals, including in-car signals, shall comply with Section 407.2.2.

❖ Signals that indicate what elevator is arriving at the elevator lobby may be provided outside or inside the elevator cab. Hall signals must comply with the provisions for audible and visual notification. Distinct requirements are provided for destination-oriented elevators based on each element's unique form of operation.

407.2.2.1 Visible and Audible Signals. A visible and audible signal shall be provided at each hoistway entrance to indicate which car is answering a call and the car's direction of travel. Where in-car signals are provided they shall be visible from the floor area adjacent to the hall call buttons.

EXCEPTIONS:

1. Destination-oriented elevators shall not be required to comply with Section 407.2.2.1, provided visible and audible signals complying with Section 407.2.1.7 are provided.

2. In existing elevators, a signal indicating the direction of car travel shall not be required.

❖ Typically, the arriving elevator is announced to the passengers waiting in the elevator lobby by a visible and audible signal located on the wall to the side of the elevator door (see Section 407.2.2.2), so it can be seen above the heads of the other passengers waiting in the lobby. The use of in-car lanterns is acceptable, but

they will affect door open time, slowing elevator service in the building. Door open time is calculated from the sounding of the audible signal and illumination of the directional lantern, so the person waiting for the car is notified which car is responding to his call.

See Sections 407.2.1.7 and 407.2.2.4 for the signals for destination-oriented elevators. Some hall signals are associated with the keypad itself and other hall signals are associated with the elevator car.

407.2.2.2 Visible Signals. Visible signal fixtures shall be centered at 72 inches (1830 mm) minimum above the floor. The visible signal elements shall be $2^1/_2$ inches (64 mm) minimum measured along the vertical centerline of the element. Signals shall be visible from the floor area adjacent to the hall call button.

EXCEPTIONS:

1. Destination-oriented elevators shall be permitted to have signals visible from the floor area adjacent to the hoistway entrance.

2. Existing elevators shall not be required to comply with Section 407.2.2.2.

❖ The visible signals can be in a vertical or a horizontal arrangement with two signal elements such as arrows or triangles if the signal elements serve to indicate direction. Color distinctions are not acceptable because some people are color blind.

The specified minimum height and size allows the visible signal to be seen when persons in the elevator lobby are standing at the call button (see Figure 407.2.2.2).

If in-car lanterns are used, the door would have to be opened before minimum door timing (see Section 407.3.4) would start. Floor lanterns and audible sig-

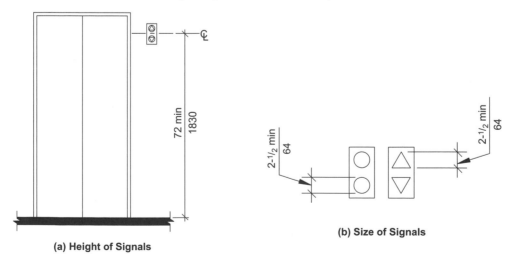

(a) Height of Signals

(b) Size of Signals

Fig. 407.2.2.2
Elevator Visible Signals

nals, on the other hand, can announce the car before it reaches a floor and the door opens, to allow people to gather near the car before the door opens.

Because the call controls have indicated which car will be responding to a particular call, the user knows at what elevator to wait; therefore, the visible signals for arrival must be seen only from immediately in front of the elevator entrance. In-car signals are not permitted.

407.2.2.3 Audible Signals. Audible signals shall sound once for the up direction and twice for the down direction, or shall have verbal annunciators that indicate the direction of elevator car travel. Audible signals shall have a frequency of 1500 Hz maximum. Verbal annunciators shall have a frequency of 300 Hz minimum and 3,000 Hz maximum. The audible signal or verbal annunciator shall be 10 dBA minimum above ambient, but shall not exceed 80 dBA, measured at the hall call button.

EXCEPTIONS:

1. Destination-oriented elevators shall not be required to comply with Section 407.2.2.3, provided the audible tone and verbal announcement is the same as those given at the call button or call button keypad.

2. The requirement for the frequency and range of audible signals shall not apply in existing elevators.

❖ The sound level specified is intended to make sure the signal can be heard above ambient noise but not cause damage to a person's hearing.

See Sections 407.2.1.7 and 407.2.2.4 for the signals for destination-oriented elevators. Some hall signals are associated with the keypad itself and other hall signals are associated with the elevator car.

407.2.2.4 Differentiation. Each destination-oriented elevator in a bank of elevators shall have audible and visible means for differentiation.

❖ Destination-oriented elevators provide a unique approach for visual and audible differentiation. Visible designations follow the same form as standard elevators; however, the lights typically also have a letter or number for car identification.

For verbal differentiation, following bar key activation and entry of a floor destination, a verbal announcement confirming the floor number and designation of what car (e.g., car "A", "B", etc.) to take will occur. The keypad speaker will then emit a unique audible tone, assigned to the specific car. A speaker at the car will emit the same tone at intervals for the duration of the notification time. The duration will correspond to the distance from the particular keypad in question to a point directly in front of the specified car

(see the commentary to Section 407.3.4). Supplementary verbal announcements are often provided, but not required, example: "there is no floor 13."

407.2.3 Hoistway Signs. Signs at elevator hoistways shall comply with Section 407.2.3.

❖ Tactile signage communicates vital information to people with vision impairments. It is also useful information for those with hearing impairments, as well as the general public. Plates that have the appropriate raised characters are acceptable if the plates are permanently fixed to the hoistway entrance jambs.

407.2.3.1 Floor Designation. Floor designations shall be provided in tactile characters complying with Section 703.3 located on both jambs of elevator hoistway entrances. Tactile characters shall be 2 inches (51 mm) minimum in height. A tactile star shall be provided on both jambs at the main entry level.

❖ Information regarding the floor level that the elevator has arrived at must be provided on both jambs of the elevator hoistway entrance. Tactile information must include both raised numbers and Braille. The main entry floor is always the first floor per Section 407.4.6.2.2. The main entrance level must be identified with a star in addition to the number (see Figure 407.2.3.1). This is coordinated with the requirement for a 'star' symbol on the control panel.

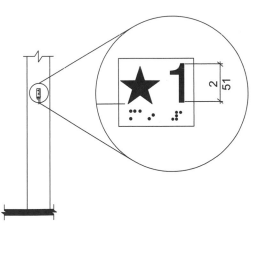

Fig. 407.2.3.1
Floor Designation

407.2.3.2 Car Designations. Destination-oriented elevators shall provide car identification in tactile characters complying with Section 703.3 located on both jambs of the hoistway immediately below the floor designation. Tactile characters shall be 2 inches (51 mm) minimum in height.

❖ As further correlation, the specified car identification (e.g., car "A", "B", etc.) is placed on both jambs immediately below the floor designation. The floor designation is always numeric to match the keypad and the car designation is always alphabetic. The five pointed raised star to indicate the main entry is next to the main floor designation. In most cases the "Main" entry will be floor 1; however, some new buildings are adopting the convention used in most other countries and calling it floor "0". The next floor is identified as 1 and one floor below is identified as -1.

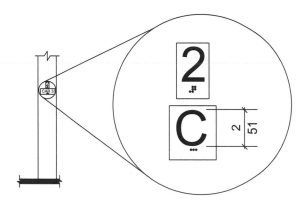

Fig. 407.2.3.2
Designation-oriented Elevator Car Identification

407.2.4 Destination Signs. Where signs indicate that elevators do not serve all landings, signs in tactile characters complying with Section 703.3 shall be provided above the hall call button fixture.

EXCEPTION: Destination oriented elevator systems shall not be required to comply with Section 407.2.4.

❖ When the elevator system is zoned, (i.e., elevators serve only certain floors), signs are typically located at the entrance to each bank indicating what floor levels are served. This information must be repeated on a tactile sign (i.e., raised letters/numbers and Braille) above the hall call buttons. Because destination-oriented elevators do not limit their operation to only certain floors, this type of system is not considered a zoned system, and signage is not required.

407.3 Elevator Door Requirements. Hoistway and elevator car doors shall comply with Section 407.3.

❖ Elevator doors are both the doors to the elevator shaft and the doors on the cabs themselves. These doors must meet the provisions for type, width, operation, reopening devices and timing specified in Sections 407.3.1 through 407.3.6.

407.3.1 Type. Elevator doors shall be horizontal sliding type. Car gates shall be prohibited.

❖ Typical passenger elevator entrances are the horizontal sliding type. The upper and/or lower section of a vertically sliding door could become a bump and/or a trip hazard for the visually impaired. The lower section of a vertically sliding door is difficult for wheelchairs to cross.

Separate car gates that are operated manually once a person is inside of the elevator (e.g., construction elevators) are not permitted in accessible elevators.

407.3.2 Operation. Elevator hoistway and car doors shall open and close automatically.

EXCEPTION: Existing manually operated hoistway swing doors shall be permitted, provided:

a) they comply with Sections 404.2.2 and 404.2.8;

b) the car door closing is not initiated until the hoistway door is closed.

❖ With automatic doors, a person with limited mobility can enter the car, access controls and exit the car without turning around in the car or requiring assistance.

Some existing elevators have manual swing doors on the hoistway with automatic doors on the car. These are permitted when doors provide a clear width of 32 inches (815 mm) (Section 404.2.2), meet the door opening forces (Section 404.2.8) and the automatic car (interior) door is not activated until the manual hoistway door is closed.

407.3.3 Reopening Device. Elevator doors shall be provided with a reopening device complying with Section 407.3.3 that shall stop and reopen a car door and hoistway door automatically if the door becomes obstructed by an object or person.

EXCEPTION: In existing elevators, manually operated doors shall not be required to comply with Section 407.3.3.

❖ A noncontact door-reopening device will stop the door and reopen it if the doorway opening becomes obstructed. The noncontact device remains effective for 20 seconds, i.e., it will stop and reopen the door if a person passes the device. Once the next person intercepts the noncontact device, the door will stop and reopen. This requirement does not mandate that the door remain open for 20 seconds, only that the reopening device be alert for people passing through the door for 20 seconds or until the door has fully closed.

The required door-reopening device holds the door open for 20 seconds if the doorway remains continuously obstructed. After 20 seconds, the door is permitted to begin closing. However, if designed in accordance with ASME A17.1, the door closing movement is still stopped if a person or object exerts sufficient force at any point on the door edge. Sufficient force is defined by ASME A17.1 as 30 pounds-force (134 N). If all door-reopening devices are rendered inoperative, the ASME A17.1 Standard also requires the average kinetic energy of the door system be reduced from 7 ft-lbf to $2^1/_2$ ft-lbf (9.5 to 3.4 J).

Because to the kinetic nature of the motion, reversal of the closing door is not instantaneous. Until the continued movement of the door is arrested, it is possible that limited movement of the door may cause it to come in contact with a person or object in its path.

407.3.3.1 Height. The reopening device shall be activated by sensing an obstruction passing through the opening at 5 inches (125 mm) nominal and 29 inches (735 mm) nominal above the floor.

❖ See the commentary for Section 407.3.3.

407.3.3.2 Contact. The reopening device shall not require physical contact to be activated, although contact shall be permitted before the door reverses.

❖ See the commentary for Section 407.3.3.

407.3.3.3 Duration. The reopening device shall remain effective for 20 seconds minimum.

❖ See the commentary for Section 407.3.3.

407.3.4 Door and Signal Timing. The minimum acceptable time from notification that a car is answering a call until the doors of that car start to close shall be calculated from the following equation:

$T = D/(1.5 \text{ ft/s})$ or $T = D/(455 \text{ mm/s}) = 5$ seconds minimum, where T equals the total time in seconds and D equals the distance (in feet or millimeters) from the point in the lobby or corridor 60 inches (1525 mm) directly in front of the farthest call button controlling that car to the centerline of its hoistway door.

EXCEPTIONS:

1. For cars with in-car lanterns, T shall be permitted to begin when the signal is visible from the point 60 inches (1525 mm) directly in front of the farthest hall call button and the audible signal is sounded.

2. Destination-oriented elevators shall not be required to comply with Section 407.3.4.

❖ This provision allows variation in the location of call buttons, advance time for warning signals and the door-holding period used to meet the time requirement. Examples of the application of this provision are shown in commentary Figure C407.3.4.

This requirement gives sufficient time for a person outside the car to gain access to an elevator based on studies completed at Syracuse University in the mid-1970s, which indicated that the disabled needed $1^1/_2$ seconds for each 1 foot (305 mm) of travel. This requirement gives the disabled time to move into the path of the car door. The provision for door reopening (Section 407.3.3) allows sufficient time to move through the open door.

On a destination elevator, the passenger is immediately advised what car to take and can go directly to it. Thus the timing starts at the keypad, calculates the time to reach the hoistway entrance, adds door open-

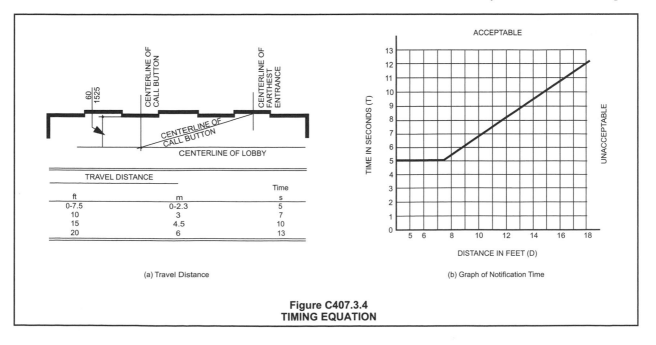

(a) Travel Distance

(b) Graph of Notification Time

Figure C407.3.4
TIMING EQUATION

ing time and time to move into the path of the open door.

407.3.5 Door Delay. Elevator doors shall remain fully open in response to a car call for 3 seconds minimum.

❖ The length of time that elevator doors remain open can typically be adjusted, but this standard requires the doors to remain open for not less than 3 seconds after reaching the fully opened position. This is the least amount of time deemed necessary to enable a person within the car to fully enter the path of the elevator doors and activate the noncontact door-reopening device.

407.3.6 Width. Elevator door clear opening width shall comply with Table 407.4.1.

> **EXCEPTION:** In existing elevators, a power-operated car door complying with Section 404.2.2 shall be permitted.

❖ The tolerance in car door widths in Table 407.4.1 is to allow for hard metric door sizes. See commentary Section 407.4.1.

407.4 Elevator Car Requirements. Elevator cars shall comply with Section 407.4.

❖ The elevator car has specific requirements for items such as dimensions, floor surfaces, platform to hoistway clearances, leveling, illumination, car controls, car position indicators and emergency communication.

Accessibility, is a function of the inside car dimension, door location and size, and access to controls, especially in smaller cars. Because of automatic operation of the doors, a turning space within the elevator car itself is not required.

407.4.1 Car Dimensions. Inside dimensions of elevator cars shall comply with Table 407.4.1.

> **EXCEPTION:** Existing elevator car configurations that provide a clear floor area of 16 square feet (1.5 m^2) minimum, and provide a clear inside dimension of 36 inches (915 mm) minimum in width and 54 inches (1370 mm) minimum in depth, shall be permitted.

❖ The specified dimensions are based on industry standard car arrangements that can be found in the *Building Transportation Standards and Guidelines*, NEII-1, available free at www.neii.org. Both imperial and hard metric elevator configurations are included in NEII-1. The industry standards are based on studies performed at Syracuse University in the mid 1970s. Accessibility in the smaller size cars is dependent on the inside floor area and location of the car door. This was taken into account when Table 407.4.1 was developed. Note 2 states that any elevator car that provides a clear door width of at least 36 inches (915 mm) and a turning space (i.e., circular or T-turn) within the cab would be considered accessible.

The exception recognizes that the size of an existing elevator is fixed. As an example the industry standard 2000 pound (907 kg) elevator was reconfigured in the mid 1970s to permit the turning of a wheelchair. Elevators of this capacity and others that predate that change cannot be reconfigured. If full compliance with Table 407.4.1 was mandated, the existing elevator would need to be completely replaced and a new hoistway constructed to allow for the reconfigured platform size.

407.4.2 Floor Surfaces. Floor surfaces in elevator cars shall comply with Section 302.

❖ The surface features of elevator car floors are just as critical as other floor or ramp surfaces used by people with disabilities, and are required to comply with Section 303.

407.4.3 Platform to Hoistway Clearance. The clearance between the car platform sill and the edge of any hoistway landing shall be in compli-

Table 407.4.1—Minimum Dimensions of Elevator Cars

Door Location	Door Clear Opening Width	Inside Car, Side to Side	Inside, Car, Back Wall to Front Return	Inside Car, Back Wall to Inside Face of Door
Centered	42 inches (1065 mm)	80 inches (2030 mm)	51 inches (1295 mm)	54 inches (1370 mm)
Side (Off Center)	36 inches (915 mm)[1]	68 inches (1725 mm)	51 inches (1295 mm)	54 inches (1370 mm)
Any	36 inches 915 mm)[1]	54 inches (1370 mm)	80 inches (2030 mm)	80 inches (2030 mm)
Any	36 inches 915 mm)[1]	60 inches (1525 mm)[2]	60 inches (1525 mm)[2]	60 inches (1525 mm)[2]

[1] A tolerance of minus $^5/_8$ inch (16 mm) is permitted.
[2] Other car configurations that provide a 36-inch (915 mm) door clear opening width and a turning space complying with Section 304 with the door closed are permitted.

ance with ASME/ANSI A17.1 listed in Section 105.2.5.

❖ The vertical and horizontal clearance between the car platform sill and the edge of any hoistway landing is a required running clearance for movement of the elevator. This clearance received much attention in the early 1970s. Persons using wheelchairs wanted the clearance to be close to zero. A large gap can be cum-

bersome to traverse with a wheelchair, especially for the front wheels. It wasn't until the industry explained and demonstrated that a running clearance was required that the tolerance was agreed upon. The requirement in ASME A17.1 for the horizontal clearance between the platform sill and the edge of the landing sill is 1¼ inches (32 mm) maximum.

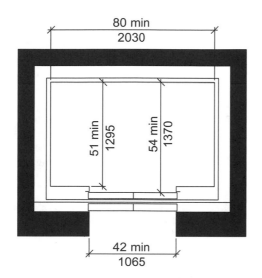

(a) Centered Door Location

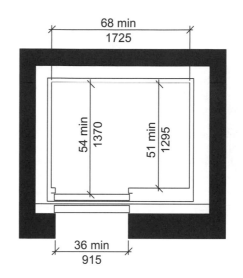

(b) Side (Off-Centered Door) Location

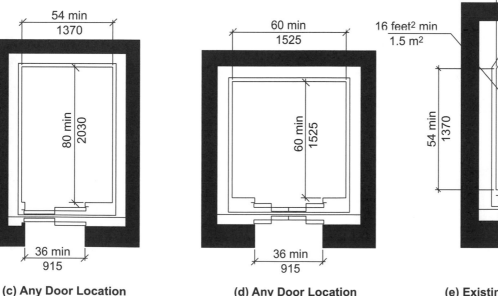

(c) Any Door Location

(d) Any Door Location

(e) Existing Car Configurations

Fig. 407.4.1
Inside Dimensions of Elevator Cars

407.4.4 Leveling. Each car shall be equipped with a self-leveling feature that will automatically bring and maintain the car at floor landings within a tolerance of $^1/_2$ inch (13 mm) under rated loading to zero loading conditions.

❖ A full elevator car may stop within $^1/_2$ inch (13 mm) of a floor landing only to creep to greater distance as people get on and off and the load increases or decreases on the elevator. This change in loading will cause the elevator to move away or toward the landing. Without releveling to the $^1/_2$-inch (13 mm) of the landing, the resulting vertical level change may make the car inaccessible to many persons with disabilities.

407.4.5 Illumination. The level of illumination at the car controls, platform, car threshold and car landing sill shall be 5 foot-candles (54 lux) minimum.

❖ A minimum amount of illumination is necessary for the benefit of all people, but is especially important for people with limited mobility who must use greater care in moving about. The illumination level required by the model building codes for general means of egress purposes is 1 footcandle (11 lux). The illumination level is the less than that required by the referenced edition of ASME A17.1. The 2000 edition of

ASME A17.1 has raised the illumination level to 10 footcandles (108 lux).

407.4.6 Elevator Car Controls. Where provided, elevator car controls shall comply with Sections 407.4.6 and 309.

EXCEPTION: In existing elevators, where a new car operating panel complying with Section 407.4.6 is provided, existing car operating panels shall not be required to comply with Section 407.4.6.

❖ Car controls are the buttons inside the car that allow users to indicate the desired floor they wish to travel to with the associated designation immediately adjacent (see Section 407.4.7). In addition to the controls being in an accessible location (e.g., a clear floor space in front of the controls and controls within reach ranges), there are concerns for button size, arrangement and designation for persons with limited dexterity or visual impairments (see commentary Figure C407.4.6). The 'where provided' language is in consideration of destination-oriented elevators that do not have car controls in the cab.

In existing elevators, if a second operating panel is installed that complies with the new provisions, the original control panel may remain in place.

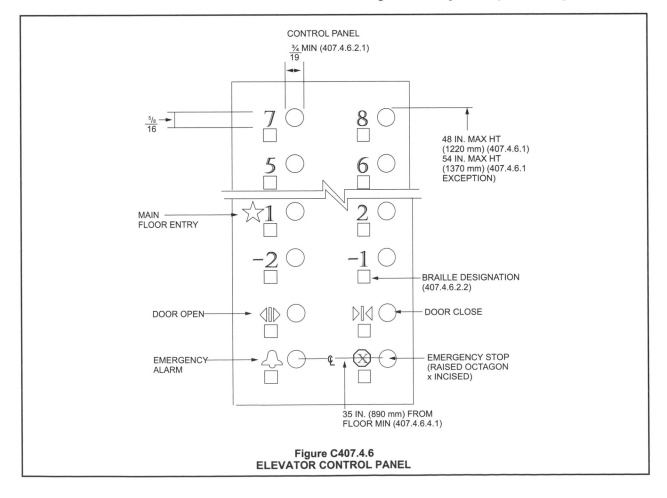

Figure C407.4.6
ELEVATOR CONTROL PANEL

407.4.6.1 Location. Controls shall be located within one of the reach ranges specified in Section 308.

EXCEPTIONS:

1. Where the elevator panel serves more than 16 openings and a parallel approach to the controls is provided, buttons with floor designations shall be permitted to be 54 inches (1370 mm) maximum above the floor.

2. In existing elevators, where a parallel approach is provided to the controls, car control buttons with floor designations shall be permitted to be located 54 inches (1370 mm) maximum above the floor. Where the panel is changed, it shall comply with Section 407.4.6.1.

❖ These provisions are intended to ensure that controls are located within reach of a person in a wheelchair. In most cases, it is possible to locate the highest control on elevator panels within 48 inches (1220 mm) of the floor. See commentary Figure C407.4.6 and Section 407.4.6.4.

When the elevator serves more than 16 openings (regulated by "openings" rather than "landings" to accommodate cars with front and rear openings) there may not be sufficient space in the front return panel to fit all the buttons within 48 inches (1220 mm) of the floor. Research using industry standard 2000 pound and 2500 pound (907 and 1134 kg) capacity elevators indicates that side reach from a facing position is not possible unless flush-mounted car controls are located 23.5 inches (595 mm) or more from a corner. This is not possible in these cars.

When Exception 1 is used, the elevator must have sequential step scanning in accordance with Section 407.4.8.

In existing elevators, existing control panels may remain at the higher reach. When a panel is replaced, it must comply with the new provisions for panels.

407.4.6.2 Buttons. Car control buttons with floor designations shall be raised or flush, and shall comply with Section 407.4.6.2.

EXCEPTION: In existing elevators, buttons shall be permitted to be recessed.

❖ Car controls are the buttons inside the car that allow uses to indicate the desired floor they wish to travel to. In addition to the controls being in an accessible location (e.g., a clear floor space in front of the controls and controls within reach ranges), there are concerns for button size and designation for person with limited dexterity or visual impairments. Buttons must be raised from or flush with the faceplate or trim ring if provided.

The exception establishes that for existing elevators, compliance with the provisions for arrangement of the control buttons within the operating panel is not required unless the operating panel is changed. It is considered impractical, and in many cases impossible, to rearrange the buttons within an existing operating panel in full compliance with Section 407.4.6.2. These constraints do not exist when the entire operating panel is replaced.

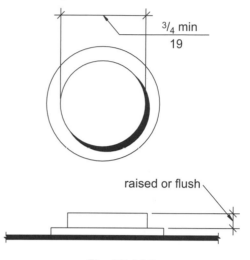

Fig. 407.4.6.2
Elevator Car Control Buttons

407.4.6.2.1 Size. Buttons shall be ³/₄ inch (19 mm) minimum in their smallest dimension.

❖ See commentary for Section 407.4.6.2 and commentary Figure C407.4.6.

407.4.6.2.2 Arrangement. Buttons shall be arranged with numbers in ascending order. Floors shall be designated . . . -4, -3, -2, -1, 0, 1, 2, 3, 4, et cetera, with floors below the main entry floor designated with minus numbers. Numbers shall be permitted to be omitted, provided the remaining numbers are in sequence. Where a telephone keypad arrangement is used, the number key ("#") shall be utilized to enter the minus symbol ("-"). When two or more columns of buttons are provided they shall read from left to right.

❖ Because of the confusion for persons unfamiliar with the building, a standard designation in the elevator for the different floors up and down from the entry level is required. This avoids unique designations such as 'M' for mezzanine or 'B2' for the basement levels. Even though the '0' designation may be popular in Europe, most buildings in the Unites States designate the entry level as Floor 1. Note the allowance to omit numbers. When there are enough floor levels that columns of buttons must be used, the buttons should first read from left to right and then move up a row (see commentary Figure C407.4.6).

An alternative arrangement for multiple buttons would be a scrolling option, when persons hold down a button until their floor designation lights up and then they release to register that call. See commentary under Section 407.4.6.3 if a keypad is chosen to enter floor calls.

407.4.6.3 Keypads. Car control keypads shall be in a standard telephone keypad arrangement and shall comply with Section 407.4.7.2.

❖ An alternative to rows of buttons is a keypad entry system. If this option is chosen, the keypad should follow the telephone arrangement in Section 707.5. The number 5 must have a raised dot. The # key is used to enter negative numbers for level below the entry floor. See Sections 407.4.7.2 and 707.5.

407.4.6.4 Emergency Controls. Emergency controls shall comply with Section 407.4.6.4.

❖ Emergency controls are typically the "HELP" button used to summon assistance if the elevator malfunctions or becomes stuck for some reason and "DOOR OPEN" button to stop an automatic closing door. It is important that these pieces of equipment be accessible for everyone when needed. The 35 inch (890 mm) value was chosen because the lower end of the reach ranges [i.e., 15 inches (380 mm)] was considered too low for proper access for taller persons. For consistency in elevators, they should always be located below the car controls.

In-car switches not intended for passenger use (e.g., fireman's operation) do not have be accessible.

407.4.6.4.1 Height. Emergency control buttons shall have their centerlines 35 inches (890 mm) minimum above the floor.

❖ See commentary for Section 407.4.6.4.

407.4.6.4.2 Location. Emergency controls, including the emergency alarm, shall be grouped at the bottom of the panel.

❖ See commentary for Section 407.4.6.4.

407.4.7 Designations and Indicators of Car Controls. Designations and indicators of car controls shall comply with Section 407.4.7.

EXCEPTIONS:

1. In existing elevators, where a new car operating panel complying with Section 407.4.7 is provided, existing car operating panels shall not be required to comply with Section 407.4.7.

2. Where existing building floor designations differ from the arrangement required by Section 407.4.6.2.2, or are alphanumeric, a new operating panel shall be permitted to use such existing building floor designations.

❖ Car controls are identified with tactile and Braille information. In addition, the buttons must indicate when a call has been registered.

The exceptions allow redundant controls in an elevator and allow the new control to follow the same designation as the existing panel. On some existing car control panels, the control buttons are crowded too close together to permit the installation of raised letter/Braille marking plates. Where locating the markings "as near to the control as possible" remains impractical, installation of a new panel conforming to Section 407.4.6 should be considered.

407.4.7.1 Buttons. Car control buttons shall comply with Section 407.4.7.1.

❖ Buttons shall comply with the requirements for identification, location, symbols and visible indicators in Sections 407.4.7.1.1 through 407.4.7.1.4.

407.4.7.1.1 Type. Control buttons shall be identified by tactile characters complying with Section 703.3.

❖ Permanently applied plates that have the appropriate raised characters/symbols and Braille are an acceptable means of providing raised control designations when nontelephone type key pads are provided.

407.4.7.1.2 Location. Tactile character and braille designations shall be placed immediately to the left of the control button to which the designations apply. Where a negative number is used to indicate a negative floor, the braille designation shall be a cell with the dots 3 and 6 followed by the ordinal number.

EXCEPTION: Where space on an existing car operating panel precludes tactile markings to the left of the control button, markings shall be placed as near to the control button as possible.

❖ Raised numbers and Braille designations must be placed immediately to the left of each control button (see commentary Figure C407.4.6). For Braille numbers, see commentary Figure C407.4.7.1.2(a). The main floor must also have the star symbol. The Braille symbol for the negative number is the bottom two dots in the Braille cell (see commentary Figure C407.4.7.1.2(b) and Section 407.4.6.2.2).

407.4.7.1.3 Symbols. The control button for the emergency stop, alarm, door open, door close, main entry floor, and phone, shall be identified with tactile symbols as shown in Table 407.4.7.1.3.

❖ Common controls found inside elevator cabs must be identified with both raised symbols and Braille designations as indicated in Table 407.4.7.1.3.

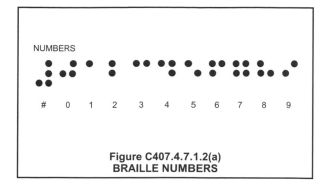

Figure C407.4.7.1.2(a)
BRAILLE NUMBERS

BRAILLE CELL

1 ○ ○ 4
2 ○ ○ 5
3 ○ ○ 6

Figure C407.4.7.1.2(b)
BRAILLE CELLS

407.4.7.1.4 Visible Indicators. Buttons with floor designations shall be provided with visible indicators to show that a call has been registered. The visible indication shall extinguish when the car arrives at the designated floor.

❖ Visible indicators do not have to be proved by the button itself. Lights beside buttons are permitted but cannot interfere with the placement of the raised and Braille characters.

407.4.7.2 Keypads. Keypads shall be identified by visual characters complying with Section 703.2 and shall be centered on the corresponding keypad button. The number five key shall have a single raised dot. The dot shall have a base diameter of 0.118 inch (3 mm) minimum to 0.120 inch (3.05 mm) maximum, and a height of 0.025 inch (0.6 mm) minimum to 0.037 inch (0.9 mm) maximum.

❖ Telephone type key pad arrangements were addressed in the 1998 standard for the first time. For tactile information where the standard telephone arrangement is used [see Figure 707.5(a)], there is a tactile dot on the number "5" key. The remainder of the keys are identified visually. For consistency the star appearing on the lower left key will be visually the same as the 5 pointed star in Table 407.4.7.1.3 and when pushed will enter a call to the "Main" floor designated for the elevator. Entering the "Main" floor number will do the same. The "Pound" key position in the lower right hand position is used to enter minus "-" floors such as below-grade levels or parking. The "Pound" key position and then a number in succession will enter the appropriate calls to these below-grade floors. To enter floor calls above the "Main" floor such as floor 15, it is only necessary to push "1" and then "5" in succession.

407.4.8 Elevator Car Call Sequential Step Scanning. Elevator car call sequential step scanning shall be provided where car control buttons are provided more than 48 inches (1220 mm) above the floor, as permitted by Section 407.4.6.1, Exception #1. Floor selection shall be accomplished by applying momentary or constant pressure to the up or down scan button.

The up scan button shall sequentially select floors above the current floor. The down scan button shall sequentially select floors below the current floor. When pressure is removed from the up or down scan button for more than 2 seconds, the last floor selected shall be registered as a car call. The up and down scan button shall be located adjacent to or immediately above the emergency control buttons.

❖ Persons who are short of stature and some people who use wheelchairs may not be able to reach the upper buttons when Exception 1 to Section 407.4.6.1 is permitted. The sequential step scanner provides an alternative means that would allow a person to choose a floor. Sequential step scanning works like the up/down button on a TV. When the "up" button is pressed floor selection proceeds in a sequential order (car floor buttons light up) until the "up" button is released. The last floor selected is registered as a car call.

407.4.9 Car Position Indicators. Audible and visible car position indicators shall be provided in elevator cars.

❖ During the ascent or descent of an elevator car, information must be provided inside the car that indicates the car's location. This information must be provided visibly and audibly as indicated in Sections 407.4.9.1 through 407.4.9.2.3.

407.4.9.1 Visible Indicators. Visible indicators shall comply with Section 407.4.9.1.

❖ The location and size of the visible indicator must be readily seen by everyone in the car, but most importantly, it must be in a standardized location so people will become accustomed to it being in the same location in all accessible elevators.

407.4.9.1.1 Size. Characters shall be $\frac{1}{2}$ inch (13 mm) minimum in height.

❖ See commentary for Section 407.4.9.1.

407.4.9.1.2 Location. Indicators shall be located above the car control panel or above the door.

❖ See commentary for Section 407.4.9.1.

Table 407.4.7.1.3—Control Button Identification

Control Button	Tactile Symbol	Braille Message	Proportions Open circles indicate unused dots within each Braille Cell
DOOR OPEN		OP"EN"	
REAR/SIDE DOOR OPEN		REAR/SIDE OP"EN"	
DOOR CLOSE		CLOSE	
REAR/SIDE DOOR CLOSE		REAR/SIDE CLOSE	
MAIN		MA"IN"	
ALARM		AL"AR"M	
PHONE		PH"ONE"	
EMERGENCY STOP (WHEN PROVIDED) X on face of octagon is not required to be tactile		"ST"OP	

407.4.9.1.3 Floor Arrival. As the car passes a floor and when a car stops at a floor served by the elevator, the corresponding character shall illuminate.

> **EXCEPTION:** Destination-oriented elevators shall not be required to comply with Section 407.4.9.1.3, provided the visible indicators extinguish when the call has been answered.

❖ The indicators above the car control or above the door are location indicators that indicate progress up and down the hoistway. They can be on a strip where the floor number illuminates at approximately the time the car passes each floor; or they can be a changing number display.

For destination-oriented elevators, the indicators are the same size and in the same location, but the information is displayed slightly differently. See the commentary for Section 407.4.9.1.4.

407.4.9.1.4 Destination Indicator. In destination-oriented elevators, a display shall be provided in the car with visible indicators to show car destinations.

❖ In destination-oriented elevators the in-car display provides information regarding what floor the car is traveling to next. The visible indicators on the in-car display will remain lit until the floor designated has been reached. The visible indication is extinguished after the call has been answered. Other enhancements such as having the next designated stop begin to flash are used, but are not required.

407.4.9.2 Audible Indicators. Audible indicators shall comply with Section 407.4.9.2.

❖ A verbal announcement is preferred by persons with visual impairments and the general public. A nonverbal, audible signal is difficult to use in high-rise buildings and when nonstandard floor arrangements (e.g., basement, lobby, mezzanine, 2nd floor, 12th floor, 14th floor, etc.) are used.

407.4.9.2.1 Signal Type. The signal shall be an automatic verbal annunciator that announces the floor at which the car is about to stop. The verbal announcement indicating the floor shall be completed prior to the initiation of the door opening.

> **EXCEPTION:** For elevators other than destination-oriented elevators that have a rated speed of 200 feet per minute (1 m/s) or less, a non-verbal audible signal with a frequency of 1500 Hz maximum that sounds as the car passes or is about to stop at a floor served by the elevator shall be permitted.

❖ See the commentary to Section 407.4.9.2.

407.4.9.2.2 Signal Level. The verbal annunciator shall be 10 dBA minimum above ambient, but shall not exceed 80 dBA, measured at the annunciator.

❖ A minimum sound pressure level is necessary to ensure that the audible signal can be reasonably heard over and above ambient noise levels in the elevator car. The sound level specified is intended to make sure the signal can be heard above ambient noise but not cause damage to a persons hearing.

407.4.9.2.3 Frequency. The verbal annunciator shall have a frequency of 300 Hz minimum to 3,000 Hz maximum.

❖ See the commentary to Section 407.4.9.2.2.

407.4.10 Emergency Communications. Emergency two-way communication systems between the elevator car and a point outside the hoistway shall comply with Section 407.4.10 and ASME/ANSI A17.1 listed in Section 105.2.5.

❖ The referenced edition of ASME A17.1, Rule 2.27.1, requires that a means to activate two-way communication "HELP" button be provided in elevators. These provisions address the details that are necessary to ensure that the emergency communications devices are accessible to and usable by people who are unable to use voice communication (e.g., people with speech/hearing impairments). A telephone symbol with Braille is generally used to identify the two-way communications means, which may be an intercom or a telephone. A device that requires no handset is required by A117.1 and is easier to use by people who have difficulty reaching.

It is not the intent of this section to apply to any two-way communication equipment for use only by the fire-department.

407.4.10.1 Height. The highest operable part of a two-way communication system shall comply with Section 308.

❖ All operable parts of the emergency communication equipment must be within the reach ranges of Section 308.

407.4.10.2 Identification. Tactile characters complying with Section 703.3 and symbols complying with Section 407.4.7.1.3 shall be provided adjacent to the device.

❖ The raised phone symbol and Braille information must be provided in accordance with Table 407.4.1.3.

408 Limited-Use/Limited-Application Elevators

408.1 General. Limited-use/limited-application elevators shall comply with Section 408 and ASME A17.1 listed in Section 105.2.5. Elevator operation shall be automatic.

❖ The organization of this section is similar to that of the elevator section; elevator landing (Section 408.2), elevator doors (Section 408.3), and elevator cars (Section 408.4).

A Limited-Use/Limited-Application (LULA) elevator is defined by ASME A17.1 as "a power passenger elevator where the use and application is limited by size, capacity, speed and rise." LULA elevators are generally used where installation of a full passenger elevator is not practical or economically feasible. LULA elevators provide many of the same features as full passenger elevators and provide accessibility in situations where access may otherwise not be provided.

ASME A17.1 provides comprehensive safety requirements for the installation of LULA elevators. For example, LULA elevators are restricted to 25 feet (7620 mm) of travel, a speed of 30 feet per minute (9145 mm/min), an 18 square foot (1.7 m²) car size and 1400 pound (635 kg) capacity. Because of their limited travel and smaller size, firefighter emergency operation is not required on LULA elevators (see commentary Figure C408.1).

For purposes of accessibility, elevators that are attendant operated are not considered acceptable because of the potential for the attendant not being readily available. Also, elevator controls that require continuous pressure for operation are not allowed, because they may not be suitable for people who have limited use of their hands.

Figure C408.1
LULA ELEVATOR

408.2 Elevator Landing Requirements. Landings serving limited-use/limited application elevators shall comply with Section 408.2.

❖ Similar to other types of passenger elevators, at each floor level that is served by the LULA elevator, there are provisions for controls to call the car, the signals for car arrival at the floor level and floor level information on the elevator door jambs.

408.2.1 Call Controls. Elevator call buttons and keypads shall comply with Section 407.2.1.

❖ Car controls in LULA elevator must comply with the same provisions as other types of passenger elevators. This would include access to the controls, car button requirements, visual and audible indicators, etc. There should never be a problem with meeting the reach ranges because of the limited levels served. See Section 407.2.1.

408.2.2 Hall Signals. Hall signals shall comply with Section 407.2.2.

❖ Hall signals for LULAs are the same as for other types of passenger elevators. This includes both visual and audible signals. This is mostly to address the direction of travel rather than which elevator is arriving because it is very unusual for more than one LULA to be installed in a building.

408.2.3 Hoistway Signs. Signs at elevator hoistways shall comply with Section 407.2.3.

❖ LULA elevators must have raised and Braille floor level identification at each hoistway entrance similar to the general elevator requirements. This would include a raised star at the main level.

Tactile signage communicates vital information to people with vision impairments. It is also useful information for those with hearing impairments, as well as the general public. Plates that have the appropriate raised characters are acceptable if the plates are permanently fixed to the hoistway entrance jambs.

408.3 Elevator Door Requirements. Elevator hoistway doors shall comply with Section 408.3.

❖ LULA elevators may use swinging or sliding doors that operate automatically. The car door width and location affects the accessibility of the LULA elevator. Vertical sliding doors are not allowed.

408.3.1 Sliding Doors. Sliding hoistway and car doors shall comply with Sections 407.3.1 through 407.3.3, and 408.3.3.

❖ By the reference to Sections 407.3.1 through 407.3.3, sliding doors on the car and on the hoistway must meet the provisions in the general elevator requirements for the horizontal sliding type, operate automatically and be equipped with a reopening device. The reference to Section 408.3.3 stipulates minimum width and location relative to the car shape.

408.3.2 Swinging Doors. Swinging hoistway doors shall open and close automatically and shall comply with Sections 408.3.2, 404, and 407.3.2.

❖ Some LULA elevators have a swinging door at the hoistway openings. These doors must be automatic (Section 407.3.2) and meet the power operation and duration requirement in the subsections of Section 408.3.2. In addition, the door must meet the provisions in Section 404.3 for automatic doors. Because the car door is horizontal sliding and automatic, the car and hoistway doors are not considered doors in a series (See Section 404.3.4).

408.3.2.1 Power Operation. Swinging doors shall be power-operated and shall comply with ANSI/BHMA A156.19 listed in Section 105.2.3.

❖ The building hardware industry has developed consensus standards for automatic doors. Issues such as safety, durability, usability, operation and installation are covered. The standard is available from the American National Standards Institute, 25 West 43rd Street, Fourth Floor, New York, New York 10036.

408.3.2.2 Duration. Power-operated swinging doors shall remain open for 20 seconds minimum when activated.

❖ The intent of the 20 seconds is to allow sufficient time for passengers to enter the elevator without the door closing on them.

408.3.3 Door Location and Width. Car doors shall provide a clear opening width of 32 inches (815 mm) minimum. Car doors shall be positioned at a narrow end of the car.

EXCEPTION: Car doors that provide a clear opening width of 36 inches (915 mm) minimum shall be permitted to be located on adjacent sides of cars that provide a clear floor area of 51 inches (1295 mm) in width and 51 inches (1295 mm) in depth.

❖ In a standard LULA elevator with one door, minimally, the door must have a clear width of 32 inches (815 mm) and be located at the narrow end of the 42 inch by 54 inch (1065 mm) car (See Figure 408.4.1).
LULA elevators may sometimes have two doors. If doors are at opposite ends, the requirements are the same as for a single car door. If doors are on adjacent walls, the minimum clear width is increased to 36 inches (915 mm) for both doors, and the minimum car size is increased to 51 inches by 51 inches (1295 by 1295 mm) (see commentary Figure C408.3.3).

408.4 Elevator Car Requirements. Elevator cars shall comply with Section 408.4.

❖ LULA cars must comply with provisions for minimum dimensions, floor surface, platform to hoistway clearances, leveling of the car, illumination, in-car controls, floor designations and car location information and emergency communication. Many of these requirements are the same as those for general passenger elevators.

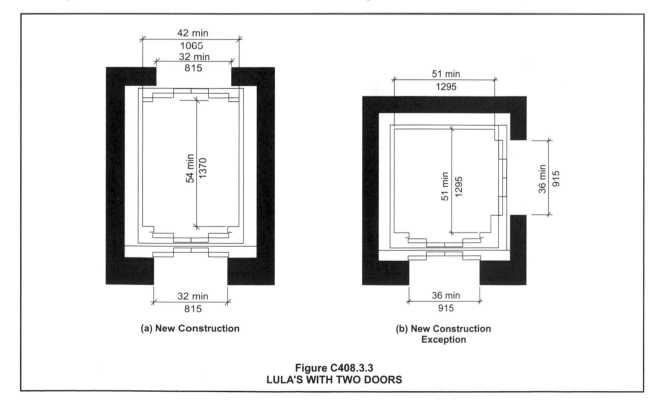

Figure C408.3.3
LULA'S WITH TWO DOORS

408.4.1 Inside Dimensions of Elevator Cars.
Elevator cars shall provide a clear floor area of 42 inches (1065 mm) minimum in width, and 54 inches (1370 mm) minimum in depth.

EXCEPTIONS:

1. Cars that provide a 51 inches (1295 mm) minimum clear floor width shall be permitted to provide 51 inches (1295 mm) minimum clear floor depth.

2. For installations in existing buildings, elevator cars that provide a clear floor area of 15 square feet (1.4 m^2) minimum, and provide a clear inside dimension of 36 inches (915 mm) minimum in width

and 54 inches (1370 mm) minimum in depth, shall be permitted.

❖ The inside dimensions of the elevator car provide adequate space for a person using a wheelchair to enter the car, operate the controls and exit the car. Per Section 408.3.3, doors are positioned on the narrow ends of the platform to allow the user to go in and out of the elevator car without turning. The car doors are required to meet the same 32 inch (815 mm) clear width as other accessible doors.

The first exception is to provide correlation with the exception permitted in Section 408.3.3 that deals with two doors on adjacent walls and minimum car size. This same minimum car size is permitted with one door [see Figure 408.4.1(b) and commentary Figure C408.3.3(b)].

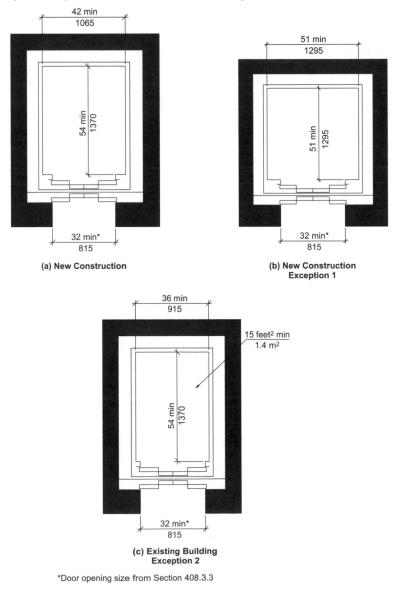

(a) New Construction

(b) New Construction
Exception 1

(c) Existing Building
Exception 2

*Door opening size from Section 408.3.3

Fig. 408.4.1
Inside Dimensions of Limited Use/Limited Application (LULA) Elevator Cars

Existing conditions sometimes require the use of a smaller car. The dimensions of 36 inches by 54 (915 by 1370 mm) inches allow for this, while still providing adequate room for the user to enter, operate the controls and exit the lift. The *Building Transportation Standards and Guidelines*, NEII-1 also provides standard industry car dimensions and door arrangements that comply with A117.1. NEII-1 is available free of charge at www.neii.org.

408.4.2 Floor Surfaces. Floor surfaces in elevator cars shall comply with Section 302.

❖ The surface features of elevator car floors are just as critical as other floor or ramp surfaces used by people with disabilities, and are required to comply with Section 302. See also Section 407.4.2.

408.4.3 Platform to Hoistway Clearance. The clearance between the car platform sill and the edge of any hoistway landing shall be in compliance with ASME/ANSI A17.1 listed in Section 105.2.5.

❖ This provision restricts the horizontal clearance between the car platform sill and the edge of any hoistway landing to a maximum of $1^1/_4$ inches (32 mm) as required by ASME A17.1. See also Section 407.4.3.

408.4.4 Leveling. Elevator car leveling shall comply with Section 407.4.4.

❖ LULA elevators are required to initially level at the landings the same as other passenger elevators. If the car is not required to stop within $^1/_2$ inch (13 mm) of the landing for all loading conditions, the resulting vertical level change may make this car inaccessible to many persons with disabilities. Because of the limited capacity, LULA elevators do not require a releveling feature.

408.4.5 Illumination. Elevator car illumination shall comply with Section 407.4.5.

❖ A minimum amount of illumination is necessary for the benefit of all people, but is especially important for people with limited mobility who must use greater care in moving about. The illumination level required by the model building codes for general means of egress is 1 footcandle (11 lux). The illumination level of 5 footcandles (54 lux) at the car controls, platform and car threshold is less than that required by the referenced edition of ASME A17.1. The 2000 edition of ASME A17.1 has raised the requirement to 10 footcandles (108 lux).

408.4.6 Elevator Car Controls. Elevator car controls shall comply with Section 407.4.6. Control panels shall be centered on a side wall.

❖ In LULA elevators, the car controls within the cab must meet the same provisions as for typical passenger elevators in Section 407.4.6. This includes provisions for control height, button style and emergency controls. See Section 407.4.6.

In LULA elevators, for easy access, controls should be centered on a side wall. The controls in the elevator car are most conveniently located for the person using a wheelchair from a side reach. The size and configuration of the elevator car does not allow for the user to complete a turn, and, therefore, the controls cannot be on the end walls. If the controls are moved toward a corner, they may end up behind the shoulder of the person entering the cab and the result could be that they were not reachable given the tight space of the cab floor.

408.4.7 Designations and Indicators of Car Controls. Designations and indicators of car controls shall comply with Section 407.4.7.

❖ Car controls are identified with raised numbers and Braille information, including a star at the main floor. Permanently applied plates that have the appropriately raised characters and symbols are an acceptable means of providing raised control designations. In addition, the buttons must indicate what calls have been registered. See Sections 407.4.7 though 407.4.7.2.

408.4.8 Emergency Communications. Car emergency signaling devices complying with Section 407.4.10 shall be provided.

❖ The referenced edition of ASME A17.1, Rule 2.27.1, requires that a means to activate two-way communication "HELP" button be provided in elevators. These provisions address the details that are necessary to ensure that the emergency communications devices are accessible to and usable by people who are unable to use voice communication (e.g., people with speech/hearing impairments). A telephone symbol with Braille is generally used to identify the two-way communications means, which may be an intercom or a telephone. A device that requires no handset is required by A117.1 and is easier for people who have difficulty reaching to use.

409 Private Residence Elevators

409.1 General. Private residence elevators shall comply with Section 409 and ASME/ANSI A17.1 listed in Section 105.2.5. Elevator operation shall be automatic.

EXCEPTION: Elevators complying with Section 407 or 408.

❖ Private residence elevators must comply with Section 5.3 of ASME A17.1. Operation of the elevator must be automatic. The only elevator landing requirement is call buttons (Section 409.2). For car and hoistway door requirements, see Section 409.3. Car requirements are in Section 409.4.

Private residence elevators are limited by the standard to a maximum of 50 feet (15 240 mm) vertical travel distance, and a maximum speed of 40 feet per minute (12 190 mm/min). The standard also limits the application of these types of elevators to within an individual unit or private access to an individual unit (see commentary Figure C409.1).

The requirements for private residence elevators are not as restrictive as the provisions for passenger elevators or LULAs because of the familiarity of the users. The majority of private residence elevators are connected within a vertical shaft. Most have a pit with a depth of about 6 inches (150 mm).

Private residence elevators can be used as part of the required accessible route in Accessible or Type A units. When private residence elevators are installed within individual townhouse style units with four or more units in a structure, Type B unit requirements are applicable to units with elevators.

The exception allows for elevators installed within a single dwelling unit or providing private access to a single dwelling unit to be passenger elevators, LULAs or private residence elevators.

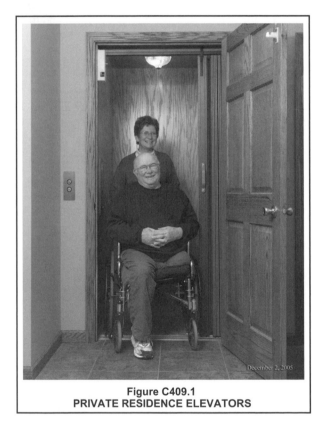

Figure C409.1
PRIVATE RESIDENCE ELEVATORS

409.2 Call Buttons. Call buttons at elevator landings shall comply with Section 309. Call buttons shall be $^3/_4$ inch (19 mm) minimum in their smallest dimension.

❖ Call buttons must meet all the provisions for operable parts: clear floor space, height and operation. Typically, buttons are located between 35 and 48 inches (890 and 1220 mm) above the floor (see Section 407.2.1.1). Minimum dimensions for the buttons ensure that the buttons are suitable for people who have limited use of their hands.

When a private residence elevator is accessed from a public area, the call is required by ASME A17.1 to be via key operation for security, similar to locking your front door.

409.3 Doors and Gates. Elevator car and hoistway doors and gates shall comply with Sections 409.3 and 404.

EXCEPTION: The maneuvering clearances required by Section 404.2.3 shall not apply for approaches to the push side of swinging doors.

❖ Two doors are installed at each elevator opening, one for the car and one for the hoistway. Typically, the car door slides sideways, and the hoistway door is a swinging door. Both doors must comply with this section specific to elevator doors, and the general provisions for doors in Section 404. These doors would not be considered doors in a series. Because of the small size of the elevator cab, the maneuvering clearances for doors are not required on the elevator side for the hoistway door.

409.3.1 Power Operation. Elevator car doors and gates shall be power operated and shall comply with ANSI/BHMA A156.19 listed in Section 105.2.3. Elevator cars with a single opening shall have low energy power operated hoistway doors and gates.

EXCEPTION: For elevators with a car that has more than one opening, the hoistway doors and gates shall be permitted to be of the manual-open, self-close type.

❖ When the elevator cab has only one door, both the door to the cab and the door to the hoistway must be power operated because the person using a wheelchair in this elevator would be dealing with a pull in-back out situation. The exception allows the doors to the hoistway to be manual if the elevator has a door on each end of the cab. In this situation, the person using the wheelchair would be dealing with a pull in-pull out situation. Doors must be self-closing to allow the elevator to operate effectively. If the door is not closed, the elevator cannot be called.

409.3.2 Duration. Power operated doors and gates shall remain open for 20 seconds minimum when activated.

❖ The power operated door device holds the doors open for 20 seconds if the doorway remains continuously obstructed. After 20 seconds, the door is permitted to begin closing. However, if designed in accordance with ASME A17.1, the door closing movement is still stopped if a person or object exerts sufficient force at any point on the door edge. Sufficient force is defined by ASME A17.1 as 30 pounds-force (134 N). If all door reopening devices are rendered inoperative the ASME A17.1 Code also requires the average kinetic energy of the door system be reduced from 7 ft-lbf to $2^1/_2$ ft-lbf (9.5 J to 3.4 J).

409.3.3 Door or Gate Location. Car gates or doors shall be positioned at a narrow end of the clear floor area required by Section 409.4.1.

❖ Given the size of the cab in Section 409.4, cab doors and hoistway doors must provide a 32-inch (815 mm) clear width (Section 404.2.2 and 409.3) and be located at the narrow end of the cab. At this time, the alternative of a side door is not prescribed for private residence elevators. However, the cab size and configuration is similar to a platform lift. Side doors for platform lifts are discussed in Section 410.2.1.

409.4 Elevator Car Requirements. Elevator cars shall comply with Section 409.4.

❖ The elevator car must comply with the car size, floor surface, clearance between hoistway and cab, illumination, car controls and emergency communication requirements in this section.

409.4.1 Inside Dimensions of Elevator Cars. Elevator cars shall provide a clear floor area 36 inches (915 mm) minimum in width and 48 inches (1220 mm) minimum in depth.

❖ The minimum cab size is consisted with the alcove provisions in Section 305.7.2. The car size must be a minimum of 36 inches (915 mm) wide and 48 inches (1220 mm) deep, which computes as a minimum area of 12 square feet (1.1 m^2). The ASME A17.1 limits the maximum cab size in a private residence elevator to 15 square feet (1.4 m^2).

409.4.2 Floor Surfaces. Floor surfaces in elevator cars shall comply with Section 302.

❖ The floor surface in the elevator cab must be stable, firm and slip resistant. If carpet is installed, the carpet must meet the requirements in Section 302.2. By reference in Section 302, any changes in elevation along the floor of the cab must be limited to the change in level provisions in Section 303.

409.4.3 Platform to Hoistway Clearance. The clearance between the car platform sill and the edge of any hoistway landing shall be 1$^1/_4$ inches (32 mm) maximum.

❖ The vertical and horizontal clearance between the car platform sill and the edge of any hoistway landing, is a required running clearance for movement of the elevator. This clearance received much attention in the early 1970s. Persons using wheelchairs wanted the clearance to be close to zero. A large gap can be cumbersome to traverse with a wheelchair, especially for the front wheels. It wasn't until the industry explained and demonstrated that a running clearance was required that the tolerance was agreed upon.

The referenced edition of ASME A17.1 allows for a 1$^1/_2$ inch (38 mm) clearance for private residence elevators. ICC A117.1 is more restrictive, but is consis-

tent with the hoistway clearance for passenger elevators and LULAs.

409.4.4 Leveling. Each car shall automatically stop at a floor landing within a tolerance of $^1/_2$ inch (13 mm) under rated loading to zero loading conditions.

❖ When the car is at rest, the floor of the car must be within $^1/_2$ inch (13 mm) up or down from the floor of the level served.

409.4.5 Illumination. The level of illumination at the car controls, platform, and car threshold and landing sill shall be 5 foot-candles (54 lux) minimum.

❖ A minimum amount of illumination is necessary for the benefit of all people, but is especially important for people with limited mobility who must use greater care in moving about. The illumination level required by the model building codes for general means of egress purposes is 1 footcandle. The illumination level is the same as required by the referenced edition of ASME A17.1-1996.

409.4.6 Elevator Car Controls. Elevator car controls shall comply with Sections 409.4.6 and 309.4.

❖ Basically car controls must be located so that the controls are reachable by a person using a wheelchair. Controls must also meet operation requirements found in the operable parts provisions in Section 309.4.

409.4.6.1 Buttons. Control buttons shall be $^3/_4$ inch (19 mm) minimum in their smallest dimension. Control buttons shall be raised or flush.

❖ Minimum dimensions for the buttons ensure that the buttons are suitable for people who have limited use of their hands.

409.4.6.2 Height. Buttons with floor designations shall comply with Section 309.3.

❖ Car control buttons must be located within the reach ranges. Typically, buttons are located between 35 and 48 inches (890 and 1220 mm) above the floor (see Section 407.4.6.1). Controls located lower may be blocked by a wheelchair in the elevator.

409.4.6.3 Location. Controls shall be on a sidewall, 12 inches (305 mm) minimum from any adjacent wall.

❖ The location of controls within the cab will result in controls that are at the shoulder location or forward for a person using a wheelchair. Locating the controls closer to the end walls could result in controls that were effectively behind the user and would be unreachable.

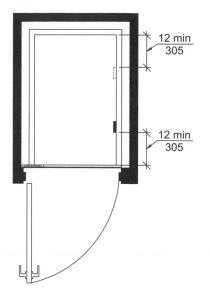

Fig. 409.4.6.3
Location of Controls in Private Residence Elevators

409.4.7 Emergency Communications. Emergency communications systems shall comply with Section 409.4.7.

❖ Private residence elevators must have emergency communication devices in case of an elevator malfunction or power outage.

409.4.7.1 Type. A telephone and emergency signal device shall be provided in the car.

❖ A phone that is connected to a central telephone exchange must be located within the cab. The phone line is typically located in the cab traveling cable. A cell phone is not acceptable because of concerns over batteries in the phones possibly running out, signal strength and power outages making the phones inoperable.

An emergency signaling device is also required in the elevator. This alarm is intended for internal notification and need not be connected to an outside alarm. If no one is in the house to assist, help can be summoned with the phone.

409.4.7.2 Operable Parts. The telephone and emergency signaling device shall comply with Section 309.3.

❖ The phone and the emergency signaling device must be located within reach ranges. Typically these devices are located adjacent to or under car controls. A consideration should be that a wheelchair in the cab would not block access to the phone and the emergency signaling system.

409.4.7.3 Compartment. If the device is in a closed compartment, the compartment door hardware shall comply with Section 309.

❖ If either the phone or the alarm is located in a closed compartment, the door hardware must meet the operable parts provisions including clear floor space, height and operation.

409.4.7.4 Cord. The telephone cord shall be 29 inches (735 mm) minimum in length.

❖ So that the phone cord will extend far enough for easy use, the cord must be a minimum of 29 inches (735 mm) long.

410 Platform Lifts

❖ During the development of the 2003 edition of ICC A117.1, platform lift requirements were editorially reformatted to harmonize with the April 2002 draft of the ADA/ABA Accessibility Guidelines. The authority having jurisdiction provides scoping for when platform lifts may be used as part of an accessible route for ingress and/or egress.

Platform lifts may move vertically or inclined. There are many different types of lifts. Some types require pits or floor depressions. Space for operational equipment is typically required immediately adjacent to the lift. See commentary Figure C410 for examples of different types.

410.1 General. Platform lifts shall comply with Section 410 and ASME/ANSI A18.1 listed in Section 105.2.6. Platform lifts shall not be attendant operated and shall provide unassisted entry and exit from the lift.

❖ A platform lift consists of a platform designed to carry a user, traveling on an incline [see commentary Figure C410.1(a)], such as along stairways, or vertically [see commentary Figure C410.1(b)] to accomplish movement from one floor level to another. Typical building code scoping provisions permit these mechanisms to serve as part of an accessible route in new construction into limited applications, such as performing areas, wheelchair viewing areas, small areas not open to the general public, raised areas in courtrooms, amusement rides, play components, team or player seating, and within dwelling units. Platform lifts can also be part of the accessible means of egress when supplied with standby power. In existing buildings lifts can be used for any application requiring access if they are installed in compliance with the requirements of the referenced edition of ASME A18.1. Please see the building codes for specific scoping provisions.

The referenced edition of ASME A18.1 contains comprehensive requirements for the installation of platform lifts. For example, lifts are limited to penetrating one floor, and vertical platform lifts may not travel more than 12 feet (3660 mm). The A18.1 is currently being modified to allow for a maximum travel distance of 14 feet (4265 mm).

Platform lifts are not permitted to be of the attendant-operated type. To provide an appropriate degree of accessibility, the lift must be arranged to allow unassisted entry, operation and egress from the lift. Unassisted access is one of the reasons ASME A18.1 requires push button controls. The requirements for inclined lifts were changed in ASME 1a-2001. The new requirements eliminated the requirement for attendant operation by adding barrier arms around the perimeter of the platform to enclose the user. This change allows the incline lifts to be in compliance with this standard.

ASME A18.1 has a requirement that permits a fold-down seat on inclined platform lifts for use by ambulatory persons. Further, it does not prohibit a similar fold-down seat to accommodate ambulatory persons on vertical lifts. Persons with other types of mobility aids may also use these lifts [see commentary Figure C410.1(c)]. For this reason and to coordinate with ASME A18.1, the term "platform" has replaced the term "wheelchair" to help clarify that ambulatory disabled persons can also use these lifts.

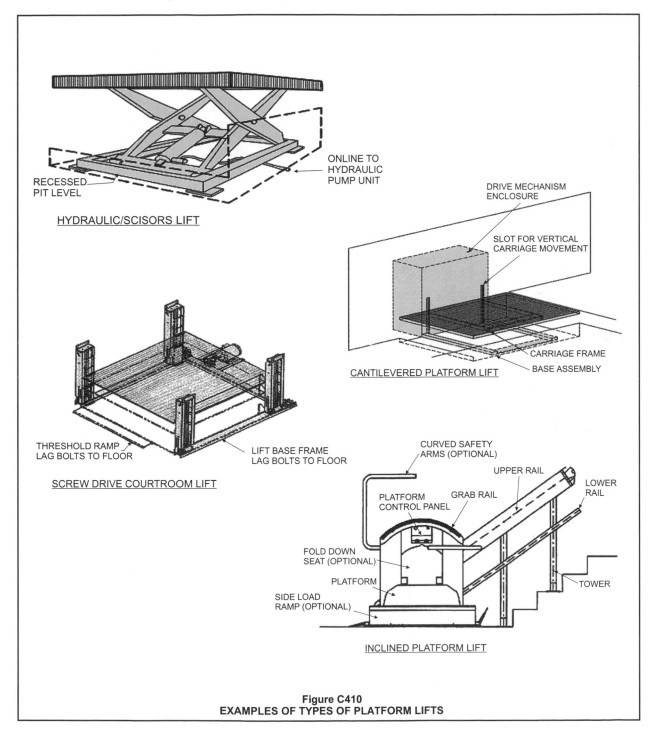

Figure C410
EXAMPLES OF TYPES OF PLATFORM LIFTS

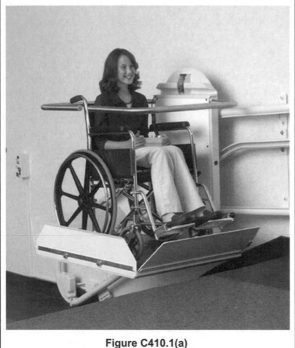

Figure C410.1(a)
INCLINED PLATFORM LIFT

Figure C410.1(b)
VERTICAL LIFT

Figure C410.1(c)
PERSON USING A SCOOTER ON A PLATFORM LIFT

minimum. Side door clear opening width shall be 42 inches (1065 mm) minimum.

> **EXCEPTION:** Lifts serving two landings maximum and having doors or gates on opposite sides shall be permitted to have self-closing manual doors or gates.

❖ Lifts are required to have power operated doors or gates to make them more accessible. The power doors or gates are required to meet the same guidelines as other power operated doors (Section 404.3). Doors or gates should remain open for 20 seconds minimum to allow the user ample time to enter or exit the lift. Doors positioned on the narrow end of the platform are required to meet the same 32 inch (815 mm) minimum clear opening as other doors on an accessible route. Doors on the long side of a platform that have a 90 degree (1.6 rad) turn, need to be wider [42 inches (1065 mm) clear] to allow the user to complete the turn as they are entering or exiting the lift. Lifts that both serve only two landing and that use doors or gates on opposite ends of the platform are not required to have power gates because the configuration allows the user to move straight forward when entering and exiting the lift in all entry and exit scenarios. See the commentary Figure C410.2.1 for configurations where the exception would and would not be applicable.

410.2 Lift Entry. Lifts with doors or gates shall comply with Section 410.2.1. Lifts with ramps shall comply with Section 410.2.2.

❖ Many lifts have doors or gates. Some lifts may include ramps to provided access onto the platform. This section does not require these items, but if they are installed, they must comply with the applicable section.

410.2.1 Doors and Gates. Doors and gates shall be low energy power operated doors or gates complying with Section 404.3. Doors shall remain open for 20 seconds minimum. End door clear opening width shall be 32 inches (815 mm)

410.2.2 Ramps. End ramps shall be 32 inches (815 mm) minimum in width. Side ramps shall be 42 inches (1065 mm) minimum in width.

❖ When ramps provide access to the floor of the platform lift, ramps must be the same width as the platform door served. Ramps must also meet the slope,

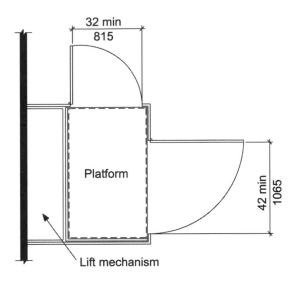

Fig. 410.2.1
Platform Lift Doors and Gates

cross slope and edge protection restrictions found in Section 405.

410.3 Floor Surfaces. Floor surfaces of platform lifts shall comply with Section 302.

❖ The floor surface in the platform must be stable, firm and slip resistant. If carpet is installed, the carpet must meet the requirements in Section 302.2. By the reference in Section 302, any changes in elevation along the floor of the cab must be limited to the change-in-level provisions in Section 303. The criterion in Section 410.4 is more specific to this particular situation; therefore, Section 302.3 would not be applicable to the platform-to-runway clearance.

410.4 Platform to Runway Clearance. The clearance between the platform sill and the edge of any runway landing shall be $1^1/_4$ inch (32 mm) maximum.

❖ The vertical and horizontal clearance between the car platform sill and the edge of any runway landing is a required running clearance for movement of the lift. This clearance received much attention in the early 1970s. Persons using wheelchairs wanted the clearance to be close to zero. A large gap can be cumbersome to traverse with a wheelchair, especially for the front wheels. It wasn't until the industry explained

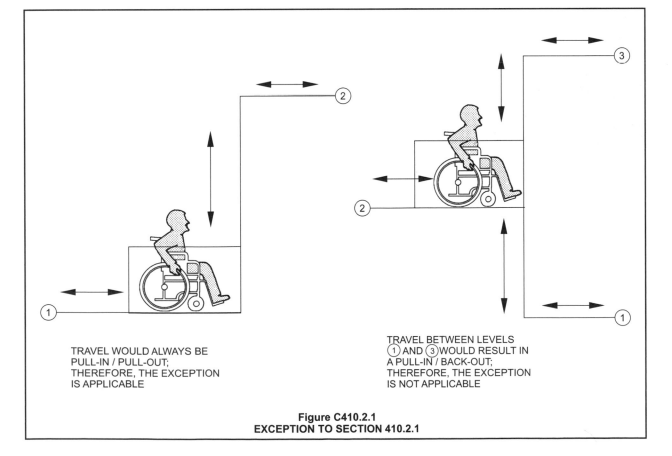

TRAVEL WOULD ALWAYS BE
PULL-IN / PULL-OUT;
THEREFORE, THE EXCEPTION
IS APPLICABLE

TRAVEL BETWEEN LEVELS
①AND③WOULD RESULT IN
A PULL-IN / BACK-OUT;
THEREFORE, THE EXCEPTION
IS NOT APPLICABLE

Figure C410.2.1
EXCEPTION TO SECTION 410.2.1

and demonstrated that a running clearance was required that the tolerance was agreed upon.

410.5 Clear Floor Space. Clear floor space of platform lifts shall comply with Section 305.

❖ The space available on the floor of the platform lift must provide clear floor space consistent with Section 305. A space sized for a wheelchair is 30 by 48 inches (765 by 1220 mm) based on Section 305.3, which is consistent with many of the platform sizes for lifts currently manufactured. Although a platform lift is confined on three sides when entering and four sides during the time when the platform is moving, the doors are either automatic or situated for each access (see Section 410.2.1). Therefore in many situations, especially with the pull-in/pull-out configuration, the alcove provisions in Section 305.6 would not be applicable. In these configurations the accessible route is not permanently confined on three sides; therefore, the additional maneuvering space to get in and out would not be needed.

410.6 Operable Parts. Controls for platform lifts shall comply with Section 309.

❖ Basically platform lift controls, both inside and outside the lift, must be located so that the controls are reachable by a person using a wheelchair. Consideration should be given to the physical location of a wheelchair on the lift so the wheelchair will not block access to the controls. Controls must also meet operation requirements found in the operable parts provisions in Section 309.4.

Chapter 5. General Site and Building Elements

❖ Chapter 5 contains technical criteria for elements that are typically found outside a building, but on the site (e.g., parking spaces and passenger loading zones). This chapter also includes some specific building elements that may be specifically scoped by the authority having jurisdiction to be accessible (e.g., stairways and windows).

- Section 501 is a general statement about the Chapter 5 criteria being applicable for site and building elements that are referenced to this standard by the authority having jurisdiction.

- Section 502 contains criteria for car-accessible and van-accessible parking spaces and their associated signage.

- Section 503 provides criteria for passenger loading and drop off zones.

- When stairways must be accessible, Section 504 provides provisions for stairway construction as well as lighting and striping.

- The provisions in Section 505 are handrail requirements that are referenced from stairways (Section 504.6), ramps (Section 405.8) and when handrails are required along walking surfaces (see Section 403.5).

- Section 506 provides a reference to operable parts requirements for windows that are required to be accessible.

501 General

501.1 Scope. General site and building elements required to be accessible by the scoping provisions adopted by the administrative authority shall comply with the applicable provisions of Chapter 5.

❖ This chapter mainly deals with general site elements such as parking and passenger loading zones and general building elements such as stairways, including handrails, and windows. Note that these provisions apply to site and building elements required by the scoping provisions (see Section 201).

502 Parking Spaces

502.1 General. Accessible car and van parking spaces shall comply with Section 502.

❖ This section provides the technical requirements for accessible parking spaces for both cars and vans. Typically zoning ordinances establish the number of parking spaces required and the scoping documents (e.g., model codes) specify the number of accessible

spaces required. Parking spaces designated for persons with physical disabilities are required by the model codes to be located on the shortest accessible circulation route to an accessible entrance of the building. In separate parking structures or lots that do not serve a particular building, a parking space for a person with a physical disability must be located on the shortest accessible circulation route to an accessible pedestrian entrance of the parking facility (see commentary Figure C502.1).

Figure C502.1
ACCESSIBLE PARKING SPACES

502.2 Vehicle Space Size. Car parking spaces shall be 96 inches (2440 mm) minimum in width. Van parking spaces shall be 132 inches (3350 mm) minimum in width.

EXCEPTION: Van parking spaces shall be permitted to be 96 inches (2440 mm) minimum in width where the adjacent access aisle is 96 inches (2440 mm) minimum in width.

❖ The minimum width of the accessible car parking space is required to be 96 inches, while the accessible van space can be either 132 inches or 96 inches depending on the width of the associated access aisle (see also the commentary for Section 502.4.2). The combination of the parking space and the associated access aisle is what makes the total accessible parking space. The length of the space is left up to the designer of the parking lot because the length is dependent on the types of vehicles the lot will serve. The length of an average car is 19 feet (5795 mm).

502.3 Vehicle Space Marking. Car and van parking spaces shall be marked to define the width. Where parking spaces are marked with lines, the width measurements of parking spaces and adjacent access aisles shall be made from the centerline of the markings.

> **EXCEPTION:** Where parking spaces or access aisles are not adjacent to another parking space or access aisle, measurements shall be permitted to include the full width of the line defining the parking space or access aisle.

❖ The width of parking spaces must be designated in some manner. The most common way is painting stripes on the paved surface, but it could be some other alternative. This section provides guidance for specific points to measure the width of the accessible

parking space. For the aisle see Section 502.4.4. Where accessible parking spaces are part of a row of parking spaces or on the side adjacent to the access aisle, the width is measured to the center of the dividing/marking lines. An exception is allowed if the accessible space is adjacent to a curb or drive. Then the width can be measured to the outside edge of the line or whatever marks the edge of the space.

502.4 Access Aisle. Car and van parking spaces shall have an adjacent access aisle complying with Section 502.4.

❖ Each accessible space must have an associated access aisle where persons may transfer from their vehicle. The access aisle must meet the location, width, length and marking requirements in the following subsection.

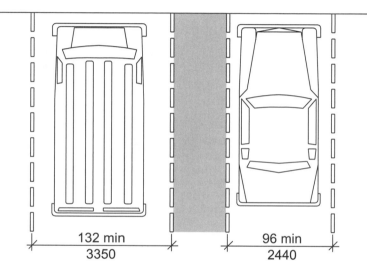

Fig. 502.2
Vehicle Parking Space Size

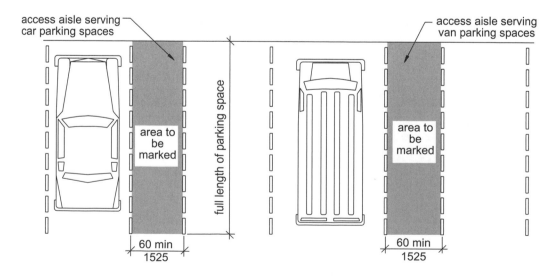

Fig. 502.4
Parking Space Access Aisle

502.4.1 Location. Access aisles shall adjoin an accessible route. Two parking spaces shall be permitted to share a common access aisle. Access aisles shall not overlap with the vehicular way. Parking spaces shall be permitted to have access aisles placed on either side of the car or van parking space. Van parking spaces that are angled shall have access aisles located on the passenger side of the parking space.

❖ The access aisle is often the start or end of the accessible route between the accessible parking space the accessible entrance. As such, the access aisle must meet the accessible route requirements, including the 1:48 maximum slope and width. The accessible route from other parking spaces or site arrival point may overlap the access aisle; however, if a built up curb ramp is used, it must not intrude over the access aisle. It is important that the slope in this area be minimized to facilitate transfers. Often, the circulation route to and from parking spaces is located immediately adjacent to and across the front of the parking spaces. In this event, the front (or rear) of the vehicles could possibly overhang the curb and extend into the circulation path. The accessible route requirements prohibit such vehicle overhangs from reducing the required clear width of the circulation route. This can be accomplished by providing curb stops that limit the distance a vehicle can extend into the circulation path or by providing a circulation path width sufficient to accommodate the vehicle overhang [see commentary Figure C502.4.1(a)].

To minimize the amount of space committed to parking, the standard allows two adjacent accessible parking spaces to share a common access aisle. This is considered reasonable based on the unlikelihood of vehicles arriving simultaneously at both spaces and the occupants using the access aisle at the same time. If that does occur, one can wait while the other loads or unloads. In most situations it is anticipated that a driver would back into a parking space if necessary to orient the access aisle to the transfer side of the vehicle. However, because van access is almost always from the passenger side, when angled parking is provided for the van space, the access aisle must be on the passenger side. Because most converted vans provide access through the passenger side, even in straight-in parking, it would be beneficial to locate the van access aisle on the passenger side.

For safety reasons, it is important that the access aisle not overlap the road or driveway where vehicles could possibly strike the person emerging from their vehicle. This is especially important when the option of parallel parking is provided [see commentary Figure C502.4.1(b)]. The configuration would allow for either the driver or a passenger to transfer out of the vehicle.

502.4.2 Width. Access aisles serving car and van parking spaces shall be 60 inches (1525 mm) minimum in width.

❖ The required width of the parking space and adjacent access aisle is necessary to provide sufficient space for a person in a wheelchair to enter and exit a vehicle and to do so without being in the vehicular way.

The 'universal space' for vans is a 132-inch (3350 mm) wide parking space with a 60-inch (1525 mm) wide access aisle. The exception to Section 502.2 would still permit the 96-inch (2440 mm) wide van parking space adjacent to the 96-inch (2440 mm) wide

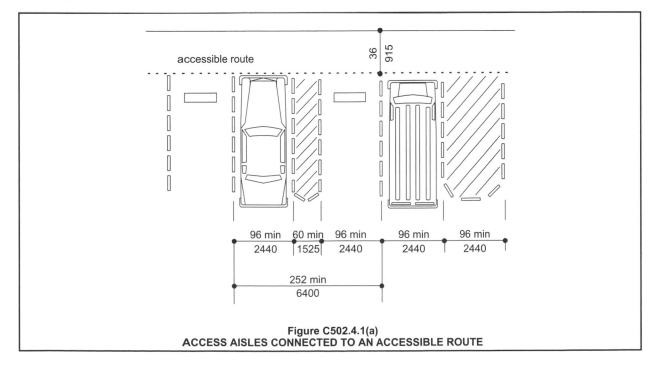

Figure C502.4.1(a)
ACCESS AISLES CONNECTED TO AN ACCESSIBLE ROUTE

access aisle. Both spaces result in a total width of 182 inches (4880 mm). Using the 60 inch (1025 mm) aisle for both van and car spaces may help discourage parking in the access aisle.

A side lift mechanism that operates perpendicular to the van requires an aisle that is 96 inches (2440 mm) wide. The required 96 inches (2440 mm) is based on the distance the lift extends out from the side of the vehicle, i.e., 48 inches (1220 mm) for the lift and 48 inches (1220 mm) for the wheelchair that exits the lift perpendicular to the side of the vehicle (see commentary Figure C502.4.2).

502.4.3 Length. Access aisles shall extend the full length of the parking spaces they serve.

❖ Vehicles vary in length. The access aisle must be the same length as the parking space it serves, be it com-

pact car, van or bus. The average length for a parking space is 19 feet (5795 mm).

502.4.4 Marking. Access aisles shall be marked so as to discourage parking in them. Where access aisles are marked with lines, the width measurements of access aisles and adjacent parking spaces shall be made from the centerline of the markings.

EXCEPTION: Where access aisles or parking spaces are not adjacent to another access aisle or parking space, measurements shall be permitted to include the full width of the line defining the access aisle or parking space.

❖ The access aisle should be marked or surfaced in a manner that makes it clear the access aisle is not a parking space. The access aisle must remain clear to

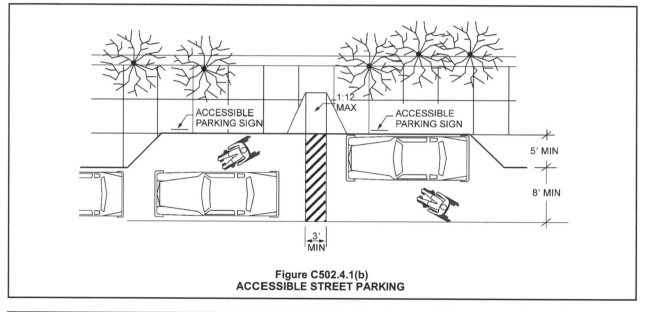

Figure C502.4.1(b)
ACCESSIBLE STREET PARKING

Figure C502.4.2
ACCESSIBLE VAN

allow for a person to approach the vehicle in a wheelchair and transfer into the car. The most common method is striping on the paved surface. It is recommended that the access aisle should not be painted a different color over the entire surface. The epoxy paint typically used on parking lots is exceptionally slippery when wet and could cause problems during the approach and transfer to the vehicle.

The width of the access aisle must be designated in some manner. The most common way is painting stripes on the paved surface, but it could be some other alternative. This section provides guidance for specific points to measure the width of the access aisle. For the space see Section 502.3. Where accessible parking spaces and access aisles are part of a row of parking spaces or on the side adjacent to the accessible parking space, the width of the access aisle is measured to the center of the dividing/marking lines. The exception allows for if the access aisle is adjacent to a curb or drive. Then the width can be measured to the outside edge of the line or whatever marks the edge of the space.

502.5 Floor Surfaces. Parking spaces and access aisles shall comply with Section 302 and have surface slopes not steeper than 1:48. Access aisles shall be at the same level as the parking spaces they serve.

❖ The accessible parking space and access aisles must be at the same elevation to facilitate entering and exiting a vehicle by a person in a wheelchair. It would be unreasonably difficult to do so if the parking space and the access aisle adjacent to the vehicle are not level (with a slope of 1:48 maximum), with a stable surface. Built-up curb ramps must be located so that they do not overlap the access aisle.

The suitability of an accessible route depends on certain characteristics of the surface itself. This section requires compliance with the general provisions of Section 302, which addresses characteristics that relate to both safety (slip resistance) and usability (stable and firm). Note that Section 104.4 states that the term floor surface refers to the finished floor or ground surface, as applicable.

Ambulatory and semi-ambulatory people who have difficulty maintaining balance and those with restricted gaits are particularly sensitive to slipping and tripping hazards. For such people, a stable and regular surface is necessary to walk safely. Wheelchairs are propelled most easily on surfaces that are hard, stable and regular. Soft, loose surfaces such as loose sand, gravel, crushed stone or wet clay, and irregular surfaces such as cobblestone, significantly impede movement of a wheelchair.

A stable surface is one that remains unchanged by contaminants or applied force, so that when the contaminant or force is removed, the surface returns to its original condition. A firm surface resists deformation by either indentation or particles moving on its sur-

face. It is not the intent of the standard to require only paved surfaces; however, any other types (e.g., wood chips, gravel) would need to be evaluated.

Slip resistance is based on the frictional force necessary to keep a shoe or crutch tip from slipping on a walking surface under the conditions of use likely to be found on the surface. For example, outside surfaces or entryways may be wet from rain or snow and should be evaluated under those conditions. Although it is known that the static coefficient of friction is one basis of slip resistance, there is not as yet a generally accepted method to evaluate the slip resistance of walking surfaces for all use conditions.

502.6 Vertical Clearance. Parking spaces for vans, access aisles serving them, and vehicular routes from an entrance to the van parking spaces, and from the van parking spaces to a vehicular exit serving them shall provide a vertical clearance of 98 inches (2490 mm) minimum.

❖ A height of 98 inches (2490 mm) minimum will accommodate most high-top lift-equipped vans. Vans retrofitted with lifts may have a higher profile because the roof of the van is raised to provide headroom within the van for someone sitting in a wheelchair. This is typically a concern in parking garages. The clearance must be maintained for the entire route from the entrances to the garage, to the accessible space, and back out of the garage (including garage doors).

Although not required, because parking garages typically do not have adequate clearance throughout the garage, signage indicating the route to the van accessible spaces and the route to exit from those spaces would be beneficial to the user of the space as well as to the garage owner/operator.

502.7 Identification. Where accessible parking spaces are required to be identified by signs, the signs shall include the International Symbol of Accessibility complying with Section 703.6.3.1. Signs identifying van parking spaces shall contain the designation "van accessible." Such signs shall be 60 inches (1525 mm) minimum above the floor of the parking space, measured to the bottom of the sign.

❖ The international symbol of accessibility identifies the space as reserved for authorized vehicles. Typically, state Department of Transportation regulations have an additional requirement for text on the accessible parking signage, including fines for illegal parking. The required "van accessible" designation is intended to be informative, not restrictive, in identifying those spaces that are better suited for van use (see commentary Figure C502.7).

Signs designating parking spaces for a person with a physical disability are seen from a driver's seat if the signs are mounted high enough above the ground and located at the front of a parking space. This provision effectively means that painting a symbol on the surface of the parking space does not by itself comply with the standard because it will be obscured when a vehicle is parked in the space or when there may be snow on the ground. Vehicle and traffic laws in many jurisdictions require that the symbol be mounted both on a post or wall in front of the space and painted on the ground surface within the parking space. The sign for the space must be located or configured so that it will not be a protruding object (see commentary Section 307.3).

Figure C502.7
EXAMPLE OF ACCESSIBLE PARKING SPACE SIGNAGE

502.8 Relationship to Accessible Routes. Parking spaces and access aisles shall be designed so that cars and vans, when parked, cannot obstruct the required clear width of adjacent accessible routes.

❖ The access aisle is often the start or end of the accessible route between the accessible parking space and the accessible entrance. Often, the circulation route to and from parking spaces is located immediately adjacent to and across the front of the parking spaces. In this event, the front (or rear) of the vehicles will overhang the curb and extend into the circulation path.

The accessible route requirements prohibit vehicle overhangs from reducing the required clear width of the circulation route. This can be accomplished by providing curb stops that limit the distance a vehicle can extend into the circulation path or by providing a wider circulation path width sufficient to accommodate the vehicle overhang [see commentary Figure C502.4.1(a)].

503 Passenger Loading Zones

503.1 General. Accessible passenger loading zones shall comply with Section 503.

❖ Passenger loading zones are typically required at institutional facilities such as assisted living facilities, hospitals and nursing homes. Passenger loading zones, when voluntarily provided, should also comply with these provisions.

Passenger loading zones that serve a particular building entrance should be located on the shortest accessible circulation route to an accessible entrance of the building (see commentary Figure C503.1).

Passenger loading zones area fairly common at hotels; assembly occupancies such as theaters, convention facilities, places of worship and restaurants; and at larger office and mercantile buildings. Where a parking valet service is provided, a passenger loading zone will be present.

503.2 Vehicle Pull-up Space Size. Passenger loading zones shall provide a vehicular pull-up space 96 inches (2440 mm) minimum in width and 20 feet (6100 mm) minimum in length.

❖ Passenger loading zones function in much the same manner as the access aisle adjacent to an accessible parking space except that they are not located at a permanent parking space. Passenger loading zones serve areas at which a vehicle will temporarily stop to load and unload passengers, and then depart. The vehicle space must be at least as wide as an accessible parking space and be the same length as the associated access aisle (see Section 503.3.3).

503.3 Access Aisle. Passenger loading zones shall have an adjacent access aisle complying with Section 503.3.

❖ An access aisle that serves as the passenger drop off must be of a stable and firm surface and be connected to an accessible route. This is typically accomplished by either a curb cut or the passenger drop off and access aisle being constructed at the same elevation as the adjacent sidewalk. The subsections contain criteria for the adjacency of the access aisle, the size and the markings.

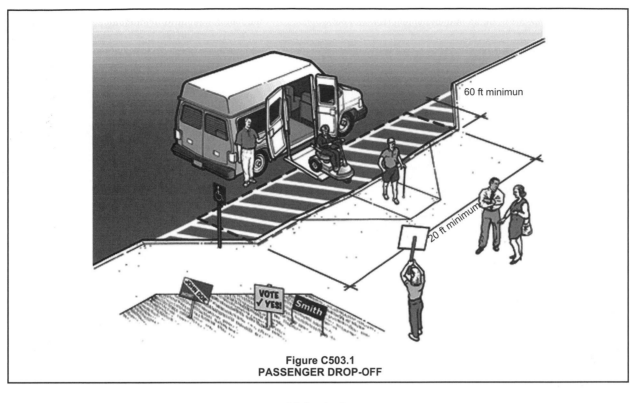

Figure C503.1
PASSENGER DROP-OFF

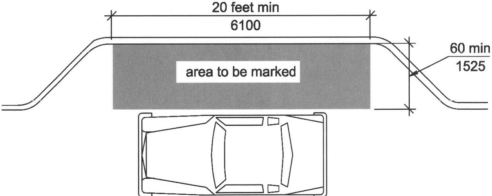

Fig. 503.3
Passenger Loading Zone Access Aisle

503.3.1 Location. Access aisles shall adjoin an accessible route. Access aisles shall not overlap the vehicular way.

❖ There must be an accessible route between the passenger drop off zone and the accessible entrance. For safety the access aisle must not overlap any portion where there may be other moving vehicles, such as a car aisle or driveway (see commentary Figure C503.1).

503.3.2 Width. Access aisles serving vehicle pull-up spaces shall be 60 inches (1525 mm) minimum in width.

❖ The access aisle must be the same width as that required for an accessible parking space (see Section 502.4.2).

The width of the parking space and adjacent access aisle must provide sufficient space for a person in a wheelchair to enter and exit a vehicle and to do so without being in the vehicular way.

503.3.3 Length. Access aisles shall be 20 feet (6100 mm) minimum in length.

❖ The required length of 20 feet (6 m) provides the necessary range in which a vehicle can maneuver into and out of the space with the door of the vehicle positioned within the loading zone.

503.3.4 Marking. Access aisles shall be marked so as to discourage parking in them.

❖ The access aisle should be marked or surfaced in a manner that makes it clear the access aisle is not a parking space (see commentary Figure C503.1). The access aisle must remain clear to allow a person in a wheelchair to approach the vehicle and transfer into the car. The most common method is striping on the paved surface. The access aisle should not be painted a different color over the entire surface. The epoxy paint typically used on parking lots is exceptionally slippery when wet and could cause problems during the approach and transfer to the vehicle.

503.4 Floor Surfaces. Vehicle pull-up spaces and access aisles serving them shall comply with Section 302 and shall have slopes not steeper than 1:48. Access aisles shall be at the same level as the vehicle pull-up space they serve.

❖ The accessible passenger loading zone and access aisle must be at the same elevation to facilitate a person in a wheelchair entering and exiting a vehicle. It would be unreasonably difficult to do so if the access aisle adjacent to the vehicle is not level (with a slope of 1:48 maximum), and does not have a stable surface. Note that Section 104.4 states that the term floor surface refers to the finished floor or ground surface, as applicable.

Ambulatory and semi-ambulatory people who have difficulty maintaining balance and those with restricted gaits are particularly sensitive to slipping and tripping hazards. For those people, a stable and regular surface is necessary to walk safely. Wheelchairs are propelled most easily on surfaces that are hard, stable and regular. Soft, loose surfaces such as loose sand, gravel, crushed stone or wet clay, and irregular surfaces such as cobblestone, significantly impede movement of a wheelchair.

A stable surface is one that remains unchanged by contaminants or applied force, so that when the contaminant or force is removed, the surface returns to its original condition. A firm surface resists deformation by either indentation or particles moving on its surface. It is not the intent of the standard to require only paved surfaces; however, any other types (e.g., wood chips, gravel) would need to be evaluated.

Slip resistance is based on the frictional force necessary to keep a shoe or crutch tip from slipping on a walking surface under the conditions of use likely to be found on the surface. For example, outside surfaces or entryways may be wet from rain or snow and should be evaluated under those conditions. Although it is known that the static coefficient of friction is one basis of slip resistance, there is not as yet a generally accepted method to evaluate the slip resistance of walking surfaces for all uses.

503.5 Vertical Clearance. Vehicle pull-up spaces, access aisles serving them, and a vehicular route from an entrance to the passenger loading zone, and from the passenger loading zone to a vehicular exit serving them, shall provide a vertical clearance of 114 inches (2895 mm) minimum.

❖ A height of 114 inches (2895 mm) minimum will accommodate most high-top lift-equipped vans and small buses. A van retrofitted with a lift may have a higher profile because the roof of the van is raised to provide headroom within the van for someone sitting in a wheelchair. This is typically a concern at entrance canopies (see commentary Figure 503.5).

Figure C503.5
EXAMPLE OF ENTRANCE CANOPY

504 Stairways

504.1 General. Accessible stairs shall comply with Section 504.

❖ Stairs cannot be part of an accessible route intended for use by persons who use wheelchairs. Stairs are "accessible" only to the extent that they comply with Section 504. These criteria for stairs provide greater usability for persons who are ambulatory, but have a mobility disability; in this case, stairs can be used as a means of ingress and egress. Use of these criteria throughout a building or complex of buildings will also provide consistency that persons with vision impairments can rely on in their travels.

The model codes contain provisions for stairways that are more extensive than the provisions in this section. For example, there are no provisions in this standard for guards at drop-offs adjacent to stairs or consistency/variation in the riser height along a stairway run. Neither does this standard address specifics that are unique to spiral and curved stairways.

504.2 Treads and Risers. All steps on a flight of stairs shall have uniform riser height and uniform tread depth. Risers shall be 4 inches (100 mm) minimum and 7 inches (180 mm) maximum in height. Treads shall be 11 inches (280 mm) minimum in depth.

❖ A great deal of research has been conducted and much debate over appropriate tread and riser dimensions has occurred, much of it in the forums for development of the model building codes. The tread and riser dimensions specified in this standard are consistent with those in the model building codes with the exception of within individual dwelling units. The tread depth is based on the largest shoe size found within 95 percent of the adult population. An 11-inch (280 mm) tread allows for an appropriate amount of overhang beyond the tread nosing in descent. The combination of an 11-inch (280 mm) tread and a 7-inch (180 mm) rise provides a favorable stairway geometry for user comfort, expenditure of energy and rate of misstep as measured in research. If a nosing is provided in accordance with Section 504.5, the minimum tread depth must be measured past the nosing to allow for proper foot placement when descending the stairs (see commentary Figure C504.2).

Dimensional uniformity in riser and tread dimensions greatly reduces the tripping hazard for all users. Minimum requirements for variation along a stair flight are addressed in the model codes.

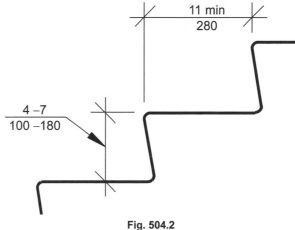

Fig. 504.2
Treads and Risers for Accessible Stairways

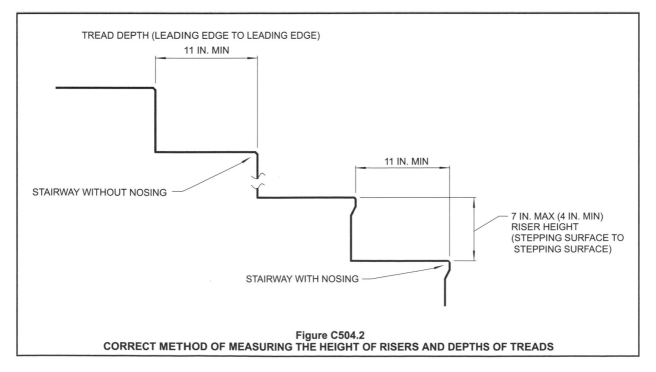

Figure C504.2
CORRECT METHOD OF MEASURING THE HEIGHT OF RISERS AND DEPTHS OF TREADS

504.3 Open Risers. Open risers shall not be permitted.

❖ Open risers present a detection problem for long-cane users. Open risers also increase the potential for the toe of the foot to catch on the underside of the tread above in ascent, possibly resulting in a misstep or preventing further ascent.

504.4 Tread Surface. Stair treads shall comply with Section 302 and shall have a slope not steeper than 1:48.

❖ Stair treads must be a stable and firm surface. Opening in the tread surface are limited to $1/2$ inch (13 mm). Grating may be necessary so that the surfaces will not accumulate snow or water in outdoor locations. Treads must be level, but may be sloped to drain where needed.

Ambulatory and semi-ambulatory people who have difficulty maintaining balance and those with restricted gaits are particularly sensitive to slipping and tripping hazards. For those people, a stable and regular surface is necessary to walk safely.

A stable surface is one that remains unchanged by contaminants or applied force, so that when the contaminant or force is removed, the surface returns to its original condition. A firm surface resists deformation by either indentation or particles moving on its surface.

Slip resistance is based on the frictional force necessary to keep a shoe or crutch tip from slipping on a walking surface under the likely conditions of use. For example, outside steps or steps near entryways may be wet from rain or snow and should be evaluated under those conditions; surfaces on the inside stairway would typically not be influenced by outside weather and should be evaluated in a dry condition. Although it is known that the static coefficient of friction is one basis of slip resistance, there is not as yet a generally accepted method to evaluate the slip resistance of walking surfaces for all use conditions.

504.5 Nosings. The radius of curvature at the leading edge of the tread shall be $1/2$ inch (13 mm) maximum. Nosings that project beyond risers shall have the underside of the leading edge curved or beveled. Risers shall be permitted to slope under the tread at an angle of 30 degrees maximum from vertical. The permitted projection of the nosing shall be $1^1/2$ inches (38 mm) maximum over the tread or floor below. The leading 2 inches (51 mm) of the tread shall have visual contrast of dark-on-light or light-on-dark from the remainder of the tread.

❖ Nosing dimensions are important to smooth, stable stairway usage. On descent, an excessively beveled nosing can reduce the available tread depth to the extent that this may cause the foot to pitch forward or slide off the tread. On ascent, these criteria minimize the potential for the toe of a shoe to catch and be held by the underside of the tread above (see commentary Figure C504.5).

The intent of the striping is to allow persons with visual impairments to identify the forward edge or each tread and landing. The change from the level walking surface to steps may be a tripping hazard for persons with visual impairments.

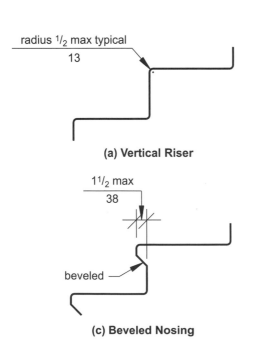

(a) Vertical Riser

(c) Beveled Nosing

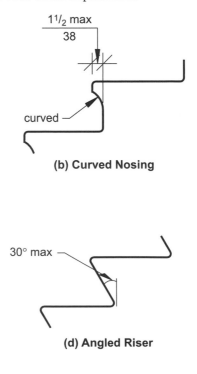

(b) Curved Nosing

(d) Angled Riser

**Fig. 504.5
Stair Nosings**

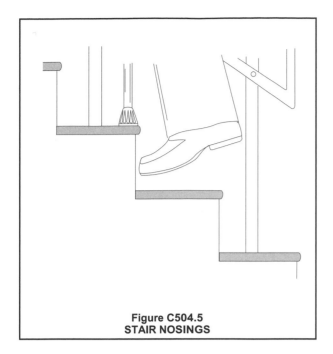

Figure C504.5
STAIR NOSINGS

504.6 Handrails. Stairs shall have handrails complying with Section 505.

❖ Handrails are a critical safety element for stairway users. See Section 505.

504.7 Wet Conditions. Stair treads and landings subject to wet conditions shall be designed to prevent the accumulation of water.

❖ The accumulation of water on stairways, landings and approaches to stairways has significant safety implications for all users, not just those with disabilities. Wet conditions could be outside where the stairs are exposed to rain or snow, or inside adjacent to entrances where water could be carried in from the outside, or in areas near swimming pools or other water sources. In areas subject to freezing, stairs should not be located under roof gutters.

504.8 Lighting. Lighting for interior stairways shall comply with Section 504.8.

❖ The following subsections contain technical criteria for the intensity of lighting on stairways and the controls for that lighting.

504.8.1. Illumination Level. Lighting facilities shall be capable of providing 10 foot-candles (108 lux) of illuminance measured at the center of tread surfaces and on landing surfaces within 24 inches (610 mm) of step nosings.

❖ Model codes typically require a minimum of 1 footcandle (11 lux) for the path for means of egress from a building. This section specifies that the light fixtures for the stairways must be capable of providing a minimum of 10 footcandles (108 lux). For treads, the lighting level should be measured at the center of stair-

way width and tread depth at the surface of the tread. For a landing, the light level should be measured within 24 inches (610 mm) from the edge of the landing on the side adjacent to the stairway run, in the center of the stairway width and at the landing surface.

504.8.2. Lighting Controls. If provided, occupancy-sensing automatic controls shall activate the stairway lighting so the illuminance level required by Section 504.8.1 is provided on the entrance landing, each stair flight adjacent to the entrance landing, and on the landings above and below the entrance landing prior to any step being used.

❖ This section does not require automatic lighting controls (e.g., motion detectors to automatically turn on lights), but if provided, they must activate the lights for the one flight up and one flight down from the landing the occupant entered. The lighting must be available quickly enough that the occupants have not started up or down the steps. For example, low-voltage florescents take a few minutes to come to full power, and therefore would not meet this provision.

504.9 Stair Level Identification. Stair level identification signs in tactile characters complying with Section 703.3 shall be located at each floor level landing in all enclosed stairways adjacent to the door leading from the stairwell into the corridor to identify the floor level. The exit door discharging to the outside or to the level of exit discharge shall have a tactile sign stating "EXIT."

❖ Raised numbers and Braille signage must be provided adjacent to each door in a stairway indicating the floor level. This is in addition to the signage required by the model codes where floor levels must be identified on the wall across from the door so that occupants or emergency responders in the stairway can identify the level they are on.

At the door that leads to the outside, there should be additional raised and Braille signage indicating 'Exit.' This requirement should still be followed even when the stairway discharges to a lobby or exit passageway instead of directly to the exterior.

505 Handrails

505.1 General. Handrails required by Section 405.8 for ramps, or Section 504.6 for stairs, shall comply with Section 505.

❖ This standard is generally consistent with the requirements in the model building codes for handrail requirements. In the event of a conflict, the building code will typically supersede the standard. Structural requirements for handrails are also contained in the model building codes.

Handrails are required on ramp runs with a rise of more than 6 inches (150 mm) (see Section 405.8) and accessible stairways (see Section 504.6). Handrails are not required on curb ramps (see Section 406.9). Handrails are not required on walking surfaces with running slopes less than 1:20 (see the definition for 'Ramp' in Section 106.5). However, handrails must comply with Sections 505.4 through 505.9 (see Section 403.6) when they are required in corridors (e.g., nursing homes or hospitals).

505.2 Location. Handrails shall be provided on both sides of stairs and ramps.

> **EXCEPTION:** Aisle stairs and aisle ramps provided with a handrail either at the side or within the aisle width.

❖ Handrails are an important safety consideration in the use of stairways and ramps for all people, not just people with disabilities. Because people can travel on either side of a stairway or a ramp, it is appropriate to require handrails on both sides to ensure that a handrail is available. This also enables persons with a mobility impairment to use the side of the ramp or stairway that corresponds to their strength, which may be significantly greater on their left or right.

Additional intermediate handrails can be provided if desired on ramps [see commentary Figure C505.2(b)]. The building codes require additional handrails based on capacity requirements for stairways.

In the case of aisle stairs and aisle ramps, typically occurring in assembly occupancies, requiring handrails on both sides is generally unnecessary and may unduly impede access to and egress from assembly seating. The standard, therefore, allows a single handrail either at one side or in the center of the ramp or stairway [see commentary Figure C505.2(a)].

505.3 Continuity. Handrails shall be continuous within the full length of each stair flight or ramp run. Inside handrails on switchback or dogleg stairs or ramps shall be continuous between flights or runs. Other handrails shall comply with Sections 505.10 and 307.

> **EXCEPTION:** Handrails in aisles serving seating.

❖ Continuity of handrails is important so that gaps do not occur that would require people to release their grip and thus no longer be able to arrest their fall or steady themselves should they slip or misstep at that point. The exception recognizes the practical necessity of breaking the handrail for aisle seating to allow access to seats [see commentary Figure C505.2(a)].

It is reasonable to require the inside handrail of a stairway or ramp that turns or reverses direction to be continuous around the turn. This also provides the user with a continuous gripping surface while the turn is being negotiated and staging for the set of steps or ramp slope. Additionally, the continuous handrail may act as an indicator to users who are blind or have low vision that a stair run has not terminated and allows the user to anticipate additional steps.

The references to Sections 307 and 505.10 indicate that the handrail ends must comply with the applicable extensions and return in a manner that will make the ends detectable and not protruding objects.

Figure C505.2(a)
AISLE STAIR HANDRAILS

Figure C505.2(b)
INTERMEDIATE HANDRAILS

505.4 Height. Top of gripping surfaces of handrails shall be 34 inches (865 mm) minimum and 38 inches (965 mm) maximum vertically above stair nosings, ramp surfaces and walking surfaces. Handrails shall be at a consistent height above stair nosings, ramp surfaces and walking surfaces.

❖ The specified range for handrail heights corresponds to that determined appropriate for effectively arresting a fall on the stairway or ramp. Consistency of the handrail height is important so as not to affect the balance and cadence of the user.

  The heights for handrails are based on adults. When children are the principal user of a building (e.g., elementary school, children's museum) a second set of handrails at an appropriate height can assist them. A maximum height of 28 inches (715 mm) to the top of the gripping surface is recommended for handrails designed for children. Sufficient vertical clearance between upper and lower handrails, 9 inches (230 mm) minimum, should be provided to help prevent entrapment. Concerns for the climbability of the two handrail configuration should be considered as part of the design to help prevent children from attempting to climb and end up falling over the guard along the side of the stair.

505.5 Clearance. Clearance between handrail gripping surface and adjacent surfaces shall be 1¹/₂ inches (38 mm) minimum.

❖ The clearance required between a handrail and the adjacent wall surface is the minimum clearance necessary to allow the hand to fully grasp the handrail. The required clearance is a minimum dimension, unlike the absolute dimension required for grab bars. A clearance more than 1¹/₂ inches (38 mm) is permitted for handrails because they are not used in the same manner as grab bars.

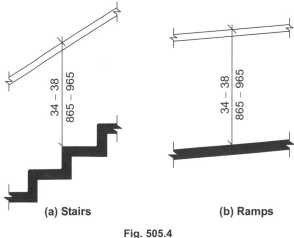

(a) Stairs   **(b) Ramps**

Fig. 505.4
Handrail Height

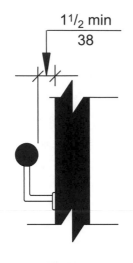

Fig. 505.5
Handrail Clearance

505.6 Gripping Surface. Gripping surfaces shall be continuous, without interruption by newel posts, other construction elements, or obstructions.

EXCEPTIONS:

1. Handrail brackets or balusters attached to the bottom surface of the handrail shall not be considered obstructions, provided they comply with the following criteria:

   a) not more than 20 percent of the handrail length is obstructed,

   b) horizontal projections beyond the sides of the handrail occur $1^1/_2$ inches (38 mm) minimum below the bottom of the handrail, and provided that for each $^1/_2$ inch (13 mm) of additional handrail perimeter dimension above 4 inches (100 mm), the vertical clearance dimension of $1^1/_2$ inch (38 mm) can be reduced by $^1/_8$ inch (3.2 mm), and

   c) edges shall be rounded.

2. Where handrails are provided along walking surfaces with slopes not steeper than 1:20, the bottoms of handrail gripping surfaces shall be permitted to be obstructed along their entire length where they are integral to crash rails or bumper guards.

❖ Requiring continuity of the gripping surface affects specific details of the installation and mounting method for the handrail. As the hand slides along the handrail, no interruptions or obstructions can be encountered that will require users to release their grip to bypass the obstruction. For example, a handrail

bracket that attaches to the side of the handrail will not allow the hand to slide past it without releasing the grip. Conversely, a bracket can be attached to the bottom surface of the handrail so that it will pass between the tips of the fingers as the hand slides past the bracket. The larger handrail size permits shorter brackets because geometrically the finger clearance is still maintained.

When combined crash rails and handrails are installed along the walls for balance assistance, the bottom of the handrail may be continually obstructed (see commentary Figure C505.6).

505.7 Cross Section. Handrails shall have a cross section complying with Section 505.7.1 or 505.7.2.

❖ A handrail must be graspable with a power grip, not a pinching grip. Choices for either a circular cross section or shapes that provide equivalent graspability are indicated in the subsections that follow.

505.7.1 Circular Cross Section. Handrails with a circular cross section shall have an outside diameter of $1^1/_4$ inches (32 mm) minimum and 2 inches (51 mm) maximum.

❖ The shape of a handrail affects the ability to secure a power grip on the handrail. Shapes that are too narrow or too large in cross-section will not allow a grip sufficient to enable the user to arrest a fall. These criteria are based on geometry that enables an average able-bodied person to securely grasp the handrail.

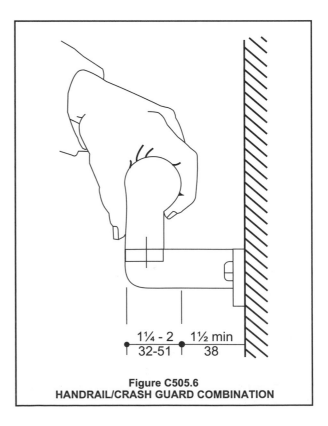

Figure C505.6
HANDRAIL/CRASH GUARD COMBINATION

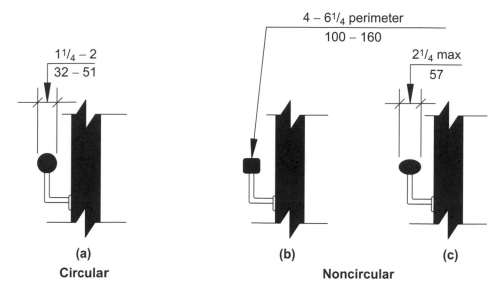

Fig. 505.7
Handrail Cross Section

505.7.2 Noncircular Cross Sections. Handrails with a noncircular cross section shall have a perimeter dimension of 4 inches (100 mm) minimum and $6^{1}/_{4}$ inches (160 mm) maximum, and a cross-section dimension of $2^{1}/_{4}$ inches (57 mm) maximum.

❖ It is not necessary to limit the cross-section shape of handrails to that of a circle if the shape otherwise provides a suitable gripping surface. The standard provides for the acceptance of other shapes based on a determination of equivalency.

505.8 Surfaces. Handrails, and any wall or other surfaces adjacent to them, shall be free of any sharp or abrasive elements. Edges shall be rounded.

❖ Handrails may be made of any material that conforms to this requirement. The purpose of this provision is to avoid surface features that may cause an injury resulting from accidental or unavoidable contact with sharp or abrasive surface elements.

505.9 Fittings. Handrails shall not rotate within their fittings.

❖ Persons having certain mobility impairments and using certain orthotics may have an increased need for support when walking on an inclined surface. In addition, many elderly persons and those lacking stamina depend on handrails for support. This support could be lost if the handrail is mounted in a manner that allows it to rotate or otherwise move when grasped. Loosely mounted handrails or handrails that can rotate represent a significant hazard to all users.

505.10 Handrail Extensions. Handrails shall extend beyond and in the same direction of stair flights and ramp runs in accordance with Section 505.10.

EXCEPTIONS:

1. Continuous handrails at the inside turn of stairs and ramps.

2. Extensions are not required for handrails in aisles serving seating where the handrails are discontinuous to provide access to seating and to permit crossovers within the aisle.

3. In alterations, full extensions of handrails shall not be required where such extensions would be hazardous due to plan configuration.

❖ Horizontal extensions and continuity at turns are beneficial for all users. Handrail extensions are especially needed by persons who wear leg braces or have similar disabilities. People with balance concerns use the handrail to balance themselves as they make the transition between the stepped or sloping surfaces and the landings. Bending the handrail extension at 90 degrees (1.6 rad) to the direction of travel puts the extension out of reach and defeats its purpose; therefore, the handrail top and bottom extension must extend in the same direction as the stair flight or ramp run. Exception 3 allows for the condition in existing buildings where handrails extending in the direction of the stairway may result in handrail extensions blocking the means of egress that runs perpendicular to the stairway run (see commentary Figure C505.10).

Exception 1 allows the inside rail to be continuous and not extend at landings where the stairway or ramp continues. Continuous, inside handrails on switchback or dogleg stairs can indicate to the person with a visual impairment that another stair flight or ramp run begins immediately after the turn. The handrail should be installed at a consistent height as much as practicable so that the handrail has the same slope as the stairs or ramps.

Exception 2 allows for handrails to not have top and bottom extensions on the discontinuous handrails along stairs and ramps that serve assembly seating areas. The handrail extension would block access to seats and possibly obstruct cross aisles, thus proving to be more of a hazard than a benefit [see commentary Figure C505.2(a)].

505.10.1 Top and Bottom Extension at Ramps. Ramp handrails shall extend horizontally above the landing 12 inches (305 mm) minimum beyond the top and bottom of ramp runs. Extensions shall return to a wall, guard, or floor, or shall be continuous to the handrail of an adjacent ramp run.

❖ An extension of 12 inches (305 mm) will provide a sufficient length of handrail to enable users to complete the travel on the ramp and reach stable, level floor area before having to release their grip. The requirement that the handrail return to the wall, guard or floor, or be continuous to the next segment is intended to avoid a handrail end projecting out in mid-air and thus having the potential for a person to sustain injury from accidental impact with the handrail end.

Handrails should return to the wall, guard, ground or support. There are two concerns. The handrail extension must be formed so that clothes would not catch on the end. The handrail extension when it returns to the support must also be detectable by persons using a long cane and not become a protruding object for people crossing perpendicular to the ramp (see Figure 505.10.1).

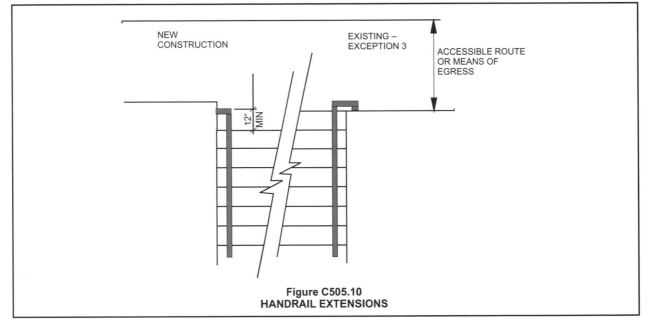

Figure C505.10
HANDRAIL EXTENSIONS

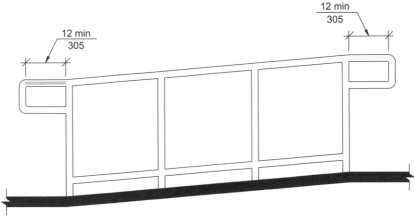

Fig. 505.10.1
Top and Bottom Handrail Extensions at Ramps

505.10.2 Top Extension at Stairs. At the top of a stair flight, handrails shall extend horizontally above the landing for 12 inches (305 mm) minimum beginning directly above the landing nosing. Extensions shall return to a wall, guard, or the landing surface, or shall be continuous to the handrail of an adjacent stair flight.

❖ The most critical transition from level walking to stair use is at the top of a flight. One should be able to reach and grasp the handrail(s) in advance of attempting the very critical, first descent step. Therefore, Section 505.10.2 is presented as a safety convention helpful for all users and as an additional aid for those with perceptual or mobility disabilities. It also provides assistance for users who need to pull themselves to the level surface at the top of the stairs.

Handrails should return to the wall, guard, ground or support. There are two concerns. The handrail extension must be formed so that clothes would not catch on the end. The handrail extension when it returns to the support must also be detectable by persons using a long cane and not become a protruding object for people crossing perpendicular to the top of the stair (see Figure 505.10.2 and commentary Figure C505.10.2).

505.10.3 Bottom Extension at Stairs. At the bottom of a stair flight, handrails shall extend at the slope of the stair flight for a horizontal distance equal to one tread depth beyond the bottom tread nosing. Extensions shall return to a wall, guard, or the landing surface, or shall be continuous to the handrail of an adjacent stair flight.

❖ A less critical, but still important, transition is at the bottom of a stair flight. Section 505.10.3 requires continuation of the handrail at stair flight slope for the equivalent of one tread at the landing, which means that a person's hand will find the end of the handrail at about the same instant as the leading foot contacts the landing surface. An extension equal to the dimension of one tread anticipates that the bottom landing immediately at the riser effectively serves as a tread when descending because the user must step down to that surface before completing the stair-stepping cadence. Thus, the handrail is required to extend to the point at which the landing surface effectively serves as a tread. An additional horizontal extension is not required at this point, however, if it is provided, this exceeds requirements.

Handrails should return to the wall, guard, ground or support. There are two concerns. The handrail extension must be formed so that clothes would not catch on the end. The handrail extension when it returns to the support must also be detectable by persons using a long cane and not become a protruding object for people crossing perpendicular to the top of the stair (see Figure 505.10.3).

Figure C505.10.2
EXAMPLE OF TOP EXTENSION AT STAIRS

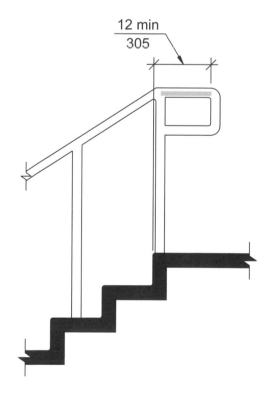

12 min
305

Fig. 505.10.2
Top Handrail Extensions at Stairs

x = tread depth

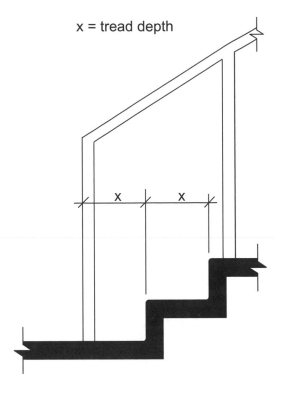

Fig. 505.10.3
Bottom Handrail Extensions at Stairs

506 Windows

506.1 General. Accessible windows shall have operable parts complying with Section 309.

❖ For those windows that must be accessible, it is logical to ensure that the mechanisms that lock and unlock or open and close must be positioned for accessibility, including clear floor space, reach ranges and graspability of the mechanisms. Examples of required operable windows would be egress windows in bedrooms and windows in spaces where natural ventilation is required. Examples of the types of operable windows include double-hung, sliding, casement and awning windows.

Chapter 6. Plumbing Elements and Facilities

❖ Chapter 6 deals with fixtures that would be connected to a building's water supply. This includes plumbing fixtures, as well as the requirements for other related items such as water closet stalls, laundry equipment, etc. Kitchens and Kitchenettes (Section 804) references the sink requirements in Section 606. Although Chapter 6 is referenced in Chapter 10 for some of the criteria for toilet rooms or bathrooms located within or serving only Accessible, Type A or Type B dwelling units or sleeping units, (e.g., congregate residences, apartments, hotel rooms, nursing homes— refer to the appropriate scoping document) should first follow the provisions in Chapter 10 for the appropriate level of accessibility.

- Section 601 is a general scoping provision to indicate that the requirements in this chapter are applicable when referenced by the authority having jurisdiction.
- Section 602 deals with built-in drinking fountains.
- Section 603 contains the general requirements for the rooms that contain toilet and/or bathing facilities.
- Section 604 deals with the water closets (toilets) themselves. This includes the stall requirements for wheelchair-accessible and ambulatory stalls.
- Section 605 contains the technical requirements for accessible urinals.
- Section 606 contains criteria for both lavatories and sinks. Lavatories are typically used for hand washing. Sinks are typically used for other types of clean up or work (lab sink, kitchen sink).
- Bathtub requirements are covered in Section 607. Bathtubs may include portable seats or built-in seats at the foot of the tub.
- Section 608 contains information for transfer, roll-in and an alternate roll-in shower compartment.
- The general grab bar information in Section 609 is referenced in the sections dealing with water closets, bathtubs and showers.
- Section 610 provides general information for the seats found in bathtubs and showers.
- Section 611 contains criteria for laundry equipment, both washers and dryers.

There are specific exemptions for toilet or bathing rooms accessed only through a private office. These can be found in Sections 603.2.3, 604.4, 604.5,

606.2, 606.3, 607.4, 608.3 and 608.4. The exceptions allow for adaptable features in this portion of an individual's work space, which includes reversal of the door to the toilet room; any height for the water closet; installation of blocking for future installation of grab bars at the water closet, bathtub or shower, or seats in the shower; and no clear floor space or height restrictions for the lavatory. The room and fixtures must also meet other provisions for accessibility.

There are specific requirement for drinking fountains and toilet rooms sized for children. The standard does not require a designer to use the child size provisions, but once the choice is made for the drinking fountain or toilet room, all the pieces of the package must be followed. For example, the water closet would not be as usable if the child-size seat height was used with the adult height for grab bars. See Sections 602.2, 604.1, 604.8.2, 604.8.5, 604.10 through 604.10.8, 606.2 and 609.4. Section 602.2 contains technical criteria for children's accessible drinking fountains. Provisions for child size toilet rooms call for water closets closer to the wall with the grab bar, lower water closet seat height, lower flush controls, a lower reach range for the toilet paper dispenser, lower lavatories (including a possible side approach) and lower grab bars. Provisions for child size toilet compartments also include higher toe clearance requirements for stalls partitions, as well as larger compartment sizes for stalls with wall-hung water closets.

601 General

601.1 Scope. Plumbing elements and facilities required to be accessible by scoping provisions adopted by the administrative authority shall comply with the applicable provisions of Chapter 6.

❖ The provisions in this chapter are intended to cover the requirements for plumbing fixtures found in general use toilet rooms and bathrooms. Toilet rooms and bathrooms associated with Accessible, Type A and Type B dwelling and sleeping units are more specifically addressed in Chapter 10. Chapter 10 references Chapter 6 when applicable. Note that these provisions apply to plumbing elements required by the scoping documents (see Section 201).

602 Drinking Fountains

❖ This standard does not require drinking fountains, but once they are provided, the percentages specified by the scoping document must meet the requirements in this Section. Typically, the locally adopted plumbing code specifies the number of required drinking fountains based on the number of occupants and use of the space. This section includes provisions for drinking fountains for standing persons, as well as accessible drinking fountains for adults and children that use wheelchairs.

602.1 General. Accessible drinking fountains shall comply with Sections 602 and 307.

❖ This section is not intended to cover bottle-type water coolers, which generally rely on paper cups and are not permanently piped. This section is intended to address the clear floor space and access to the controls and water for built-in drinking fountains. Please be aware that accessible drinking fountains by their clearance requirements are not within the detectable range for a cane user; therefore, provisions for protruding objects and alcoves are additional concerns. This is may be even more of a concern for the drinking fountains raised for standing persons. Drinking fountains may be located in an alcove or provide adjacent barriers that are detectable by a person with a long cane (see commentary Figure C602.1 and Section 307).

Figure C602.1
DRINKING FOUNTAINS IN ALCOVE

602.2 Clear Floor Space. A clear floor space complying with Section 305, positioned for a forward approach to the drinking fountain, shall be provided. Knee and toe space complying with Section 306 shall be provided. The clear floor space shall be centered on the drinking fountain.

EXCEPTIONS:

1. Drinking fountains for standing persons.

2. Drinking fountains primarily for children's use shall be permitted where the spout is 30 inches (760 mm) maximum above the floor, and a parallel approach complying with Section 305, centered on the drinking fountain, is provided.

3. In existing buildings, existing drinking fountains providing a parallel approach complying with Section 305, centered on the drinking fountain, shall be permitted.

4. Where specifically permitted by the administrative authority, a parallel approach complying with Section 305, centered on the drinking fountain, shall be permitted for drinking fountains that replace existing drinking fountains with a parallel approach.

❖ In addition to having accessible spout design and controls, a water fountain must be located on an accessible route, have appropriate knee and toe clearance, and have clear floor space. The space required in Section 305 must be provided to ensure that the person can maneuver from the accessible route directly to the water fountain or into an alcove to get into position to drink [see commentary Figure C602.2(a) and (b)].

The height and shape of the drinking fountain must permit an individual in a wheelchair to access the fixture. A cantilevered unit at least 17 inches (430 mm) deep allows the legs and feet of the user to be positioned under the unit. The knee and toe clearances required in Sections 306.2 and 306.3 are consistently required throughout the standard for a forward approach.

Drinking fountains for standing persons are not required to meet the clear floor space and knee and toe clearance requirements in this Section (Exception 1).

Accessible drinking fountains with the spout at 36 inches (915 mm) (Section 602.4) have been found to be outside of the reach of children using wheelchairs. However, if the spout outlet height is installed at 30 inches (760 mm) maximum, the knee and toe clearances are not typically available. Therefore, a parallel side approach, centered on the drinking fountain is required (Exception 2).

Exceptions 3 and 4 deal with the constraints that may occur in an existing building. Existing drinking fountains having a parallel approach are permitted to remain. If a parallel approach drinking fountain is replaced, the new drinking fountain should be a front approach drinking fountain unless there is difficulty with the placement. For example, if the front approach drinking fountain would block the accessible route or means of egress past the drinking fountain, a parallel approach drinking fountain may be approved by the local building official (see commentary Figure C602.2(c)].

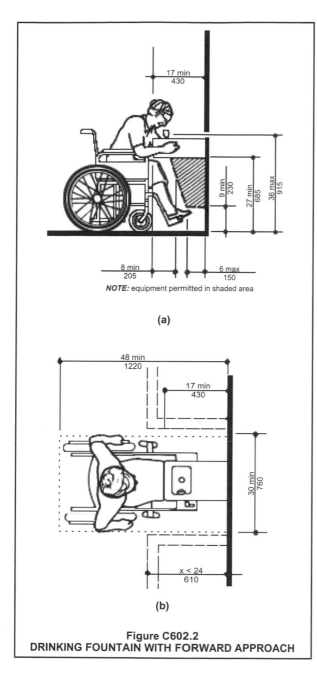

NOTE: equipment permitted in shaded area

(a)

(b)

Figure C602.2
DRINKING FOUNTAIN WITH FORWARD APPROACH

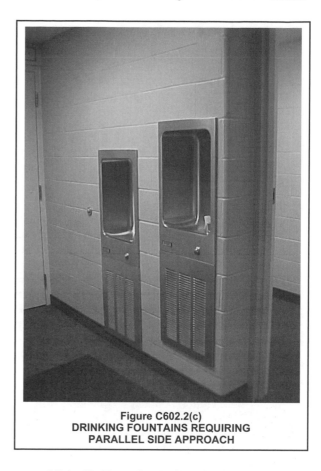

Figure C602.2(c)
DRINKING FOUNTAINS REQUIRING
PARALLEL SIDE APPROACH

602.3 Operable Parts. Operable parts shall comply with Section 309.

❖ Operable parts of the drinking fountain include controls to activate the water flow. These controls must comply with Section 309 for height and operation. The clear floor space can be the same as that provided for the drinking fountain itself.

Although it is the intent for the drinking fountains for standing persons to meet the height and operation requirements in Sections 309.2 and 309.3, the clear floor spaces required in Section 309.1 are not required because of the specific exception to clear floor space

established in Exception 1 of Section 602.1. The operable parts requirements are beneficial for persons with limited use of their hands.

Although not specifically required, it may be desirable when designing for children to use the reach ranges indicated in Table C308.1.

602.4 Spout Outlet Height. Spout outlets of wheelchair accessible drinking fountains shall be 36 inches (915 mm) maximum above the floor. Spout outlets of drinking fountains for standing persons shall be 38 inches (965 mm) minimum and 43 inches (1090 mm) maximum above the floor.

❖ The height of 36 inches (915 mm) has been established as the maximum for a person to be able to drink water from a spout from a seated position. For persons who have difficulty bending over, the 43 inch (1090 mm) maximum height results in a higher level of comfort.

This requirement is not intended to require two drinking fountains—there is a choice of providing separate drinking fountains or combined drinking fountains. There are commercially available drinking fountains that have two spouts at varying heights which are ideally suited both for people in wheelchairs and people who find it difficult or awkward to bend low. One spout is located at the 36-inch (915 mm) height and the higher spout at the 43-inch (1090 mm) height.

If designing an accessible drinking fountain for children, the maximum spout outlet height is 30 inches (760 mm) as stated in Exception 2, Section 602.2.

602.5 Spout Location. The spout shall be located 15 inches (380 mm) minimum from the vertical support and 5 inches (125 mm) maximum from the front edge of the drinking fountain, including bumpers. Where only a parallel approach is provided, the spout shall be located 3½ inches (89 mm) maximum from the front edge of the drinking fountain, including bumpers.

❖ Criteria are provided for both a parallel and a forward approach. See Exceptions 2, 3 and 4, Section 602.2, regarding when a parallel approach is permitted. For a parallel approach, it is difficult to lean laterally over the wheelchair arms, and the spout must be located within 3½ inches (89 mm) of the front edge of the unit. Because it is less difficult to lean forward than to twist and lean laterally, this dimension may be increased to 5 inches (125 mm) in a forward approach. If the spout is located lower or farther forward or both, the maximum distance from the front edge becomes less critical. The front edge is the unit edge, not the location of the controls.

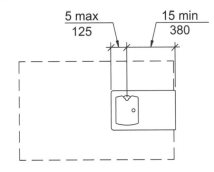

(a) Forward Approach

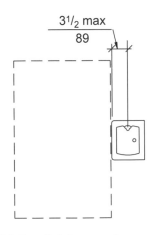

(b) Parallel Approach

Fig. 602.5
Drinking Fountain Spout Location

Knee and toe clearances are also needed for a forward approach. The 15-inch (380 mm) dimension from the vertical support locates the spout far enough away from the wall so the user's knees and toes may extend below the unit.

Because no clearances are required for drinking fountains for standing persons, there are no spout location requirements.

602.6 Water Flow. The spout shall provide a flow of water 4 inches (102 mm) minimum in height. The angle of the water stream from spouts within 3 inches (76 mm) of the front of the drinking fountain shall be 30 degrees maximum, and from spouts between 3 inches (76 mm) and 5 inches (125 mm) from the front of the drinking fountain shall be 15 degrees maximum, measured horizontally relative to the front face of the drinking fountain.

❖ This requirement permits the drinking fountain to serve the greatest number of individuals. It is difficult, if not impossible, for some individuals to lean and drink from the spout. These requirements allow for the insertion of a cup or glass under the flow of water. The position of the spout dictates the angle that the stream of water should project. The farther the spout is from the user, the smaller the angle must be.

603 Toilet and Bathing Rooms

❖ This section addresses toilet and bathing rooms for all uses other than within Accessible, Type A and Type B dwelling and sleeping units. For toilet and bathing rooms in Accessible, Type A and Type B units, see the more specific criteria in Chapter 10. Chapter 10 references back to Sections 604 through 610, as applicable.

Toilet rooms typically include water closets and lavatories. The room can also contain urinals. Bathing rooms may include water closets, urinals, lavatories and bathing fixtures (bathtubs or showers). Sometimes some of the plumbing fixtures are located in a separate room or area. For example, in locker rooms the showers may be in a separate area from the lavatories and water closets; some elementary schools are placing the lavatories in the hall immediately outside the room with the water closets so teachers can monitor hand washing. Separating the fixtures into different areas is not prohibited, but the room requirements may need to be applied in both locations. Section 603 contains general provisions for these rooms or spaces. See Sections 604 through 608 for individual plumbing fixture requirements.

603.1 General. Accessible toilet and bathing rooms shall comply with Section 603.

❖ When required to be accessible, all of these facilities must be located on an accessible route and have doors, clear floor space and operable parts that meet the requirements established and discussed in the following sections. Other amenities that commonly occur in these rooms (mirrors, coat hooks and shelves) are also addressed.

603.2 Clearances.

❖ The intent of the clearance requirements is to assure that a person using a wheelchair can enter the room, close the door, access the fixtures and exit the room.

Floor drains located in front of accessible plumbing fixtures can create slopes that cause undesired movement of a wheelchair or walking aid when using plumbing fixtures (see Section 305.2).

603.2.1 Turning Space. A turning space complying with Section 304 shall be provided within the room.

❖ A 60-inch (1525 mm) turning circle or a 60-inch T-turn space is required within the bathing room or toilet room. This assures that persons using the room can turn to address each fixture or operable part they may need to access. These turning spaces can use knee and

toe clearances under the lavatory or toe clearance at the water closet as indicated in Section 304.3.

603.2.2 Overlap. Clear floor spaces, clearances at fixtures, and turning spaces shall be permitted to overlap.

❖ It is important to understand that the clear floor space, or location where a wheelchair would sit when using a fixture, is permitted to overlap. However, the fixture itself cannot overlap the clear floor space of another. The most common mistake in public single user toilet rooms is to locate the lavatory adjacent to the water closet and over the water closet clear floor space. With the lavatory at this location the clear floor space required for a side transfer to the water closet is not available. Because the clear floor space at fixtures and the turning space are permitted to overlap, portions of the turning space may extend underneath the lavatory. See the commentary for Section 604.3.2 and the examples in commentary Figure C603.2.2.

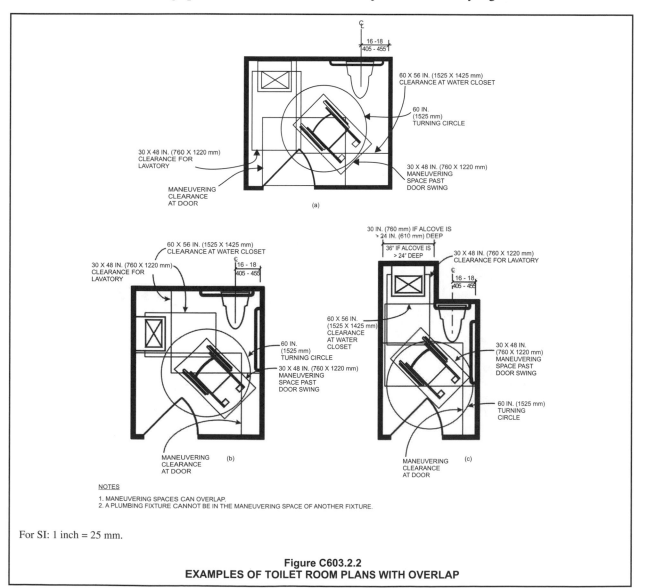

NOTES

1. MANEUVERING SPACES CAN OVERLAP.
2. A PLUMBING FIXTURE CANNOT BE IN THE MANEUVERING SPACE OF ANOTHER FIXTURE.

For SI: 1 inch = 25 mm.

Figure C603.2.2
EXAMPLES OF TOILET ROOM PLANS WITH OVERLAP

603.2.3 Door Swing. Doors shall not swing into the clear floor space or clearance for any fixture.

EXCEPTIONS:

1. Doors to a toilet and bathing room for a single occupant, accessed only through a private office and not for common use or public use shall be permitted to swing into the clear floor space, provided the swing of the door can be reversed to meet Section 603.2.3.

2. Where the room is for individual use and a clear floor space complying with Section 305.3 is provided within the room beyond the arc of the door swing.

❖ In a multi-user bathroom, the locations where a person in a wheelchair may be sitting to use a fixture must be out of the swing of the door. This is to prevent the wheelchair from being struck when others leave or enter the room. Although not the best design alternative, the door may swing over the turning space within the room. The turning space is part of the accessible route, not a clear floor or ground space for a fixture.

The intent of Exception 1 is to allow for bathrooms accessed only through a private office to have some items readily adaptable. Either the door can swing into the room if a 30-inch by 48-inch (760 by 1220 mm) clear floor space will be available after the room is modified (Exception 2), or the door must be reversible to swing out of the room. In either case, the room must be sized so that it can be made accessible.

A "bathroom for individual use" refers to a bathroom for private use by one individual at a time (single occupant bathrooms with a water closet and lavatory) or in bathrooms provided for an individual who may need assistance ("family" or "assisted use" bathrooms). The door may encroach on all fixture-clear floor spaces in the bathroom because it is assumed that no one else will be using the fixtures as the door is being opened. However, a fixture cannot overlap the maneuvering space required for the door to the room. The 30-inch by 48-inch (760 by 1220 mm) clear floor space is required to be beyond the arc of the door swing to ensure that the person using the wheelchair is positioned to be able to enter the room and close the door. When a door opens into a bathroom, sufficient maneuvering space must be provided within the room for a person using a wheelchair to enter, close the door, use the fixtures, reopen the door and exit without undue difficulty (see commentary Figure C603.2.3).

603.3 Mirrors. Mirrors located above lavatories, sinks or counters shall be mounted with the bottom edge of the reflecting surface 40 inches (1015 mm) maximum above the floor. Mirrors not located above lavatories, sinks or counters shall be mounted with the bottom edge of the reflecting surface 35 inches (890 mm) maximum above the floor.

❖ The normal eye level of a person using a wheelchair, 43 inches to 51 inches (1090 to 1295 mm), provides an angle of incidence sufficient for reflection from a mirror with a maximum bottom edge of 40 inches (1015 mm) above the floor to have an adequate field of view to accomplish the desired activities while allowing for clearance over the backsplash on the lavatory or counter [see commentary Figure C102(a)].

If mirrors are to be used by both ambulatory people and wheelchair users, design standards recommend that the top most edge be at a minimum 74-inch (1880 mm) height. It would typically be considered best design practice to make the mirror over the accessible sink the accessible mirror, but a mirror in another location within the room, maybe even a full length mirror, would accommodate all people, including children. If a mirror is not located over the accessible lavatory, but in another location in the space, the bottom edge can be at a minimum of 35 inches (890 mm) above the floor because the lavatory is not in conflict with the bottom edge of the mirror.

603.4 Coat Hooks and Shelves. Coat hooks shall be located within one of the reach ranges specified in Section 308. Shelves shall be 40 inches (1015 mm) minimum and 48 inches (1220 mm) maximum above the floor.

❖ The provisions for coats hooks and shelves within accessible toilet rooms are consistent with those provisions for wheelchair and ambulatory accessible stalls in Section 604.11. These items are not required, but to provide equal access, if provided for general use, they should be installed in an accessible location.

Coat hooks must be located within reach ranges. Measurements are to be taken to the top of the shelf or coat hook. If a shelf is provided, it should be located within reach ranges and also so that it won't interfere with maneuvering within the space. There are no spe-

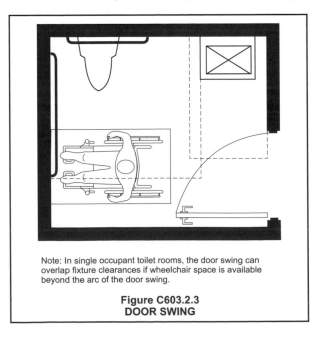

Note: In single occupant toilet rooms, the door swing can overlap fixture clearances if wheelchair space is available beyond the arc of the door swing.

Figure C603.2.3
DOOR SWING

cific provisions for child sizes because the expected reach ranges (see Table C308.1) are lower than that permitted for adults.

604 Water Closets and Toilet Compartments

❖ This section addresses water closets and toilet compartments.

- Sections 604.2 through 604.4 deal with the water closet requirements.

- Section 604.5 deals with grab bar orientation and length.

- Section 604.6 addresses flush controls.

- Section 604.7 contains technical criteria for toilet paper dispensers.

- Sections 604.8 and 604.9 have the technical criteria for accessible and ambulatory stalls. The criteria for these two types of stalls are different because they are intended for two different groups of mobility impairments.

- Children's requirements in Section 604.10 provide either specific criteria or appropriate reference for the water closet, grab bars, flush controls, toilet paper dispensers and compartments sized for children.

- The criteria for the coat hooks and shelves provided within stalls addressed in Section 604.11 are the same as required for within the toilet room specified in Section 603.4.

604.1 General. Accessible water closets and toilet compartments shall comply with Section 604. Compartments containing more than one plumbing fixture shall comply with Section 603. Wheelchair accessible compartments shall comply with Section 604.8. Ambulatory accessible compartments shall comply with Section 604.9.

EXCEPTION: Water closets and toilet compartments primarily for children's use shall be permitted to comply with Section 604.10 as applicable.

❖ The maneuvering space, seat height, grab bars, controls and dispensers must be located to permit use by a person with a disability. This section addresses water closets in uses other than dwellings and sleeping units. See Chapter 10 for water closets in dwellings and sleeping units.

If a toilet compartment contains a lavatory and a water closet, it must meet the same provisions as a single occupant toilet room. The criteria for wheelchair-accessible and ambulatory-accessible stalls are different because they are intended for two different groups of mobility impairments.

The exception allows for bathrooms or toilet compartments specifically designed for children to be appropriately sized for their different wheelchair sizes and reach ranges. If this option is chosen, the criteria must be followed for all applicable elements. The option does not allow picking and choosing between the different elements (e.g., grab bar height, water closet location, stall size). Children's requirements in Section 604.10 provide either specific criteria or appropriate reference for the water closet, grab bars, flush controls, toilet paper dispensers and compartments sized for children.

604.2 Location. The water closet shall be located with a wall or partition to the rear and to one side. The centerline of the water closet shall be 16 inches (405 mm) minimum to 18 inches (455 mm) maximum from the side wall or partition. Water closets located in ambulatory accessible compartments specified in Section 604.9 shall have the centerline of the water

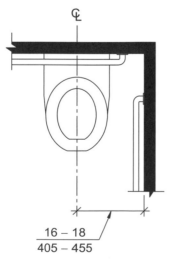

(a) Accessible Water Closets

16 – 18
405 – 455

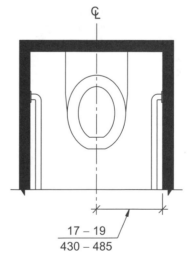

(b) Ambulatory Accessible Water Closets

17 – 19
430 – 485

Fig. 604.2
Water Closet Location

closet 17 inches (430 mm) minimum to 19 inches (485 mm) maximum from the side wall or partition.

❖ Sixteen inches (405 mm) to 18 inches (455 mm) has been established as the optimal dimension from a side wall or partition to the center line of the water closet to allow optimum bearing and reach for the grab bar. The 17 inch to 19 inch (430 to 485 mm) dimension for ambulatory stalls permits a similar 2-inch (55 mm) tolerance. Once everything is installed, this 2-inch tolerance addresses differences that occur between the plumbing rough-in and the finished wall to water closet measurement.

See Section 604.10.2 for provisions for water closet location in toilet rooms or stalls designed specifically for children's use.

604.3 Clearance.

❖ This section addresses the clearances around the water closet in the single occupant toilet room and what is permissible to overlap that clearance. Section 604.10.3 references this provision for clearances in toilet rooms or stalls designed specifically for children.

604.3.1 Size. A clearance around a water closet 60 inches (1525 mm) minimum, measured perpendicular from the sidewall, and 56 inches (1420 mm) minimum, measured perpendicular from the rear wall, shall be provided.

❖ The 60 inch (1525 mm) requirement provides approximately 30 inches (760 mm) between the water closet and the nearest wall or fixture. This space allows the wheelchair user to back into the space and accomplish a side transfer from the wheelchair to the water closet [see commentary Figure C604.3.1(a)]. This transfer requires less maneuvering than a diagonal or front transfer [see commentary Figure C604.3.1(b)]. Diagonal or front transfers are difficult, if not impossible, for persons who have no use of their legs or need assistance to transfer. Another fixture (e.g., lavatory) is not permitted within this clear floor space (see Section 604.3.2).

The 56-inch (1220 mm) minimum depth is intended to be consistent with the requirements in water closet compartments for clearances around the water closet.

604.3.2 Overlap. The required clearance around the water closet shall be permitted to overlap the water closet, associated grab bars, paper dispensers, sanitary napkin receptacles, coat hooks, shelves, accessible routes, clear floor space at other fixtures and the turning space. No other fixtures or obstructions shall be within the required water closet clearance.

❖ The water closet clearance can overlap elements of the accessible route (path of travel, door clearance) including the turning space required in the toilet room (see Section 603.2) [see commentary Figures C604.3.2(a), C603.2.2(a), C603.2.2(b) and C603.2.2(c)].

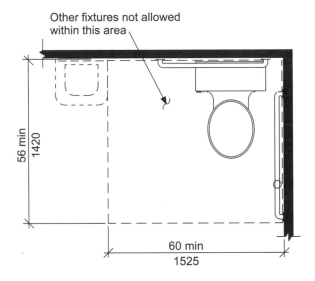

Other fixtures not allowed within this area

56 min
1420

60 min
1525

Fig 604.3
Size of Clearance for Water Closet

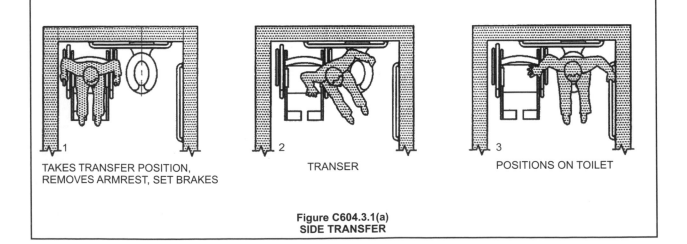

TAKES TRANSFER POSITION, REMOVES ARMREST, SET BRAKES

TRANSER

POSITIONS ON TOILET

Figure C604.3.1(a)
SIDE TRANSFER

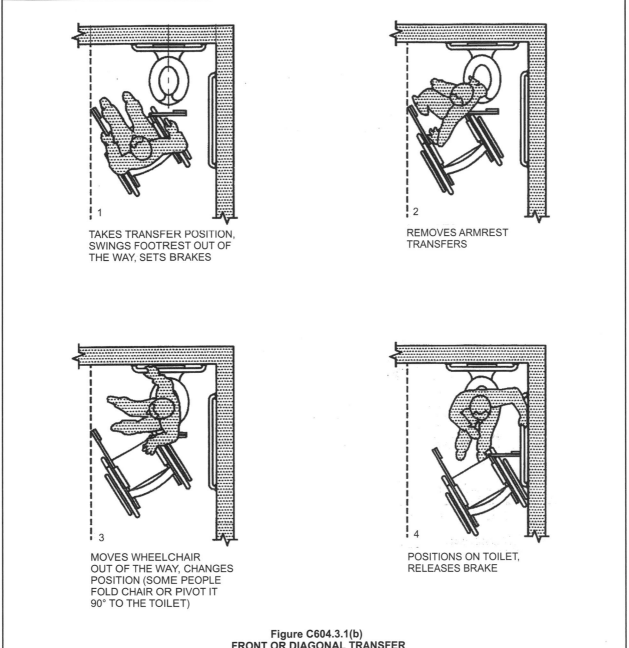

1 TAKES TRANSFER POSITION, SWINGS FOOTREST OUT OF THE WAY, SETS BRAKES

2 REMOVES ARMREST TRANSFERS

3 MOVES WHEELCHAIR OUT OF THE WAY, CHANGES POSITION (SOME PEOPLE FOLD CHAIR OR PIVOT IT 90° TO THE TOILET)

4 POSITIONS ON TOILET, RELEASES BRAKE

Figure C604.3.1(b)
FRONT OR DIAGONAL TRANSFER

Items that can overlap the clear floor space of the water closet without blocking access to the water closet include grab bars and the tissue dispenser. Items that cannot overlap the clear floor space for the water closet include counters or the accessible lavatory. Because there is an assumption that only one person will be using the toilet room facilities at a time, the spaces at other fixtures where the wheelchair user would sit to use those fixtures may overlap the clear floor space at the water closet [see commentary Figures C604.3.2(b), C604.3.2(c), C603.2.2(a), C603.2.2(b) and C603.2.2(c)].

Other items listed, such as paper dispensers, sanitary napkin receptacles, coat hooks and shelves, are items commonly found in toilet rooms or toilet stalls. Other items that are also often found in the bathroom are seat cover dispensers and fold-up diaper changing tables. It is not the intent of this section to prohibit these items within the toilet room or stall, but rather to make sure that these items are located so that they do not block access to the water closet within the room or stall.

Diaper changing stations when in the down position should meet the requirements for work surfaces in Section 902.

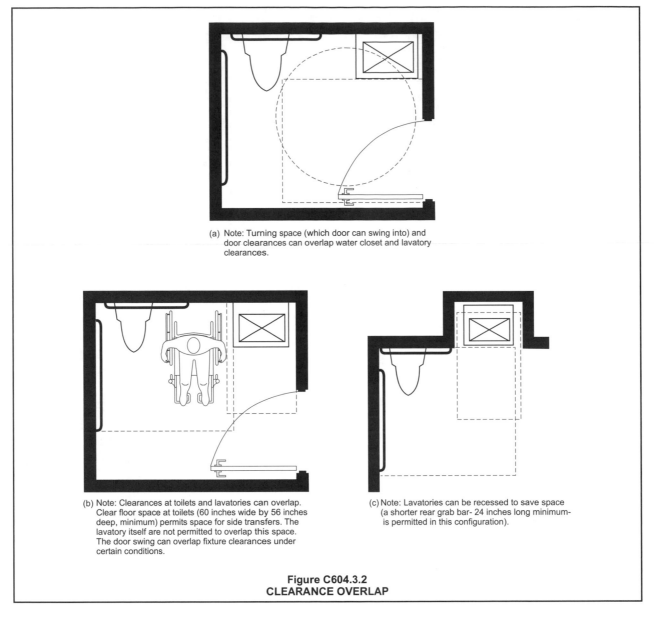

(a) Note: Turning space (which door can swing into) and door clearances can overlap water closet and lavatory clearances.

(b) Note: Clearances at toilets and lavatories can overlap. Clear floor space at toilets (60 inches wide by 56 inches deep, minimum) permits space for side transfers. The lavatory itself are not permitted to overlap this space. The door swing can overlap fixture clearances under certain conditions.

(c) Note: Lavatories can be recessed to save space (a shorter rear grab bar- 24 inches long minimum- is permitted in this configuration).

Figure C604.3.2
CLEARANCE OVERLAP

604.4 Height. The height of water closet seats shall be 17 inches (430 mm) minimum and 19 inches (485 mm) maximum above the floor, measured to the top of the seat. Seats shall not be sprung to return to a lifted position.

EXCEPTION: A water closet in a toilet room for a single occupant, accessed only through a private office and not for common use or public use, shall not be required to comply with Section 604.4.

❖ Preferences for the heights of toilet seats vary considerably among persons with disabilities. Higher seat heights are an advantage to some ambulatory persons with disabilities, but a disadvantage for some persons who use wheelchairs and others. Toilet seats that are approximately 17 inches to 19 inches (430 to 485

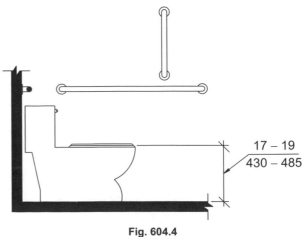

17 – 19
430 – 485

Fig. 604.4
Water Closet Height

mm) high is a reasonable compromise. Seats and filler rings of various thicknesses are available to adapt china-fixture rims, which vary from 14 inches to 18 inches (355 to 455 mm) high.

A 17-inch to 19-inch water closet seat height is based on the assumption that a typical wheelchair seat height, with or without a cushion, would fall within that range. Both the seat of the wheelchair and the water closet must be as level as possible for ease of transfer. Although it would be easier to transfer "down" to a seat, more strength would be required to transfer back "up" to the wheelchair. An upward spring-loaded toilet seat will interfere with the user's transfer.

The exception for both the water closet seat height and the sprung seat is part of the private office toilet room exceptions discussed in the general commentary to Chapter 6.

See Section 604.10.4 for provisions for toilet seat height in toilet rooms or stalls designed specifically for children's use.

604.5 Grab Bars. Grab bars for water closets shall comply with Section 609 and shall be provided in accordance with Sections 604.5.1 and 604.5.2. Grab bars shall be provided on the rear wall and on the side wall closest to the water closet.

EXCEPTIONS:

1. Grab bars are not required to be installed in a toilet room for a single occupant, accessed only through a private office and not for common use or public use, provided reinforcement has been installed in walls and located so as to permit the installation of grab bars complying with Section 604.5.

2. In detention or correction facilities, grab bars are not required to be installed in housing or holding cells or rooms that are specially designed without protrusions for purposes of suicide prevention.

3. In Type A units, grab bars are not required to be installed where reinforcement complying with Section 1003.11.4 is installed for the future installation of grab bars.

4. In Type B units located in institutional facilities and assisted living facilities, two swing-up grab bars shall be permitted to be installed in lieu of the rear wall and side wall grab bars. Swing-up grab bars shall comply with Sections 604.5.3 and 609.

5. In a Type B unit, where fixtures are located on both sides of the water closet, a swing-up grab bar complying with Sections 604.5.3 and 609 shall be permitted. The swing-up grab bar shall be installed on the side of the water closet with the 18 inch (455 mm) clearance required by Section 1004.11.3.1.2.

❖ See Section 609 for specific requirements for grab bar size, wall clearance, height and installation requirements. Side and rear grab bars are required at all water closets. Section 604.10.5 references this provision for grab bar length and orientation in toilet rooms or stalls designed specifically for children's use.

A wall immediately adjacent to the water closet provides a solid support for grab bars. Grab bars mounted wall-to-floor without lateral bracing tend to become loose and contribute to a feeling of insecurity in users. Swing-down bars mounted behind the water closet may serve a person wearing leg braces or having a similar mobility impairment, but may not be stable enough to provide assistance in a transfer by most wheelchair users.

Side and rear grab bars should be mounted horizontally. Grab bars mounted vertically, diagonally or in locations other than on the walls behind and adjacent to the water closet, do not provide equivalent stability or graspability for transfer from a wheelchair. A grab bar that is one piece that is located along the entire range for the two separate grab bars is acceptable. Commentary Figures C604.3.1(a) and C604.3.1(b) show the diagonal and side approaches used to transfer from a wheelchair to a water closet.

There are several exceptions to this section.

Exception 1 allows for just the blocking to be provided for the future installation of grab bars as part of the private office toilet room exceptions discussed in the general commentary to Chapter 6.

Exception 2 is limited to detention and correctional facilities and to areas within those facilities that are specifically designed for suicide prevention. Even though the exception would specifically exempt grab bars, there are grab bars made that have a continuous support so that there is no 'bar' to allow someone to hook something through to potentially strangle themselves [see commentary Figure C604.5(a)].

Exception 3 verifies that Type A units at the time of initial construction are required to have the blocking for grab bars, but not the grab bars installed. Grab bars can be added later as a modification based on the occupant's needs. This is also true for Type B units, but because of a

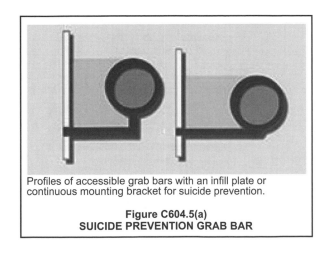

Profiles of accessible grab bars with an infill plate or continuous mounting bracket for suicide prevention.

Figure C604.5(a)
SUICIDE PREVENTION GRAB BAR

difference in the language in Chapter 10, a correlative exception was not needed for Type B units.

Type B units are the only location where blocking for swing-up grab bars or the installation of swing-up grab bars is permitted instead of the blocking or installation of fixed-rear and side grab bars. As stated in Exception 4, within the Type B units required in institutional facilities (e.g., nursing homes) and assisted living facilities, two swing-up grab bars are permitted in place of the rear and side grab bars. This is in recognition of two commonalities in Type B units in these facilities: 1) there may be additional space adjacent to the water closet to allow for nurse assistance; or 2) the occupant may be using mobility aids such as a walker or cane, so the grab bar is for assistance in rising or sitting, not transfer. Exception 5 is in recognition that Option A bathrooms in Type B units allow for the water closet to be located between a tub and a lavatory; therefore, a wall is located only behind the water closet. A swing-up grab bar is a viable alternative for the side and rear grab bar. Although a swing-up grab bar is not ideal for transfer, providing a fixed grab bar would block access to the tub. For persons with mobility impairments, Option A configurations allow a person to sit down at or transfer to the water closet, swing up the bar, and transfer to the tub. This can reduce the chance of a fall getting in and out of the tub [see commentary Figure C604.5(b)].

604.5.1 Fixed Side Wall Grab Bars. Fixed sidewall grab bars shall be 42 inches (1065 mm) minimum in length, located 12 inches (305 mm) maximum from the rear wall and extending 54 inches (1370 mm) minimum from the rear wall. In addition, a vertical grab bar 18 inches (455 mm)

minimum in length shall be mounted with the bottom of the bar located between 39 inches (990 mm) and 41 inches (1040 mm) above the floor, and with the center line of the bar located between 39 inches (990 mm) and 41 inches (1040 mm) from the rear wall.

EXCEPTIONS:

1. In Type A and Type B units, the vertical grab bar component is not required.

2. In a Type B unit, when a side wall is not available for a 42-inch (1065 mm) grab bar, the sidewall grab bar shall be permitted to be 18 inches (455 mm) minimum in length, located 12 inches (305 mm) maximum from the rear wall and extending 30 inches (760 mm) minimum from the rear wall.

❖ The grab bar located on the side wall must be properly located and of sufficient length to allow the user to place an arm on the grab bar while transferring between the water closet and the wheelchair.

The vertical bar on the side wall was added to aid a person who may use other types of mobility aids and needs assistance to rise or sit on the water closet. To grab the horizontal grab bar to rise would require twisting of the wrist and provides minimal leverage.

Exception 1 is in recognition that windows are often located on the wall adjacent to the water closet within dwelling units, therefore blocking for the vertical grab bar is not required in Type A and Type B units.

Exception 2 is limited to Type B units and is applicable when the side wall provided does not allow for blocking for a full length side bar. This may occur when the water closet is adjacent to a shower or tub enclosure or the door into the room is on the side wall. Blocking for the shorter bar is acceptable (see commentary Figure C604.5.1).

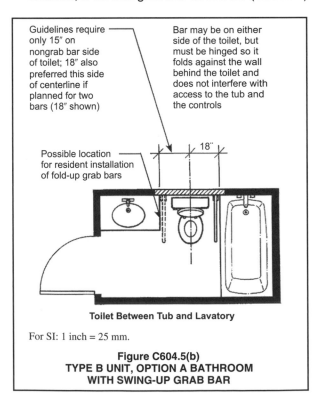

Guidelines require only 15″ on nongrab bar side of toilet; 18″ also preferred this side of centerline if planned for two bars (18″ shown)

Bar may be on either side of the toilet, but must be hinged so it folds against the wall behind the toilet and does not interfere with access to the tub and the controls

Possible location for resident installation of fold-up grab bars

18″

Toilet Between Tub and Lavatory

For SI: 1 inch = 25 mm.

Figure C604.5(b)
TYPE B UNIT, OPTION A BATHROOM
WITH SWING-UP GRAB BAR

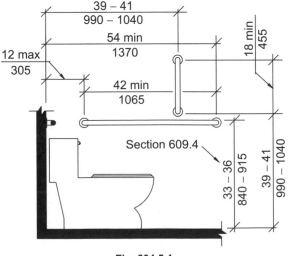

39 – 41
990 – 1040
54 min
1370
12 max
305
42 min
1065
18 min
455

Section 609.4

33 – 36
840 – 915

39 – 41
990 – 1040

Fig. 604.5.1
Side Wall Grab Bar for Water Closet

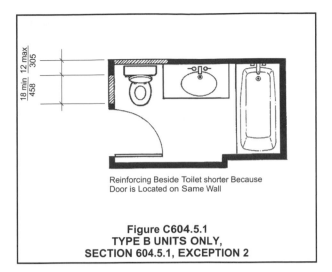

Reinforcing Beside Toilet shorter Because
Door is Located on Same Wall

**Figure C604.5.1
TYPE B UNITS ONLY,
SECTION 604.5.1, EXCEPTION 2**

604.5.2 Rear Wall Grab Bars. The rear wall grab bar shall be 36 inches (915 mm) minimum in length, and extend from the centerline of the water closet 12 inches (305 mm) minimum on the side closest to the wall, and 24 inches (610 mm) minimum on the transfer side.

EXCEPTIONS:

1. The rear grab bar shall be permitted to be 24 inches (610 mm) minimum in length, centered on the water closet, where wall space does not permit a grab bar 36 inches (915 mm) minimum in length due to the location of a recessed fixture adjacent to the water closet.

2. In a Type A or Type B unit, the rear grab bar shall be permitted to be 24 inches (610 mm) minimum in length, centered on the water closet, where wall space does not permit a grab bar 36 inches (915 mm) minimum in length.

3. Where an administrative authority requires flush controls for flush valves to be located in a position that conflicts with the location of the rear grab bar, that grab bar shall be permitted to be split or shifted to the open side of the toilet area.

❖ A 36-inch (915 mm) long grab bar will provide 24 inches (610 mm) on the side of the water closet opposite the wall. This will enable the person who must reach across his body to reach the grab bar and make a transfer.

Exception 1 permits a 24-inch rear grab bar, centered on the water closet, in the configuration shown in commentary Figure C604.3.2(c).

Exception 2 is in recognition that in Type A and Type B units, clearances in Sections 1003.11.7, 1004.11.3.1.2 and 1004.11.3.2.2, would allow for a lavatory to overlap the clear floor space needed for the water closet. In some situations, this would result in the lavatory or counter obstructing the possible future installation of the 36-inch (915 mm) rear grab bar. In these configurations, blocking for the 24-inch (610 mm) rear grab bar is sufficient.

In some public bathrooms with heavy usage, a designer may choose to use a flush-o-meter system rather than a tank system (see commentary Figure C604.5.2). The system has less maintenance and fewer chances for vandalism than the tank type. The flush-o-meter could possibly conflict with the rear grab bar. In such situations, per Exception 3, a split rear grab bar would be acceptable.

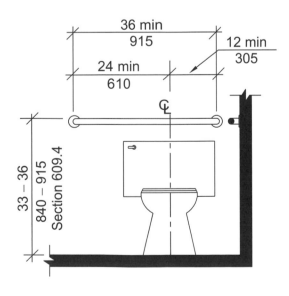

**Fig. 604.5.2
Rear Wall Grab Bar for Water Closet**

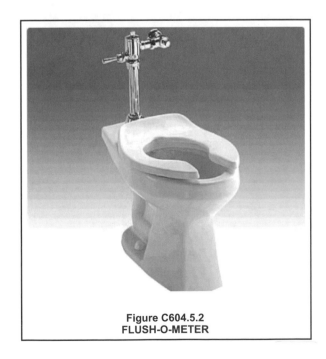

**Figure C604.5.2
FLUSH-O-METER**

604.5.3 Swing-up Grab Bars. Where swing-up grab bars are installed, a clearance of 18 inches (455 mm) minimum from the centerline of the water closet to any side wall or obstruction shall be provided. A swing-up grab bar shall be installed with the centerline of the grab bar $15^3/_4$ inches (400 mm) from the centerline of the water closet. Swing-up grab bars shall be 28 inches (710 mm) minimum in length, measured from the wall to the end of the horizontal portion of the grab bar.

❖ The swing-up grab bars are permitted as required grab bars only in Type B units (see Section 604.5, Exceptions 4 and 5). The intent of the center line dimension for the swing-up grab bars is to locate the bar in the same orientation to the side of the water closet as if there was a wall mounted bar. The length is based on three considerations: 1) the length is consistent with the shorter length permitted in Section 604.5.1 Exception 2; 2) the support for this length/cantilever is achievable with a standard wall system; 3) this length is commonly available so that future modification is readily achievable (see commentary Figure C604.5.3).

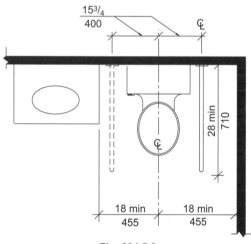

Fig. 604.5.3
Swing-up Grab Bar for Water Closet

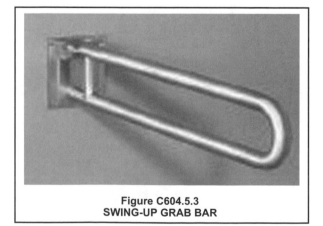

Figure C604.5.3
SWING-UP GRAB BAR

604.6 Flush Controls. Flush controls shall be hand operated or automatic. Hand operated flush controls shall comply with Section 309. Flush controls shall be located on the open side of the water closet.

EXCEPTION: In ambulatory accessible compartments complying with Section 604.9, flush controls shall be permitted to be located on either side of the water closet.

❖ The reference to Section 309 assumes that the controls are operable. The controls must be within reach of a user sitting on the side from which the transfer is made. Automatic controls have no additional requirements.

Flush controls for tank-type toilets have a standardized mounting location on the left side of the tank (facing the tank). Tanks are available by special order with controls mounted on the right side. Tanks must not block access to the grab bar. See the commentary to Section 609.3 for clearances below the grab bar.

Flush-o-meters are an option if the controls are oriented toward the wide side of the clearance.

Although the controls in an ambulatory stall are required to meet operable parts provision, the controls can be located on either side of the tank or flush-o-meter.

See Section 604.10.6 for provisions for flush controls in toilet rooms or stalls designed specifically for children.

604.7 Dispensers. Toilet paper dispensers shall comply with Section 309.4 and shall be 7 inches (180 mm) minimum and 9 inches (230 mm) maximum in front of the water closet measured to the centerline of the dispenser. The outlet of the dispenser shall be 15 inches (380 mm) minimum and 48 inches (1220 mm) maximum above the floor, and shall not be located behind the grab bars. Dispensers shall not be of a type that control delivery, or do not allow continuous paper flow.

❖ The dispenser must be located within the prescribed dimensions, which fall within the reaches established in Section 308. A common problem within toilet rooms and compartments is that the dispensers are located so that they interfere with the use of the grab bars. See Section 609.3 for clearance requirements. Paper dispensers that require a high level of dexterity or effort are not acceptable.

See Section 604.10.7 for provisions for dispensers in toilet rooms or stalls designed specifically for children.

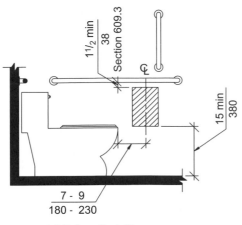

(a) Below Grab Bar

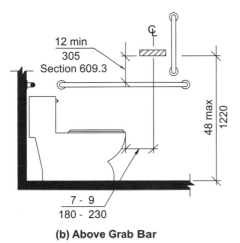

(b) Above Grab Bar

Fig. 604.7
Dispenser Location

604.8 Wheelchair Accessible Compartments.

❖ A wheelchair-accessible compartment provides sufficient space for a person using a wheelchair to completely enter the water closet compartment and close the door.

Section 604.10.8 references this provision for toilet stalls designed specifically for children.

604.8.1 General. Wheelchair accessible compartments shall comply with Section 604.8.

❖ This standard recognizes two types of stalls: wheelchair accessible and ambulatory accessible. Scoping provisions adopted by the administrative authority will specify how many of each design are required.

Requirements for toilet fixture height, clear floor space, grab bars, flush controls and dispensers in Section 604 are the same for toilet stalls and separate toilet rooms. If a lavatory is also provided within the accessible toilet compartment, the compartment must comply

with the same provisions as a single-occupant toilet room.

604.8.2 Size. The minimum area of a wheelchair accessible compartment shall be 60 inches (1525 mm) minimum in width measured perpendicular to the side wall, and 56 inches (1420 mm) minimum in depth for wall hung water closets, and 59 inches (1500 mm) minimum in depth for floor mounted water closets measured perpendicular to the rear wall. The minimum area of a wheelchair accessible compartment for primarily children's use shall be 60 inches (1525 mm) minimum in width measured perpendicular to the side wall, and 59 inches (1500 mm) minimum in

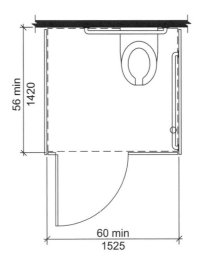

(a) Wall-Hung Water Closet - Adult

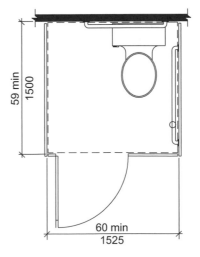

(b) Floor-Mounted Water Closet - Adult
Wall-Hung and
Floor-Mounted Water Closet - Children

Fig. 604.8.2
Wheelchair Accessible Toilet Compartments

depth for wall-hung and floor-mounted water closets measured perpendicular to the rear wall.

❖ The compartment is sized to allow the person using the wheelchair to maneuver within so the occupant gains full and easy access to the water closet and its controls. The length is dependent on the type of water closet installed. Because floor-mounted water closets encroach on toe clearances, the compartment must be 3 inches (75 mm) longer than for the wall-mounted water closet.

A 60-inch (1525 mm) wide compartment would permit a wheelchair user to transfer to the water closet by pulling up parallel to the fixture and affecting a side transfer. More individuals are able to transfer from a position parallel to the water closet than diagonal to the fixture. This configuration is also easier when a person needs assistance to transfer from the wheelchair to the water closet and back [see commentary Figure C604.3.1(a)].

The centerline of the water closet must be 16 inches to 18 inches (405 to 455 mm) from an adjacent wall or partition (see Section 604.2). A common design error is to locate the water closet centered in the stall, which renders the compartment virtually useless for someone who needs to do a side transfer to the water closet.

The size for the children's wheelchair accessible stall is the same, 60 inches by 59 inches (1525 by 1500 mm), for both wall-hung and floor-mounted toilets. The height of the children's footplates is higher than for an adult; therefore, they cannot take advantage of the space under the wall-hung toilet [see Figure 604.8.5(b)].

604.8.3 Doors. Toilet compartment doors, including door hardware, shall comply with Section 404.1, except if the approach is to the latch side of the compartment door clearance between the door side of the stall and any obstruction shall be 42 inches (1065 mm) minimum. Doors shall be located in the front partition or in the side wall or partition farthest from the water closet. Where located in the front partition, the door opening shall be 4 inches (100 mm) maximum from the side wall or partition farthest from the water closet. Where located in the side wall or partition, the door opening shall be 4 inches (100 mm) maximum from the front partition. The door shall be self-closing. A door pull complying with Section 404.2.6 shall be placed on both sides of the door near the latch. Toilet compartment doors shall not swing into the required minimum area of the compartment.

❖ The reference to the general Section 404.1, results in toilet compartment doors that must comply with all door provisions. There is a reduction in depth for door maneuvering clearances for latch approach, pull side [see Figure 404.2.3.1(f)] from 54 inches to 42 inches (1370 to 1065 mm). The location of the door allows the door to align with the clear space adjacent to the water closet to allow easier movement into the stall (see Figure 604.8.3). A self closer will allow someone to enter

the accessible stall and not have to worry about reaching back out to close the stall door. Door pulls on both sides of the doors and the security latch must not require tight grasping, pinching or twisting of the wrist to operate. Both the door pull and the privacy latch must be between 34 inches and 48 inches (865 and 1220 mm) above the floor.

There is an alternate wheelchair accessible stall that allows a narrower approach path. Thirty-six inches (915 mm) minimum of additional depth is needed to let the door swing into the stall and still allow the user to enter, maneuver and close the compartment door (see commentary Figure C604.8.3).

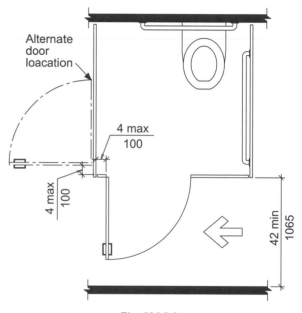

Fig. 604.8.3
Wheelchair Accessible Compartment Doors

604.8.4 Approach. Wheelchair accessible compartments shall be arranged for left-hand or right-hand approach to the water closet.

❖ Both left-hand and right-hand approaches are acceptable as may be dictated by the proposed layout.

604.8.5 Toe Clearance. The front partition and at least one side partition shall provide a toe clearance of 9 inches (230 mm) minimum above the floor and extending 6 inches (150 mm) beyond the compartment side face of the partition, exclusive of partition support members. Compartments primarily for children's use shall provide a toe clearance of 12 inches (305 mm) minimum above the floor and extending 6 inches (150 mm) beyond the compartment side face of the partition, exclusive of partition support members.

EXCEPTIONS:

1. Toe clearance at the front partition is not required in a compartment greater than

62 inches (1575 mm) in depth with a wall-hung water closet, or greater than 65 inches (1650 mm) in depth with a floor-mounted water closet. In a compartment primarily for children's use, greater than 65 inches (1650 mm) in depth, toe clearance at the front partition is not required.

2. Toe clearance at the side partition is not required in a compartment greater than 66 inches (1675 mm) in width.

❖ The toe clearance beneath the partition is used for maneuvering. Partitions around stalls for children have a higher toe clearance requirement than for adults. If the size of the stall exceeds 65 inches (1650 mm) in depth and 66 inches (1675 mm) in width, a toe clearance is not required. If the stall exceeds the mini-

mum dimension in only one direction, the toe clearance is not required on that side.

604.8.6 Grab Bars. Grab bars shall comply with Section 609. Side wall grab bars complying with Section 604.5.1 located on the wall closest to the water closet, and a rear wall grab bar complying with Section 604.5.2, shall be provided.

❖ See Section 609 for specific requirements for size, wall clearance, height and installation requirements.

Requirements for grab bars within wheelchair accessible toilet stalls are the same as those for water closets in a room. Side grab bars include both the horizontal and vertical grab bars. See Sections 604.5.1 and 604.5.2. The use of swing-up grab bars is limited to Type B units found in Section 604.5, Exceptions 4 and 5.

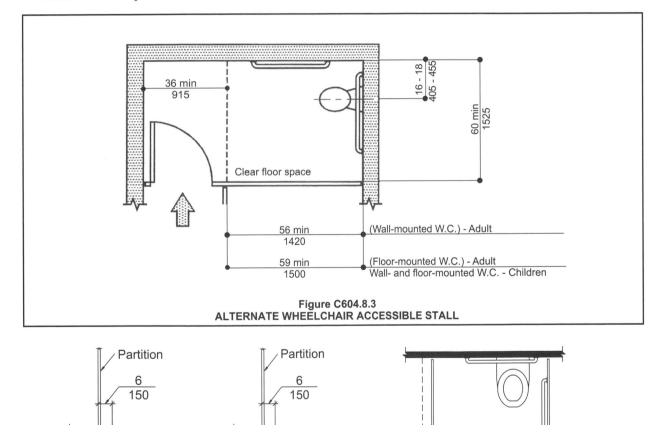

Figure C604.8.3
ALTERNATE WHEELCHAIR ACCESSIBLE STALL

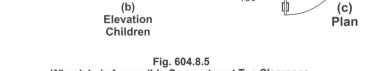

(a)
Elevation
Adult

(b)
Elevation
Children

(c)
Plan

Fig. 604.8.5
Wheelchair Accessible Compartment Toe Clearance

604.9 Ambulatory Accessible Compartments.

❖ An ambulatory accessible stall can be used by a person with a mobility impairment that may require additional support. Ambulatory stalls are typically scoped in the building codes so they occur when six or more water closets and urinals are provided within a single toilet room. This is in addition to the accessible wheelchair stall requirements, not an exception.

Section 604.10.8 references this provision for toilet stalls designed specifically for children.

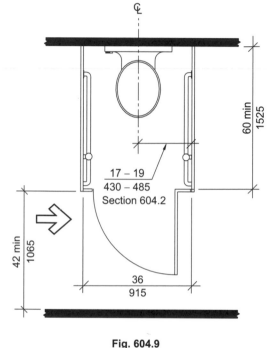

Fig. 604.9
Ambulatory Accessible Compartment

604.9.1 General. Ambulatory accessible compartments shall comply with Section 604.9.

❖ This standard recognizes two types of stalls: wheelchair accessible and ambulatory accessible. Scoping provisions adopted by the administrative authority will specify the number of each design required.

Requirements for toilet fixture height, clear floor space, grab bars, flush controls and dispensers in Section 604 are the same for toilet stalls and separate toilet rooms.

604.9.2 Size. The minimum area of an ambulatory accessible compartment shall be 60 inches (1525 mm) minimum in depth and 36 inches (915 mm) in width.

❖ The width dimension is absolute. A common mistake is to make the ambulatory stall wider, with the intent to better facilitate wheelchair access. However, the purpose of the ambulatory stall is more to serve per-

sons with mobility impairments who may be using a walker, cane or crutches. In an ambulatory stall, both grab bars are typically used simultaneously. The 36 inch (915 mm) dimension provides an optimum spread to best use the grab bars to maneuver both into and out of the stall. A wider spread would reduce the ability of the user to use the grab bars for balance and optimum leverage. It would make raising and lowering more difficult because the advantage of the use of the upper body for pulling or pushing is reduced.

604.9.3 Doors. Toilet compartment doors, including door hardware, shall comply with Section 404, except if the approach is to the latch side of the compartment door the clearance between the door side of the compartment and any obstruction shall be 42 inches (1065 mm) minimum. The door shall be self-closing. A door pull complying with Section 404.2.6 shall be placed on both sides of the door near the latch. Compartment doors shall not swing into the required minimum area of the compartment.

❖ The reference to the general Section 404, results in toilet compartment doors that must comply with all door provisions. There is a reduction in depth for door maneuvering clearances for latch approach, pull side [see Figure 404.2.3.1(f)] from 54 inches to 42 inches (1370 to 1065 mm). The 32-inch (815 mm) clear width for doors in Section 404.2.2 is applicable to allow clearance for a walker or crutches.

When in the compartment with the door swinging out, it is difficult for someone with limited arm and hand movement to close a toilet stall door from the inside. Without a handle or self-closing hinges, it is difficult for someone with limited arm and hand movement to close a toilet stall door from the inside. A self closer allows someone to enter the accessible stall and not have to worry about reaching back to close the stall door. Door pulls on both sides of the doors and the security latch must not require tight grasping, pinching or twisting of the wrist to operate. Both the door pull and the privacy latch must be between 34 inches (865 mm) and 48 inches (1220 mm) above the floor.

604.9.4 Grab Bars. Grab bars shall comply with Section 609. Side wall grab bars complying with Section 604.5.1 shall be provided on both sides of the compartment.

❖ See Section 609 for specific requirements for size, wall clearance, height and installation requirements.

Side grab bars, both horizontal and vertical, are required on both sides of an ambulatory accessible stall. These bars provide balance and stability to a person while maneuvering in or out of the stall. See Section 604.5.1.

604.10 Water Closets and Toilet Compartments for Children's Use.

❖ These provisions are intended for water closets and toilet compartments specifically designed for children. The anticipated age is 3 to 12 years. The anthropometrics for children are different from those of the average adult male. The U.S. Access Board has reviewed provisions for children. Commentary Table C308.1 is based on that research and provides guidance on unobstructed reach ranges for children according to age when building elements such as coat hooks or operable parts are designed for use primarily by children. The dimensions apply to either forward or side reaches. In addition, Table C604.10 provides guidance in applying the specifications for water closets for children according to the age group served and reflects specifications that correspond to the age of the primary use group. The specifications of one age group should be applied consistently in the installation of water closets and related items. These tables are information only and are not intended to present requirements.

604.10.1 General. Accessible water closets and toilet compartments primarily for children's use shall comply with Section 604.10.

❖ The standard does not require water closets or toilet compartments for children's use; however, if a designer wants to design for children (e.g., day care facilities, elementary schools) they must follow all the provisions in Section 604.10 and the associated references. The exception in Section 604.1 is a general reference to the child size provisions in Section 604.10.

604.10.2 Location. The water closet shall be located with a wall or partition to the rear and to one side. The centerline of the water closet shall be 12 inches (305 mm) minimum to 18 inches (455 mm) maximum from the side wall or partition. Water closets located in ambulatory accessible toilet compartments specified in Section 604.9 shall be located as specified in Section 604.2.

❖ In single occupant rooms or wheelchair accessible stalls designed for children, the center of the water closet can be located closer to the wall than required for adults (see Section 604.2). The center of the water closet in an ambulatory accessible stall is the same as for adults.

604.10.3 Clearance. A clearance around a water closet complying with Section 604.3 shall be provided.

❖ The clearance around a water closet in an accessible toilet room designed for children is the same as for adults (see Section 604.3). The lavatory or any fixture other than the water closet must not overlap this clear floor space.

604.10.4 Height. The height of water closet seats shall be 11 inches (280 mm) minimum and 17 inches (430 mm) maximum above the floor, measured to the top of the seat. Seats shall not be sprung to return to a lifted position.

❖ The height for the water closet in accessible single occupant rooms, wheelchair accessible stalls or ambulatory accessible stalls designed for children can have the height of the water closet lower than the 17-inch to 19-inch (430 to 485 mm) required for adults in Section 604.4.

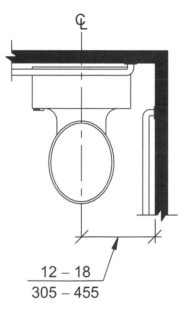

**Fig. 604.10.2
Children's Water Closet Location**

Table C604.10		
ADVISORY SPECIFICATIONS FOR WATER CLOSETS SERVING CHILDREN AGES 3 THROUGH 12		
	Ages 3 and 4	**Ages 5 through 8**	**Ages 9 through 12**
Water closet centerline	12 inches (305 mm)	12 to 15 inches (305 to 380 mm)	15 to 18 inches (380 to 455 mm)
Toilet seat height	11 to 12 inches (280 to 305 mm)	12 to 15 inches (305 to 380 mm)	15 to 17 inches (380 to 430 mm)
Grab bar height	18 to 20 inches (455 to 510 mm)	20 to 25 inches (510 to 635 mm)	25 to 27 inches (635 to 685 mm)
Dispenser height	14 inches (355 min)	14 to 17 inches (355 to 430 mm)	17 to 19 inches (430 to 485 mm)

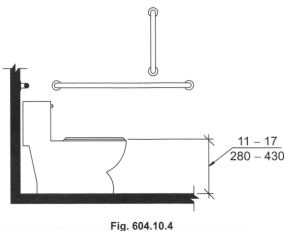

**Fig. 604.10.4
Children's Water Closet Height**

604.10.5 Grab Bars. Grab bars for water closets shall comply with Section 604.5.

❖ The length and relative orientation of the grab bars in single occupant toilet rooms, wheelchair accessible stalls and ambulatory accessible stalls designed for children is the same as those for adults (see Section 604.5). However, the height of the grab bars for children is lowered (see Section 609.4). The location for vertical grab bars in Section 604.5.1 is based on the adult provisions for grab bar height in Section 609.4. An alternative permitted by Section 103 would allow for locating the vertical grab bar relative to the horizontal grab bars (see commentary Table C604.10) and reach (see commentary Table C308.1) for the age group that the toilet room was being designed for.

604.10.6 Flush Controls. Flush controls shall be hand operated or automatic. Hand operated flush controls shall comply with Sections 309.2 and 309.4 and shall be installed 36 inches (915 mm) maximum above the floor. Flush controls shall be located on the open side of the water closet.

> **EXCEPTION:** In ambulatory accessible compartments complying with Section 604.9, flush controls shall be permitted to be located on either side of the water closet.

❖ Provisions for flush controls for adults are addressed in Section 604.6. Although the provisions for children are basically the same, the difference is that the upper reach range for flush controls is 36 inches (915 mm) rather than 48 inches (1220 mm). This results from the specifics in this section rather than the direct reference to Section 309.3. This is consistent with the reach ranges for 3 and 4 year olds indicated in commentary Table C308.1.

604.10.7 Dispensers. Toilet paper dispensers shall comply with Section 309.4 and shall be 7 inches (180 mm) minimum and 9 inches (230

mm) maximum in front of the water closet measured to the center line of the dispenser. The outlet of the dispenser shall be 14 inches (355 mm) minimum and 19 inches (485 mm) maximum above the floor. There shall be a clearance of $1^1/_2$ inches (38 mm) minimum below the grab bar. Dispensers shall not be of a type that control delivery or do not allow continuous paper flow.

❖ The provisions for toilet paper dispensers for adults are located in Section 604.7. The main difference is that the outlet of the dispenser is 14 inches to 19 inches (355 to 485 mm) rather than 15 inches to 48 inches (380 to 1220 mm). This effectively prohibits toilet paper dispensers installed over the grab bar. The general provisions for grab bars in Section 609.3 will require a minimum of $1^1/_2$ inches (38 mm) clearance below the grab bars for adults as well as for children.

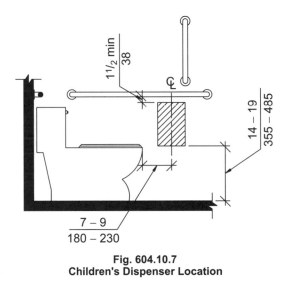

**Fig. 604.10.7
Children's Dispenser Location**

604.10.8 Toilet Compartments. Toilet compartments shall comply with Sections 604.8 and 604.9, as applicable.

❖ The general provisions for wheelchair accessible stalls and ambulatory accessible stalls are referenced for children. However, Section 604.8.2 contains child specific provisions for wheelchair accessible stall dimensions and Section 604.8.5 details child specific provisions for higher toe clearance requirements.

604.11 Coat Hooks and Shelves. Coat hooks provided within toilet compartments shall be 48 inches (1220 mm) maximum above the floor. Shelves shall be 40 inches (1015 mm) minimum and 48 inches (1220 mm) maximum above the floor.

❖ The provisions for coats hooks and shelves within ambulatory accessible and wheelchair accessible stalls are consistent with those provisions for toilet rooms in Section 603.4. These items are not required, but to provide equal access, if they are installed in the general stalls, they should be installed in the accessible stalls and meet the requirements in this section.

Coat hooks installed in accessible toilet rooms or stalls must be located within reach ranges. Measurements are to be taken to the top of the shelf or coat hook. If a shelf is installed, it should be located both so that it is within reach ranges and so that it won't interfere with maneuvering within the space or use of the grab bars.

There are no specific provisions for children sizes because the expected reach ranges (see commentary Table C308.1) are lower than that permitted for adults.

605 Urinals

❖ The intent of Section 605 is to address urinals for all uses other than within Accessible, Type A and Type B units. However, because urinals are not typically found in bathrooms in dwellings or sleeping units, requirements for urinals are not found in Chapter 10.

There are no specific provisions for urinals that are being designed for children.

605.1 General. Accessible urinals shall comply with Section 605.

❖ For urinals to be considered accessible, the height, clear floor space and location of controls must be as indicated below. If privacy shields are installed, the alcove provisions in Section 305.7 may be applicable (see commentary Figure C605.1).

605.2 Height. Urinals shall be of the stall type or shall be of the wall hung type with the rim at 17 inches (430 mm) maximum above the floor.

❖ A stall type urinal is floor mounted and extends up the wall. A wall hung urinal is mounted on the wall and typically stops a few inches above the floor. The 17 inch (430 mm) maximum rim height is based on the assumption that 17 inches is a typical wheelchair seat height (see Figure 605.2).

Stall type urinals may be considered more accessible for a broader range of individuals, including people of short stature. A minimum depth of 13^1/$_2$ inches (340 mm) from the outer face of the rim to the back surface of the fixture has been recommended as a usable depth for persons with disabilities.

Figure C605.1
URINAL AND PARTITIONS

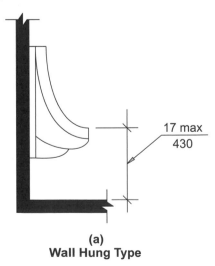

(a)
Wall Hung Type

17 max
430

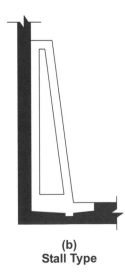

(b)
Stall Type

Fig. 605.2
Height of Urinals

605.3 Clear Floor Space. A clear floor space complying with Section 305, positioned for forward approach, shall be provided.

❖ The typical 30-inch by 48-inch (760 by 1220 mm) wheelchair space is required for a forward approach to urinals. The clear floor space should not extend under the urinal front rim. A person would need to stand up in front of a wheelchair to use the urinal.

To ensure a front approach, the urinal partition shall not extend past the front edge of the rim unless partitions are spaced at least 30 inches (760 mm) apart. If privacy partitions or adjacent walls extend more than 24 inches (610 mm) past the urinal rim, the clearances for alcoves in Section 305.7 would require a 36 inch (915 mm) minimum width.

605.4 Flush Controls. Flush controls shall be hand operated or automatic. Hand operated flush controls shall comply with Section 309.

❖ Manual flush controls must be located within reach ranges, and the controls themselves must meet the operable parts operation requirements. The best design practice would be that the clear floor space for the urinal is the same as the clear floor space required to access the flush controls, but that is not a requirement. Alternatively, automatic flush controls may be installed.

606 Lavatories and Sinks

❖ This section addresses requirements for lavatories and sinks that must be accessible. Lavatories would typically be found in toilet and bathing rooms and used for bathing purposes such as washing hands. A sink is typically used for purposes other than bathing. Scoping provisions adopted by the administrative authority may exempt some types of sinks, such as service and mop sinks, from accessibility requirements. Special provisions for children are located in Section 606.2, Exceptions 3 and 4.

Accessible, Type A and Type B units will reference Chapter 6 for sinks and lavatories where applicable. See Chapter 10 for applicable requirements and references.

606.1 General. Accessible lavatories and sinks shall comply with Section 606.

❖ The clear floor space, knee and toe clearances, height and pipe protection for sinks and lavatories must be within the limitations in the standard to be accessible. The requirements for the faucets, soap dispensers, towel dispensers and hand dryers are to facilitate access to controls.

606.2 Clear Floor Space. A clear floor space complying with Section 305.3, positioned for forward approach, shall be provided. Knee and toe clearance complying with Section 306 shall be provided. The dip of the overflow shall not be considered in determining knee and toe clearances.

EXCEPTIONS:

1. A parallel approach complying with Section 305 shall be permitted to a kitchen sink in a space where a cook top or conventional range is not provided.

2. The requirement for knee and toe clearance shall not apply to a lavatory in a toilet and bathing facility for a single occupant, accessed only through a private office and not for common use or public use.

3. A knee clearance of 24 inches (610 mm) minimum above the floor shall be permitted at lavatories and sinks used primarily by children ages 6 through 12 where the rim or counter surface is 31 inches (785 mm) maximum above the floor.

4. A parallel approach complying with Section 305 shall be permitted at lavatories and sinks used primarily by children ages 5 and younger.

5. The requirement for knee and toe clearance shall not apply to more than one bowl of a multibowl sink.

6. A parallel approach shall be permitted at wet bars.

❖ For access to lavatories and sinks, knee and toe clearances and clear floor space must be considered. The 30-inch by 48-inch (760 by 1220 mm) dimensions in Section 305.3 are required in front of a sink or lavatory. This rectangular space may extend under the sink up to 25 inches (635 mm). An extension of not less than 17 inches (430 mm) is required for a forward approach [see commentary Figures C306.1(b) and C306.1(c)].

The knee and toe clearances required in Sections 306.2 and 306.3 are consistently required throughout the standard for work areas. Pipes below the fixture must not restrict access to the lavatory or sink. The dip or overflow on a sink can result in a bump along the front and bottom edge of the bowl. Because this would typically be between a user's legs when they approached the sink, this should not be considered when determining whether adequate knee and toe clearances have been provided [see commentary Figure C606.2(a)].

The first and sixth exceptions acknowledge that in kitchenette type areas, such as coffee stations in office buildings or wetbars in hotel rooms, there is not typically a need to wash dishes on a regular or extensive basis in this sink; therefore, a side approach is a viable alternative. The 34-inch (865 mm) maximum sink height in Section 606.3 is still applicable. Typically, because these areas are only 3 feet to 6 feet (915 to 1830 mm) in length, the entire counter is installed below 34 inches (865 mm), not just the sink [see commentary Figure C606.2(b)].

Exception 2 allowance for no knee and toe clearances is part of the private office toilet room exceptions discussed in the general commentary to Chapter 6. This is coordinated with the lavatory height exception in Section 606.3. The room must be sized so that clear floor space will be available if the lavatory is modified in the future.

Exceptions 3 and 4 provide for lower lavatories and sinks designed for use by children. For children age 5 and younger, a side approach is permitted. Even though the maximum height for the sink or lavatory is 34 inches (865 mm) (see Section 606.3), a lower height is permissible so

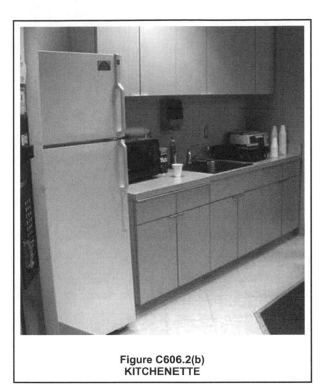

Figure C606.2(b)
KITCHENETTE

the sink or lavatory can be used by all the children in the class. Exception 4 effectively allows any sink height at 34 inches (865 mm) or lower with no knee and toe clearances. For children 6 to 12 years old, the sink/counter maximum height is at the lower height of 31 inches (790 mm) with a minimum knee clearance of 24 inches (610 mm) instead of the 27 inches (685 mm) in Section 306.3.

Per Exception 5, when a double bowl sink is installed, the knee and toe clearances are required under only one bowl. This allows for installation of a garbage disposal underneath one of the bowls of a double bowl sink.

606.3 Height. The front of lavatories and sinks shall be 34 inches (865 mm) maximum above the floor, measured to the higher of the rim or counter surface.

EXCEPTION: A lavatory in a toilet and bathing facility for a single occupant, accessed only through a private office and not for common use or public use, shall not be required to comply with Section 606.3.

❖ The 34 inch (865 mm) maximum height of lavatories and sinks ensures usability with an obstructed reach range. Built-in lavatories in countertops should be placed as close as possible to the front edge of the counter top.

The exception allowance for no height restriction for the lavatory is part of the private office toilet room exceptions discussed in the general commentary to Chapter 6. This is coordinated with the knee and toe clearance exception in Section 606.2. A lavatory with removable cabinets would exceed code requirements.

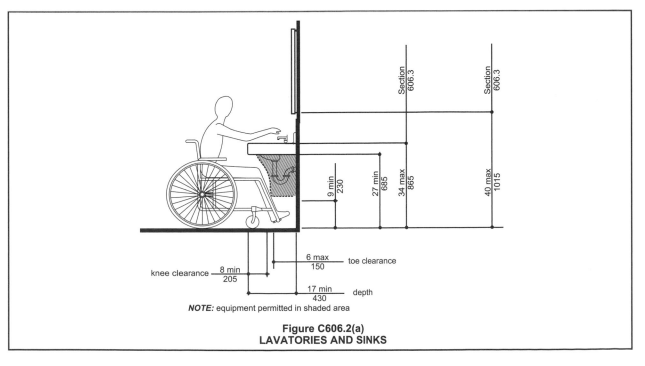

Figure C606.2(a)
LAVATORIES AND SINKS

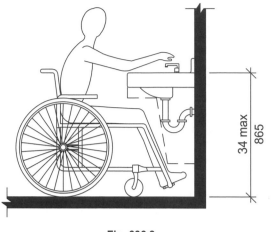

Fig. 606.3
Height of Lavatories and Sinks

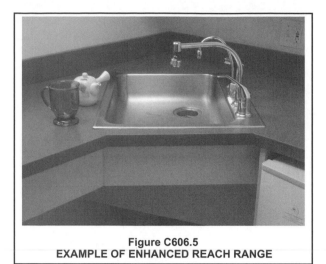

Figure C606.5
EXAMPLE OF ENHANCED REACH RANGE

606.4 Faucets. Faucets shall comply with Section 309. Hand-operated metering faucets shall remain open for 10 seconds minimum.

❖ Conventional one-quarter-turn, lever-operated, push-type and automatically controlled mechanisms are examples of acceptable designs. See commentary to Section 309 regarding the operable parts of the faucet. The 10 second time limit allows a person time to wash their hands once the faucet has been opened.

The model plumbing codes have 'tempered' water requirements for some bathing fixtures—which limit the temperature at the fixture to less than 110°F (43°C).

606.5 Lavatories with Enhanced Reach Range. Where enhanced reach range is required at lavatories, faucets and soap dispenser controls shall have a reach depth of 11 inches (280 mm) maximum or, if automatic, shall be activated within a reach depth of 11 inches (280 mm) maximum. Water and soap flow shall be provided with a reach depth of 11 inches (280 mm) maximum.

EXCEPTION: In Type A and Type B units, reach range for lavatory faucets and soap dispensers is not required.

❖ This standard requires enhanced reach range for lavatory faucets and soap dispensers when required by the authority having jurisdiction. When required, the faucets and soap dispenser must be located on the side of the lavatory [i.e., 11 inches (280 mm) maximum from the front edge of the counter] rather than at the back of the lavatory or on the back wall. This is beneficial for persons who are short in stature or have limited reach over the 34 inch (865 mm) lavatory or counter (see commentary Figure C606.5). Alternatively, access could be provided from the side of the lavatory as well as from the front.

The exception recognizes that this requirement was not intended to be scoped in Type A and Type B dwelling units.

Where the accessible and enhanced reach range lavatories are separate fixtures, accessible lavatories (i.e., without enhanced reach range requirements) must have faucets and soap dispenser controls that meet the general operable parts requirements in Section 309.

606.6 Exposed Pipes and Surfaces. Water supply and drainpipes under lavatories and sinks shall be insulated or otherwise configured to protect against contact. There shall be no sharp or abrasive surfaces under lavatories and sinks.

❖ Hot, cold and abrasive surfaces may cause harm to persons using a wheelchair because the ability to feel and react to such hazards may be diminished significantly as a result of paralysis or loss of sensation.

This protection can be provided by padding, apron walls, recessing the pipes, etc. This protection is not required to be the type of insulation required for steam pipes, hot water heating pipes or other types of extreme temperatures system piping.

The model plumbing codes have 'tempered' water requirements for some lavatory fixtures—which limit the temperature at the fixture to less than 110°F (43°C).

606.7 Operable Parts. Operable parts on towel dispensers and hand dryers shall comply with Table 606.7.

❖ Towel dispensers or hand dryers associated with the accessible lavatory have requirements that are more restrictive than the typical obstructed reach range requirements in Sections 308.2.2 and 308.3.2. With the lavatory at 34 inches (865 mm) in height, the towel dispenser or hand dryer must be on a side wall where the maximum reach depth is 11 inches (280 mm). If the towel dispenser or hand dryer is located somewhere else in the room, the height can be higher, but the reach over an obstruction underneath is less. For example, a wall mounted towel dispenser can have the outlet at 48 inches (1220 mm), but the waste receptacle underneath cannot stick out more than ¹/₂ inch (13 mm) (see commentary Figure C606.7).

Table 606.7
Maximum Reach Depth and Height

Maximum Reach Depth	0.5 inch (13 mm)	2 inches (50 mm)	5 inches (125 mm)	6 inches (150 mm)	9 inches (230 mm)	11 inches (280 mm)
Maximum Reach Height	48 inch (1220 mm)	46 inch (1170 mm)	42 inch (1065 mm)	40 inches (1015 mm)	36 inches (915 mm)	34 inches (865 mm)

Figure C606.7
TOWEL DISPENSER

607 Bathtubs

❖ Bathtubs and showers are both considered bathing facilities. This section addresses bathtubs. Technical criteria are stated for the situation where the tub is surrounded on three sides by walls. If a different configuration is constructed, Section 103 would allow for alternatives that provide the same or a higher level of accessibility.

Accessible, Type A and Type B units will reference Chapter 6 for bathtubs where applicable. See Chapter 10 for applicable requirements and references.

607.1 General. Accessible bathtubs shall comply with Section 607.

❖ For a bathtub to be accessible, the clear floor space, seat, grab bars and location of controls must comply with this section.

For purposes of this standard, the 'control end' is the end of the bathtub with the controls (e.g., faucets,

shower head and spout). The 'head end' is the end opposite the controls.

607.2 Clearance. A clearance in front of bathtubs extending the length of the bathtub and 30 inches (760 mm) minimum in depth shall be provided. Where a permanent seat is provided at the head end of the bathtub, the clearance shall extend 12 inches (305 mm) minimum beyond the wall at the head end of the bathtub.

❖ The floor space needed to approach a bathtub differs depending on whether a removable or permanent seat is installed.

For a parallel approach with a removable in-tub seat, a space 30 inches wide (760 mm) and the full length of the tub is needed for a lateral transfer from a parallel position. A typical tub provides a minimum length of 60 inches (1525 mm).

For a parallel approach to a tub with a fixed seat at the head of the tub, the clear floor space must be at least 30 inches (760 mm) wide by the full length of the tub and seat, plus an additional 12 inches (305 mm) past the seat. With a standard 60 inch (525 mm) tub, the minimum seat depth of 15 inches (380 mm) (see Section 610.2), and the additional 12 inches (305 mm) past the seat, the typical clear length would be a minimum of 87 inches (2210 mm). The additional 12 inch (305 mm) space is needed to permit the alignment of the wheelchair seat with the fixed tub seat to complete the transfer.

No other fixture or counter may overlap any portion of this clear floor space (see Figure 607.2).

607.3 Seat. A permanent seat at the head end of the bathtub or a removable in-tub seat shall be provided. Seats shall comply with Section 610.

❖ Section 610 addresses the minimum size and structural strength for the seats found either in or at the head of the bathtubs. The depth must be a minimum of 15 inches (380 mm), and the height must be between 17 and 19 inches (430 and 485 mm). The seat serves as either a bathing platform or as a transfer location to move into the tub. This effectively sets the height for the tub rim.

607.4 Grab Bars. Grab bars shall comply with Section 609 and shall be provided in accordance with Section 607.4.1 or 607.4.2.

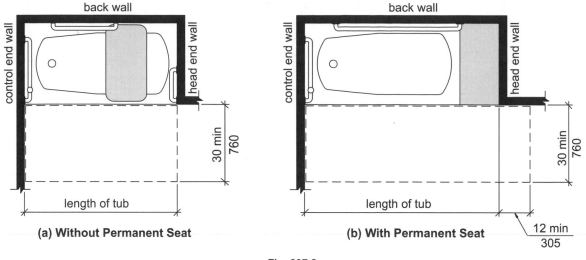

(a) Without Permanent Seat

(b) With Permanent Seat

**Fig. 607.2
Clearance for Bathtubs**

EXCEPTIONS:

1. Grab bars shall not be required to be installed in a bathing facility for a single occupant accessed only through a private office and not for common use or public use, provided reinforcement has been installed in walls and located so as to permit the installation of grab bars complying with Section 607.4.

2. In Type A units, grab bars are not required to be installed where reinforcement complying with Section 1003.11.4 is installed for the future installation of grab bars.

❖ Properly located grab bars enable the user to transfer from a wheelchair to the tub, as well as the lowering or raising of oneself in and out of the tub. Specific criteria are provided for both bathtubs with permanent seats at the head end and bathtubs with removable seats. See Section 609 for specific requirements for size, wall clearance, height and installation requirements.

Exception 1 allows for just the blocking to be provided for the future installation of grab bars as part of the private office toilet room exceptions discussed in the general commentary to Chapter 6.

Exception 2 verifies that Type A units at the time of initial construction are required to have the blocking for grab bars, but not the grab bars, installed. Grab bars can be added later as a modification based on occupants needs. This is also true for Type B units, but because of a difference in the language in Chapter 10, a correlative exception was not needed for Type B units.

607.4.1 Bathtubs with Permanent Seats. For bathtubs with permanent seats, grab bars complying with Section 607.4.1 shall be provided.

❖ When a permanent seat is installed at the head of the tub, a one horizontal and one vertical grab bar are required at the control end and a double bar is required at the back wall. Any controls or built in soap dishes should be located where they will not conflict with access to the grab bars. Grab bars are not required at the head end of the tub because the seat itself provides stability during transfer and the bar would conflict with leaning back on the seat.

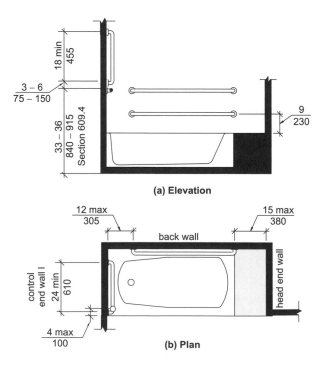

(a) Elevation

(b) Plan

**Fig. 607.4.1
Grab Bars for Bathtubs with Permanent Seats**

607.4.1.1 Back Wall. Two horizontal grab bars shall be provided on the back wall, one complying with Section 609.4 and the other 9 inches (230 mm) above the rim of the bathtub. Each grab bar shall be located 15 inches (380 mm) maximum from the head end wall and extend to 12 inches (305 mm) maximum from the control end wall.

❖ Two grab bars are required on the back wall. The top one is used during the transfer; the lower bar is used to move down into or up from the bottom of the tub. The placement of grab bars is essential to allow the person to transfer from the seat to the tub. Therefore, the end of the grab bar mounted on the back wall (opposite the open side) must be approximately even with the front edge of the seat at the head end of the bathtub.

607.4.1.2 Control End Wall. Control end wall grab bars shall comply with Section 607.4.1.2.

> **EXCEPTION:** An L-shaped continuous grab bar of equivalent dimensions and positioning shall be permitted to serve the function of separate vertical and horizontal grab bars.

❖ A horizontal and vertical bar are required on the control wall of the bathtub. These bars can be separate, or they can be one continuous bar. Alternatively, the horizontal bar along the control end and the top grab bar on the rear wall can be one continuous bar.

607.4.1.2.1 Horizontal Grab Bar. A horizontal grab bar 24 inches (610 mm) minimum in length shall be provided on the control end wall at the front edge of the bathtub.

❖ This additional grab bar is used to move within the tub to gain access to the controls (see Figure 607.4.1).

607.4.1.2.2 Vertical Grab Bar. A vertical grab bar 18 inches (455 mm) minimum in length shall be provided on the control end wall 3 inches (75 mm) minimum to 6 inches (150 mm) maximum above the horizontal grab bar, and 4 inches (100 mm) maximum inward from the front edge of the bathtub.

❖ This vertical grab bar is intended to be an aid for stability for persons with mobility impairments as they step into or out of the bathtub (see Figure 607.4.1).

607.4.2 Bathtubs without Permanent Seats. For bathtubs without permanent seats, grab bars complying with Section 607.4.2 shall be provided.

❖ When a removable seat is provided within the tub, one horizontal and one vertical grab bar are required at the control end, one bar is required at the head end and a double bar is required at the back wall. Any controls or built-in soap dishes should be located where they will not conflict with access to the grab bars.

607.4.2.1 Back Wall. Two horizontal grab bars shall be provided on the back wall, one complying with Section 609.4 and the other 9 inches (230 mm) above the rim of the bathtub. Each grab bar shall be 24 inches (610 mm) minimum in length, located 24 inches (610 mm) maximum from the head end wall and extend to 12 inches (305 mm) maximum from the control end wall.

❖ Two grab bars are required on the back wall. The top one is used during transfer; the lower bar is used to move down into or up from the bottom of the tub. The placement of grab bars is essential to allow the person to transfer from the seat to the tub. With a removable seat, a grab bar shorter than the bars required for bathtubs with permanent seats is sufficient. Therefore, the grab bar mounted on the back wall (opposite the open side) must be within 24 inches (610 mm) of the wall at the head end (opposite the controls).

607.4.2.2 Control End Wall. Control end wall grab bars shall comply with Section 607.4.2.2.

> **EXCEPTION:** An L-shaped continuous grab bar of equivalent dimensions and positioning shall be permitted to serve the function of separate vertical and horizontal grab bars.

❖ A horizontal and a vertical bar are required on the control wall of the bathtub. These bars can be separate or they can be one continuous bar. Alternatively, the horizontal bar along the control end and the top grab bar on the rear wall can be one continuous bar.

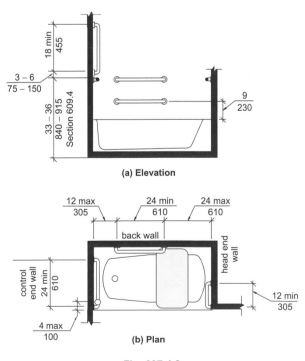

(a) Elevation

(b) Plan

Fig. 607.4.2
Grab Bars for Bathtubs without Permanent Seats

607.4.2.2.1 Horizontal Grab Bar. A horizontal grab bar 24 inches (610 mm) minimum in length shall be provided on the control end wall beginning near the front edge of the bathtub and extend toward the inside corner of the bathtub.

❖ This additional grab bar is used to move within the tub to gain access to the controls (see Figure 607.4.2).

607.4.2.2.2 Vertical Grab Bar. A vertical grab bar 18 inches (455 mm) minimum in length shall be provided on the control end wall 3 inches (76 mm) minimum to 6 inches (150 mm) maximum above the horizontal grab bar, and 4 inches (102 mm) maximum inward from the front edge of the bathtub.

❖ This vertical grab bar is intended to be an aid for stability for persons with mobility impairments as they step into or out of the bathtub (see Figure 607.4.2).

607.4.2.3 Head End Wall. A horizontal grab bar 12 inches (305 mm) minimum in length shall be provided on the head end wall at the front edge of the bathtub.

❖ A grab bar at the end away from the controls is required to assist in the transfer. This bar is not required when a fixed seat is installed at the head end (see Section 607.4.1), which provides the support necessary for the transfer.

607.5 Controls. Controls, other than drain stoppers, shall be provided on an end wall, located between the bathtub rim and grab bar, and between the open side of the bathtub and the midpoint of the width of the bathtub. Controls shall comply with Section 309.4.

❖ The controls must not be obstructed by the grab bars and vise versa. The controls are located toward the outside edge of the tub so they are more reachable by persons located in the adjacent clear floor space. Controls must also meet the operation requirements in Section 309.4.

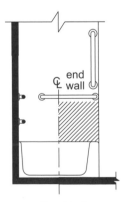

Fig. 607.5
Location of Bathtub Controls

607.6 Hand Shower. A hand shower with a hose 59 inches (1500 mm) minimum in length, that can be used as both a fixed shower head and as a hand shower, shall be provided. The hand shower shall have a control with a nonpositive shut-off feature. An adjustable-height hand shower mounted on a vertical bar shall be installed so as to not obstruct the use of grab bars.

❖ In conjunction with the bathtub fixtures, when the unit is also intended to serve as a shower, a hand-held shower spray unit is also required. A hand-held shower head that is capable of being adjusted up and down on a bar is preferred, as long as the grab bars are not obstructed.

The shower head must be useable in both a typical shower configuration and as a hand held unit. A shower head with a volume control mechanism (e.g., nonpositive shut-off feature) on the handset is a good design feature. This allows the shower occupant or attendant to reduce the flow of water to allow the handset to hang down while soaping or shampooing. Section 609.3, Exception 1, allows the vertical bar for the shower unit to extend within $1^1/_2$ inches (38 mm) above the grab bar.

607.7 Bathtub Enclosures. Enclosures for bathtubs shall not obstruct controls or transfer from wheelchairs onto bathtub seats or into bathtubs. Enclosures on bathtubs shall not have tracks installed on the rim of the bathtub.

❖ Enclosures shall be mounted in a manner that allows the user full accessibility without defeating any of the design features required by the standard. Curtains on a standard rod would typically not block a transfer; however, shower doors would most likely be an obstruction. Tracks on the bathtub rim are very uncomfortable to traverse while making the transfer.

607.8 Water Temperature. Bathtubs shall deliver water that is 120 degrees F (49 degrees C) maximum.

❖ The temperature limitation for the water is to prevent accidental scalding. Options for controlling the temperature of the water at the tub are a balanced-pressure, thermostatic, or a combination balanced-pressure/thermostatic valve.

608 Shower Compartments

❖ Bathtubs and showers are both considered bathing facilities. This section addresses showers. Technical criteria are provided for the situation where the shower is surrounded on three sides by walls. If a different configuration is constructed, Section 103 allows for alternatives that result in the same or a higher level of accessibility.

Where applicable, Accessible, Type A and Type B units will reference Chapter 6 for showers where applicable. See Chapter 10 for applicable requirements and references.

608.1 General. Accessible shower compartments shall comply with Section 608.

❖ For a shower to be accessible, the stall size, clear floor space, seat, grab bars and location of controls must comply with this section.

608.2 Size and Clearances.

❖ The size and clearances are different for transfer-type showers, roll-in-type showers and alternate roll-in shower compartments.

608.2.1 Transfer-Type Shower Compartments.
Transfer-type shower compartments shall have a clear inside dimension of 36 inches (915 mm) in width and 36 inches (915 mm) in depth, measured at the center point of opposing sides. An entry 36 inches (915 mm) minimum in width shall be provided. A clearance of 48 inches (1220 mm) minimum in length measured perpendicular from the control wall, and 36 inches (915 mm) minimum in depth shall be provided adjacent to the open face of the compartment.

❖ A transfer-type stall is a shower fixture at which a person using a wheelchair can transfer from the chair to the required seat within the shower stall.

Once a person transfers into the shower, the 36-inch by 36-inch (915 by 915 mm) inside finished dimensions allows a person of average size to reach and operate the controls without difficulty, while providing reasonable knee space for larger users. A transfer-type shower stall is also intended to serve persons without disabilities so a folding seat would provide more space for a standing person. Rounding of corners as necessitated in the manufacture of prefabricated shower stalls does not interfere with use. Therefore, the dimensions are measured at the center point of the walls rather than at the corners, and at a midpoint in the height (approximately shoulder height of a seated person), not at the base. The 36-inch (915

mm) minimum width entrance is required so that access to the transfer seat is not blocked.

A 36 inch by 48 inch (915 by 1220 mm) clear floor space is required to allow a person in a wheelchair outside of the shower to work the controls and adjust the water flow and temperature before they transfer. A common mistake is to put a wall at both ends of this clear floor space. The intent is typically to provide a small private dressing area, however, this space must also meet the alcove provisions in Section 305.7. Therefore, the space in front of the transfer shower must be a minimum of 60 inches (1525 mm) wide (see commentary Figure C608.2.1).

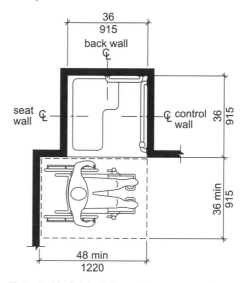

Note: inside finished dimensions measured at the center points of opposing sides

**Fig. 608.2.1
Transfer-Type Shower
Compartment Size and Clearance**

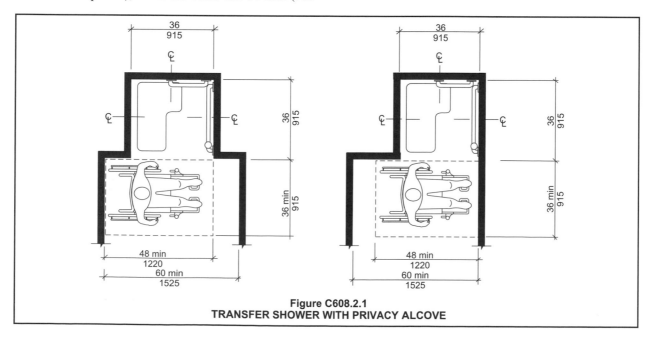

**Figure C608.2.1
TRANSFER SHOWER WITH PRIVACY ALCOVE**

608.2.2 Standard Roll-in-Type Shower Compartments. Standard roll-in-type shower compartments shall have a clear inside dimension of 60 inches (1525 mm) minimum in width and 30 inches (760 mm) minimum in depth, measured at the center point of opposing sides. An entry 60 inches (1525 mm) minimum in width shall be provided. A clearance of 60 inches (1525 mm) minimum in length adjacent to the 60-inch (1525 mm) width of the open face of the shower compartment, and 30 inches (760 mm) minimum in depth, shall be provided. A lavatory complying with Section 606 shall be permitted at the end of the clearance opposite the shower compartment side where shower controls are positioned. Where shower controls are located on the back wall and no seat is provided, the lavatory shall be permitted at either end of the clearance.

❖ The roll-in-type shower stall in Figure 608.2.2 will fit into the space commonly provided for a bathtub. A roll-in shower is sized to allow a person that uses a bathing wheelchair to move the wheelchair into the stall. Some roll-in showers also come equipped with folding seats so that they can also be used as transfer showers. If there is a desire to make the stall deeper, and a seat is included, it is important to keep the length of the seat consistent with the distance from the front edge and back wall (see Section 610). The seat wall should not exceed 36 inches (915 mm) because it would become difficult to slide into the corner if the user needed the wall support.

Rounding of corners, as necessitated in the manufacture of prefabricated shower stalls or bases, does not interfere with use. Typically, the dimensions would be measured at the center point of the walls rather than at the corners, and at a midpoint in the height (approximately shoulder height of a seated person), not at the base.

A 30 inch by 60 inch (760 by 1525 mm) clear floor space is required to allow a person in a wheelchair to move into the space in front of the shower. If the controls are on a side wall, the person can sit outside of the shower to work the controls and adjust the water flow and temperature before they move into the shower. To facilitate transfer to a seat, an additional 12 inches (305 mm) may be desired past the wall behind the seat [see commentary Figure C608.2.2(a)].

Providing a seat is optional (see Section 608.4). Controls may be located on a side wall or the back wall (see Section 608.5.2). When a seat is installed, the grab bars should not be located over the seat because this stops a person from leaning against the wall for support (see Section 608.3.2). In addition, the controls should be reachable from the seat (see Section 608.5.2).

A lavatory with knee and toe clearances may be located within the clear floor space outside of the shower if it does not block access to the controls or transfer to the seat [see commentary Figure C608.2.2(b)].

The concern about a dressing area/alcove in front of the roll-in shower is not the same as it is for a transfer shower. A roll-in shower plus its clear floor space should accommodate a 60 inch (1525 mm) turning space or a T-turn when there is knee space under the lavatory.

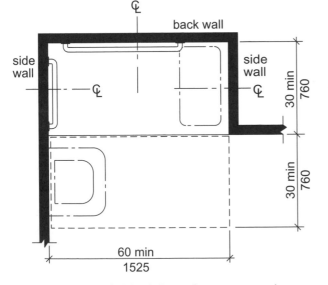

Note: inside finished dimensions measured at the center points of opposing sides

Fig. 608.2.2
Standard Roll-in-Type Shower
Compartment Size and Clearance

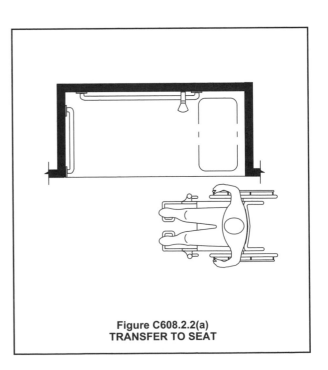

Figure C608.2.2(a)
TRANSFER TO SEAT

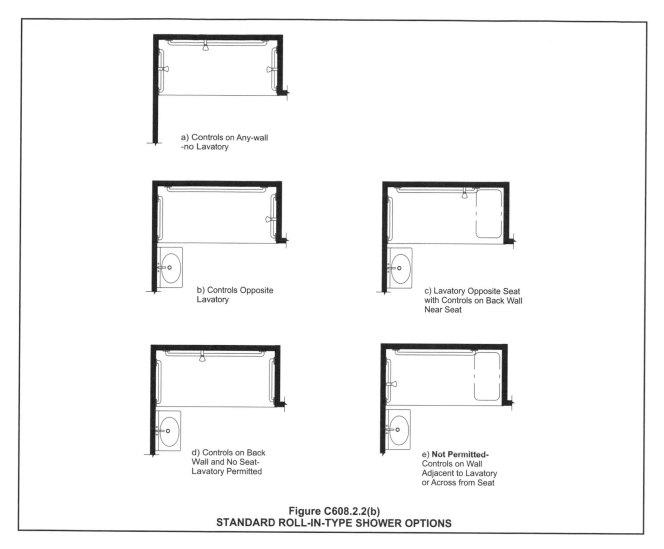

Figure C608.2.2(b)
STANDARD ROLL-IN-TYPE SHOWER OPTIONS

608.2.3 Alternate Roll-in-Type Shower Compartments. Alternate roll-in shower compartments shall have a clear inside dimension of 60 inches (1525 mm) minimum in width, and 36 inches (915 mm) in depth, measured at the center point of opposing sides. An entry 36 inches (915) mm) minimum in width shall be provided at one end of the 60-inch (1525 mm) width of the compartment. A seat wall, 24 inches (610 mm) minimum and 36 inches (915 mm) maximum in length, shall be provided on the entry side of the compartment.

❖ The alternate roll-in-type shower is intended to serve the purpose of both a roll-in and a transfer shower. Although a clear floor space is not required in front of the shower unit, the entrance must be located on an accessible route [see commentary Figure C608.2.3(a)].

Once a person moves into the shower and/or transfers to the seat, the controls located on the back wall across from the seat or adjacent to the seat will allow a person of average size to reach and operate the controls without difficulty [see commentary Figure C608.2.3(b)]. To allow a viable transfer seat, the

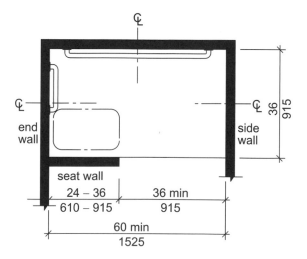

Note: inside finished dimensions measured at the center points of opposing sides

Fig. 608.2.3
Alternate Roll-in Type Shower
Compartment Size and Clearance

length of the seat wall is 24 inches to 36 inches (610 to 915 mm). This will typically result in the size of the of the shower stall being 36 inches (915 mm) deep and between 60 inches and 72 inches (1525 and 1830 mm) wide.

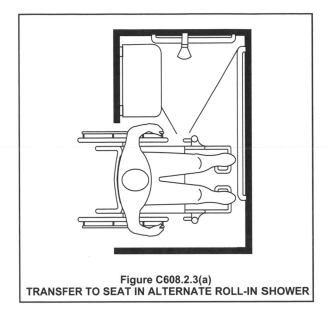

Figure C608.2.3(a)
TRANSFER TO SEAT IN ALTERNATE ROLL-IN SHOWER

608.3 Grab Bars. Grab bars shall comply with Section 609 and shall be provided in accordance with Section 608.3. Where multiple grab bars are used, required horizontal grab bars shall be installed at the same height above the floor.

EXCEPTIONS:

1. Grab bars are not required to be installed in a shower facility for a single occupant,

accessed only through a private office and not for common use or public use, provided reinforcement has been installed in walls and located so as to permit the installation of grab bars complying with Section 608.3.

2. In Type A units, grab bars are not required to be installed where reinforcement complying with Section 1003.11.4 is installed for the future installation of grab bars.

❖ Separate requirements for grab bars for transfer-type and roll-in type showers are discussed in the following sections. The reference to Section 609 covers size, wall clearance, height and installation requirements. Fixture controls and other installed items, such as soap dishes, must be located so they do not interfere with access to the grab bars. Horizontal grab bars around the water closet, shower or tub should be at the same elevation. This provides a higher level of stability.

Exception 1 allows for just the blocking to be provided for future installation of grab bars as part of the private office bathing room exceptions discussed in the general commentary to Chapter 6.

Exception 2 verifies that Type A units at the time of initial construction are required to have the blocking for grab bars, but not the grab bars installed. Grab bars can be added later as a modification based on the occupant's needs. This is also true for Type B units, but due to a difference in the language in Chapter 10, a correlative exception is not needed.

608.3.1 Transfer-Type Showers. Grab bars for transfer type showers shall comply with Section 608.3.1.

❖ Transfer showers are required to have horizontal bars and a vertical bar.

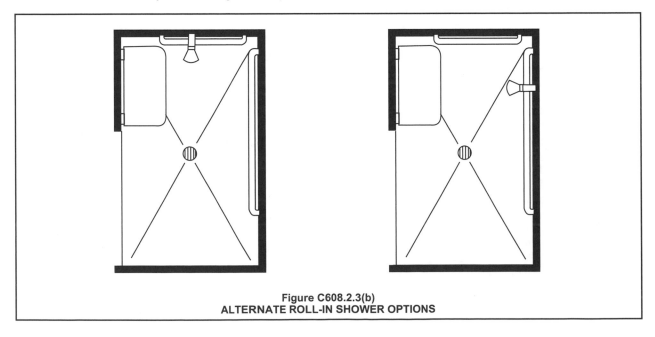

Figure C608.2.3(b)
ALTERNATE ROLL-IN SHOWER OPTIONS

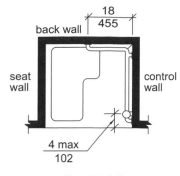

Fig. 608.3.1
Grab Bars in Transfer-Type Showers

608.3.1.1 Horizontal Grab Bars. Horizontal grab bars shall be provided across the control wall and on the back wall to a point 18 inches (455 mm) from the control wall.

❖ Improperly located grab bars are likely to interfere with the transfer from a wheelchair to the seat or make the seat unusable if a grab bar is mounted over the seat.

A horizontal bar should be installed on the wall across from the seat and on the back wall in front of the seat. The seat in a transfer shower can be the fold-up type (see Section 608.4), so the grab bars may be used by a sitting or standing person. This can be one bar or two bars. If two horizontal bars are used, they should be installed at the same height. This bar will be used by persons with mobility impairments for transfer, rising, sitting or additional stability.

608.3.1.2 Vertical Grab Bar. A vertical grab bar 18 inches (455 mm) minimum in length shall be provided on the control end wall 3 inches (75 mm) minimum to 6 inches (150 mm) maximum above the horizontal grab bar, and 4 inches (100 mm) maximum inward from the front edge of the shower.

❖ This vertical grab bar is intended to be an aid for stability for persons with mobility impairments as they step into or out of the shower (see Figure 608.3.1).

608.3.1.3 Grab Bar Configuration. Grab bars complying with Sections 608.3.1.1 and 608.3.1.2 shall be permitted to be separate bars, a single piece bar, or combination thereof.

❖ The grab bars, both horizontal and vertical, can be individual bars or some type of combined bar. If two horizontal bars are used, they should be installed at the same height.

608.3.2 Standard Roll-in-Type Showers. In standard roll-in type showers, grab bars shall be provided on three walls of showers without seats. Where a seat is provided in a standard roll-in type shower, grab bars shall be provided on the back wall and on the wall opposite the seat. Grab bars shall not be provided above the seat. Grab bars shall be 6 inches (150 mm) maximum from the adjacent wall.

❖ Some persons who use wheelchairs or persons who use other types of mobility aid devices can stand to use a shower if grab bars are readily available to aid in achieving balance. In a standard roll-in-type shower, three separate grab bars or a single, wraparound grab bar can be used. To provide the higher level of stability, if separate bars are used they should be installed at the same height. For situations where standard roll-in showers also include transfer seats, grab bars should not be located over the seat.

608.3.3 Alternate Roll-in-Type Showers. In alternate roll-in type showers, grab bars shall be provided on the back wall and the end wall adjacent to the seat. Grab bars shall not be provided above the seat. Grab bars shall be 6 inches (150 mm) maximum from the adjacent wall.

❖ If grab bars are readily available to aid in achieving balance, some persons who use wheelchairs or persons who use other types of mobility aid devices can stand to use a shower. The grab bars in alternate roll-in showers may be considered a hybrid of the transfer and standard roll-in-type grab bar configuration (see Figure 608.3.3). Two separate grab bars or a single, wraparound grab bar can be used. If separate

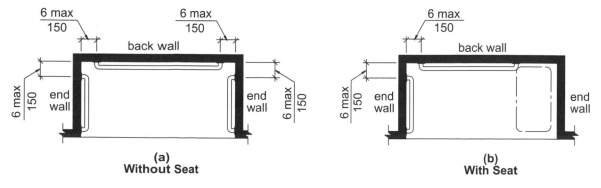

(a)
Without Seat

(b)
With Seat

Fig. 608.3.2
Grab Bars in Standard Roll-in-Type Showers

horizontal bars are used they should be installed at the same height to provide a higher level of stability.

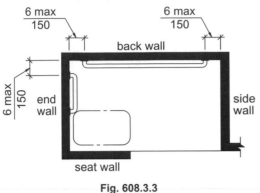

Fig. 608.3.3
Grab Bars in Alternate Roll-in-Type Showers

608.4 Seats. A folding or nonfolding seat shall be provided in transfer-type shower compartments. A seat shall be provided in an alternate roll-in-type shower compartment. In standard and alternate roll-in-type showers where a seat is provided, if the seat extends over the minimum clear inside dimension required by Section 608.2.2 or 608.2.3, the seat shall be a folding seat. Seats shall comply with Section 610.

EXCEPTIONS:

1. A shower seat is not required to be installed in a shower facility for a single occupant, accessed only through a private office and not for common use or public use, provided reinforcement has been installed in walls and located so as to permit the installation of a shower seat complying with Section 608.4.

2. In Type A units, a shower seat is not required to be installed where reinforcement complying with Section 1003.11.4 is installed for the future installation of a shower seat.

❖ Transfer seats in transfer showers can be either fixed or folding type. The transfer shower compartment would be more usable by the general population if a folding seat is installed. When transfer seats are installed in roll-in or alternate roll-in showers, they must be a folding type (Section 610.3) so that the shower will serve both transfer and roll-in purposes. In a combination roll-in/transfer shower where the seat was located outside of the minimum floor space, a fixed seat could be an alternative. Seats must always be permanently installed.

The shape of the seat provides support when the user's back is placed in the corner for support during the shower. The seat must be essentially the full depth of the stall; it must be within 3 inches (75 mm) of the front edge of the seat wall to minimize the distance between the seat and the wheelchair, and facilitate a transfer. A grab bar should not be located over the seat

(i.e., back or side) to allow a person to slide onto the seat and brace themselves in the corner for support. An "L" shaped seat allows the user to get additional stability from the adjacent walls.

Exception 1 allows for just the blocking to be provided for future installation of grab bars as part of the private office bathing room exceptions discussed in the general commentary to Chapter 6.

Exception 2 verifies that Type A units at the time of initial construction must have the blocking for grab bars, but not the grab bars, installed. Grab bars can be added later as a modification based on the occupants needs. This is also true for Type B units, but because of a difference in the language in Chapter 10, a correlative exception is not needed.

608.5 Controls and Hand Showers. Controls and hand showers shall comply with Sections 608.5 and 309.4.

❖ Controls for all types of accessible showers are addressed in the following subsection. All controls must meet the operation requirements in Section 309.4. In addition, hand showers must comply with Section 608.6.

608.5.1 Transfer-Type Showers. In transfer-type showers, the controls and hand shower shall be located on the control wall opposite the seat, 38 inches (965 mm) minimum and 48 inches (1220 mm) maximum above the shower floor, within 15 inches (380 mm), left or right, of the centerline of the seat.

❖ In showers that include transfer seats, controls must be located so they are within the reach range of the person sitting on the transfer seat (see commentary Figure C608.2.1 and Figure 608.5.1). The specific height provisions are consistent with the exception to the minimum grab bar clearances in Section 609.3.

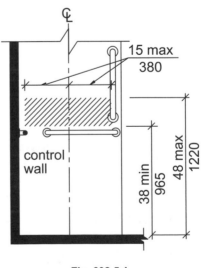

Fig. 608.5.1
Transfer-Type Shower
Controls and Handshowers Location

608.5.2 Standard Roll-in Showers. In standard roll-in showers, the controls and hand shower shall be located 38 inches (965 mm) minimum and 48 inches (1220 mm) maximum above the shower floor. In standard roll-in showers with seats, the controls and hand shower shall be located on the back wall, no more than 27 inches (685 mm) maximum from the end wall behind the seat.

❖ In a roll-in shower, controls must be within the reach of the person in the wheelchair and can be on any wall. In showers that include transfer seats, controls must be located so that they are within the reach range of the person sitting on the transfer seat [see commentary Figure C608.2.2(b) and Figure 608.5.2]. The specific height provisions are consistent with the exception to the minimum grab bar clearances in Section 609.3.

608.5.3 Alternate Roll-in Showers. In alternate roll-in showers, the controls and hand shower shall be located 38 inches (965 mm) minimum and 48 inches (1220 mm) maximum above the shower floor. In alternate roll-in showers with controls and hand shower located on the end wall adjacent to the seat, the controls and hand shower shall be 27 inches (685 mm) maximum from the seat wall. In alternate roll-in showers with the controls and hand shower located on the back wall opposite the seat, the controls and hand shower shall be located within 15 inches (380 mm), left or right, of the centerline of the seat.

EXCEPTION: A fixed shower head with the controls and shower head located on the back wall opposite the seat shall be permitted.

❖ Alternate roll-in showers are a hybrid of the roll-in and transfer situations. In an alternate roll-in shower a transfer seat is required by Section 608.4. Therefore, controls must be located so that they are within the reach range of the person sitting on the transfer seat [see commentary Figure C608.2.3(b) and Figure 608.5.3]. The specific height provisions are consistent with the exception to the minimum grab bar clearances in Section 609.3.

The exception was intended as a coordination with the exception in Section 608.6.

608.6 Hand Showers. A hand shower with a hose 59 inches (1500 mm) minimum in length, that can be used both as a fixed shower head and as a hand shower, shall be provided. The hand shower shall have a control with a nonpositive shut-off feature. An adjustable-height shower head mounted on a vertical bar shall be installed so as to not obstruct the use of grab bars.

EXCEPTION: A fixed shower head shall be permitted in lieu of a hand shower where the scoping provisions of the administrative authority require a fixed shower head.

❖ The shower head must be useable in both a typical shower configuration and as a hand held unit. A shower head with a volume control mechanism (e.g., nonpositive shut-off feature) on the handset is a good design feature. This allows the shower occupant or attendant to reduce the flow of water and allows the handset to hang down while soaping or shampooing. Section 609.3 allows for a minimum of $1^1/_2$ inches (38 mm) above the grab bar for the vertical bar supporting the hand shower.

A jurisdiction may determine that a fixed shower head is required instead of the hand-held. For example, in facilities where vandalism causes a maintenance problem, such as in isolated or unmonitored areas, a fixed shower head could be used in lieu of a hand-held shower head. The fixed shower head should be mounted 48 inches (1220 mm) maximum above the shower floor so it is still within reach ranges.

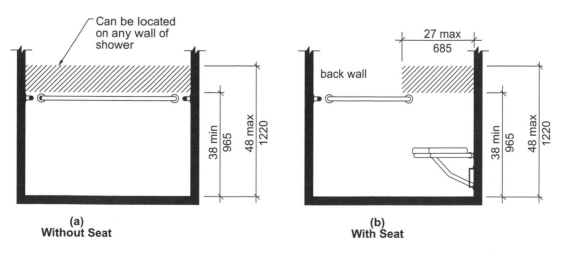

(a)
Without Seat

(b)
With Seat

Fig. 608.5.2
Standard Roll-in-Type Shower Control and Handshower Location

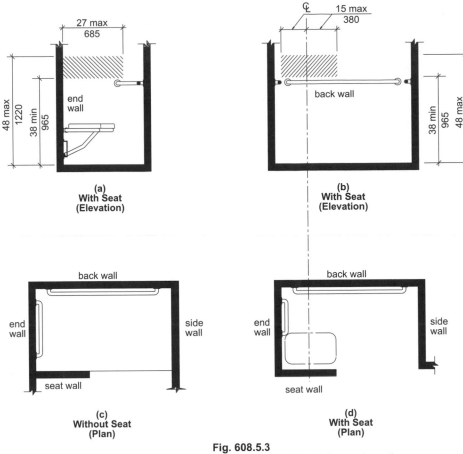

Fig. 608.5.3
Alternate Roll-in-Type Shower Control and Handshower Location

608.7 Thresholds. Thresholds in roll-in-type shower compartment shall be $\frac{1}{2}$ inch (13 mm) maximum in height in accordance with Section 303. In transfer-type shower compartments, thresholds $\frac{1}{2}$ inch (13 mm) maximum in height shall be beveled, rounded, or vertical.

EXCEPTION: In existing facilities, in transfer-type shower compartments where provision of a threshold $\frac{1}{2}$ inch (13 mm) in height would disturb the structural reinforcement of the floor slab, a threshold 2 inches (51 mm) maximum in height shall be permitted.

❖ A threshold with a $\frac{1}{2}$ inch (13 mm) maximum height will help reduce the amount of water that will reach the bathroom floor while allowing the front wheels of many wheelchairs access to the shower stall. There are wheelchairs that have very small wheels which cannot be moved easily, or in some instances safely, over a threshold. In roll-in showers, if the height is more than $\frac{1}{4}$ inch (6 mm) the change must be beveled. See commentary to Section 303. In transfer showers, the $\frac{1}{2}$ inch (13 mm) threshold is not required to meet the bevel provisions in Section 303 (see commentary Figure C608.7).

In existing facilities, there are limited situations where a 2 inch (50 mm) threshold is permitted.

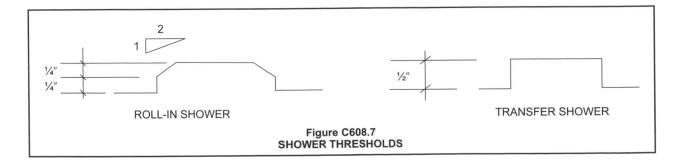

Figure C608.7
SHOWER THRESHOLDS

608.8 Shower Enclosures. Shower compartment enclosures for shower compartments shall not obstruct controls or obstruct transfer from wheelchairs onto shower seats.

❖ Enclosures must be mounted in a manner that allows the user full accessibility without defeating any of the design features required by the standard. Curtains on a standard rod would typically not block a transfer; however, shower doors would most likely be an obstruction. Tracks on the shower threshold may prevent access into the shower stall. Even in a transfer situation, the wheelchair user may need to move the small front wheels of the chair into the stall to make the transfer.

608.9 Water Temperature. Showers shall deliver water that is 120 degrees °F (49 degrees °C) maximum.

❖ Options for controlling the temperature of the water at the shower are a balanced-pressure, thermostatic, or a combination balanced-pressure/thermostatic valve.

609 Grab Bars

❖ These specific provisions for grab bars are referenced throughout the standard where it is necessary to install such features. When this section is referenced for blocking locations, the blocking should extend the full range of the permissible grab bar locations. The extent of the blocking must also include provisions for the mounting plates and adequate edge distance for the mounting screws.

609.1 General. Grab bars in accessible toilet or bathing facilities shall comply with Section 609.

❖ This section addresses grab bar requirements for shape, size, clearance, height and installation.

Many people with disabilities rely heavily on grab bars to maintain balance and prevent serious falls. Many brace their forearms between supports and walls to give them more leverage and stability in maintaining balance or for lifting. The clearance of 1¹/₂ inches (38 mm) required between the bar and the wall surface is a safety clearance to prevent injuries from arms slipping through the opening. This clearance also provides a minimum space for gripping.

609.2 Cross Section. Grab bars shall have a cross section complying with Section 609.2.1 or 609.2.2.

❖ Grab bars can have a shape that is either round (Section 609.2.1) or a noncircular shape (Section 609.2.2) that is graspable.

609.2.1 Circular Cross Section. Grab bars with a circular cross section shall have an outside diameter of 1¹/₄ inch (32 mm) minimum and 2 inches (51 mm) maximum.

❖ The cross-sectional shape of a grab bar is limited in size to afford optimum graspability. The grab bar is typically a round section or shape such as a pipe.

Equivalent gripping surface, though not specifically defined, pertains to the ability to wrap one's fingers completely around the bar to achieve a "power grip." A "pinch grip" does not provide the needed stability for which grab bars are used, even for people with ordinary hand dexterity.

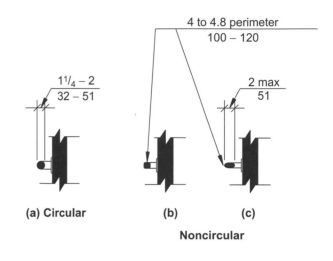

Fig. 609.2
Size of Grab Bars

609.2.2 Noncircular Cross Section. Grab bars with a noncircular cross section shall have a cross section dimension of 2 inches (51 mm) maximum, and a perimeter dimension of 4 inches (102 mm) minimum and 4.8 inches (122 mm) maximum.

❖ These provisions should allow an equivalent level of graspability for shapes other than the round bars in Section 609.2.1.

609.3 Spacing. The space between the wall and the grab bar shall be 1¹/₂ inches (38 mm). The space between the grab bar and projecting objects below and at the ends of the grab bar shall be 1¹/₂ inches (38 mm) minimum. The space between the grab bar and projecting objects above the grab bar shall be 12 inches (305 mm) minimum.

EXCEPTIONS:

1. The space between the grab bars and shower controls, shower fittings, and other grab bars above the grab bar shall be permitted to be 1¹/₂ inches (38 mm) minimum.

2. Swing-up grab bars shall not be required to comply with Section 609.3.

❖ The 1¹/₂ inch (38 mm) spacing between the grab bar and the wall is absolute. Anything smaller would prevent gripping around the grab bar circumference, and a larger space would create the risk of trapping a person's forearm when leaning on the bar during a transfer. There is a 12 inch (305 mm) minimum space required above the grab bars to allow for sufficient access and the possibility that a person may lean on the top of the bar for support.

Exception 1 permits the listed items to be located closer to the grab bars than the 12 inch (305 mm) minimum clearance in the main text. To require these items to be located a minimum of 12 inches (305 mm) above the grab bar would take them out of the reach ranges. The specific allowances for fixture controls in showers and bathtubs in Sections 607.6, 608.5 and 608.6 would permit a 1½ inch (38 mm) clearance above the grab bars to those particular items.

Exception 2 exempts swing-up grab bars from the wall clearance and projection requirements. Because the swing-up grab bar is not near a wall, the arm entrapment danger is not there, nor are there items that would block access to the bar.

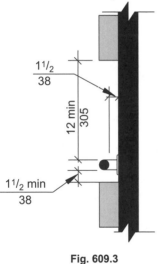

Fig. 609.3
Spacing of Grab Bars

609.4 Position of Grab Bars. Grab bars shall be installed in a horizontal position, 33 inches (840 mm) minimum and 36 inches (915 mm) maximum above the floor measured to the top of the gripping surface. At water closets primarily for children's use complying with Section 604.10, grab bars shall be installed in a horizontal position 18 inches (455 mm) minimum to 27 inches (685 mm) maximum above the floor measured to the top of the gripping surface.

EXCEPTIONS:

1. The lower grab bar on the back wall of a bathtub required by Section 607.4.1.1 or 607.4.2.1.

2. Vertical grab bars required by Sections 604.5.1, 607.4.1.2.2, 607.4.2.2.2, and 608.3.1.2.

❖ The dimensions are from the floor to the top of the grab bar. In addition to the required grab bars, supplemental grab bars may be added without meeting the location and size requirements contained in this standard. However, they must not be positioned where they interfere with the use of the required bars.

There is a different height allowance for grab bars adjacent to water closets, or around bathtubs or showers specifically designed for use by children. The height of the grab bar is correlated to the height of the toilet seat in Section 604.10. There are not similar allowances for the height for shower or tub seats.

Exception 1 is to allow for the double grab bar required on the rear wall at bathtubs.

Exception 2 reaffirms that vertical grab bar locations are fully addressed in listed sections.

609.5 Surface Hazards. Grab bars, and any wall or other surfaces adjacent to grab bars, shall be free of sharp or abrasive elements. Edges shall be rounded.

❖ Wall surfaces and other features adjacent to grab bars can be hazardous to users if they are abrasive or sharp. Cuts and abrasions may result, as well as the user's reluctance to use the bar when needed.

609.6 Fittings. Grab bars shall not rotate within their fittings.

❖ The bar must be firmly attached to the fittings that support the bar. If the bar rotates or spins within the fitting while the user is exerting a force on the bar, the person's grip may be lost, which could result in injury.

609.7 Installation. Grab bars shall be installed in any manner that provides a gripping surface at the locations specified in this standard and does not obstruct the clear floor space.

❖ Grab bars that are wall mounted do not affect the measurement of required clear floor space where the space below the grab bar is clear and does not present a knee space encroachment as provided in Section 306. However, a floor mounted grab bar system, depending on the specific configuration, may encroach on knee space and would affect how required clear floor space is measured. This requirement is included to ensure that the grab bar installation does not obstruct the required clear floor space.

609.8 Structural Strength. Allowable stresses shall not be exceeded for materials used where a vertical or horizontal force of 250 pounds (1112 N) is applied at any point on the grab bar, fastener mounting device, or supporting structure.

❖ The structural strength of a grab bar is dependent on the material used as well as the design. This provision requires that all of the components of the grab bar be strong enough to resist a 250 pound (1112 N) concentrated force applied either horizontally or vertically. There is no way of knowing in which direction the forces will be applied to the grab bar in a real installation. For instance, a user may apply weight to the top, pull to the side to get up, push on the side to get up, pull up on the bar to avoid tipping over, and so on. This provision may be more difficult to meet for some installations than others. For example, floor mounted grab bars may require elaborate anchoring devices and heavy duty components to resist the horizontal forces. Further, the floor, wall or other structural element to which the bar is attached must be considered. Unless that element and the connection to it is able to transfer the loads, the strength of the grab bar itself will not compensate for the lack of stability in the connection.

610 Seats

❖ Seats are referenced from bathtubs and showers. Bathtubs may have removable seats in the tub or fixed seats at the head end of the tub. Transfer showers and alternate roll-in-showers must have seats. Seats are an alternative for standard roll-in showers. See Sections 607.3 and 608.4.

610.1 General. Seats in accessible bathtubs and shower compartments shall comply with Section 610.

❖ This section addresses the size and shape for seats within bathtubs and showers that include a transfer seat. All seats must also meet the structural strength specified.

610.2 Bathtub Seats. The height of bathtub seats shall be 17 inches (430 mm) minimum to 19 inches (485 mm) maximum above the bathroom floor, measured to the top of the seat. Removable in-tub seats shall be 15 inches (380 mm) minimum and 16 inches (405 mm) maximum in depth. Removable in-tub seats

shall be capable of secure placement. Permanent seats shall be 15 inches (380 mm) minimum in depth and shall extend from the back wall to or beyond the outer edge of the bathtub. Permanent seats shall be positioned at the head end of the bathtub.

❖ The seat installed in the tub is typically used as a transfer surface for people to sit on while transferring down into the tub. Some users do bathe directly from the moveable seat without transferring into the tub. It is assumed that a permanent seat will extend the full width of the tub. The 17-inch to 19-inch (430 to 485 mm) height is a typical seat height for wheelchairs (see Figure 610.2). This will effectively set a rim height for the tub.

Both this section and Section 607.3 require the permanent seat at the tub to be located at the head end.

610.3 Shower Compartment Seats. Where a seat is provided in a standard roll-in shower compartment, it shall be a folding type and shall be on the wall adjacent to the controls. The height of the seat shall be 17 inches (430 mm) minimum and 19 inches (485 mm) maximum above the bathroom floor, measured to the top of the seat. In transfer-type and alternate roll-in-type showers, the seat shall extend along the seat wall to a point within 3 inches (75 mm) of the compartment entry. In standard roll-in-type showers, the seat shall extend from the control wall to a point within 3 inches (75 mm) of the compartment entry. Seats shall comply with Section 610.3.1 or 610.3.2.

❖ Transfer seats in the 36-inch by 36-inch (915 by 915 mm) transfer showers can be either fixed or folding

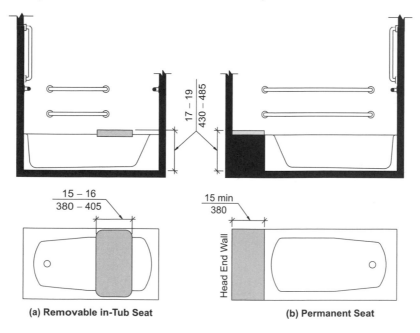

(a) Removable in-Tub Seat   **(b) Permanent Seat**

Fig. 610.2
Bathtub Seats

types. The transfer shower compartment is more usable by the general population if a folding seat is installed. When transfer seats are installed in standard and alternate roll-in showers, they must be folding types so the shower will work as both transfer and roll-in. In a combination roll-in/transfer shower where the seat is located outside of the minimum floor space, a fixed seat could be an alternative (see Section 608.4).

The shape of the seat provides support when the user's back is placed in the corner for support while the shower is in use. The seat must be essentially the full depth of the stall; it must be within 3 inches (75 mm) of the front edge of the seat wall to minimize the distance between the seat and the wheelchair to facilitate a transfer. The seat wall must be free of grab bars to allow a person to slide onto the seat and a portion of the adjacent back wall must be without a grab bar so the person's back can be placed against the walls for support (Sections 608.3.1, 608.3.2 and 608.3.3). An L-shaped seat allows the user to get additional stability from the adjacent walls.

610.3.1 Rectangular Seats. The rear edge of a rectangular seat shall be $2^1/_2$ inches (64 mm) maximum and the front edge 15 inches (380 mm) minimum to 16 inches (405 mm) maximum from the seat wall. The side edge of the seat shall be $1^1/_2$ inches (38 mm) maximum from the back wall of a transfer-type shower and $1^1/_2$ inches (38 mm) maximum from the control wall of a roll-in-type shower.

❖ Although the seat should extend the full width of the shower compartment, the total depth of the seat must be between 15 inches and 16 inches (380 and 405 mm). The maximum gap permissible across the back of the seat is $2^1/_2$ inches (64 mm) and between the seat and the rear wall is $1^1/_2$ inch (38 mm).

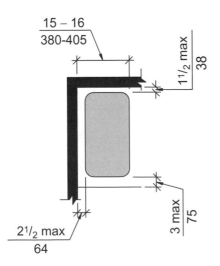

Fig. 610.3.1
Rectangular Shower Compartment Seat

610.3.2 L-Shaped Seats. The rear edge of an L-shaped seat shall be $2^1/_2$ inches (64 mm) maximum and the front edge 15 inches (380 mm) minimum to 16 inches (405 mm) maximum from the seat wall. The rear edge of the "L" portion of the seat shall be $1^1/_2$ inches (38 mm) maximum from the wall and the front edge shall be 14 inches (355 mm) minimum and 15 inches (380 mm) maximum from the wall. The end of the "L" shall be 22 inches (560 mm) minimum and 23 inches (585 mm) maximum from the main seat wall.

❖ The leg of the L-shaped seat is similar to that of the rectangular seat. The arm of the "L" shape of the seat is provided across the back wall. An L-shaped seat allows the user to get additional stability from the adjacent walls.

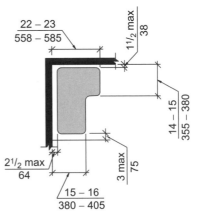

Fig. 610.3.2
L-Shaped Shower Compartment Seat

610.4 Structural Strength. Allowable stresses shall not be exceeded for materials used where a vertical or horizontal force of 250 pounds (1112 N) is applied at any point on the seat, fastener mounting device, or supporting structure.

❖ The seat and attachments must comply with the structural strength requirements to avoid failure and possible injury during use.

611 Washing Machines and Clothes Dryers

❖ For public use laundry facilities, the authority having jurisdiction will specify the number of washing machines and clothes dryers that must be accessible and comply with this section. Laundry equipment within an individual dwelling or sleeping unit in Accessible, Type A or Type B units is addressed in Chapter 10 with reference to this section as applicable.

611.1 General. Accessible washing machines and clothes dryers shall comply with Section 611.

❖ Laundry facilities present some complex problems of accessibility to the disabled person in a wheelchair. The reach ranges provided in Section 308 do not include criteria for accessing things that require bending the elbow joint such as reaching over the top of and into the basket of a top loading clothes washing machine or down and into the front of a front loading washer or dryer. Many devices are used to aid the user in reaching into these appliances to retrieve clothes at the bottom of the washer basket or rear of the dryer drum.

This standard provides specifics for top and front loading laundry equipment and basically assumes separate pieces of equipment. Criteria included are clear floor space, height of the door and operational requirements for all operable parts (e.g., doors, lint traps) and controls (e.g., time or temperature settings, on/off control). It is not the intent of this standard to prohibit dual use equipment or stacked units if they are accessible (see Section 103).

611.2 Clear Floor Space. A clear floor space complying with Section 305, positioned for parallel approach, shall be provided. The clear floor space shall be centered on the appliance.

❖ A 30 inch by 48 inch (760 by 1220 mm) clear floor space must be provided in front of and centered on both the washer and dryer to allow for access to the controls and access within the appliances themselves. If access to the washer or dryer is located within an alcove, the clear floor space must also meet the alcove provisions in Section 305.7.

611.3 Operable Parts. Operable parts, including doors, lint screens, detergent and bleach compartments, shall comply with Section 309.

❖ The appliances must have controls that are provided with a clear floor space, within the reach ranges and can be operated with minimum hand dexterity. Operable parts include the on/off switch, any time/temperature water level settings, filters, doors, detergent and fabric softener ports, and anything unique to normal operation of the pieces of equipment.

611.4 Height. Top loading machines shall have the door to the laundry compartment 36 inches (915 mm) maximum above the floor. Front loading machines shall have the bottom of the opening to the laundry compartment 15 inches (380 mm) minimum and 34 inches (865 mm) maximum above the floor.

❖ This section assumes that front loading appliances are more accessible than top loading appliances. The 36 inch (915 mm) height for top loading machines does cover most commonly available top loading machines on the market. Operating a front loading machine may be easier than operating a top loading machine. Some appliances have been developed with features to enhance accessibility. For example, some models are available with drawers under the units to raise the front loading machines and provide easier access into the drum.

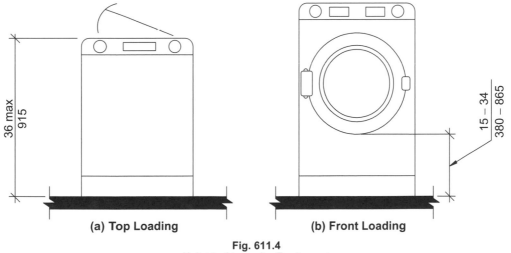

(a) Top Loading

(b) Front Loading

Fig. 611.4
Height of Laundry Equipment

Chapter 7. Communication Elements and Features

❖ Chapter 7 includes elements that are used for communication of information. Information can be general (e.g., evacuation alarms, signage, detectable warnings) or private (e.g., phones, ATMs). Although the other chapters of this standard mainly dealt with mobility impairments, this chapter is more for persons with visual or hearing impairments.

Communication features that are specific to dwelling units are covered in Section 1005.

- Section 701 is a general scoping provision that indicates that the requirements in this chapter are applicable when referenced by the authority having jurisdiction.

- Section 702 deals with visible and audible alarms. These devices are typically used to make occupants aware of an emergency evacuation that is necessary because of a fire in the building, but they can be used to inform occupants for other types of emergencies that may require evacuation or lock-down.

- Section 703 contains information on a variety of signage: tactile (i.e., raised and Braille) and visual (i.e., text and pictograms). New technologies have also lead to technical criteria for remote infrared audible sign systems and pedestrian signals.

- Section 704 deals with telephone access for persons using wheelchairs and for persons with hearing impairments.

- Section 705 contains the technical criteria for detectable warnings on walking surfaces. The authority having jurisdiction dictates when the detectable warnings must be provided.

- Section 706 concerns assistive listening systems. These systems are commonly used in assembly spaces such as theaters, sports arenas and courtrooms.

- Section 707 provides tactile and audible requirements for ATMs and fare machines.

- Section 708 deals with two-way communication systems. These systems are commonly found at controlled entrances, within elevator cars (Section 407.4.10) or within areas of refuge.

701 General

❖ The national census has identified the population over 65 years of age as the fastest growing number in the United States. The percentage of people who have mobility, hearing and vision impairments increases as the general population of the United States ages. Following are brief descriptions of what constitutes a hearing or visual impairment.

"Blindness cuts you off from things; deafness cuts you off from people." — Helen Keller

Hearing Impairments

A hearing impairment is a full or partial decrease in the ability to detect or understand sounds. One American in a hundred has a profound hearing loss; nearly one in 10 has a significant loss. Many hearing losses can be improved with hearing aids; however, a person with a moderate to profound hearing loss is dependent on visual cues for normal interaction, as well as to alert them to emergencies.

A hearing loss can be over the full range of frequencies or within a partial range, such as a high frequency range loss caused by exposure to loud noises. The U.S. Environmental Protection Agency (EPA) has set noise standards to protect people from these adverse health risks. The EPA has identified the level of 70 decibels for 24-hour exposure as the level necessary to protect the public from hearing loss. Normal speech sounds are within the 25 decibel to 35 decibel range. Living near an airport or a highway could expose someone to a 65 decibel to 75 decibel range and over time cause a hearing loss.

The severity of hearing loss is measured by how much louder, as measured in decibels, a sound must be made over the usual levels before being detected by an individual. The following list shows the rankings and their corresponding decibel ranges:

- Mild:
  - For adults: between 25 and 40 dB
  - For children: between 15 and 40 dB
- Moderate: between 41 and 55 dB
- Moderately severe: between 56 and 70 dB
- Severe: between 71 and 90 dB
- Profound: 90 dB or greater

Sound waves vary in amplitude and in frequency. Amplitude is the sound wave's highest point of oscillation. Frequency is the speed of sound divided by the wavelength of the sound wave, which is referred to as the pitch of the sound. The term "hearing impairment" is often reserved for people who have relative insensitivity to sound in the speech frequencies. Losing the ability to detect some frequencies creates some form of hearing impairment.

Many people with a hearing loss have better hearing in the lower frequency ranges (low tones), and cannot hear as well or at all in the higher frequencies. Noisy situations are especially difficult because hearing loss not only affects the ability to hear sounds, but also to localize and filter out background noise. People with unilateral hearing loss (single-sided deafness/SSD) lose their ability to localize sounds (i.e., unable to tell where a sound is coming from) and are unable to process out background noise in a noisy environment. A room with a high ceiling and hard surfaces for the walls and floors will have a lot of reverberation; therefore, acoustics can greatly affect a person's hearing ability. Difficulties can also arise for the listener trying to lip-read if the speaker is sitting with his back against the light source, obscuring his face.

Visual Impairments

The American Foundation for the Blind estimates that one in five people in the United States is visually impaired. "Visual impairment" is a term experts use to describe any kind of vision loss, whether it's someone who cannot see at all or someone who has partial vision loss. Some vision impairments can be improved with glasses or contacts, but not all. Persons with severe impairments may rely on a guide animal or a long cane for guidance.

Vision impairments in the young are more typically a result of an injury or congenital blindness. As part of the process of ageing, visual impairment may be caused by cataracts, diabetic retinopathy, glaucoma or macular degeneration.

Some people are completely blind, but many others have what's called legal blindness. They haven't lost their sight completely but have lost enough vision that they have to stand 20 feet from an object to see it as well as someone with perfect vision could from 200 feet away.

Color blindness is the inability to see parts of the color spectrum. This affects approximately 10 percent of males and 0.5 percent of females. People with color blindness usually have trouble discriminating reds and greens.

701.1 Scope. Communications elements and features required to be accessible by the scoping provisions adopted by the administrative authority shall comply with the applicable provisions of Chapter 7.

❖ The provisions in this chapter are intended to cover the requirements for communication features that are installed in a building. Even though signage is found in almost every building, other items are prescribed by the authority having jurisdiction (e.g., alarm systems) or are dependent on the type of activities within the building (e.g., assisted listening devices in a courthouse). Communication features specific to residential type facilities are specifically addressed in Section 1005. Note that these provisions apply to communica-

tion elements required in the scoping provisions (see Section 201).

702 Alarms

❖ Alarms serve to alert the occupants of a building of some event or condition. Fire, smoke, tornadoes, earthquakes and police emergencies are a few of the things for which people are notified by an audible or visual signal. These provisions address the technical requirements for the signaling devices used to notify occupants of fire emergencies (see commentary Figure C702).

This standard does not mandate that fire alarm systems be installed in buildings. It provides only the technical requirements for such systems to be considered accessible. The systems are typically mandated by the model codes, state laws or local ordinances. In alterations, where a new alarm system is installed or an existing system is replaced or upgraded, the degree of compliance is determined by the scope of the work and technical feasibility.

Audible alarms have been a standard feature of building construction since the early 1900s. However, visible signals did not appear even in accessibility codes until 1980. Early standards required relatively dim flashing lights at exit signs, effective only along the exit route. As accessibility and building codes were revised they began to incorporate alarm technology that was developed for use in schools for persons who are deaf and in factories where ambient noise levels made audible alarms ineffective.

The specifications in this section do not preclude the use of zoned or coded emergency alarm systems. In zoned systems, the visible alarm signals in an area flash whenever an audible signal sounds in the area. The standards regarding visible alarm signals provide comparable coverage and protection for persons who are deaf or hard-of-hearing, as well as for those depending on audible alarms. The provisions in this sec-

Figure C702
AUDIBLE ALARM AND VISIBLE SIGNAL APPLIANCE

tion for visible alarm signals were derived by studying facilities not designed for sleeping; e.g., business occupancies. In sleeping rooms, additional methods for waking sleeping persons who have hearing impairments may be necessary. For dwelling unit requirements see Section 1005.4.

Some facilities; for example, schools and courthouses, have started using the fire alarm system to make occupants aware of other types of emergencies, such as tornadoes or lock-downs. Typically, a different pattern is provided on the audible devices. Practice drills train the occupants to be aware of the differences. Facility alarm systems, other than the fire alarm systems, such as those used for tornado warnings and other emergencies are not required to comply with the technical provisions in Section 702. However, every effort should be made to assure that all occupants will be aware of any emergency. A full evaluation of the emergency evacuation system must be available in any building where fire safety and evacuation plans are required by the authority having jurisdiction.

702.1 General. Accessible audible and visual alarms and notification appliances shall be installed in accordance with NFPA 72 listed in Section 105.2.2, be powered by a commercial light and power source, be permanently connected to the wiring of the premises electric system and be permanently installed.

❖ The model codes and NFPA 72 use the term "visible" alarms instead of "visual alarms." The terms are both intended to describe flashing light type alarms. A visible alarm provides persons with hearing loss the same warning delivered to hearing persons by an audible alarm. Unlike audible alarms, visible alarms must be located within the space they serve so that the signal is visible. NFPA 72, *National Fire Alarm Code* is the nationally recognized technical standard for the installation of fire alarm systems. Because of the possible interpretation of language in NFPA 72 for allowance of radio-activated alarms, the A117.1 development committee wanted to emphasize that alarm systems must be permanently installed, not something that was handed to someone or moved around. Connection to the electrical system of the building will assure that batteries do not run out, resulting in the units not operating.

Some hearing aids deactivate the amplification of a sound that could result in damage to residual hearing capabilities. Therefore, it is recommended that the maximum audible sound level of audible alarms be 110 decibels. Although the 2002 edition of NFPA 72 allows a maximum decibel level of 120, revisions for the next edition will lower the maximum to 110 decibels. At locations where the alarm will not be heard above the ambient sound level, visible alarms must be provided.

Section 103 would allow for alternative alarm systems in situations where occupants may not be capable of self preservation, such as a jail or hospital. For example, in hospitals, the activation of the alarm may cause undue concerns with bedridden patients, or startle doctors and nurses during operations. Alternative solutions that provide an equivalent level of safety in these situations are permitted. The first step is notification of trained personnel through a messaging system or audible code over an intercom system. Redundant protection, such as closure of doors to create separate smoke compartments/protected areas happens automatically. Trained personnel can then respond appropriately for possible evacuation or movement of patients to adjacent protected areas.

703 Signs

❖ The authority having jurisdiction establishes when accessible signage is required; however, a designer may choose to provide accessible signage at rooms that have permanent designations. The types of signage addressed in this section are visual signs (Section 703.2), tactile signs (Sections 703.3 and 703.4) that include both raised letters and Braille, and pictograms (Section 703.5). The symbols for different accessible elements are indicated in Section 703.6.

Signage can include any combination of these types of signs (see commentary Figure C703). Some of the requirements are repeated for each signage type. Rather than have the reader bounce around by referencing back, the commentary is repeated for each type of sign with most differences identified.

An example of different types of signage are signs that provide audible information for persons with visual impairments. Technical requirements for remote infrared audible sign systems and pedestrian signals are provided in Sections 703.7 and 703.8.

703.1 General. Accessible signs shall comply with Section 703.

❖ Much of the information contained in Section 703 was developed to assist the large number of people

Figure C703
TACTILE AND VISUAL SIGNAGE WITH PICTOGRAMS

who are visually impaired but have some residual sight. In building complexes where finding locations independently on a routine basis is a necessity, tactile maps or prerecorded instructions are very helpful to visually impaired people. Several maps and auditory instructions have been developed and tested for specific applications. The types of maps or instructions are based on the information that must be communicated to the user, which in turn depends largely on the type of building as well as the user. Tactile signage is used where permanent signs are required to identify rooms and spaces such as, but not limited to the following:

- Hotel guest rooms.
- Tenant space entrances.
- Entrances to apartment units.
- Patient rooms in medical facilities.
- Classrooms and offices in schools and colleges.
- Banquet and meeting rooms.
- Toilet and bathing rooms.
- Areas of refuge.

Landmarks easily distinguished by individuals with a visual impairment are useful as orientation cues. Such cues include changes in illumination level, bright colors, unique patterns, wall murals, location of special equipment, or other architectural features. Many people with disabilities have limitations in movement of their head and reduced peripheral vision. Thus, signage positioned perpendicular to the path of travel is easiest for them to notice. People generally distinguish signage within an angle of 30 degrees to either side of the centerline of their line of sight without being required to move their heads.

703.2 Visual Characters.

❖ Examples of signs that provide visual information only would be exit signage, overhead signage and egress path information [see commentary Figures C703.2(a) and (b)].

Figure C703.2(a)
VISUAL SIGNAGE

703.2.1 General. Visual characters shall comply with Section 703.2.

EXCEPTION: Visual characters complying with Section 703.3 shall not be required to comply with Section 703.2.

❖ For visual signage, the legibility of printed characters is a function of the viewing distance, character proportions, font and the contrast between character and background, the finish, and the lighting.
Signage that is both tactile and visual must meet the more restrictive of the two provisions.

703.2.2 Case. Characters shall be uppercase, lowercase, or a combination of both.

❖ Even though tactile letters are required to be uppercase only (Section 703.3.3), visual signage can be uppercase and lowercase.
Signage that is both tactile and visual must have uppercase letters (Section 703.3.3).

703.2.3 Style. Characters shall be conventional in form. Characters shall not be italic, oblique, script, highly decorative, or of other unusual forms.

❖ Visual signs are not required to be sans serif like tactile signs (Section 703.3.4); however, typefaces without excessive flourishes or deviation in stroke width have been found to be the most legible. A severely nearsighted person has to be much closer to see a character of a given size accurately than a person with normal visual acuity.

Figure C703.2(b)
VISUAL SIGNAGE

Signage that is both tactile and visual must be sans serif (Section 703.3.4).

703.2.4 Character Height. The uppercase letter "I" shall be used to determine the allowable height of all characters of a font. The uppercase letter "I" of the font shall have a minimum height complying with Table 703.2.4. Viewing distance shall be measured as the horizontal distance between the character and an obstruction preventing further approach towards the sign.

❖ Proportions of visual lettering are a function of character width (Section 703.2.5), height (Section 703.2.4), stroke width (Section 703.2.6) and character spacing (Section 703.2.7). The uppercase letter "I" in a font is the baseline to determine the "character height" for the entire font chosen for the sign. Therefore, some lower case letters may actually be smaller than the minimum dimensions in Table 703.2.4 and the sign would still meet requirements. This same baseline is used to determine the relationship for character width, stroke width and spacing.

Character proportions in visual signage are very important to legibility. Very thick or thin characters are difficult to read. Characters placed close together can cause confusion with words like "MIN." Society for Environmental Graphic Design (SEGD) recommends using the capital "O" and the capital "I" for calculating proportions for text. If numbers are used to identify spaces, use the numbers "0" and "1." Uniform stroke width also increases legibility.

The height for visual characters is based on viewing distance. If the sign is overhead, a person may need to stand back to read the sign. If moving forward to the signage is blocked by some type of barricade the viewing distance is from that barricade.

For signage that is both tactile and visual:

- Character width requirements in Section 703.2.5 and 703.3.6 are the same.
- Character height requirements are specifically addressed in Section 703.3.5.
- Specifics in Section 703.3.7.2 will result in the stroke width requirements being the same as those in Section 703.2.6.
- Character spacing requirements in Section 703.3.8 are specific to a maximum character height of 2 inches, however, the intent is to be consistent with the character spacing percentage in Section 703.2.7.

703.2.5 Character Width. The uppercase letter "O" shall be used to determine the allowable width of all characters of a font. The width of the uppercase letter "O" of the font shall be 55 percent minimum and 110 percent maximum of the height of the uppercase "I" of the font.

❖ See the commentary in Section 703.2.4. For an example of proportion based on width see commentary Figure C703.3.6. Assuming characters within the font are proportional, some characters, such as "W," could actually be wider than the 110 percent required for the "O" and the font would still be compliant.

Table 703.2.4—Visual Character Height

Heights above Floor to Baseline of Character	Horizontal Viewing Distance	Minimum Character Height
40 inches (1015 mm) to less than or equal to 70 inches (1780 mm)	Less than 6 feet (1830 mm)	$^5/_8$ inch (16 mm)
	6 feet (1830 mm) and greater	$^5/_8$ inch (16 mm), plus $^1/_8$ inch (3.2 mm) per foot (305 mm) of viewing distance above 6 feet (1830 mm)
Greater than 70 inches (1780 mm) to less than or equal to 120 inches (3050 mm)	Less than 15 feet (4570 mm)	2 inches (51 mm)
	15 feet (4570 mm) and greater	2 inches (51 mm), plus $^1/_8$ inch (3.2 mm) per foot (305 mm) of viewing distance above 15 feet (4570 mm)
Greater than 120 inches (3050 mm)	Less than 21 feet (6400 mm)	3 inches (75 mm)
	21 feet (6400 mm) and greater	3 inches (76 mm), plus $^1/_8$ inch (3.2 mm) per foot (305 mm) of viewing distance above 21 feet (6400 mm)

❖ The actual viewing distance for a person looking at a sign varies, depending on the height of the person, the height of sign and the number of lines of information. Character height requirements are calculated using the horizontal and vertical distances between the viewer and the sign as specified in the table. The 'horizontal viewing distance' is the horizontal distance from the closest point a person can stand to view the sign, to the face of the sign. The vertical height is from the floor of the viewing position to the baseline of the highest line of the characters (see commentary Figure C703.2.4). Section 703.2.9 requires that the baseline of the lowest row of characters to be a minimum of 40 inches above the floor. Specific requirements for visual signage in elevators are listed in Sections 407, 408 and 409 depending on the type of elevator.

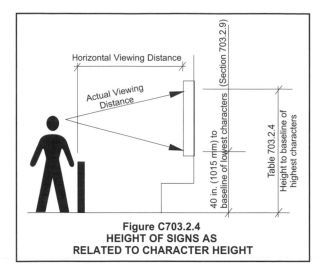

Figure C703.2.4
HEIGHT OF SIGNS AS
RELATED TO CHARACTER HEIGHT

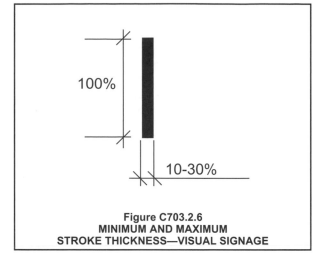

Figure C703.2.6
MINIMUM AND MAXIMUM
STROKE THICKNESS—VISUAL SIGNAGE

703.2.6 Stroke Width. The uppercase letter "I" shall be used to determine the allowable stroke width of all characters of a font. The stroke width shall be 10 percent minimum and 30 percent maximum of the height of the uppercase "I" of the font.

❖ Very thick or thin letters are difficult to read. See the commentary in Section 703.2.4 and commentary Figure C703.2.6 for additional information. Stroke thickness within a font could vary, but should always stay within the 10 to 30 percent range.

703.2.7 Character Spacing. Spacing shall be measured between the two closest points of adjacent characters within a message, excluding word spaces. Spacing between individual characters shall be 10 percent minimum and 35 percent maximum of the character height.

❖ See commentary for Section 703.2.4. The range in character spacing allows for locating sloped or curved letters closer to the adjacent letters so the font does not appear to have uneven spacing.

703.2.8 Line Spacing. Spacing between the baselines of separate lines of characters within a message shall be 135 percent minimum to 170 percent maximum of the character height.

❖ The character height is determined in Table 703.2.4 and is based on the uppercase letter "I"; therefore, line spacing is 135 percent to 170 percent of the uppercase letter "I" for the font used in the sign. This is measured from the highest letter in a row to the baseline of the row above. Tails of letters such as "g," "j" and "y" would not be considered. Equal spacing between lines increases legibility. If unrelated information is included on the same sign (e.g., signs in two languages), the line spacing may be larger between the two pieces of information.
Line spacing requirements for visual and tactile signs are the same (Section 703.3.9).

703.2.9 Height Above Floor. Visual characters shall be 40 inches (1015 mm) minimum above the floor of the viewing position, measured to the baseline of the character. Heights shall comply with Table 703.2.4, based on the size of the characters on the sign.

EXCEPTION: Visual characters indicating elevator car controls shall not be required to comply with Section 703.2.9.

❖ This 40 inch minimum measurement must be taken to the baseline of the lowest line of text. Because visual characters can be uppercase and lowercase, the baseline of the visual characters is the bottom edge of most of the letters, with the tail of some letters, like "g" and "j" going below the baseline. Note that Table 703.2.4 provides information based on the baseline to the highest line of information on the sign (see commentary Figure C703.2.4).
Requirements for visual information on elevator car controls is contained in Sections 407, 408 and 409 depending on the type of elevator.
Signs that are both visual and tactile are required to comply with Sections 703.3.10 and 703.3.11.

703.2.10 Finish and Contrast. Characters and their background shall have a non-glare finish. Characters shall contrast with their background, with either light characters on a dark background, or dark characters on a light background.

❖ A nonglare finish is typically matte or eggshell. Consideration must be given to light sources and the ambient lighting to prevent glare on sign surfaces. Light characters on a dark background are usually considered easier to read than dark characters on a light background, however, either is permitted. A contrast of at least 70 percent based on the light reflectance value is recommended.
A nonglare finish (11 to 19 degree gloss on 60 degree glossimeter) is recommended. Research indi-

cates that signs are more legible for persons with low vision when characters contrast with their background by 70 percent minimum. Contrast, in percent, is determined by:

Contrast = $[(B_1 - B_2)/B_1] \times 100$

where B_1 = light reflectance value (LRV) of the lighter area

and B_2 = light reflectance value (LRV) of the darker area.

In any application neither white nor black is ever absolute; therefore, B_1 will never equal 100, and B_2 will always be greater than 0. The greatest readability is usually achieved with the use of light-colored characters or symbols on a dark background.

Examples of acceptable and unacceptable finishes, according to Society for Environmental Graphic Design (SEGD) are included in Table C703.2.10.

If a sign is both visual and tactile, it must comply with the finish and contrast requirements that are repeated in Sections 703.2.10 and 703.3.12. Tactile signage only is addressed in the exception to Section 703.3.12.

703.3 Tactile Characters.

703.3.1 General. Tactile characters shall comply with Section 703.3, and shall be duplicated in braille complying with Section 703.4.

❖ Persons who are blind read either tactile characters or Braille; many of them do not read both. Therefore, tactile signs include both raised characters and Braille. Both tactile characters and Braille are most legible when the raised profile in cross-section (perpendicular to the face of the letter) is rounded or trapezoidal. Tactile characters and Braille having rectangular profiles are not as legible.

If a sign provides both tactile and visual characters, the sign must comply with Sections 703.3 and 703.2.

703.3.2 Depth. Tactile characters shall be raised $^1/_{32}$ inch (0.8 mm) minimum above their background.

❖ Minimum projection of characters above the background is necessary to make the characters tactile or perceptible by touch. Height limitations keep the letters in a size range that can be distinguishable by a person reading them by touch (see commentary Figure C703.3.2).

703.3.3 Case. Characters shall be uppercase.

❖ The letters are raised so they can be read by touch; restricting the letters to uppercase allows for easier reading. Signage that is for visual only can be a combination of upper and lower case (Section 703.2.2).

Table C703.2.10 FINISH AND CONTRAST RECOMMENDATIONS		
MATERIALS	**ACCEPTABLE**	**UNACCEPTABLE**
Finish paints and inks	Eggshell, matte	Gloss or semi-gloss
Acrylic sheet, mylar, frosted glass	Most nonglare types	Polished surface
Self-adhesive vinyl film	Most nonglare types	Glossy
Metal	Certain satin or random brushed finishes	Polished or directional brushed finishes

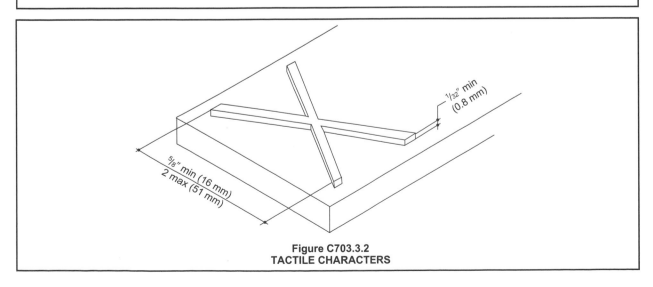

Figure C703.3.2
TACTILE CHARACTERS

703.3.4 Style. Characters shall be sans serif. Characters shall not be italic, oblique, script, highly decorative, or of other unusual forms.

❖ In typography, a sans serif typeface is one that does not have the small features called 'serifs' at the end of strokes. Sans serif typefaces or a simple serif typeface without excessive flourishes or deviation in stroke width have been found to be the most legible. A severely nearsighted person has to be much closer to see a character of a given size accurately than a person with normal visual acuity. For an example of serif and sans serif typeface, see commentary Figure C703.3.4. Stroke thickness within a font can vary from top to bottom; however, uniform thickness is easier to read.

703.3.5 Character Height. The uppercase letter "I" shall be used to determine the allowable height of all characters of a font. The height of the uppercase letter "I" of the font, measured vertically from the baseline of the character, shall be $^5/_8$ inch (16 mm) minimum, and 2 inches (51 mm) maximum.

> **EXCEPTION:** Where separate tactile and visual characters with the same information are provided, the height of the tactile uppercase letter "I" shall be permitted to be $^1/_2$ inch (13 mm) minimum.

❖ Proportions of tactile lettering are a function of character width (Section 703.3.6), height (Section 703.3.5), stroke width (Section 703.3.7) and character spacing (Section 703.3.8). The uppercase letter "I" in a font is the baseline to determine the "character height" for the entire font chosen for the sign. Because tactile signs are all uppercase (Section 703.3.3) there probably will not be any smaller letters as in visual signs (Section 703.2.4). This same baseline is used to determine the relationship for character width, stroke width and spacing.

Character proportions in tactile signage are very important to legibility. Very thick or thin characters are difficult to read. Characters placed close together can cause confusion with words like "MIN." Society for Environmental Graphic Design (SEGD) recommends using the capital "O" and the capital "I" for calculating proportions for text. If numbers are used to identify spaces, use the numbers "0" and "1." Uniform stroke width also increases legibility.

Characters used for both visual and tactile signage can be $^5/_8$ inch to 2 inches (16 to 51 mm) in height (see Figure 703.3.5). If a sign is for tactile reading only (e.g., tactile exit signage), text can be as small as $^1/_2$ inch (13 mm).

703.3.6 Character Width. The uppercase letter "O" shall be used to determine the allowable width of all characters of a font. The width of the uppercase letter "O" of the font shall be 55 percent minimum and 110 percent maximum of the height of the uppercase "I" of the font.

❖ See the commentary to Section 703.3.5. For an example of proportion based on width, see commentary Figure C703.3.6. Assuming characters within the font are proportional, some characters, such as "W" could actually be wider than the 110 percent required for the "O" and the font would still be compliant.

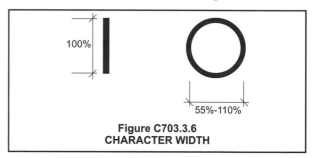

Figure C703.3.6
CHARACTER WIDTH

703.3.7 Stroke Width. Tactile character stroke width shall comply with Section 703.3.7. The uppercase letter "I" of the font shall be used to determine the allowable stroke width of all characters of a font.

❖ Very thick or thin letters are difficult to read. See the commentary for Section 703.3.5 for additional information.

703.3.7.1 Maximum. The stroke width shall be 15 percent maximum of the height of the uppercase letter "I" measured at the top surface of the character, and 30 percent maximum of the height of the uppercase letter "I" measured at the base of the character.

❖ See the commentary in Section 703.3.7 and commentary Figure C703.3.7. Stroke thickness within a font can vary from top to bottom; however, uniform thickness is easier to read.

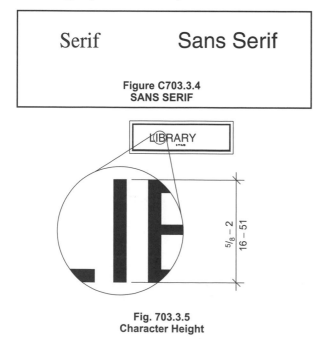

Figure C703.3.4
SANS SERIF

Fig. 703.3.5
Character Height

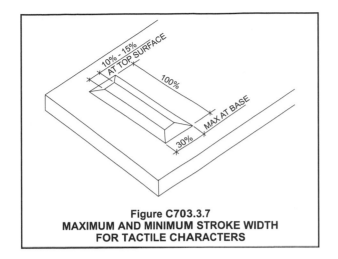

Figure C703.3.7
MAXIMUM AND MINIMUM STROKE WIDTH
FOR TACTILE CHARACTERS

703.3.7.2 Minimum. When characters are both visual and tactile, the stroke width shall be 10 percent minimum of the height of the uppercase letter "I".

❖ There are additional minimum stroke width criteria when the sign is visual and tactile. See the commentary in Sections 703.3.7 and 703.2.6 and commentary Figures C703.3.7 and C703.2.6.

703.3.8 Character Spacing. Character spacing shall be measured between the two closest points of adjacent tactile characters within a message, excluding word spaces. Spacing between individual tactile character shall be $1/8$ inch (3.2 mm) minimum measured at the top surface of the characters, $1/16$ inch (1.6 mm) minimum measured at the base of the characters, and four times the tactile character stroke width maximum. Characters shall be separated from raised borders and decorative elements $3/8$ inch (9.5 mm) minimum.

❖ The range in character spacing allows for sloped or curved letters to be located closer to the adjacent let-

ters so the font does not appear to have uneven spacing. See the commentary in Section 703.3.5.

Raised borders can confuse tactile reading or the raised and Braille characters; therefore, they should be avoided or spaced away from the main text.

703.3.9 Line Spacing. Spacing between the baselines of separate lines of tactile characters within a message shall be 135 percent minimum and 170 percent maximum of the tactile character height.

❖ The character height is determined in Section 703.3.5 and is based on the uppercase letter "I"; therefore, line spacing is 135 percent to 170 percent of the uppercase letter "I" for the font used in the sign. Proportional spacing between lines increases legibility. If nonrelated information appears on the same sign (e.g., signs in two languages), the line spacing may be larger between the two pieces of information.

703.3.10 Height above Floor. Tactile characters shall be 48 inches (1220 mm) minimum above the floor, measured to the baseline of the lowest tactile character and 60 inches (1525 mm) maximum above the floor, measured to the baseline of the highest tactile character.

EXCEPTION: Tactile characters for elevator car controls shall not be required to comply with Section 703.3.10.

❖ Because tactile characters are all uppercase, the baseline of the raised characters is the bottom edge. Note that in addition to the baseline of the raised letters needing to be within 48 inches and 60 inches (1220 to 1525 mm), the Braille must also be located within the same dimensions (Section 703.4.5). This is a convenient height in reading signs for a standing person. The tactile or Braille signage need not be located within the reach ranges in Section 308.

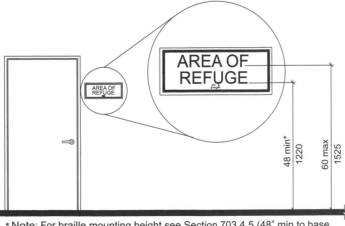

* Note: For braille mounting height see Section 703.4.5 (48″ min to base line of Braille cell).

Fig. 703.3.10
Height of Tactile Characters above Floor or Ground

Elevator car controls have requirement for tactile and Braille information. The height requirements for elevator car controls are addressed in Sections 407, 408 and 409, depending on the type of elevator.

703.3.11 Location. Where a tactile sign is provided at a door, the sign shall be alongside the door at the latch side. Where a tactile sign is provided at double doors with one active leaf, the sign shall be located on the inactive leaf. Where a tactile sign is provided at double doors with two active leaves, the sign shall be to the right of the right-hand door. Where there is no wall space on the latch side of a single door, or to the right side of double doors, signs shall be on the nearest adjacent wall. Signs containing tactile characters shall be located so that a clear floor area 18 inches (455 mm) minimum by 18 inches (455 mm) minimum, centered on the tactile characters, is provided beyond the arc of any door swing between the closed position and 45 degree open position.

EXCEPTION: Signs with tactile characters shall be permitted on the push side of doors with closers and without hold-open devices.

❖ To be usable by the visually impaired, tactile signs are placed at consistent locations. In locations having double doors, tactile signs are mounted to the right of the right-hand door, as it is approached. Thus, visually impaired travelers following customary pedestrian traffic patterns by traveling to the right side of corridors or spaces encounter signs before they encounter the associated doors.

Placement of tactile signs adjacent to doors on the latch side will allow for a person to stand outside the swing of the door when reading the sign. In addition, signs located at the hinge side are obscured when doors are open. It is important that any fixed elements not obstruct access to the sign. The wheelchair maneuvering clearance required at the pull side of the doors should allow adequate space.

When adequate wall space is not available on the latch side, signs are to be places on the adjacent wall (see commentary Figure C703.3.11).

The exception allows for placing tactile signs on the door in limited situations. With the closers operating, the door will never be held open, so the signage will always be readable.

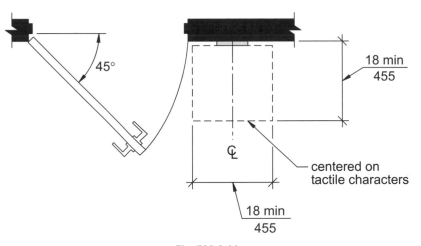

Fig. 703.3.11
Location of Tactile Signs at Doors

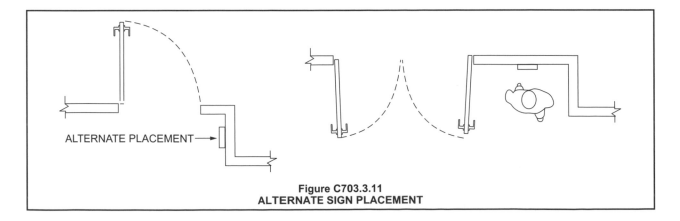

Figure C703.3.11
ALTERNATE SIGN PLACEMENT

703.3.12 Finish and Contrast. Characters and their background shall have a nonglare finish. Characters shall contrast with their background with either light characters on a dark background, or dark characters on a light background.

EXCEPTION: Where separate tactile characters and visual characters with the same information are provided, tactile characters are not required to have nonglare finish or to contrast with their background.

❖ A nonglare finish is typically matte or eggshell. Consideration must be given to light sources and the ambient lighting to prevent glare on sign surfaces. Light characters on a dark background are usually considered easier to read than dark characters on a light background; however, either is permitted. A contrast of at least 70 percent based on the light reflectance value is recommended.

A nonglare finish (11 to 19 degree gloss on 60 degree glossimeter) is recommended. Research indicates that signs are more legible for persons with low vision when characters contrast with their background by 70 percent minimum. Contrast, in percent, is determined by:

$$\text{Contrast} = [(B_1 - B_2)/B_1] \times 100$$

where B_1 = light reflectance value (LRV) of the lighter area

and B_2 = light reflectance value (LRV) of the darker area.

In any application, neither white nor black is ever absolute; therefore, B_1 will never equal 100, and B_2 will always be greater than 0. The greatest readability is usually achieved with the use of light-colored characters or symbols on a dark background.

Example of acceptable and unacceptable finishes, according to Society for Environmental Graphic Design (SEGD) are included in Table C703.2.10.

If a sign is both visual and tactile, it must comply with the finish and contrast requirements that are repeated in Sections 703.2.10 and 703.3.12. Tactile signage only is addressed in the exception to Section 703.3.12. When separate visual and tactile signage with the same information is provided, the tactile sign can have little or no contrast, including being the same color as the background.

703.4 Braille.

❖ Braille is read with a light sweeping touch using the pad of the finger, not the tip.

Braille can be Grade 1 or Grade 2. Section 703.4.1 specifies Grade 2 Braille on signage. A character symbol is used to distinguish numbers from letters because the same characters are used for both. A character symbol is also used to indicate capitalization. Unlike tactile characters, which must be in all capitals, capitals for Braille should be limited (Section 703.4.2). If a Braille sign is all capitals, the capital symbol would be required before each letter.

703.4.1 General. Braille shall be contracted (Grade 2) braille and shall comply with Section 703.4.

❖ Grade 1 Braille is a character-for-character translation of printed text. Grade 2 Braille is standard literary Braille in which numerous contractions shorten words (i.e., "contracted Braille") (see commentary Figure C703.4.1).

703.4.2 Uppercase Letters. The indication of an uppercase letter or letters shall only be used before the first word of sentences, proper nouns and names, individual letters of the alphabet, initials, or acronyms.

❖ Standard 6-dot Braille provides for 63 distinct characters, therefore, a number of distinct rule sets have been developed over the years to represent literary text, mathematics and science, computer software, music and other varieties of written material. Signage must follow the rules established for literary Braille.

Section 703.4.1 specifies Grade 2 Braille on signage. A character symbol is used to indicate capitalization. Unlike tactile characters, which must be in all capitals, capitals for Braille should be limited to the items listed in this section. If a Braille sign is all capitals, the capital symbol would be required before each letter.

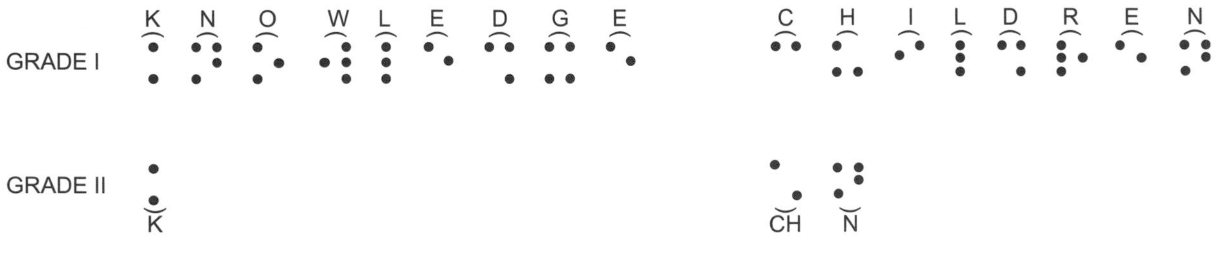

Figure C703.4.1
GRADE I AND II BRAILLE

703.4.3 Dimensions. Braille dots shall have a domed or rounded shape and shall comply with Table 703.4.3.

❖ It is important for readability that the vertical position of dots be rounded, not straight (i.e., mounds, not cylinders).

703.4.4 Position. Braille shall be below the corresponding text. If text is multi-lined, braille shall be placed below entire text. Braille shall be separated $^3/_8$ inch (9.5 mm) minimum from any other tactile characters and $^3/_8$ inch (9.5 mm) minimum from raised borders and decorative elements. Braille provided on elevator car controls shall be separated $^3/_{16}$ inch (4.8 mm) minimum either directly below or adjacent to the corresponding raised characters or symbols.

❖ The Braille equivalent of the raised text must be located below the raised text.

If multiple lines of information are provided on the sign, the raised text and Braille must be grouped to-gether to facilitate reading. The Braille letters must be spaced away from the raised letters or borders so the fingers can be flush with the sign face.

The elevator provisions in Section 407 and 408 reference this section for the elevator car controls. Because of the control buttons and the configuration of the panel, the Braille location is different from the signage requirements (i.e., location options and grouping).

703.4.5 Mounting Height. Braille shall be 48 inches (1220 mm) minimum and 60 inches (1525 mm) maximum above the floor, measured to the baseline of the braille cells.

EXCEPTION: Elevator car controls shall not be required to comply with Section 703.4.5.

❖ The lowest line of Braille text must be located between 48 inches and 60 inches (1220 and 1525 mm) above the floor so that it can be located and reached by a person with visual impairments. The tactile or Braille signage need not be located within the reach ranges in Section 308.

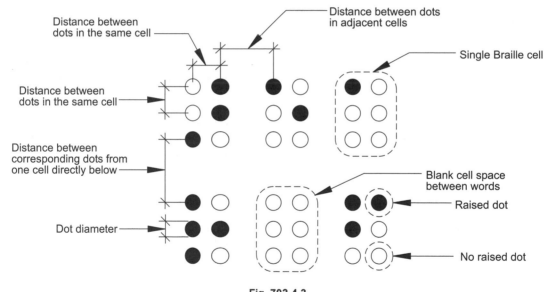

Fig. 703.4.3
Braille Measurement

Table 703.4.3—Braille Dimensions

MEASUREMENT RANGE	MINIMUM IN INCHES MAXIMUM IN INCHES
Dot base diameter	0.059 (1.5 mm) to 0.063 (1.6 mm)
Distance between two dots in the same cell	0.090 (2.3 mm) to 0.100 (2.5 mm)
Distance between corresponding dots in adjacent cells[1]	0.241 (6.1 mm) to 0.300 (7.6 mm)
Dot height	0.025 (0.6 mm) to 0.037 (0.9 mm)
Distance between corresponding dots from one cell directly below	0.395 (10.0 mm) to 0.400 (10.2 mm)

[1]Measured center to center.

All the signage information must work together. Note that Section 703.3.1 requires Braille to be located under the tactile information and Section 703.3.10 requires the tactile information to be located between 48 inches and 60 inches (1220 and 1525) above the floor to the baseline of the text. Limiting obstructions under signage as much as possible is recommended. See Section 703.3.11 for additional discussion on the mounting location at doors.

Previous editions of this standard required Braille to be between 40 inches and 60 inches (1220 and 1525 mm). The new height limitations are based on the 'reading' of the sign by standing users. Braille readers use the pads of their fingers to read. If the signage is too low, readers have to rotate their wrist, vastly complicating reading and intelligibility.

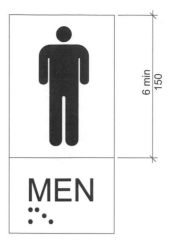

Fig. 703.5
Pictogram Field

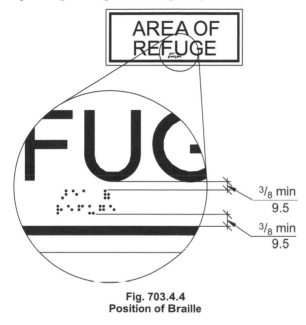

Fig. 703.4.4
Position of Braille

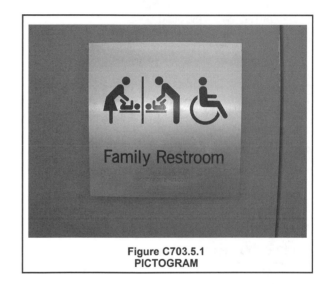

Figure C703.5.1
PICTOGRAM

703.5 Pictograms.

703.5.1 General. Pictograms shall comply with Section 703.5.

❖ Pictograms improve access for people with cognitive or learning disabilities, children and others who may have limited reading abilities. When accessible elements or spaces must be labeled with certain symbols, they must meet Section 703.6.

Pictograms which are understood by sighted persons are frequently not discernible or interpretable by visually impaired persons; therefore, pictograms are accompanied by the verbal equivalent in tactile (raised letters and Braille) text descriptors complying with Section 703.3. Requirements for tactile text apply to pictograms used to label permanent rooms or spaces (e.g., restrooms) where provided. Pictorial symbols used for other types of signs (e.g., no smoking, occupant logos) are not required to meet these provisions, including access symbols (see commentary Figure C703.5.1).

703.5.2 Pictogram Field. Pictograms shall have a field 6 inches (150 mm) minimum in height. Characters or braille shall not be located in the pictogram field.

❖ The minimum height applies to the symbol field, excluding the raised and Braille text provided below (Section 703.5.4). Because pictogram symbols vary in their shape and proportions, a minimum size is specified for the background, which effectively controls the symbol size. To avoid confusing the information, the raised and Braille characters must not overlap the pictogram.

703.5.3 Finish and Contrast. Pictograms and their fields shall have a nonglare finish. Pictograms shall contrast with their fields, with either a light pictogram on a dark field or a dark pictogram on a light field.

❖ A nonglare finish is typically matte or eggshell. Consideration must be given to light sources and the ambient lighting to prevent glare on sign surfaces. Light colors on a dark background are usually considered easier to read than dark colors on a light background; however, either is permitted. A contrast of at least 70 percent based on the light reflectance value is recommended.

A nonglare finish (11 to 19 degree gloss on 60 degree glossimeter) is recommended. Research indicates that signs are more legible for persons with low vision when symbols contrast with their background by 70 percent minimum. Contrast, in percent, is determined by:

Contrast = $[(B_1 - B_2)/B_1] \times 100$

where B_1 = light reflectance value (LRV) of the lighter area

and B_2 = light reflectance value (LRV) of the darker area.

In any application neither white nor black is ever absolute; therefore, B_1 will never equal 100, and B_2 will always be greater than 0. The greatest readability is usually achieved with the use of light-colored symbols on a dark background.

Examples of acceptable and unacceptable finishes, according to Society for Environmental Graphic Design (SEGD) are included in Table C703.2.10.

703.5.4 Text Descriptors. Where text descriptors for pictograms are required, they shall be located directly below the pictogram field. Text descriptors shall comply with Sections 703.3 and 703.4.

❖ The verbal equivalent of the pictogram must be provided below it in characters that meet the tactile (raised characters and Braille) criteria in Sections 703.3 and 703.4. Because of the pictogram, compliance with visual character requirements (Section 703.2) is optional.

703.6 Symbols of Accessibility.

703.6.1 General. Symbols of accessibility shall comply with Section 703.6.

❖ Several types of access symbols are required by the authority having jurisdiction or other sections of this standard (e.g., accessible parking in Section 502.6) to identify accessible elements. Contrast is required, but size and color are not specified.

703.6.2 Finish and Contrast. Symbols of accessibility and their backgrounds shall have a non-glare finish. Symbols of accessibility shall contrast with their backgrounds, with either a light symbol on a dark background or a dark symbol on a light background.

❖ A nonglare finish is typically matte or eggshell. Consideration must be given to light sources and the ambient lighting to prevent glare on sign surfaces. Light characters on a dark background are usually considered easier to read than dark characters on a light background; however, either is permitted. A contrast of at least 70 percent based on the light reflectance value is recommended.

A nonglare finish (11 to 19 degree gloss on 60 degree glossimeter) is recommended. Research indicates that signs are more legible for persons with low vision when

characters contrast with their background by 70 percent minimum. Contrast, in percent, is determined by:

Contrast = $[(B_1 - B_2)/B_1] \times 100$

where B_1 = light reflectance value (LRV) of the lighter area

and B_2 = light reflectance value (LRV) of the darker area.

In any application neither white nor black is ever absolute; therefore, B_1 will never equal 100, and B_2 will always be greater than 0. The greatest readability is usually achieved with the use of light-colored characters or symbols on a dark background.

Examples of acceptable and unacceptable finishes, according to Society for Environmental Graphic Design (SEGD) are included in Table C703.2.10.

703.6.3 Symbols.

703.6.3.1 International Symbol of Accessibility. The International Symbol of Accessibility shall comply with Figure 703.6.3.1.

Fig. 703.6.3.1
International Symbol of Accessibility

❖ The model building codes require identification of certain accessible elements using the International Symbol of Accessibility. The model codes do not require that all accessible elements be identified as accessible. Typically, elements such as inaccessible building entrances, inaccessible public toilets and bathing facilities, and elevators not serving an accessible route, must be marked with the International Symbol of Accessibility and directional signage indicating the accessible route to the nearest like accessible element. The International Symbol of Accessibility and appropriate directional signage are placed at inaccessible entrances indicating the direction to the nearest accessible entrance.

The International Symbol of Accessibility is used to label such items as accessible parking spaces, checkout aisles, dressing rooms, areas of refuge and exterior areas of rescue assistance. When not all similar elements are accessible, the International Symbol for Accessibility is used to identify such elements as the accessible passenger loading zone, entrances, exits, toilet and bathing rooms.

This emblem, depicting a person in a wheelchair, is standardized to be recognizable anywhere.

703.6.3.2 International Symbol of TTY. The International Symbol of TTY shall comply with Figure 703.6.3.2.

Fig. 703.6.3.2
International TTY Symbol

❖ This emblem depicts a telephone with a text type keypad indicating the telecommunication device can be used by typing messages on the keypad.

In the 1960s people who were deaf began using modified teletypewriters, which were in use at the time for printing stock quotes and typing messages to others who also had teletypewriters. They were referred to as TTYs. Technological advances in the 1970s produced smaller portable telecommunication devices for the deaf or TDDs. During the 1980s, people with normal speech and hearing began using these telecommunication devices. The new term, "text telephone" (TT), was coined to indicate that the use of these devices was not limited to the deaf or hearing impaired. There were objections to the use of this designation by members of the deaf community who rely on American Sign Language to communicate. The objection was raised because the sign language for text telephone (TT) is also used for toilet. Telecommunications for the Deaf, Inc. conducted a national survey and found that deaf individuals preferred the term "teletypewriter" (TTY).

703.6.3.3 Assistive Listening Systems. Assistive listening systems shall be identified by the International Symbol of Access for Hearing Loss complying with Figure 703.6.3.3.

Fig. 703.6.3.3
International Symbol of Access for Hearing Loss

❖ Assistive listening systems include such devices as amplifiers for the hearing impaired. The emblem depicts an ear with a diagonal stripe indicating hearing loss.

This symbol can also be use to provide notice of auxiliary aids and services such as real time captioning or sign language/oral interpretation services.

703.6.3.4 Volume-Controlled Telephones. Telephones with volume controls shall be identified by a pictogram of a telephone handset with radiating sound waves on a square field complying with Figure 703.6.3.4.

Fig. 703.6.3.4
Volume-Controlled Telephone

❖ The volume control is a form of assistive listening device installed in a telephone. It controls the receiver part of the telephone only.

703.7 Remote Infrared Audible Sign (RIAS) Systems.

❖ Remote infrared audible sign systems are a form of wireless communication that provides a means of way finding for persons with visual impairments. The system is typically made up of transmitters at key doors or elements you want people to be able to locate and the portable receivers that a person will carry.

The system consists of audio signals transmitted by invisible infrared light beams. The receivers decode the signal and deliver voice messages through a speaker or headset. The signals are directional, and the beam width and distance can be adjusted. The system can work both indoors and outside.

703.7.1 General. Remote Infrared Audible Sign Systems shall comply with Section 703.7.

❖ To work effectively, the transmitters (Section 703.7.2) installed in the buildings must be compatible with the receivers (Section 703.7.3) that are provided to or purchased by the persons using the system.

703.7.2 Transmitters. Where provided, Remote Infrared Audible Sign Transmitters shall be designed to communicate with receivers complying with Section 703.7.3.

❖ The transmitters are intended to be compatible with a variety of receivers. Typically the transmitters are installed in a building and the individuals will bring in their own receivers. See commentary Section 703.7.

703.7.3 Remote Infrared Audible Sign Receivers.

❖ Receivers are hand held and must meet frequency, optical power density, audio output, reception range and power ration specified in the following subsections.

703.7.3.1 Frequency. Basic speech messages shall be frequency modulated at 25 kHz, with a ± 2.5 kHz deviation, and shall have an infrared wavelength from 850 to 950 nanometer (nm).

❖ See commentary Sections 703.7 and 703.7.3.

703.7.3.2 Optical Power Density. Receiver shall produce a 12 decibel (dB) signal-plus-noise-to-noise ratio with a 1 kHz modulation tone at ± 2.5 kHz deviation of the 25 kHz subcarrier at an optical power density of 26 picowatts per square millimeter measured at the receiver photosensor aperture.

❖ See commentary Sections 703.7 and 703.7.3.

703.7.3.3 Audio Output. The audio output from an internal speaker shall be at 75 dBA minimum at 18 inches (455 mm) with a maximum distortion of 10 percent.

❖ See commentary Sections 703.7 and 703.7.3.

703.7.3.4 Reception Range. The receiver shall be designed for a high dynamic range and capable of operating in full-sun background illumination.

❖ See commentary Sections 703.7 and 703.7.3.

703.7.3.5 Multiple Signals. A receiver provided for the capture of the stronger of two signals in the receiver field of view shall provide a received power ratio on the order of 20 dB for negligible interference.

❖ See commentary Sections 703.7 and 703.7.3.

703.8 Pedestrian Signals. Accessible pedestrian signals shall comply with Section 4E.06 - Accessible Pedestrian Signals, and Section 4E.08 - Accessible Pedestrian Signal Detectors, of the Manual on Uniform Traffic Control Devices listed in Section 105.2.1.

EXCEPTION: Pedestrian signals are not required to comply with the requirement for choosing audible tones.

❖ Audible signals, provided at locations where traffic is controlled by traffic lights, allow for persons with vision impairments to know when they can cross the street. The sound also provides some directional information so people can stay in the crosswalk.

704 Telephones

❖ Public telephones are mounted in a variety of ways: in telephone booths, on wall surfaces, recessed in walls, enclosed in an alcove, on pylons and others. Providing access to make the telephones usable for persons with disabilities is the purpose of these provisions (see commentary Figure C704).

Many individuals with hearing impairments use certain assistive devices in their daily lives. Individuals can communicate by telephone using telecommunication devices for the deaf (TDD). This device looks like a typewriter or computer keyboard and transmits typed text over the telephone. Other names in common use are textphone and minicom. A videophone can be used for distance communication using sign language. In 2004, mobile textphone devices came onto the market for the first time allowing simultaneous two way text communication. There are telephone relay services so that a hearing impaired person can communicate with a hearing person via a human translator. Wireless, internet and mobile phone/SMS text messaging are beginning to take over the role of the TDD. Video conferencing is also a new technology that permits signed conversations as well as permitting an ASL-English interpreter to voice and sign conversations between a hearing impaired and hearing person, negating the need to use a TTY or computer keyboard.

Figure C704
TELEPHONE

704.1 General. Accessible public telephones shall comply with Section 704.

❖ Phones that may be addressed by the authority having jurisdiction are public phones, closet circuit phones for controlled access and phones at security glazing. The provisions are for persons using wheelchairs and persons with hearing and speech impairments. One phone can meet the requirements for both.

704.2 Wheelchair Accessible Telephones. Wheelchair accessible public telephones shall comply with Section 704.2.

❖ Telephones that are usable by persons in wheelchairs must comply with provisions for access and operable parts.

704.2.1 Clear Floor Space. A clear floor space complying with Section 305 shall be provided. The clear floor space shall not be obstructed by bases, enclosures, or seats.

❖ The clear floor space requirements are determined by a forward or parallel approach, and whether the phone is located in an alcove. Many elements found in typical mounting arrangements will restrict the clear floor space. Care must be taken to ensure that such elements do not interfere with the clear floor space required to make the telephone usable. A turning space is not required; however, if provided, it can use the knee and toe clearances available under any built in seats or counters.

704.2.1.1 Parallel Approach. Where a parallel approach is provided, the distance from the edge of the telephone enclosure to the face of the telephone shall be 10 inches (255 mm) maximum.

❖ The parallel approach allows a side reach for a person using a wheelchair. Only 10 inches (255 mm) is allowed from the edge of the telephone enclosure to the face of the telephone unit to ensure the receiver and controls are within the reach range. This is consistent with the maneuvering clearance provided for a side reach in accordance with Section 308.3.1. A parallel approach may provide better access for person using scooters.

704.2.1.2 Forward Approach. Where a forward approach is provided, the distance from the front edge of a counter within the enclosure to the face of the telephone shall be 20 inches (510 mm) maximum.

❖ An option for an accessible phone is to provide a front approach with knee and toe clearances under the phone. If a counter is provided, the face of the phone can be a maximum of 20 inches (510 mm) back from the front edge of the counter. This allows for the controls and handset to be within reach ranges. If the surrounding booth or walls create an alcove, the requirements of Section 305.7 are also applicable.

704.2.2 Operable Parts. The highest operable part of the telephone shall comply with Section 308. Telephones shall have push button controls where service for such equipment is available.

❖ For users with limited hand dexterity, push button controls are beneficial. Operable parts would include items such as the key pad, coin slots coin return, credit card swipes, volume controls and handsets.

704.2.3 Telephone Directories. Where provided, telephone directories shall comply with Section 309.

❖ The reference to Section 309 addresses the general provisions for making an object accessible for those who are mobility impaired. It includes provisions for maneuvering spaces for wheelchairs and reach ranges.

704.2.4 Cord Length. The telephone handset cord shall be 29 inches (735 mm) minimum in length.

❖ This minimum cord length will accommodate a standing person, a person using a wheelchair or scooter and a portable TTY.

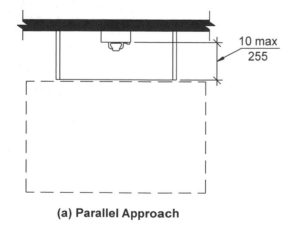

(a) Parallel Approach

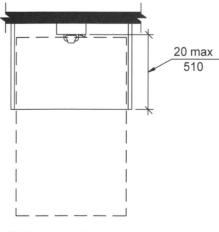

(b) Forward Approach

Fig. 704.2.1
Clear Floor Space Telephones

704.2.5 Hearing-Aid Compatibility. Telephones shall be hearing aid compatible.

❖ Many persons who are hard-of-hearing use hearing aids to enhance their ability to hear. To be accessible, telephones must be compatible with hearing aids. This is not the same as a volume control (Section 704.3). A federal law, the Hearing Aid Compatibility Act of 1998 requires all public telephones installed in the U.S. to be hearing-aid compatible. A compatible phone generates a magnetic field that can be "translated" by hearing aids with a "T" switch, which activates a telecoil. This normally results in a clearer signal than having the hearing aid reamplify the audible output of the handset. It is important that the compatible phones be shielded or located away from other electromagnetic sources which can interfere with the T-switch transmission.

704.3 Volume-Control Telephones. Public telephones required to have volume controls shall be equipped with a receive volume control that provides a gain adjustable up to 20 dB minimum. Incremental volume controls shall provide at least one intermediate step of gain of 12 dB minimum. An automatic reset shall be provided.

❖ Volume control ranges reflect a 20 dB minimum in order to make them usable. The volume control is equipped with automatic reset, which protects the next user from a potentially damaging loud volume.

Volume controls are located either on the base or on the handset. Volume controls located in handsets are most commonly used in retrofitting existing phones. Telephones that have a volume control are identified by the volume control telephone symbol in Section 703.6.3.4.

704.4 TTY. TTYs required at a public pay telephone shall be permanently affixed within, or adjacent to, the telephone enclosure. Where an acoustic coupler is used, the telephone cord shall be of sufficient length to allow connection of the TTY and the telephone handset.

❖ Requiring permanently affixed equipment precludes an arrangement that requires the user to ask an employee of an establishment to hook up a TTY. It ensures that, where required, the equipment will be available. An acoustic coupler is a device that allows the telephone receiver to be fitted into it, or with digital phones a digital/analog converter is needed. The signals will then be transmitted through the coupler to the TTY (see commentary Figure C704.4).

The TTY is a device that allows persons with hearing or speech impairments to communicate over the telephone. Like computers with modems, TTYs provide a keyboard for input and some type of visual output. Typed messages are converted in audible tones, which are transmitted through the phone lines to a receiver unit. See Section 106.5, definitions for TTY.

Signage is required at phones indicating the location of the TTY. The symbol is the International TTY symbol shown in Section 703.6.3.2.

704.5 Height. When in use, the touch surface of TTY keypads shall be 34 inches (865 mm) minimum above the floor.

EXCEPTION: Where seats are provided, TTYs shall not be required to comply with Section 704.5.

❖ The 34 inch (865 mm) height for the TTY keypad will be accessible for a person using a wheelchair or a standing person. If a seat is provided, the TTY keypad can be at a lower height.

704.6 TTY Shelf. Where pay telephones designed to accommodate a portable TTY are provided, they shall be equipped with a shelf and an electrical outlet within or adjacent to the telephone enclosure. The telephone handset shall be capable of being placed flush on the surface of the shelf. The shelf shall be capable of accommodating a TTY and shall have a vertical clearance 6 inches (150 mm) minimum in height above the area where the TTY is placed.

❖ Some people travel with their own portable TTY units. These requirements ensure that electrical power and a surface with enough vertical clearance to place the equipment are provided to make a portable TTY usable

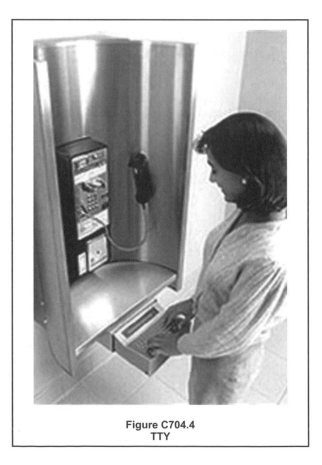

**Figure C704.4
TTY**

at pay telephones. To accommodate the full range of models, the shelf should provide a minimum clearance of 10 inches (255 mm) minimum and have the electrical outlet less than 3 feet (915 mm) from the shelf.

704.7 Protruding Objects. Telephones, enclosures, and related equipment shall comply with Section 307.

❖ Telephone equipment and enclosures are often installed projecting from walls, pylons and posts. Such projections may be detrimental to the visually impaired person. Persons who are blind and depend on canes to detect obstructions are particularly affected by such projections. Projections under which canes can sweep without being detected present a potential danger to the cane user. Telephones must be located so that they are not along a walking path, are recessed, have side panels with the bottom edge below 27 inches (685 mm) or are otherwise configured so that they do not violate the protruding-object provisions in Section 307.

705 Detectable Warnings

❖ Detectable warnings are required by this standard at raised marked crossings (Section 406.12). Detectable warnings are not required by this standard at curb ramps (Section 406.13), islands or cut-through medians (Section 406.14), but if provided, should comply with the provisions in this section. Model codes require detectable warnings at the edges of transportation platforms, such as train loading platforms (see commentary Figure C705).

Figure C705
PLATFORM EDGE

705.1 General. Detectable warning surfaces shall comply with Section 705.

❖ Detectable warnings provide a tactile clue for persons with visual impairments when they approach some type of edge. Detectable warnings are commonly used at platform edges, at the bottom of curb ramps, at traffic islands, at the front of stores along the edge of the parking lot or at the top of stairways.

Detectable warnings are intended to alert pedestrians of a hazard. Research indicates the most effective detectable warnings:

- Have a unique texture distinction from other common surfaces in the environment.

- Adjoin the hazard to signal the change.

- Extend beyond the average stride length so a person can detect and still have time to react before encountering the hazard.

At the time of the writing of this commentary, the U.S. Access Board has a committee that is reviewing the requirements for public rights of way, including detectable warnings.

705.2 Standardization. Detectable warning surfaces shall be standard within a building, facility, site, or complex of buildings.

EXCEPTION: In facilities that have both interior and exterior locations, detectable warnings in exterior locations shall not be required to comply with Section 705.4.

❖ Recognition of, and quick response to, detectable warnings is maximized by standardization of material as well as surface texture and color. Provision of too many different types of detectable and tactile warnings or failure to standardize such warnings weakens their usefulness. Detectable and tactile warnings are also visual signals to guide dogs because dogs are trained to respond to a large variety of visual cues.

The exception is in recognition that requirements for resiliency and sound-on-cane contact is applicable only in interior environments.

705.3 Contrast. Detectable warning surfaces shall contrast visually with adjacent surfaces, either light-on-dark or dark-on-light.

❖ Different colors for the main floor surface and for the domes and their immediate surrounding surfaces assists persons with vision impairments to identify the location of detectable warnings. When choosing a color, keep in mind persons with color blindness as well as the issue of contrast. The recommended minimum light reflectance contrast is 70 percent.

705.4 Interior Locations. Detectable warning surfaces in interior locations shall differ from adjoining walking surfaces in resiliency or sound-on-cane contact.

❖ Interior applications require that the warning feature contrast in resilience or sound when sensed with a cane. This requirement is not applicable for exterior locations (Section 705.2 Exception).

705.5 Truncated Domes. Detectable warning surfaces shall have truncated domes complying with Section 705.5.

❖ Truncated domes are typically placed in a strip 24 inches (610 mm) wide.

705.5.1 Size. Truncated domes shall have a base diameter of 0.9 inch (23 mm) minimum to 1.4 inch (36 mm) maximum, and a top diameter of 50 percent minimum to 65 percent maximum of the base diameter.

❖ See Figure 705.5 for a graphic indication of dome size.

705.5.2 Height. Truncated domes shall have a height of 0.2 inch (5.1 mm).

❖ See Figure 705.5 for a graphic indication of dome size.

705.5.3 Spacing. Truncated domes shall have a center-to-center spacing of 1.6 inches (41 mm) minimum and 2.4 inches (61 mm) maximum, and a base-to-base spacing of 0.65 inch (16.5 mm) minimum, measured between the most adjacent domes on the grid.

❖ See Figure 705.5 for a graphic indication of dome spacing.

705.5.4 Alignment. Truncated domes shall be aligned in a square grid pattern.

❖ See Figure 705.5 for a graphic indication of dome alignment. The square grid pattern was chosen over the diagonal grid pattern so persons using a wheelchair can locate their wheels between rows of domes to cross the detectable warning. The diagonal grid used in the past was difficult to maneuver over and could cause some discomfort for persons using wheelchairs as they crossed them.

706 Assistive Listening Systems

❖ Assistive listening systems are required by the model codes in assembly areas, such as a live theater, lecture hall, courtroom or movie theater. They work by increasing the loudness of sounds, minimizing background noise, reducing the effect of distance and overriding poor acoustics. The number of system receivers required is based on seating capacity. It is important that some of the receivers be compatible with hearing aids. Availability of assistive listening systems must be identified by posting the international symbol for access for hearing loss (Section 703.6.3.3).

In the past, a hard-wired system was used; however, listeners had to sit in certain locations and use headphones. With the new technologies, almost all assisted listening systems are wireless. Portable systems are feasible for special accommodations; however, the required systems must be permanently installed.

The three types of wireless devices are the FM system, the audio induction loop and the infrared system. Each system has advantages and benefits for particular uses.

All three types of systems require that the person who is speaking use a microphone. Sound is converted and transferred by radio waves (FM), invisible light waves (infrared) or electromagnetic field (audio induction loop) to the listener. The listener uses a receiver with headphones to hear the speaker. If the listener wears hearing aids or a cochlear implant processor which has a telecoil (T-coil), a neckloop can be used in place of the headphones with the FM or infrared systems. Neckloops transmit the sound directly from the receiver into the aid or processor. Sound pro-

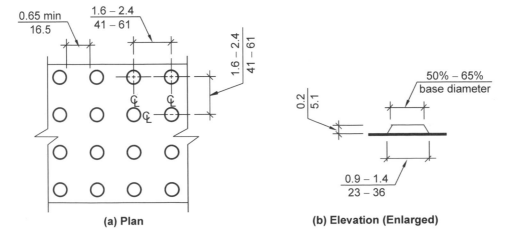

(a) Plan   (b) Elevation (Enlarged)

Fig. 705.5
Truncated Dome Size and Spacing

vided by an audio induction loop can be heard by a wearer of hearing aids or a cochlear implant processor with T-coils, without an additional receiver or neckloop. All systems can be integrated with existing PA systems.

There is no difference in the amount of understanding provided by the three systems (refer to Table C706) which are used as public accommodations, as long as they are of good quality. The choice of which system should be provided will depend on other factors, such as the need for confidentiality.

No matter what system is used, selection of the microphone is critical. For best sound quality microphones should:

- Limit background noise,
- Provide the highest gain signal,

- Accommodate speech over all frequencies and
- Be used with an automatic mixer where multiple microphones are used.

706.1 General. Accessible assistive listening systems in assembly areas shall comply with Section 706.

❖ An assistive listening system is used in conjunction with an audio amplification system to assist those individuals who are hard of hearing to have the same audio information as is being transmitted to the general public at the event. The scoping provisions from the jurisdiction having authority typically require these systems when the audio information provided over the audio amplification system is necessary for the understanding of the event.

Table C706
SUMMARY OF ASSISTIVE LISTENING DEVICES

SYSTEM	ADVANTAGES	DISADVANTAGES	TYPICAL APPLICATIONS
INDUCTION LOOP Transmitter: Transducer wired to induction loop around listening area. Receiver: Self-contained induction receiver or personal hearing aid with telecoil.	Accommodate a large group of people or an individual based on size of loop Cost-effective Low maintenance Easy to use Unobtrusive May be possible to integrate into existing public address system. Some hearing aids can function as receivers	With large loops, signal spills over to adjacent rooms Susceptible to electrical interference Limited portability Inconsistent signal strength Head position affects signal strength Lack of standards for induction coil performance Receivers with a telecoil are required for people who do not have a telecoil in their hearing aid	Meeting areas Theaters Churches and Temples Conference rooms Classrooms TV viewing
FM Transmitter: Flashlight sized worn by speaker Receiver: With personal hearing aid via DAI or induction neck loop and telecoil; or self-contained with earphone(s)	Highly portable Can be used indoors or outdoors Covers large areas Different channels allow use by different groups within the same facility High user mobility Variable for large range of hearing losses	Signal spills over to adjacent rooms Subject to interference High cost of receivers Equipment obtrusive Custom fitting to individual user may be required	Classrooms Tour Groups Meeting areas Outdoor events One-on-one
INFRARED Transmitter: Emitter in line-of-sight with receiver Receiver: Self-contained or with personal hearing aid via DAI or induction neck loop and telecoil	Easy to use Ensures privacy or confidentiality Moderate cost Can often be integrated into existing public address system	Line-of-sight required between emitter and receiver Ineffective outdoors Limited portability Requires installation	Theaters Churches and Temples Auditoriums Meetings requiring confidentiality Courtrooms

Source: Rehab Brief, National Institute on Disability and Rehabilitation Research, Washington, DC, Vol. XII, No. 10, (1990).

706.2 Receiver Jacks. Receivers required for use with an assistive listening system shall include a ¹/₈-inch (3.2 mm) standard mono jack.

❖ The intent of the requirement for receiver jacks is to ensure compatibility with standard headphones or earbuds.

706.3 Receiver Hearing-Aid Compatibility. Receivers required to be hearing aid compatible shall interface with telecoils in hearing aids through the provision of neck loops.

❖ The intent of the requirement for receivers is to ensure compatibility with hearing aids.

706.4 Sound Pressure Level. Assistive listening systems shall be capable of providing a sound pressure level of 110 dB minimum and 118 dB maximum, with a dynamic range on the volume control of 50 dB.

❖ The increase in sound levels should allow the user to hear above the ambient noise of the room.

706.5 Signal-to-Noise Ratio. The signal-to-noise ratio for internally generated noise in assistive listening systems shall be 18 dB minimum.

❖ The electronic noise in the system can be a problem for the listener. The tolerance of noise to the amount of noise in the system is the signal to noise ratio.

706.6 Peak Clipping Level. Peak clipping shall not exceed 18 dB of clipping relative to the peaks of speech.

❖ The distortion caused when the gain of an amplifier is increased to a point where the high points, or peaks, of the signal or waveform are cut off at a level where the amplifying circuits are driven beyond their overload point. This is also called over-modulation. Peak clipping can be avoided by gain reduction, compression of the signal or the use of a limiter.

707 Automatic Teller Machines (ATMs) and Fare Machines

❖ Although this section is specifically geared toward ATMs and fare machines, similar machines must comply as much as applicable. For example, there are now machines that dispense lottery tickets, or many movie theaters allow people to buy tickets through an automated machine (see commentary Figure C707).

707.1 General. Accessible automatic teller machines and fare machines shall comply with Section 707.

❖ Requirements are applicable to automatic teller machines wherever walk-up access is provided, and to fare machines such as those in transportation facilities. Basic accessibility is provided by requiring a way to the machine, clear floor space, height, reach range and display requirements.

707.2 Clear Floor Space. A clear floor space complying with Section 305 shall be provided in front of the machine.

EXCEPTION: Clear floor space is not required at drive up only automatic teller machines and fare machines.

❖ The ATM can be accessed by either a front approach or a parallel approach. A clear floor space is not required at drive-up facilities. With a front approach, clearance must be provided to the front of the unit because effective reach is not much past the toes of the person in the wheelchair. Providing knee and/or toe clearance would make access easier because it would allow for a closer approach. Where a parallel approach is provided, the clear floor space should be centered on the controls.

707.3 Operable Parts. Operable parts shall comply with Section 309. Each operable part shall be able to be differentiated by sound or touch, without activation.

EXCEPTION: Drive up only automatic teller machines and fare machines shall not be required to comply with Section 309.2 or 309.3.

❖ All operable parts, including items such as keypad, deposit slots, money or ticket dispensing and coin slots must be within the 15 inch to 48 inch (380 to 1220 mm) reach range. To assist persons with visual impairments, each operable part must be distinguishable by either touch or sound without activation. For example, the keypad can meet the provisions of Section 707.5. Drive-up machines are not required to provide the clear floor space or reach ranges in Section 309, but the operable parts must still meet the operational requirements in Section 309.4. Controls for user activation must:

- Be automatic or operable with one hand;
- Operate without tight grasping, pinching or twist of the wrist;
- Require no more than 5 pounds (22 N) force to activate.

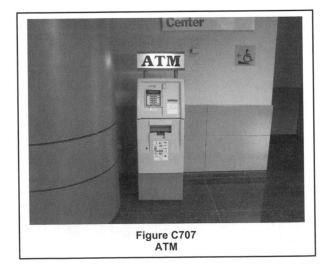

Figure C707
ATM

707.4 Privacy. Automatic teller machines shall provide the opportunity for the same degree of privacy of input and output available to all individuals.

❖ In addition to people with visual impairment, people who are short of stature cannot effectively block the video screen with their bodies, so they may prefer to use speech output. Screen output users can benefit from an option to render the screen blank, thereby affording them greater privacy and personal security.

An audio output or large print display that can be seen or heard by persons other than the person using the machine may create a privacy concern. Options could be a telephone handset or audio plugs so that a person could use a headset to hear audio output during the transaction.

707.5 Numeric Keys. Numeric keys shall be arranged in a 12-key ascending or descending telephone keypad layout. The number Five key shall have a single raised dot.

❖ Telephone keypads have numbers in an ascending order [Figure 707.5(a)] while computer keypads have numbers in a descending order [Figure 707.5(b)]. Both types of keypads are acceptable. The number 5 key must be designated tactilely with a raised dot.

707.6 Function Keys. Function keys shall comply with Section 707.6.

❖ Function keys are the buttons on an ATM or fare machine other than numeric keypads. Examples on an ATM are the 'Enter' or 'Clear' button. Examples on a fare machine might be the key for the desired station or zone or add/subtract value keys used to change the amount of money you want in the transportation card. Cues for the visually impaired are arrangement, marking and color coding.

707.6.1 Tactile Symbols. Function key surfaces shall have raised tactile symbols as shown in Table 707.6.1.

❖ It is not the intent to require these particular function keys, but if provided, standard tactile cues on the typical function keys will provide additional assistance for persons with visual impairments.

Table 707.6.1—Tactile Symbols

KEY FUNCTION	DESCRIPTION OF TACTILE SYMBOL	TACTILE SYMBOL
Enter or Proceed:	CIRCLE	○
Clear or Correct:	LEFT AROW	←
Cancel:	"X"	×
Add Value:	PLUS SIGN	+
Decrease Value:	MINUS SIGN	−

707.6.2 Contrast. Function keys shall contrast visually from background surfaces. Characters and symbols on key surfaces shall contrast visually from key surfaces. Visual contrast shall be either light-on-dark or dark-on-light.

EXCEPTION: Tactile symbols required by Section 707.6.1 shall not be required to comply with Section 707.6.2.

❖ The function buttons/keys must contrast with the surrounding surfaces. The requirement is for the keys themselves, not the tactile symbols in Section 707.6.1. A contrast of at least 70 percent based on the light reflectance value is recommended. See commentary for Section 703.2.10.

707.7 Display Screen. The display screen shall comply with Section 707.7.

❖ Video display screens are found on almost all ATMs and some fare machines. Even though tactile cues used for keys would not be technically feasible, the screens can improve access with good design for viewing height, contrast and fonts.

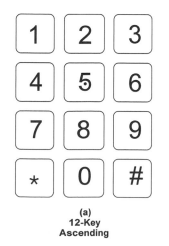

(a)
**12-Key
Ascending**

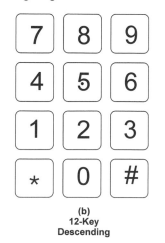

(b)
**12-Key
Descending**

**Fig. 707.5
Numeric Key Layout**

707.7.1 Visibility. The display screen shall be visible from a point located 40 inches (1015 mm) above the center of the clear floor space in front of the machine.

EXCEPTION: Drive up only automatic teller machines and fare machines shall not be required to comply with Section 707.7.1.

❖ The average eye height for an adult male using a wheelchair is from 43 inches to 51 inches (1090 to 1295 mm). The visibility of the screen is also an issue for persons who are short of stature.

The screen need not be located at 40 inches (1015 mm) above the floor, but rather it must be seen from a point 40 inches above the floor. This requirement is not applicable for drive-up machines.

707.7.2 Characters. Characters displayed on the screen shall be in a sans serif font. The uppercase letter "I" shall be used to determine the allowable height of all characters of the font. The uppercase letter "I" of the font shall be $^3/_{16}$ inch (4.8 mm) minimum in height. Characters shall contrast with their background with either light characters on a dark background, or dark characters on a light background.

❖ In typography, a sans serif typeface is one that does not have the small features called 'serifs' at the end of strokes. Sans serif typefaces or a simple serif typeface without excessive flourishes or deviation in stroke width have been found to be the most legible. A severely nearsighted person has to be much closer to see a character of a given size accurately than a person with normal visual acuity. For an example of serif and sans serif typeface, see commentary Figure C703.3.4.

The Society for Environmental Graphic Design (SEGD) recommends using the capital "O" and the capital "I" for calculating proportions for text. If numbers are used to identify spaces, use the numbers "0" and "1." Uniform stroke width also increases legibility. See Section 703.2 for additional guidance on visual characters.

Light characters on a dark background are usually considered easier to read than dark characters on a light background; however, either is permitted. A contrast of at least 70 percent based on the light reflectance value is recommended. Possible glare on the screen should also be considered.

707.8 Speech Output. Machines shall be speech enabled. Operating instructions and orientation, visible transaction prompts, user input verification, error messages, and all displayed information for full use shall be accessible to and independently usable by individuals with vision impairments. Speech shall be delivered through a mechanism that is readily available to all users including, but not limited to, an industry standard connector or a tele-phone handset. Speech shall be recorded or digitized human, or synthesized.

EXCEPTIONS:

1. Audible tones shall be permitted in lieu of speech for visible output that is not displayed for security purposes, including but not limited to, asterisks representing personal identification numbers.

2. Advertisements and other similar information shall not be required to be audible unless they convey information that can be used in the transaction being conducted.

3. Where speech synthesis cannot be supported, dynamic alphabetic output shall not be required to be audible.

❖ Visual instructions are provided on all ATMs or fare machines for persons who may not be familiar with their operation. This information must be available in an audible format as well. The intent for this section is a performance standard so that manufacturers can develop solutions that take advantage of new technologies.

707.8.1 User Control. Speech shall be capable of being repeated and interrupted by the user. There shall be a volume control for the speech function.

EXCEPTION: Speech output for any single function shall be permitted to be automatically interrupted when a transaction is selected.

❖ See the commentary in Section 707.8.

707.8.2 Receipts. Where receipts are provided, speech output devices shall provide audible balance inquiry information, error messages, and all other information on the printed receipt necessary to complete or verify the transaction.

EXCEPTIONS:

1. Machine location, date and time of transaction, customer account number, and the machine identifier shall not be required to be audible.

2. Information on printed receipts that duplicates audible information available on-screen shall not be required to be presented in the form of an audible receipt.

3. Printed copies of bank statements and checks shall not be required to be audible.

❖ Information available on the printed receipt must be available audibly, the same as the requirements for audio output for performing the transaction (Section 707.8).

The exceptions are recognition of irrelevant information, duplicated information or information that may be lengthy.

707.9 Input Controls. At least one tactually discernible input control shall be provided for each function. Where provided, key surfaces not on active areas of display screens shall be raised above surrounding surfaces. Where membrane keys are the only method of input, each shall be tactually discernable from surrounding surfaces and adjacent keys.

❖ Not all machines use standard key pads or buttons. The intent for this section is a performance standard so that manufacturers could develop solutions that can take advantage of new technologies.

707.10 Braille Instructions. Braille instructions for initiating the speech mode shall be provided. Braille shall comply with Section 703.4.

❖ Braille instructions must be provided to initiate the speech output required in Section 707.8. Braille must be the Grade 2 literary Braille specified in Section 703.4. This information should also be available on a sign for persons who may have difficulty reading the display screen.

708 Two-Way Communication Systems

❖ Two-way communication systems are used at security entrances, for closed circuit entry systems, from areas of refuge, etc. These systems must be available for person with hearing impairments.

708.1 General. Accessible two-way communication systems shall comply with Section 708.

❖ The authority having jurisdiction specifies when these systems are required (e.g., areas of refuge), however, when systems are provided voluntarily (e.g., security entrances, closed circuit entry systems) the systems should still comply. In addition, the system must also meet the general requirement for operable parts in Section 309.

708.2 Audible and Visual Indicators. The system shall provide both visual and audible signals.

❖ Different systems and purposes will result in different application needs. Visual indicators, such as a flashing light or text output, as appropriate, will make this system available to persons with hearing impairments. Audible information, provided by a speaker or a recording, as appropriate, will make this system available to persons with vision impairments.

708.3 Handsets. Handset cords, if provided, shall be 29 inches (735 mm) minimum in length.

❖ If a telephone handset is used, the cord should be a minimum of 29 inches (740 mm) long so that it could be used by a person using a wheelchair or scooter or a standing person. The handset should also be configured to address the needs of persons who have hearing impairments. See the provisions for telephones in Section 704 for additional information.

Chapter 8. Special Rooms and Spaces

❖ Chapter 8 contains the technical requirements for spaces with unique types of usage. This includes assembly seating; dressing, fitting and locker rooms; kitchens and kitchenettes; transportation facilities; holding and housing cells; courthouses.

- Section 801 is a general statement about the Chapter 8 criteria being applicable for the special types of spaces addressed in this chapter when required by the authority having jurisdiction.

- Section 802 contains criteria for fixed assembly seating arrangements.

- Section 803 provides technical criteria for spaces where a person may need to change clothes, such as a dressing room, fitting room or locker room.

- Section 804 addresses requirements for kitchens that are found outside of a Type A or Type B dwelling unit. Kitchens in Accessible units (Section 1002.12) reference Section 804 for requirements. There are also provisions for kitchenettes and wet bars that may be found in such areas as office break rooms.

- Section 805 deals with all types of transportation facilities such as bus stops and train stations.

- Requirements for holding cells and housing cells, such as those found in police stations, jails and courthouses, are covered in Section 806.

- Criteria unique to courtrooms are addressed in Section 807.

801 General

801.1 Scope. Special rooms and spaces required to be accessible by the scoping provisions adopted by the administrative authority shall comply with the applicable provisions of Chapter 8.

❖ The provisions in this chapter are intended to state requirements for the specialized use areas that may not be addressed elsewhere in the standard but are required for accessibility and usability by people with physical impairments. It is not the intent for the provisions in this chapter to exclude the application of any provision required elsewhere. All applicable accessibility requirements contained elsewhere in this standard, or required in the scoping documents adopted by the administrative authority, are to be applied in addition to the requirements in this chapter. Note that these provisions apply to these special rooms and spaces when required by the scoping provisions (see Section 201).

802 Assembly Areas

802.1 General. Wheelchair spaces and wheel chair space locations in assembly areas with spectator seating shall comply with Section 802.

❖ Although there are many types of assembly areas, the criteria in this section deals specifically with fixed seating arrangements. These requirements can be applicable to a variety of venues: including spaces such as theaters, sports arenas, churches, courtroom gallery seating, lecture halls, grandstands at high school football fields and bleachers at Little League baseball parks. Planned wheelchair positions for viewing speakers, performances, sporting events or other productions in a place of assembly enhance the viewing for those persons using wheelchairs and the general safety of the entire audience (see commentary Figure C802.1).

In the past, many places of assembly placed persons using wheelchairs in aisles and cross aisles, drawing unnecessary attention to the person with a disability and possibly obstructing required aisles for everyone. Having persons in wheelchairs sit in ramped aisles also made for unstable seating. Creating a special section where people were segregated was not a successful solution. Often, these areas did not provide a view similar to the options available to the general audience.

The criteria in this section have been extensively expanded in this edition to address concerns about dispersion and line-of-sight for seating locations for persons using wheelchairs or scooters and their companions. Wheelchair spaces are locations for individuals using a wheelchair or scooter. The number of wheelchair spaces required is based on the number of seats in the venue and is specified by the authority having jurisdiction. When benches, bleachers or pews are provided, the number of seats is typically based on one occupant for each 18 inches of seating length in most building codes.

Each 'wheelchair space' must have an associated companion seat (Section 802.7). The requirements for size (Sections 802.3 and 802.4), approach (Section 802.5), overlap (Section 802.5.1), integration (Section 802.6) and companion seat adjacency and alignment (Section 802.7) must work together for proper placement of the wheelchair space within the seating rows.

Groups of wheelchair spaces and their associated companion spaces are called 'wheelchair space locations.' Concerns about the quality and variety of choices of the wheelchair seating are addressed in sections on integration (Section 802.6), line of sight (Section 802.9), and dispersion of locations from side-to-side (Section 802.10.1), front-to-back (Section 802.10.2) and by type (Section 802.10.3). There are also unique requirements for movie theaters (Section 802.10.4).

Designated aisle seats are seating that can be used by persons with mobility impairments who have difficulty moving into the aisle accessway between rows (Section 802.8).

**Figure C802.1
ASSEMBLY SEATING**

802.2 Floor Surfaces. The floor surface of wheelchair space locations shall have a slope not steeper than 1:48 and shall comply with Section 302.

❖ The wheelchair space location must be substantially level for safety and comfort. See Section 302 for surface requirements.

The wheelchair space will typically have more depth than one row of general seats. When the wheelchair space is in seating having a tiered or sloped floor, a curb or barrier may be necessary at the edge of a raised wheelchair space location to provide a higher level of safety for persons that may be sitting near the edge of that raised area. If the drop-off is high enough, a guard may be required by the building code for issues of safety with the minimum height determined by whether or not it constrains the line of sight for a person seated on that wheelchair space location (see commentary Figure C802.2).

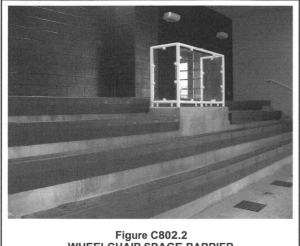

Figure C802.2
WHEELCHAIR SPACE BARRIER

802.3 Width. A single wheelchair space shall be 36 inches (915 mm) minimum in width. Where two adjacent wheelchair spaces are provided, each wheelchair space shall be 33 inches (840 mm) minimum in width.

❖ The width of a single wheelchair space is 6 inches (150 mm) greater than the clear floor or ground space required by Section 305 for maneuvering clearances within seating. When two wheelchair spaces are provided adjacent to each other, a slightly narrower wheelchair space is permitted because they share maneuvering space (see Figure 802.3 and commentary Figure C802.3).

Note that Section 802.7 requires a companion seat on at least one side of each wheelchair space, therefore, the maximum number of wheelchair spaces immediately adjacent to each other would be two.

802.4 Depth. Where a wheelchair space location can be entered from the front or rear, the wheelchair space shall be 48 inches (1220 mm) minimum in depth. Where a wheelchair space location can only be entered from the side, the wheelchair space shall be 60 inches (1525 mm) minimum in depth.

❖ When a person can pull into a wheelchair space forward or backwards, the required depth is the same as a clear floor or ground space (Section 305.3). If a person can make a full turn into the full depth of the space, similar to the allowances for accessible routes in Chapter 4, the wheelchair space is required to be 48 inches in depth minimum. Side approach to the wheelchair space requires maneuvering into a position with movements similar to parallel parking. This requires more space than the forward or rear approach. The parallel approach depth is similar to that required for the alcove provisions (Section 305.7) (see Figure 802.4 and commentary Figure C802.3).

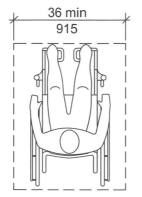

36 min
915

(a) Single Space

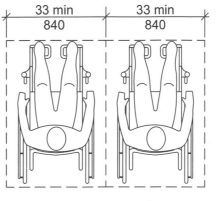

33 min | 33 min
840 | 840

(b) Multiple Adjacent Spaces

Fig. 802.3
Width of a wheelchair Space in Assembly Areas

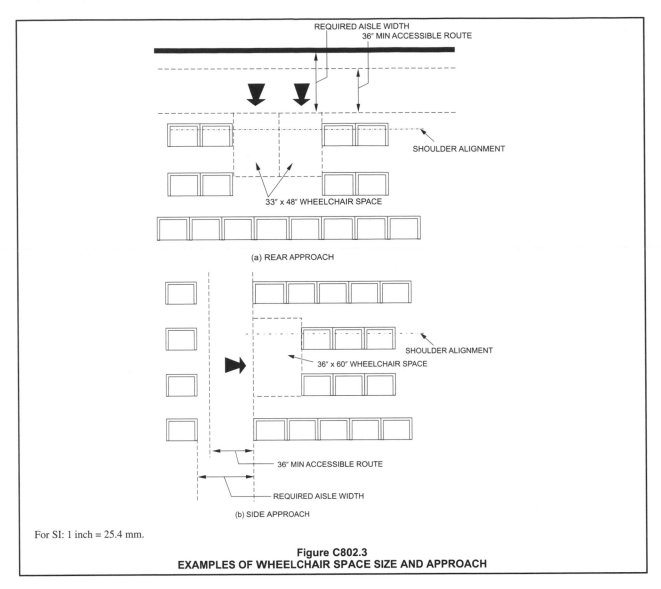

For SI: 1 inch = 25.4 mm.

Figure C802.3
EXAMPLES OF WHEELCHAIR SPACE SIZE AND APPROACH

Note that Section 802.5 requires that the approach to a wheelchair space be from an accessible route; therefore, a side approach wheelchair space will be a single wheelchair space requiring both greater width and depth than clear floor or ground space.

802.5 Approach. The wheelchair space location shall adjoin an accessible route. The accessible route shall not overlap the wheelchair space location.

❖ An accessible route must connect the wheelchair viewing space with the accessible entrances and any services, such as beverage and food stands, souvenir stands, toilet rooms, etc. The wheelchair space cannot overlap the accessible route, so the wheelchair space must either be the end point of an accessible route, or the route must be along one side of the wheelchair space. The route cannot pass through one wheelchair space to get to another wheelchair space (see commentary Figure C802.3).

The location of the accessible route and aisle (Section 802.5.1), should be measured from the wheelchair space when the wheelchair is positioned for shoulder alignment with the companion seat (Section 802.7.2). The wheelchair user should not have to move forward to get out of the aisle or accessible route, even when additional space is provided in front of the space.

802.5.1 Overlap. A wheelchair space location shall not overlap the required width of an aisle.

❖ The intent of this requirement is that a person occupying the wheelchair space would not obstruct the main exit paths from seating areas, i.e., the aisle, similar to other seats (see commentary Figure C802.3 and Section 802.5).

Seating arrangements include aisles and aisle accessways. An aisle accessway is the narrow path between the rows of seats that connect to an aisle. An aisle is the path that connects aisle accessways to other components of the exit system. The minimum clear width of both aisles and aisle accessways is defined in the building codes. Where aisles are wider than required, the wheelchair space is permitted to

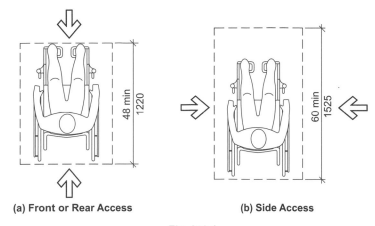

(a) Front or Rear Access

(b) Side Access

Fig. 802.4
Depth of a Wheelchair Space in Assembly Areas

overlap the portion of the aisle that is in excess of the width required. Note that Section 802.7.2 requires shoulder alignment between the wheelchair space and companion seat. Therefore, a wheelchair space needs to overlap an aisle accessway. A person using a wheelchair can move forward or backward slightly to allow someone to get to their seat from the aisle and down the aisle accessway, similar to another person standing to let them by. The number of seats along an aisle accessway is very limited compared to an aisle. Even though the wheelchair space must overlap an aisle accessway, the wheelchair space is not permitted to overlap the required width of an aisle.

802.6 Integration of Wheelchair Space Locations. Wheelchair space locations shall be an integral part of any seating area.

❖ Each wheelchair space location must be within its associated seating area as much as possible. Note that Section 802.10.3 requires wheelchair spaces to be dispersed into each type where there are multiple distinct seating areas. However, complete integration of wheelchair spaces is limited. For example, guards may be required around wheelchair space locations where they must be elevated for line of sight over standing spectators to prevent someone from accidentally rolling off the edge of the elevated area. Guard requirements can be found in the building codes.

802.7 Companion Seat. A companion seat, complying with Section 802.7, shall be provided beside each wheelchair space.

❖ Locating a wheelchair space next to a seat for a companion allows wheelchair users and at least one person accompanying them to be seated together. The companion seat should be similar to the adjacent seating and placed so that someone in a wheelchair could align their shoulders with their companion to ensure a viewing experience similar to that of others attending the event (Sections 802.7.1 and 802.7.2).

A 'wheelchair space location' that follows the repeating pattern of companion seat, two wheelchair

spaces, companion seat along a row would allow for the companion to be someone in a seat or another person using a wheelchair.

802.7.1 Companion Seat Type. The companion seat shall be comparable in size and quality to assure equivalent comfort to the seats within the seating area adjacent to the wheelchair space location. Companion seats shall be permitted to be moveable.

❖ The companion seat is essentially the same seat as provided elsewhere in the seating area. If the option of movable seats is chosen, those seats should be similar to the fixed seating. Movable seats allow greater ability to tailor the wheelchair seating location to the needs of the people wanting to sit there; however, they require greater management. Fixed seats promote less flexibility but simplify operation policies. Some venues have moved to providing a mixture of fixed and loose seating, thus providing additional flexibility and integration with the spaces available for wheelchair seating.

802.7.2 Companion Seat Alignment. In row seating, the companion seat shall be located to provide shoulder alignment with the wheelchair space occupant. The shoulder of the wheelchair space occupant is considered to be 36 inches (915 mm) from the front of the wheelchair space. The floor surface for the companion seat shall be at the same elevation as the wheelchair space floor surface.

❖ The intent of this provision is to make possible interaction between the person using the wheelchair and the person sitting next to them. The seating should be at the same floor elevation, and the shoulders of both people should align. In a front or rear approach space with a 48 inch (1220 mm) depth, the shoulder alignment is both 12 inches (305 mm) from the back and 36 inches (915 mm) from the front. This allows space for the back wheels.

In a side approach space, with a 60 inch depth (1525 mm), the shoulder alignment would be 36 inches (915 mm) from the front. However, because the person in a wheelchair aligns with the companion chair, both would have similar lines of sight regardless of whether it is 36 inches (915 mm) from the front or 12 inches (305 mm) from the back of a side approach space. The overriding criterion is the person in a wheelchair and the companion be able to sit side by side with lines of sight similar to those of other spectators (see commentary Figure C802.7.2).

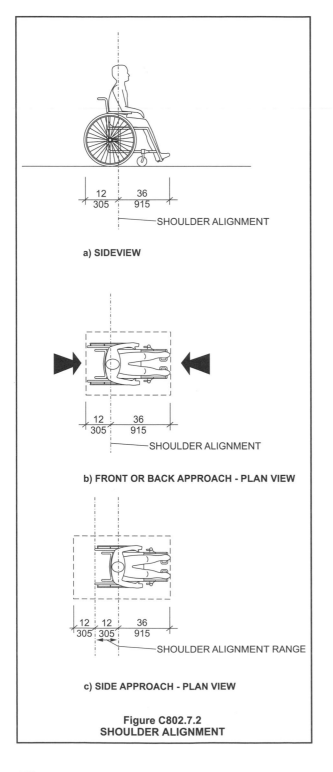

a) SIDEVIEW

b) FRONT OR BACK APPROACH - PLAN VIEW

c) SIDE APPROACH - PLAN VIEW

**Figure C802.7.2
SHOULDER ALIGNMENT**

802.8 Designated Aisle Seats. Designated aisle seats shall comply with Section 802.8.

❖ Designated aisle seats are seats located along the aisles in a fixed seating arrangement. These seats need not be located directly on an accessible route. The authority having jurisdiction determines the percentage of aisle seats required to serve as designated aisle seats. The designated aisle seats are used by persons with mobility impairments that make it difficult for them to move down the aisle accessways between the seating rows. For a description of aisles and aisle accessways, see the commentary for Section 802.5.1 (see commentary Figure C802.8).

**Figure C802.8
DESIGNATED AISLE SEATS**

802.8.1 Armrests. Where armrests are provided on seating in the immediate area of designated aisle seats, folding or retractable armrests shall be provided on the aisle side of the designated aisle seat.

❖ Armrests are not required, but if provided for the seating in the same area, armrests are required for the designated aisle seats. To accommodate persons who may need additional room to get into the seat, the armrest along the aisle must be capable of being moved out of the way. A removable or no armrest is not acceptable. The person using the seat may need the armrest for support or assistance to raise or lower themselves in the seat.

End caps on pew type seating (e.g., typically found in religious facilities or courtroom galleries, see commentary Figure C802.8.1) are not considered arm rests.

802.8.2 Identification. Each designated aisle seat shall be identified by a sign or marker.

❖ The designated aisle seats must be designated in some manner. The choice of what is acceptable is up to the designer, but should be consistent throughout the facility.

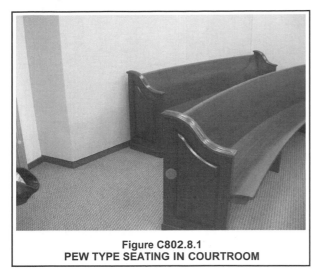

Figure C802.8.1
PEW TYPE SEATING IN COURTROOM

802.9 Lines of Sight. Where spectators are expected to remain seated for purposes of viewing events, spectators in wheelchair space locations shall be provided with a line of sight in accordance with Section 802.9.1. Where spectators in front of the wheelchair space locations will be expected to stand at their seats for purposes of viewing events, spectators in wheelchair space locations shall be provided with a line of sight in accordance with Section 802.9.2.

❖ A variety of locations and views must be available to the spectator using a wheelchair. This requirement precludes the grouping of all wheelchair spaces into one location because that would limit the sight line options available for the persons using wheelchairs and their companions. Although the average adult male seating in a wheelchair has an eye height of 43 to 51 inches (1090 to 1295 mm), the eye height of the companion will depend on the seat provided and average adult anthropometrics. The line of sight must be considered for both types of viewing.

The line of sight is dependent on the events that will occur in the venue. For example, in a courtroom or opera house, the seating is designed for seated spectators. Even though the audience in the courtroom may stand for the entrance of the judge, or stand in a theater for an ovation at the end of the performance, the audience does not typically stand during the event. In religious facilities, participants may stand for part of the services, but this is for group participation, not to view an event; therefore, seating in religious facilities is designed assuming seated spectators.

In most sports facilities, the audience is expected to stand during exciting and critical times of the event; therefore, wheelchair seating must be designed for the person in a wheelchair to see over spectators standing in front of them. The intent is to provide a line of sight for the spectator in a wheelchair the same as or better than

that of an adjacent standing spectator. A tennis stadium is an example of a sports facility where spectators are not expected to stand at exciting and critical times, so seating could be designed for seated spectators.

Within a luxury box or suite, because it is reasonable to assume the people in this area know each other and would be accomodating, line-of-site over standing spectators would not be required in the suite.

The options covered in Section 802.9 deal with typical venues. In a unique situation, such as a planetarium or omni-max, the seating arrangement should provide alternatives that meet the intent (see Section 103).

802.9.1 Line of Sight over Seated Spectators. Where spectators are expected to remain seated during events, spectators seated in wheelchair space locations shall be provided with lines of sight to the performance area or playing field comparable to that provided to spectators in closest proximity to the wheelchair space location. Where seating provides lines of sight over heads, spectators in wheelchair space locations shall be afforded lines of sight complying with Section 802.9.1.1. Where wheelchair space locations provide lines of sight over the shoulder and between heads, spectators in wheelchair space locations shall be afforded lines of sight complying with Section 802.9.1.2.

❖ The line of sight from the spectator to the event depends upon several factors, which may include items such as the vertical rise between rows of seats, the location of the focal point and/or points and the extent of event to be viewed. The line of sight may be provided between the heads of the audience members sitting in the rows in front or provided over the heads of audience members. A spectator in a wheelchair must be provided the same line of sight or better than that provided the general seating whether it is between heads or over heads.

Note that this does not require that seating be designed for spectators to see over or between heads of the spectators in front of them, but if the facility is designed in this manner, the wheelchair spaces must have a view that is the same or better than the average spectator.

802.9.1.1 Lines of Sight over Heads. Spectators seated in wheelchair space locations shall be afforded lines of sight over the heads of seated individuals in the first row in front of the wheelchair space location.

❖ In facilities where the lines of sight for spectators are designed to be unobstructed by the head of an average height spectator, spectators in wheelchairs shall be provided lines of sight unobstructed by the head of an average height spectator.

The average eye height of someone in a wheelchair is at least as high as the average eye height of a general spectator; therefore, this is typically not a problem when there is no significant difference in the vertical rise between rows of seats and those rows having wheelchair spaces.

802.9.1.2 Lines of Sight between Heads. Spectators seated in wheelchair space locations shall be afforded lines of sight over the shoulders and between the heads of seated individuals in the first row in front of the wheelchair space location.

❖ The basic requirement is to provide for a line of site similar to that provided to the surrounding seating arrangements. See the commentary for Section 802.9.1.1.

802.9.2 Line of Sight over Standing Spectators. Wheelchair space locations required to provide a line of sight over standing spectators shall comply with Section 802.9.2.

❖ In venues where the typical crowd behavior is to stand during exciting and critical times of an event, spectators in wheelchairs shall be provided the same line of sight as adjacent standing spectators. If the spectators are expected to stand, and wheelchair locations are provided where the line of sight would be over that area to the event, the line of site for the wheelchair space and the associated companion seat must be provided over the standing spectators. The designer should use the eye level of an average adult male to determine the line of site for standing spectators.

802.9.2.1 Distance from Adjacent Seating. The front of the wheelchair space location

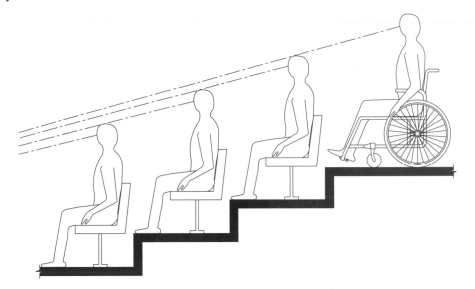

Fig. 802.9.1.1
Lines of Sight over the Heads of Seated Spectators

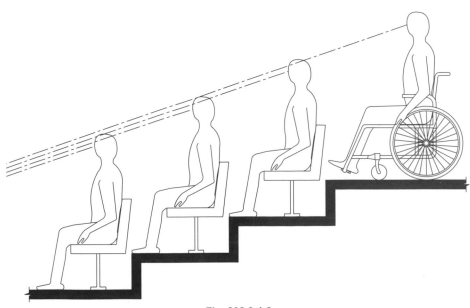

Fig. 802.9.1.2
Lines of Sight between the Heads of Seated Spectators

shall be 12 inches (305 mm) maximum from the back of the chair or bench in front.

❖ The distance between the wheelchair space and the chair in the row immediately in front is an essential criterion to provide spectators in wheelchairs with the same line of sight as standing spectators because lines of sight are based on mathematical calculation. When the wheelchair platform is at an elevation above the seating tread in front in accordance with Table 802.9.2.2 and the wheelchair space is located 12 inches (305 mm) from the chair in front, the spectator in a wheelchair is provided essentially the same lines of sight as standing spectators. Wheelchair spaces that are located closer than 12 inches (305 mm) to the row immediately in front would have better lines of sight and wheelchair spaces that are located more than 12 inches (305 mm) would see less than standing spectators. However, the designer could provide a sightline analysis to demonstrate essentially the same lines of sight as an alternative approach to Table 802.9.2.2 in support of more than 12 inches (305 mm). (see Section 103). As seen in Figure 802.9.2, the wheelchair space location may overlap a couple of rows of seats with the total depth.

802.9.2.2 Elevation. The elevation of the tread on which a wheelchair space location is located shall comply with Table 802.9.2.2. For riser heights other than those provided, interpolations shall be permitted.

❖ Table 802.9.2.2 provides the minimum height of the wheelchair space location above the tread of the row of seats in front to achieve a line of sight for persons in wheelchairs over spectators standing in front of them. Notes in Table 809.2.2 and Figure 802.9.2 provide the technical criteria based on basic geometry, assuming looking down towards an event. This type of configuration is typical for sports arenas looking down on a playing field or court. If a specific configuration is not indicated, interpolation between numbers is permitted to allow this table to cover a full range of seating options.

For example, the "tread" of a wheelchair space location associated with seating having 33 inch (835 mm) row spacing and 15 inch (380 mm) high rise between rows requires 43 inches (1090 mm) minimum height above the tread of the row in front of the wheelchair space, interpolated between 12 and 16 inch (305 and 405 mm) riser height. Likewise, the "tread" of a wheelchair space location associated with seating having 36 or 40 inch (915 or 1015 mm) row spacing and 15 inch (380 mm) high rise between rows also requires 43 inches (1090 mm) minimum height above the tread of the row in front of the wheelchair space; interpolation relates only to the height of the riser.

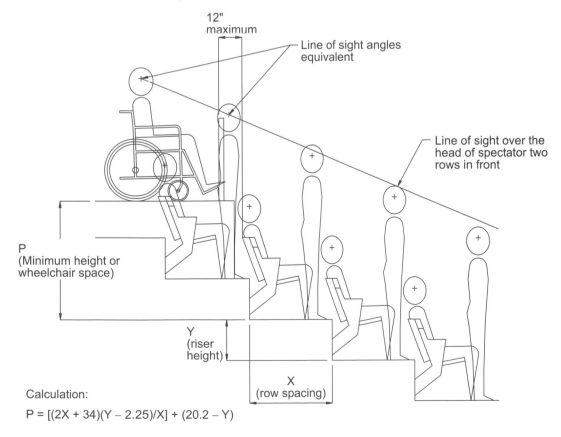

Calculation:

$$P = [(2X + 34)(Y - 2.25)/X] + (20.2 - Y)$$

**Fig. 802.9.2
Wheelchair Space Elevation**

Although this will typically result in a raised area, the wheelchair space location must be integrated into the seating as much as possible. See Section 802.6. Complete integration of wheelchair spaces is in conflict with this requirement for lines of sight over standing spectators. Building codes may require guards around wheelchair space locations because of the tread elevation of the wheelchair space location, or some other type of edge protection for safety reasons may be provided where guards are not required. If guards or barriers interfere with the line of sight, the building codes include unique provisions for sightline-constrained rails.

802.10 Wheelchair Space Dispersion. Wheelchair spaces shall be dispersed to the minimum number of locations in accordance with Table 802.10. Wheelchair space locations shall be dispersed in accordance with Sections 802.10.1, 802.10.2 and 802.10.3. In addition, in spaces utilized primarily for viewing motion picture projection, wheelchair space locations shall be dispersed in accordance with Section 802.10.4. Once the required number of wheelchair space locations has been met, further dispersion is not required.

❖ A wheelchair space location may include one wheelchair space and one companion seat or multiple wheelchair spaces and companion seats. Note that Section 802.7 requires a companion seat on at least one side of each wheelchair space; therefore, the maximum number of wheelchair spaces immediately adjacent to each other would be two. The number of wheelchair spaces required is greater than the number of wheelchair space "locations" required. Although similar in name, there are unique requirements for each. To provide a variety of choices for seating options, the wheelchair space locations must be dispersed to at least the minimum number of options indicated in Table 802.10. It is, of course, permitted to further disperse wheelchair space locations to more locations than the number required.

A common term in the assembly seating industry is to call the entire seating arrangement the 'seating bowl.' The seating bowl may be on one large sloped floor, a series of tiers or even a series of totally different floor levels (e.g., balconies). The seating bowl may totally surround the event, such as a theater in the round or a basketball arena; be in a U-shape, such as a baseball park; be on two straight sides, commonly found at a high school football stadium; or only on one side, such as in a movie projection theater, playhouse or performing arts center. The possible configurations are endless.

Table 802.9.2.2
Required Wheelchair Space Location Elevation Over Standing Spectators

Riser height	MINIMUM HEIGHT OF THE WHEELCHAIR SPACE LOCATION BASED ON ROW SPACING[1]		
	Rows less than 33 inches (840 mm)[2]	Rows 33 inches (840 mm) to 44 inches (1120 mm)[2]	Rows over 44 inches (1120 mm)[2]
0 inch (0 mm)	16 inch (405 mm)	16 inch (405 mm)	16 inch (405 mm)
4 inch (102 mm)	22 inch (560 mm)	21 inch (535 mm)	21 inch (535 mm)
8 inch (205 mm)	31 inch (785 mm)	30 inch (760 mm)	28 inch (710 mm)
12 inch (305 mm)	40 inch (1015 mm)	37 inch (940 mm)	35 inch (890 mm)
16 inch (406 mm)	49 inch (1245 mm)	45 inch (1145 mm)	42 inch (1065 mm)
20 inch (510 mm)[3]	58 inch (1475 mm)	53 inch (1345 mm)	49 inch (1245 mm)
24 inch (610 mm)	N/A	61 inch (1550 mm)	56 inch (1420 mm)
28 inch (710 mm)[4]	N/A	69 inch (1750 mm)	63 inch (1600 mm)
32 inch (815 mm)	N/A	N/A	70 inch (1780 mm)
36 inch (915 mm) and higher	N/A	N/A	77 inch (1955 mm)

[1]The height of the wheelchair space location is the vertical distance from the tread of the row of seats directly in front of the wheelchair space location to the tread of the wheelchair space location.
[2]The row spacing is the back-to-back horizontal distance between the rows of seats in front of the wheelchair space location.
[3]Seating treads less than 33 inches (840 mm) in depth are not permitted with risers greater than 18 inches (455 mm) in height.
[4]Seating treads less than 44 inches (1120 mm) in depth are not permitted with risers greater than 27 inches (685 mm) in height.

NOTE: Table 802.9.2.2 is based on providing a spectator in a wheelchair a line of sight over the head of a spectator two rows in front of the wheelchair space location using average anthropometrical data. The table is based on the following calculation: $[(2X+34)(Y-2.25)/X]+(20.2-Y)$ where Y is the riser height of the rows in front of the wheelchair space location and X is the tread depth of the rows in front of the wheelchair space location. The calculation is based on the front of the wheelchair space location being located 12 inches (305 mm) from the back of the seating tread directly in front and the eye of the standing spectator being set back 8 inches (205 mm) from the riser.

Table 802.10
Wheelchair Space Dispersion

Total seating in Assembly Areas	Minimum required number of dispersed locations
Up to 150	1
151 to 500	2
501 to 1000	3
1001 to 5,000	3, plus 1 additional space for each 1,000 seats or portions thereof above 1,000
5,001 and over	7, plus 1 additional space for each 2,000 seats or portions thereof above 5,000

When looking at the total seating arrangement or seating bowl, the intent is to disperse side to side, across or around the event (horizontal dispersion), front to back from the event (vertical dispersion) and by type of seating (e.g., box seats, seats with or without backs, reserved seating/open seating areas).

Because of the unique viewing angles inherent in the stadium style seating, now commonly offered in theaters used for viewing motion pictures, there are additional requirements for these types of venues in Section 802.10.4.

Note that dispersion is integrally related with the accessible means of egress provisions of the building code. Typically, building codes require at least two accessible means of egress where more than one exit is required. Therefore, there are practical limitations to dispersion because of accessible means of egress. In addition, dispersion is also integrally related to lines of sight over standing spectators because vertical heights necessary for such lines of sight affect options for accessible routes and accessible means of egress. (see Section 802.9.2).

802.10.1 Horizontal Dispersion. Wheelchair space locations shall be dispersed horizontally to provide viewing options. Locations shall be separated by a minimum of 10 intervening seats. Two wheelchair spaces shall be permitted to be located side-by-side.

> **EXCEPTION:** In venues where wheelchair space locations are provided on only one side or on two opposite sides of the performance area or playing field, horizontal dispersion is not required where the locations are within the 2nd or 3rd quartile of the total row length. The wheelchair space locations and companion seats shall be permitted to overlap into the 1st and 4th quartile of the total row length if the 2nd and 3rd quartile of the row length does not provide the required length for the wheelchair space locations and companion seats. All intermediate aisles shall be included in determining the total row length.

❖ Horizontal dispersion is required in order to provide viewing options around the event in a circular or U-shaped seating bowl, or from left to right in a straight line seating bowl. To be considered a different location, the wheelchair spaces must be a minimum of 10 intervening seats apart. Keep in mind that a "wheelchair space location" includes at least one wheelchair space and one companion. Therefore, the 10 intervening seats would not include the companion chair adjacent to a wheelchair space. Horizontal dispersion does not require every wheelchair space to be separated from every other wheelchair space. To allow for a companion to also use a wheelchair, two wheelchair spaces may be located between two companion seats.

The exception is to allow for the wheelchair space locations to provide for a better line of sight than the average line of sight provided for the seating bowl. For example, in a high school football stadium with seats down one or both sides of the field from goal line to goal line, if the wheelchair space locations are between the 25 yard lines, further horizontal dispersion is not required. Theses seats are considered in the location that is better than 50 percent of the general seating.

802.10.2 Dispersion for Variety of Distances from the Event. Wheelchair space locations shall be dispersed at a variety of distances from the event to provide viewing options. Locations shall be separated by a minimum of five intervening rows.

EXCEPTIONS:

1. In bleachers, wheelchair space locations shall not be required to be provided in rows other than rows at points of entry to bleacher seating.

2. In spaces utilized for viewing motion picture projections, assembly spaces with 300 seats or less shall not be required to comply with Section 802.10.2.

3. In spaces other than those utilized for viewing motion picture projections,

assembly spaces with 300 seats or less shall not be required to comply with Section 802.10.2 if the wheelchair space locations are within the front 50 percent of the total rows.

❖ Wheelchair space locations also need to provide a choice of seating from the front to the back of the seating bowl, to provides for additional viewing angles. Typically the building codes provide for vertical dispersion to different floor levels (e.g., balcony or box seating levels). This provision is for distance from the event within any seating bowl. Keep in mind that the seating bowl may be on one large sloped floor, a series of tiers or even a series of totally different floor levels (e.g., balconies). To be considered a separate wheelchair space location, the wheelchair spaces must be separated by a minimum of five intervening rows.

Bleacher seating is typically provided on its own structural frame. This is not single benches mounted on a floor or on tiered seating treads having structural framing integral with the building's floor or roof framing. Bleachers that actually fold up into a flat wall are common in schools and portions of some sporting venues. Because of safety concerns with providing portable or collapsible accessible routes into the bleacher types of seating, the exception allows for the wheelchair space locations to be incorporated only into the first row of seating [see commentary Figures C802.10.2(a) and (b)].

Even though Exception 2 would allow small motion picture theaters to not have dispersion front to back, the motion picture theater would still have to comply with the requirements in Sections 802.10.1 and 802.10.4.

Exception 3 is in recognition of what is considered the better half of the seating when moving from front to back. The exception is to allow for the wheelchair space locations to provide for a better line of sight than the average provided for the seating bowl. For example, in a typical auditorium with a front stage, if the wheelchair spaces are within the front half of the rows,

further dispersion is not required. Theses seats are considered in the location that is better than 50 percent of the general seating. Note that as a result of the different viewing angles in stadium style seating for movie projection theaters, this exception is not permitted for that particular type of seating arrangement.

802.10.3 Dispersion by Type. Where there are seating areas, each having distinct services or amenities, wheelchair space locations shall be provided within each seating area.

❖ Some venues offer a variety of types of seating; others venues have only one type of seats. Some examples would include a portion of the seating having back support and a portion that has no back support, or areas with reserved seating and areas with open seating, areas that have food or drink services available and areas that do not have such services. This provision is not meant to imply anything other than either the physical characteristics of the seats or the level of service provided.

802.10.4 Spaces Utilized Primarily for Viewing Motion Picture Projections. In spaces utilized primarily for viewing motion picture projections, wheelchair space locations shall comply with Section 802.10.4.

❖ Most of the theaters designed in the last couple of decades for viewing motion pictures have been designed using a tiered seating arrangement called 'stadium style' seating. A limited number still include the older style sloped floor seating, sometimes in rows in front of the 'stadium style' seating. The intent of this 'stadium style" is to allow for a more unobstructed view of the movie screen. Although viewing angles differ greatly in this type of venue, the main idea is that for stadium style seating, the best seats are in about the middle of the seating. The best seats in an older style sloped floor seating would include the rear of the seating because of the viewing angle relationship to the screen.

Figure C802.10.2(a)
BLEACHER SEATING EXAMPLES

Figure C802.10.2(b)
BLEACHER SEATING EXAMPLES

The average movie theater being constructed today is typical between 150 and 300 seats. Multiplex style theaters, may have a couple of auditoriums with between 300 and 500 seats.

802.10.4.1 Spaces with Seating on Risers. Where tiered seating is provided, wheelchair space locations shall be integrated into the tiered seating area.

❖ When stadium style seating is provided, at least some of the wheelchair spaces must be integrated into the tiers. If sloped seating is also provided, some of the wheelchair spaces may be located in the sloped seating if they also comply with the minimum distance from the screen indicated in Section 802.10.4.2.

802.10.4.2 Distance from the Screen. Wheelchair space locations shall be located within the rear 70 percent of the seats provided.

❖ Because the viewing angles are different for viewing a screen on the wall versus a three dimensional event on a stage or playing field, there are additional requirements for the wheelchair space locations back from the screen. The intent is for a person using a wheelchair to be in a location to view the screen that has desirable viewing angles so that they would not have to tilt their head back too far to see the extent of the screen. Wheelchair spaces located in the front of the movie seating rows would have steeper vertical viewing angles compared to seats in the rear of the movie seating rows. This provision requires that the wheelchair spaces be located in the more desirable seating of the theater. It would prohibit locating wheelchair spaces where viewing angles are too acute, which is especially important for those having limited range of head movement.

Note that there is the exception for variety of distances from the event in Exception 2 of Section 802.10.2 that is permitted for movie theaters with no more than 300 seats; however, the wheelchair space locations must still be located in the rear 70 percent of the seats. Movie theaters having more than 300 seats would still be required to vertically disperse wheelchair space locations, all of which must be located in the rear 70 percent of the seats.

When designing these types of facilities, it is important to consider the accessible route requirements for both ingress and egress from the wheelchair spaces. Access to the tiered seating, along with the exit dispersion requirements for safe evacuation found in the building codes, must be considered together.

803 Dressing, Fitting, and Locker Rooms

❖ The intent of this section is to provide requirements that would allow for a person using a mobility aid to have the ability to change clothes. Examples of these types of facilities include but are not limited to, dressing or fitting rooms in clothing retailers, dressing rooms or locker rooms in sports recreational facilities or at swimming pools, locker rooms where staff change from street clothes to uniforms. Spaces that provide storage lockers, such as at a bus depot or museum, must meet the provisions for lockers in Section 905, but not the locker room provisions of this section [see commentary Figures C803(a) and C803(b)].

Dressing rooms found in theaters may also need to comply with work station or work surface requirements found in the scoping documents and Section 902.

Small dressing areas are often provided immediately in front of shower stalls in facilities such as community pools or health clubs. Although not true dressing rooms, these are changing areas [See commentary Figure C803(c) for an example].

803.1 General. Accessible dressing, fitting, and locker rooms shall comply with Section 803.

❖ When required to be accessible, all of these facilities must be located on an accessible route and have doors, clear floor space and operable parts that meet the requirements established and discussed in the following sections. Benches are also required within the rooms (see commentary Figure C803.1).

Figure C803(a)
LOCKER AREA

803.2 Turning Space. A turning space complying with Section 304 shall be provided within the room.

❖ A 60-inch (1525 mm) diameter turning circle or a 60-inch T-turn space is required somewhere within the dressing, fitting or locker room. This section does not require individual dressing or fitting rooms; however, when individual changing areas are provided, the turning space must be available within the accessible changing room. When an open room is provided, such as a locker room, the turning space can be anywhere in the general room space. One side of the turning space can use the toe clearances under the bench required in Section 803.4 (see commentary Figure C803.1).

Figure C803(b)
LOCKER ROOM

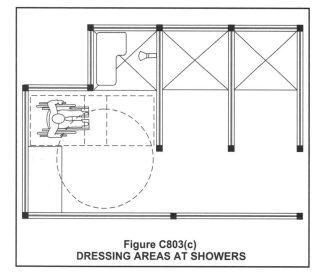

Figure C803(c)
DRESSING AREAS AT SHOWERS

803.3 Door Swing. Doors shall not swing into the room unless a clear floor space complying with Section 305.3 is provided within the room, beyond the arc of the door swing.

❖ When a door opens into a room or space, sufficient maneuvering space must be provided within the room for a person using a wheelchair to enter the room and close the door, use the facilities, and then be able to re-open the door and exit without undue difficulty.

The door swing may encroach into a clear floor space within a room or space because it is assumed that no one will be using the facility when the door is being opened. If a 30-inch by 48-inch (760 by 1220 mm) clear floor space is provided beyond the arc of the door swing, this will allow a person using a wheelchair to enter the room and close the door. Once the door is closed, the turning space required in Section 803.2 provides sufficient maneuvering space within the room for a person using a wheelchair to use the fixtures, reopen the door and exit without undue difficulty. This is consistent with the single occupant bathroom provisions in Section 602.3.2 Exception 2 (see commentary Figure C803.1).

803.4 Benches. A bench complying with Section 903 shall be provided within the room.

❖ In areas such as dressing rooms and locker rooms where people may need to get out of their wheelchair to dress or undress, an accessible bench is required.

When lockers are provided along a wall for temporary storage, a bench is not required because this situation is not considered a locker room. For example, storage lockers for bags or purses available for the public in a museum or bus station.

Accessible benches must be mounted against a wall to provide a stable surface to lean against or to provide back support (see Section 903). When considering the relationship of clear floor space to the bench, a primary consideration is transfer between a wheelchair and the bench. This can be accomplished by placing the wheelchair at the end of the bench, allowing transfer between two seats that face the same direction. For an ideal transfer, the clear floor space would extend beyond the wall at the back of the bench so that the wheelchair seat and the bench seat align. Alternatively, a bench with a back support could be provided where a transfer space

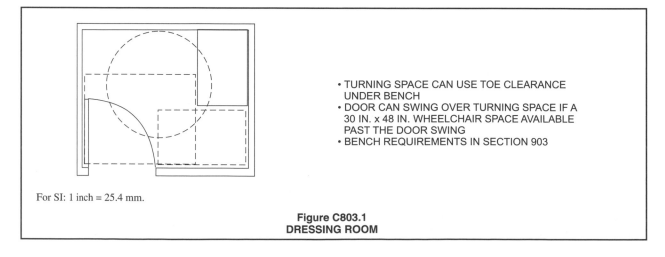

• TURNING SPACE CAN USE TOE CLEARANCE UNDER BENCH
• DOOR CAN SWING OVER TURNING SPACE IF A 30 IN. x 48 IN. WHEELCHAIR SPACE AVAILABLE PAST THE DOOR SWING
• BENCH REQUIREMENTS IN SECTION 903

For SI: 1 inch = 25.4 mm.

Figure C803.1
DRESSING ROOM

with seat alignment would be available. It is also important to recognize the barrier introduced by arm rests at the ends of benches.

In a locker room, the bench must be located so that transfer to the bench is not necessary for access to the accessible lockers. At the same time, the locker need not be within the reach range for the bench, but it is more user friendly if they are close.

Providing a grab bar on a side wall would exceed code requirements and possibly aid transfer to the bench; however, a grab bar should not be provided over the back of the bench [see commentary Figure 903.2(b)]. A grab bar on the rear wall would cause a problem with using the wall for back support.

803.5 Coat Hooks and Shelves. Accessible coat hooks provided within the room shall accommodate a forward reach or side reach complying with Section 308. Where provided, a shelf shall be 40 inches (1015 mm) minimum and 48 inches (1220 mm) maximum above the floor.

❖ Where coat hooks are provided in accessible locker rooms, dressing rooms and fitting rooms, the hooks may be accessed using either a forward approach or a parallel approach with the appropriate clear floor or ground space. Coat hooks located near or above obstructions must comply with the reach range requirements described in Section 308. The type of obstruction that must be overcome will determine the maximum allowable mounting height of coat hooks.

The location of the bench in the space (Section 803.4) must be taken into account in the design of the room. When items are hung on the coat hook, they should not obstruct the bench. Although not required, it would be more user friendly to locate at least one hook within reach of the bench so that it could be used while changing.

Fold down shelves are permitted in fitting and dressing rooms. This is typically the type of shelf used to hold a purse or bag, similar to those found in toilet stalls. The provisions in this section are intended to establish the mounting height only. A fold down shelf in the down position may overlap, but should not obstruct any of the required accessible provisions, such as clear floor space, wheelchair turning space, or the area over the bench. Fold down shelves must be designed and constructed to support the live loads for the anticipated use of the shelf.

Fixed shelves or fold down shelves may be provided at other heights if they do not overlap or obstruct the required clearances for the accessible elements. If a fold down shelf is intended to serve as a working surface (e.g., baby changing table), Section 902 is applicable.

804 Kitchens and Kitchenettes

❖ The intent of this section is to provide technical requirements for full kitchens and kitchenettes that are in shared spaces. Examples of shared kitchens are those within community buildings or some congregate residences where residents may prepare their own food, such as in dormitories or group homes. Requirements for kitchens associated with Accessible dwelling or sleeping units reference this section from Section 1002.12.

Kitchenettes, even though they do have elements similar to kitchens, do not include a stove, cooktop or range. Kitchenettes may also be referred to as wet bars or coffee counters. These types of facilities are common in offices or employee lounge areas. The food preparation and cleanup chores in these types of facilities are minimal; therefore, specific requirements for kitchenettes are addressed throughout this section by exceptions (see commentary Figure C804).

Commercial kitchens are addressed as employee work areas and specifically addressed as such in scoping requirements. Kitchens that are part of Type A and Type B dwelling units are specifically addressed in Chapter 10.

804.1 General. Accessible kitchens and kitchenettes shall comply with Section 804.

❖ The design of kitchens usable by a person with a disability demands careful consideration and thoughtful planning. Careful location of appliances, plumbing fixtures and cabinetry is essential to achieve the required maneuvering clearances and clear floor spaces that are required in the necessary functions in an accessible and functional kitchen. Careful design will produce a kitchen that provides an accessible and functionally efficient kitchen that is easily usable by a person with a disability or mobility impairment, as well as an able-bodied person.

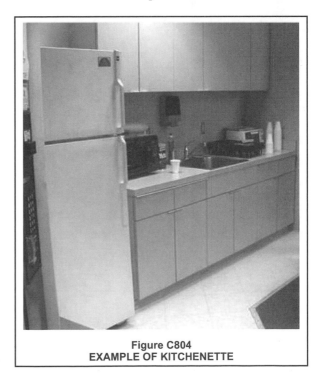

Figure C804
EXAMPLE OF KITCHENETTE

Although not as complicated as a kitchen design, accessible kitchenettes should be designed so that they are useable by persons with or without mobility impairments.

804.2 Clearance. Where a pass-through kitchen is provided, clearances shall comply with Section 804.2.1. Where a U-shaped kitchen is provided, clearances shall comply with Section 804.2.2.

EXCEPTION: Spaces that do not provide a cooktop or conventional range shall not be required to comply with Section 804.2.

❖ Kitchens include requirements for clearances between cabinets or appliances; the clearance requirements in referenced Section 804.2.1 and Section 804.2.2 are different because the two different floor plan arrangements are unique and require different types of spaces for maneuvering. The difference in the arrangement of fixtures and appliances also creates a different set of requirements for access into and egress from each kitchen type.

The exception is meant to exempt kitchenettes and wet bars from the clearance requirements for kitchens. Although the additional clearances are not required, these spaces must still meet the general accessible route provisions.

It is not the intent of these provisions to prohibit other types of kitchen layouts, such as L-shaped or kitchens with islands. If other layouts are used, the key

considerations would be maneuvering to access appliances, the sink, the work surface and storage elements.

804.2.1 Pass-through Kitchens. In pass-through kitchens where counters, appliances or cabinets are on two opposing sides, or where counters, appliances or cabinets are opposite a parallel wall, clearance between all opposing base cabinets, counter tops, appliances, or walls within kitchen work areas shall be 40 inches (1015 mm) minimum. Pass-through kitchens shall have two entries.

❖ Pass-through kitchens are typically laid out with all the appliances, counters and sink in straight lines. The appliances and fixtures can be located along one side of the kitchen, or they can be located along both sides of the kitchen. A pass-through kitchen must be open on both ends. If the pass-through kitchen is enclosed at one end by a wall or counter, the kitchen is then considered to be a U-shaped kitchen and must comply with the provisions in Section 804.2.2. The clearances in this section are the clear opening width between the faces of the cabinets and/or appliances across from each other or the wall opposite the cabinet/appliances (see Figure 804.2.1).

The need for a turning space in a kitchen is not intended to increase the 40 inch (1015 mm) width between opposing cabinets. The knee and toe clearances under the work surface (Section 804.3) or the sink

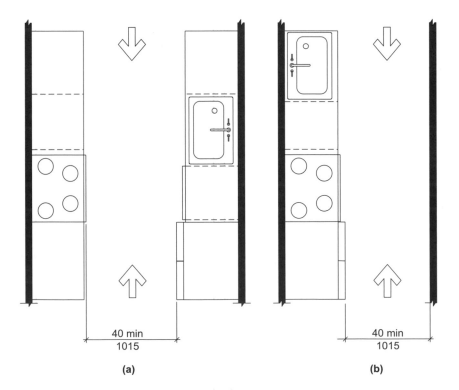

40 min
1015

(a)

40 min
1015

(b)

Fig. 804.2.1
Pass-through Kitchen Clearance

(Section 804.4) may be used to provide the turning space within the kitchen.

804.2.2 U-Shaped Areas. In kitchens enclosed on three contiguous sides, clearance between all opposing base cabinets, countertops, appliances, or walls within kitchen work areas shall be 60 inches (1525 mm) minimum.

❖ U-shaped kitchens are kitchens with cabinets and appliances on three contiguous sides. In such an arrangement, 60 inches (1525 mm) clearance is required between the faces of opposing cabinets and appliances to make all sides usable.

For galley-style kitchens with cabinet/counter on two opposing sides of a walking path with a wall at one end of the path, the kitchen is considered a U-shaped kitchen and would have to have a 60-inch (1525 mm) clear floor space.

804.3 Work Surface. Work surfaces shall comply with Section 902.

EXCEPTION: Spaces that do not provide a cooktop or conventional range shall not be required to provide an accessible work surface.

❖ An accessible work surface is a critical component of a kitchen for wheelchair users. Without an accessible work surface, many of the tasks necessary for preparing a meal, such as mixing, chopping, cutting and cleaning become very difficult, and for some wheelchair users, routine tasks may even become impossible. Sections 804.6.5.1 and 805.6.5.2 require an accessible work surface immediately adjacent to the oven. It is not the intent of this provision to require all work surfaces in the kitchen to meet Section 902. See the commentary in Section 902 for technical requirements.

If the space under the work surface is to be used for a wheelchair turning space, the minimum width of the clearance will be 36 inches (915 mm) instead of 30 inches (760 mm) (see Section 304.3.2 and commentary Figure C804.3).

The intent of the exception is to allow kitchenettes and wet bars to not include accessible work surfaces because major food preparation or clean-up is not expected in these areas.

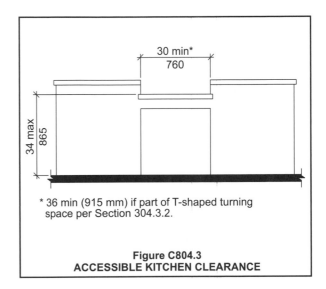

* 36 min (915 mm) if part of T-shaped turning space per Section 304.3.2.

Figure C804.3
ACCESSIBLE KITCHEN CLEARANCE

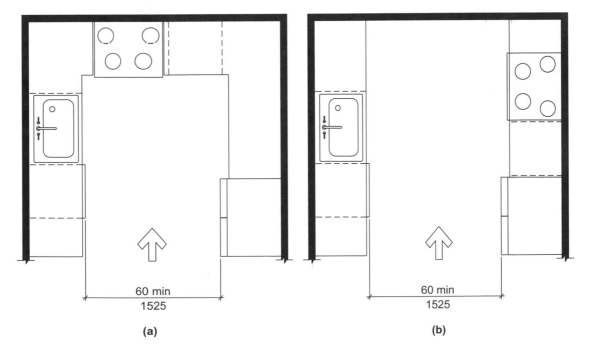

(a)   (b)

Fig. 804.2.2
U-Shaped Kitchen Clearance

804.4 Sinks. Sinks shall comply with Section 606.

❖ Sinks in kitchens shall have knee and toe clearances that allow for a front approach (including protection from the pipes), a maximum rim height of 34 inches (865 mm), and faucets that meet operable parts requirements. If a double bowl sink is installed, these requirements can be for only one bowl. This allows for the second bowl to be deeper or include a garbage disposal (see commentary Figure C804.4).

If the space under the sink is to be used for a wheelchair turning space, the minimum width of the clearance will be 36 inches (915 mm) instead of 30 inches (760 mm) (see Section 304.3.2).

Per Section 606.2, Exception 1, a side approach is a permitted alternative for sinks in kitchenettes. The sink must still meet the 34 inch (760 mm) maximum rim height provisions and have faucets that meet operable parts provisions (see commentary Figure C804).

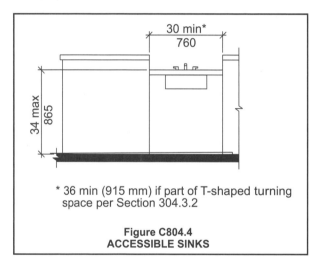

* 36 min (915 mm) if part of T-shaped turning space per Section 304.3.2

Figure C804.4
ACCESSIBLE SINKS

804.5 Storage. At least 50 percent of shelf space in cabinets shall comply with Section 905.

❖ Kitchen shelves can be provided by open shelves, within an upper or lower cabinet or within a pantry type unit. At least 50 percent of the kitchen shelves provided must be located so that a person using a wheelchair can get in front of the shelf, and the shelf must be within the 15 inch to 48 inch (380 to 1220 mm) reach range. With standard 36 inch (305 mm) base cabinets, the obstructed reach range provisions of Section 308.3.2 would not allow for standard upper cabinets to be considered within reach range because the maximum height of the obstruction is 34 inches (865 mm). Upper cabinets with a bottom shelf at 46 inches (1170 mm) located over the lower work surface or sink would meet Section 308.3.2. Drawers and open shelves could be considered equivalent to storage shelving in cabinets. Pantry style cabinets, rather than cabinets mounted over work counters, would allow for improved accessibility. Additional storage space, such as a pantry, located conveniently adjacent to kitchens could also be

considered. Any cabinet or drawer pulls or latches must meet operable parts provisions.

804.6 Appliances. Where provided, kitchen appliances shall comply with Section 804.6.

❖ Any kitchen appliance installed should meet the general requirements for clear floor space (Section 804.6.1), and any controls must be within reach range and meet operable parts provisions (Section 804.6.2). If the appliance has a door that opens for operation, the door may overlap, but not obstruct, the clear floor space. Additional provisions are included for dishwashers, ranges, cooktops, ovens and refrigerator/freezers (Sections 804.6.3 through 804.6.6).

804.6.1 Clear Floor Space. A clear floor space complying with Section 305 shall be provided at each kitchen appliance. Clear floor spaces are permitted to overlap.

❖ Unless provisions specific to a fixture or appliance are given in the following sections, a 30-inch by 48-inch (760 by 1220 mm) clear floor space must be provided which allows a forward or parallel approach to the appliance. It is important to plan the kitchen and clear floor spaces considering the way a person in a wheelchair uses the fixture or appliance. For instance, the easiest way to use the burners on the top of a range from a wheelchair is by a parallel approach, although access to the oven portion of the range may be best from a different angle. It is also important to consider how these fixtures and appliances are used in conjunction with one another. To move items from an oven to a preparation area and then to a serving dish may require counter surface to place an item on while repositioning the wheelchair.

804.6.2 Operable Parts. All appliance controls shall comply with Section 309.

EXCEPTIONS:

1. Appliance doors and door latching devices shall not be required to comply with Section 309.4.

2. Bottom-hinged appliance doors, when in the open position, shall not be required to comply with Section 309.3.

❖ Kitchen appliance controls must meet the operable part provisions for clear floor space, height and operation. Some of these may include controls for items such as a soap dispenser for the dishwasher, burner controls for a range, lights, timers and heat controls for an oven, on-off switches for a garbage disposal, openers for a trash compactor and exhaust switches for range hoods. Redundant controls, such as a wall switch for a range hood, are permitted.

Because of the physical requirements of the doors and door latches, Exception 1 states that these specific operable parts are not required to meet the one hand, no tight pinching and grasping and 5-pound (22 N) maximum force requirements in Section 309.4 for operable parts. Doors and door latches do have to meet the clear floor space and height requirements in Sections 309.2 and 309.3.

Exception 2 allows for bottom hinged appliance doors, such as commonly found on dishwashers and ovens, to not meet the lower reach range height of 15 inches (380 mm) minimum.

804.6.3 Dishwasher. A clear floor space, positioned adjacent to the dishwasher door, shall be provided. The dishwasher door in the open position shall not obstruct the clear floor space for the dishwasher or an adjacent sink.

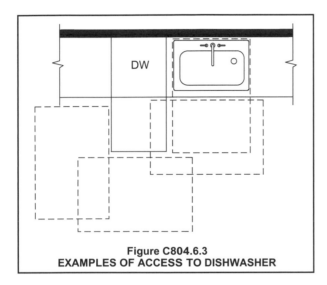

Figure C804.6.3
EXAMPLES OF ACCESS TO DISHWASHER

❖ Locating the clear floor space so that the dishwasher is usable is important. If the clear floor space is located immediately in front of the dishwasher, the door in the open position will overlap the clear floor space. By requiring that the clear floor space not be obstructed by

the dishwasher door, either the clear floor space must be located past the door, or the door could overlap the toe clearance if there was a minimum of 9 inches (225 mm) clearance under the door when open. It is important to locate the clear floor space so the dishwasher can be easily loaded and unloaded. Often, it is desirable to load the dishwasher from the sink area; therefore, it may be helpful to locate the sink and dishwasher adjacent to each other. Where a dishwasher is located adjacent to the clear floor space for a sink, the single clear floor space can be used to serve both the sink and the dishwasher (see commentary Figure C804.6.3).

804.6.4 Range or Cooktop. A clear floor space, positioned for a parallel or forward approach to the space for a range or cooktop, shall be provided. Where the clear floor space is positioned for a forward approach, knee and toe clearance complying with Section 306 shall be provided. Where knee and toe space is provided, the underside of the range or cooktop shall be insulated or otherwise configured to prevent burns, abrasions, or electrical shock. The location of controls shall not require reaching across burners.

❖ A range includes a cooktop and an oven. A range must be located for the parallel approach discussed in Section 804.6.1, not a front approach (see commentary Figure C804.6.4). This is caused by the footplates on a wheelchair stopping someone from reaching forward past their toes.

A cooktop can be provided with a parallel approach or with a front approach. When a designer chooses to provide a cooktop with a front approach, the cooktop must provide adequate clearances for a person's knees and toes underneath as well as protection from accidental bumps, cuts or burns.

To reduce the chance of accidental scalding or burns, access to controls for the burners on either a cooktop or range must not require reaching across

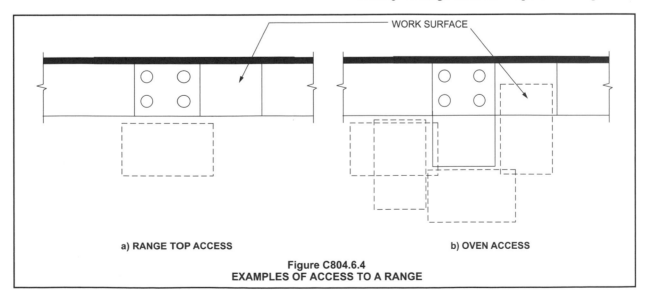

WORK SURFACE

a) RANGE TOP ACCESS

b) OVEN ACCESS

Figure C804.6.4
EXAMPLES OF ACCESS TO A RANGE

burners. Controls can be provided on the front, center or side of the burners. Access to controls for the oven that is part of the range must also be located so that a person using the range does not have to reach across burners to access the oven controls (Section 804.6.5).

804.6.5 Oven. Ovens shall comply with Section 804.6.5.

❖ Ovens may be part of a range, or they may be the wall type. Usability of the oven must be considered when choosing placement and options. Wall mounted ovens may provide better access in an accessible kitchen because the height makes access easier for persons using wheelchairs. A person would not have to reach both down and over the door to reach the rack or item in the oven. Although most standard wall ovens come with a bottom hinged door, some manufacturers are starting to offer microwave/ oven combinations with a side swing door or racks that pull out all the way without tilting.

804.6.5.1 Side-Hinged Door Ovens. Side-hinged door ovens shall have a work surface complying with Section 804.3 positioned adjacent to the latch side of the oven door.

❖ If a side opening wall oven is chosen, to facilitate transfer of dishes into and out of the oven, the latch side should be adjacent to a counter space that also serves as an accessible work surface (Sections 804.3 and 902).

804.6.5.2 Bottom-Hinged Door Ovens. Bottom-hinged door ovens shall have a work surface complying with Section 804.3 positioned adjacent to one side of the door.

❖ If a bottom-hinged oven is chosen, to facilitate transfer of dishes into and out of the oven, an adjacent counter space that also serves as an accessible work surface must be provided (Sections 804.3 and 902) (see commentary Figure C804.6.4).

804.6.5.3 Controls. Ovens shall have controls on front panels.

❖ Access to oven controls that are part of a range must not require reaching across burners. Controls for wall ovens must be within reach ranges, 15 to 48 inches (380 to 1220 mm) in height.

804.6.6 Refrigerator/Freezer. Combination refrigerators and freezers shall have at least 50 percent of the freezer compartment shelves, including the bottom of the freezer, 54 inches (1370 mm) maximum above the floor when the shelves are installed at the maximum heights possible in the compartment. A clear floor space, positioned for a parallel approach to the space dedicated to a refrigerator/freezer, shall be provided. The centerline of the clear floor space shall be offset 24 inches (610 mm) maximum from the centerline of the dedicated space.

❖ The position for the parallel approach to the refrigerator and freezer must consider how the person using a wheelchair will access the interior with the door open (see commentary Figure C804.6.6).

Refrigerator/freezer choices can have the freezer on the top, on the bottom or side-by-side. If a top freezer option is chosen, a freezer with the bottom of the compartment at a maximum of 54 inches (1370 mm) above

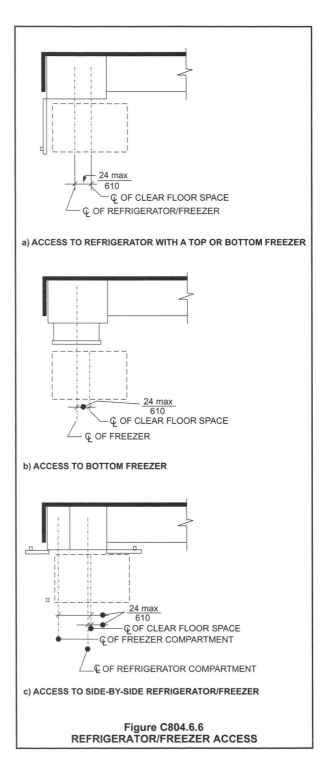

a) **ACCESS TO REFRIGERATOR WITH A TOP OR BOTTOM FREEZER**

b) **ACCESS TO BOTTOM FREEZER**

c) **ACCESS TO SIDE-BY-SIDE REFRIGERATOR/FREEZER**

Figure C804.6.6
REFRIGERATOR/FREEZER ACCESS

the ground (assuming one shelf in the freezer) will meet the freezer compartment requirements. If a bottom freezer option is chosen, at least one shelf in the freezer compartment should be 15 inches (380 mm) minimum above the floor. Side-by-side refrigerator/freezers provide the most usable freezer compartment; however, then clear floor spaces for both sides must be considered for the unit. Locating refrigerators so the doors swing back 180 degrees (3.1 rad) can provide greater accessibility for a person using a wheelchair. Although not specifically mentioned, if a refrigerator has ice or water provided through the door, or inside the appliance, that feature is considered part of the refrigerator/freezer. Therefore, those elements must also have a clear floor space for access and meet reach range and operable parts requirements.

805 Transportation Facilities

❖ Access to transportation facilities is essential for persons with disabilities, not only for reasons of equivalent access, but also because many people with disabilities cannot drive or cannot afford special converted vehicles. They rely on public transportation to get everywhere.

805.1 General. Transportation facilities shall comply with Section 805.

❖ The provisions for transportation facilities deal with elements that are unique to bus stops (Sections 805.2 through 805.4) and train stations (Sections 805.5 through 805.10). Other aspects, such as the main bus station, or other transportation, such as airports, should meet the general accessibility provisions.

805.2 Bus Boarding and Alighting Areas. Bus boarding and alighting areas shall comply with Section 805.2.

❖ When public transportation is provided by a bus system, designated bus stops and bus stations must have areas where 'kneeling' buses can deploy the ramp and people can board and disembark from the buses. These bus stop pads may be either within or outside of a shelter.

805.2.1 Surface. Bus stop boarding and alighting areas shall have a firm, stable surface.

❖ Wheelchairs are propelled most easily on surfaces that are hard, stable and regular. Soft, loose surfaces such as loose sand, gravel, crushed stone or wet clay, and irregular surfaces such as cobblestone, significantly impede movement of a wheelchair.

A stable surface is one that remains unchanged by contaminants or applied force, so that when the contaminant or force is removed, the surface returns to its original condition. A firm surface resists deformation by either indentation or particles moving on its surface. It is not the intent of the standard to require only paved surfaces; however, any other type (e.g., wood chips, gravel) would need to be evaluated.

805.2.2 Dimensions. Bus stop boarding and alighting areas shall have a 96 inches (2440 mm) minimum clear length, measured perpendicular to the curb or vehicle roadway edge, and a 60 inches (1525 mm) minimum clear width, measured parallel to the vehicle roadway.

❖ The size of the area for the bus stop pad would allow adequate space for the kneeling bus ramp to deploy and the person using the wheelchair or scooter to board or disembark from the bus (see commentary Figure C805.2.2).

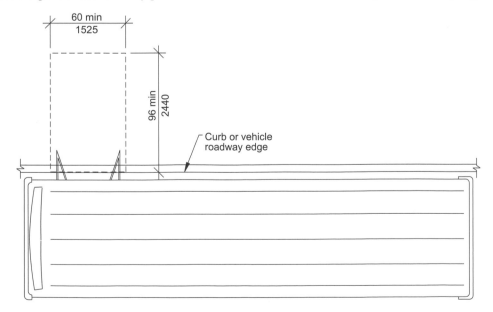

Fig. 805.2.2
Size of Bus Boarding and Alighting Areas

Figure C805.2.2
KNEELING BUS

805.2.3 Slope. The slope of the bus stop boarding and alighting area parallel to the vehicle roadway shall be the same as the roadway, to the maximum extent practicable. The slope of the bus stop boarding and alighting area perpendicular to the vehicle roadway shall be 1:48 maximum.

❖ The bus stop pad should slope with the road in the direction of travel and level back from the road edge.

805.2.4 Connection. Bus stop boarding and alighting areas shall be connected to streets, sidewalks, or pedestrian paths by an accessible route complying with Section 402.

❖ An accessible route must be available to and from the bus stop pad.

805.3 Bus Shelters. Bus shelters shall provide a minimum clear floor space complying with Section 305 entirely within the shelter. Bus shelters shall be connected by an accessible route complying with Section 402 to a boarding and alighting area complying with Section 805.2.

❖ Where bus shelters are provided, there must be within the bus shelter at least one 30 inch by 48 inch (762 by 1220 mm) clear floor space for people using wheelchairs or scooters to wait. Depending on the configuration of the shelter, the alcove provisions may be applicable. The waiting space in the bus shelter and the bus stop pad must be connected by an accessible route (see commentary Figure C805.3).

Figure C805.3
BUS SHELTER

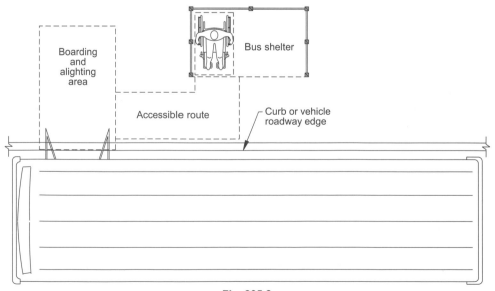

Fig. 805.3
Bus Shelters

805.4 Bus Signs. Bus route identification signs shall have visual characters complying with Sections 703.2.2, 703.2.3, and 703.2.5 through 703.2.8. In addition, bus route identification numbers shall be visual characters complying with Section 703.2.4.

> **EXCEPTION:** Bus schedules, timetables and maps that are posted at the bus stop or bus bay shall not be required to comply with Section 805.4.

❖ The intent is that bus route information should be made accessible to persons with vision impairments as much as possible. Route identification signs must meet the requirements for visual characters for case, style, character width, spacing and line spacing. In addition, bus route identification numbers must meet the minimum height requirements in Table 703.2.4. Because bus information is often posted on an overhead sign adjacent to the road, the bus route identification number will typically be over 2 inches (50 mm) in height. Although not listed as a requirement, high contrast and low glare requirements in Section 703.2.10 may be beneficial to make bus information readable. Raised lettering or Braille information is not required.

Sometimes a bus schedule, timetable or map is also posted on a side wall of the bus shelter. This information need not meet the visual signage requirements in this section.

805.5 Rail Platforms. Rail platforms shall comply with Section 805.5.

❖ Rail platforms may be elevated so that the edge of the platform lines up with the floor of the rail car. To provide open access to the cars, there are no guards provided along this edge. The requirements for slope and detectable warnings in the subsections address safety concerns for this condition.

> **805.5.1 Slope.** Rail platforms shall not exceed a slope of 1:48 in all directions.
>
> > **EXCEPTION:** Where platforms serve vehicles operating on existing track or track laid in existing roadway, the slope of the platform parallel to the track shall be permitted to be equal to the slope (grade) of the roadway or existing track.

❖ So that a person using a mobility device does not have to deal with a slope while on a train platform or while entering or exiting the cars, the platform must be basically level.

The exception allows for existing train systems to remain in operation even if they cannot meet the current provisions for level platforms as long as the platform matches the slope of the rails.

> **805.5.2 Detectable Warnings.** Platform boarding edges not protected by platform screens or guards shall have a detectable warning complying with Section 705, 24 inches (610 mm) in

width, along the full length of the public use area of the platform.

❖ Detectable warnings along the edge of the platform will alert persons with visual impairments of the edge of the platform. This is also a good safety feature that helps keep passengers from standing too close to the edge (see commentary Figure C805.5.2).

Figure C805.5.2
PLATFORM EDGE

805.6 Rail Station Signs. Rail station signs shall comply with Section 805.6.

> **EXCEPTION:** Signs shall not be required to comply with Sections 805.6.1 and 805.6.2 where audible signs are remotely transmitted to hand-held receivers, or are user- or proximity-actuated.

❖ It is important that information designating stations and routes be available for persons with visual impairments. This section does not require signage, but requires equivalent access to the information when signage is provided.

The exception allows for new technology available for wayfinding for persons with visual impairments.

Emerging technologies such as an audible sign system using infrared transmitters and receivers may provide greater accessibility in the transit environment than traditional Braille and raised letter signs. The transmitters are placed on or next to the print signs and transmit their information to an infrared receiver that is held by a person. By scanning an area, the person will hear the sign. This means that signs can be placed well out of reach of Braille readers, even on parapet walls and on walls beyond barriers. Additionally, such signs can be used to provide wayfinding information that cannot be efficiently conveyed on Braille signs.

805.6.1 Entrances. Where signs identify a station or a station entrance, at least one sign with tactile characters complying with Section 703.3 shall be provided at each entrance.

❖ At each signed entrance to a station, a sign adjacent to that entrance with both raised letters and Braille shall also be provided.

805.6.2 Routes and Destinations. Lists of stations, routes and destinations served by the station that are located on boarding areas, platforms, or mezzanines shall have visual characters complying with Section 703.2. A minimum of one tactile sign complying with Section 703.3 shall be provided on each platform or boarding area to identify the specific station.

EXCEPTION: Where sign space is limited, characters shall not be required to exceed 3 inches (76 mm) in height.

❖ Route lists must meet the visual contrast, style and size requirements in Section 703.2. At least one sign with raised and Braille characters must be provided on each platform to identify the station. Route maps need not comply with these signage requirement.

The exception is in recognition of limitations for location when a large amount of information must be provided at a high location. Table 703.2.4 requires that characters exceed 3 inches (75 mm) when the viewing distance is greater than 21 feet (6400 mm).

805.6.3 Station Names. Stations covered by this section shall have identification signs with visual characters complying with Section 703.2. The signs shall be clearly visible and within the sight lines of a standing or sitting passenger from within the vehicle on both sides when not obstructed by another vehicle.

❖ Where to disembark from the train is important information for passengers. Signage on the platform indicating the name of the station must be visible to all passengers in the train cars. This may require several signs along the length of the platform.

805.7 Public Address Systems. Where public address systems convey audible information to the public, the same or equivalent information shall be provided in a visual format.

❖ When announcements are made regarding bus or train arrivals and departures, the same information must be available for persons with hearing impairments.

805.8 Clocks. Where clocks are provided for use by the public, the clock face shall be uncluttered so that its elements are clearly visible. Hands, numerals and digits shall contrast with the background either light-on-dark or dark-on-light. Where clocks are installed overhead, numerals and digits shall be visual characters complying with Section 703.2.

❖ Departures and arrivals from transportation facilities are controlled by timed schedules. To assist persons in getting to the right place at the right time, the time is often prominently displayed in the stations. The time display can be a standard clock face or digital. Whatever option is chosen, the display must meet the visual contrast, style and height for the characters. A clock face should also meet the visual contrast requirements and be free of any types of additional information or advertising.

805.9 Escalators. Where provided, escalators shall have a 32-inch (815 mm) minimum clear width, and shall comply with Requirements 6.1.3.5.6 - Step Demarcations, and 6.1.3.6.5 - Flat Steps of ASME A17.1 listed in Section 105.2.5.

EXCEPTION: Existing escalators shall not be required to comply with Section 805.9.

❖ Even though escalators are not part of an accessible route for persons using wheelchairs or scooters, they may be usable by people with mobility impairments.

The ASME A17.1 standard for safety for elevators also includes escalator provisions. ASME A17.1, Section 6.1.3.5.6 deals with the stripe along the front edge and side of each step. ASME A17.1, Section 6.1.3.6.5 deals with the required flat area at the top and bottom of the escalator. These requirements will help persons with vision and mobility impairments negotiate the escalators. Any new escalators in transportation facilities must provide a minimum clear width of 32 inches (815 mm).

805.10 Track Crossings. Where a circulation path serving boarding platforms crosses tracks, it shall comply with Section 402.

EXCEPTION: Openings for wheel flanges shall be permitted to be $2\frac{1}{2}$ inch (64 mm) maximum.

❖ When a person with mobility impairments must cross over a track system, the rails may cause a problem. With the reference to the accessible route provisions in Section 402, the opening limitations (Section 302.3) and change in elevation (Section 303) are applicable. Therefore, the path must provide a surface level with the top of the rails, and the gap between the path and the sides of the rails must be limited to $\frac{1}{2}$ inch (13 mm) maximum. The exception does allow for additional clearance to allow for wheel flanges on the rails. In most rail systems, this $2\frac{1}{2}$ inch (63 mm) gap would be limited to the gap on the inside of the rails as indicated in Figure 805.10.

Fig. 805.10
Track Crossings

806 Holding Cells and Housing Cells

❖ The administrative authority will specify which holding cells and housing cells are required to be accessible.

Generally, for holding cells, the requirements are for one of each type at each location. For example, in a courthouse, there may be men's, women's and juvenile holding cells at a main entry level (e.g., different types) and holding cells adjacent to the courtrooms where criminal cases are heard (e.g., different locations). At least one accessible cell must be provided to serve each courtroom to avoid having to move the entire proceeding to accommodate a person who uses a wheelchair. If a pair of cells equally serve more than one courtroom, only one cell must be accessible.

Housing cells in jails may vary based on the security level within the facility or the need (e.g., every day housing, hospital cells, isolation cells). Because of security and safety concerns, Accessible cells must be available in each type, but can to be grouped in the facility.

806.1 General. Holding cells and housing cells shall comply with Section 806.

❖ Persons may be incarcerated before, during and after a trial. Holding cells are used for short term incarcerations, and are those commonly found within police stations and in courthouses. Housing cells are used for more long term incarceration and are typically found in jails. Holding cells often have bench seating, and may include a water closet and lavatory within the cell. Housing cells often include a water closet, a lavatory and a bed within the cell, and may also include a shower, bench and working surface. The nature of the facility causes almost everything to be built-in when in high security situations (see commentary Figure C806.1). Shared spaces available to Accessible jail housing cells must be also be accessible. For example, if bathing facilities are provided in a common area, the bathing facility must be accessible.

Of concern are persons with mobility impairments (Section 806.2) as well as those with hearing impairments (Section 806.3).

806.2 Features for People Using Wheelchairs or Other Mobility Aids. Cells required to have features for people using wheelchairs or other mobility aids shall comply with Section 806.2.

❖ A person with mobility impairments may be using a wheelchair, scooter, walker or other type of mobility device. The cell must be designed so that a person can access and use all elements provided in the cell.

806.2.1 Turning Space. Turning space complying with Section 304 shall be provided within the cell.

❖ Either a 60 inch (525 mm) diameter circle or a T-shaped turning space must be available within the cell. The turning space can use any knee and toe clearances available under the bed, bench, lavatory or work surfaces in the room. The door to the cell can be sliding or swing into or out of the cell. If the door swings into the cell, a 30-inch by 48-inch (760 by 1220 mm) clear floor space should be provided past the swing of the door, as in to the single occupant toilet room or dressing room.

Figure C806.1
ACCESSIBLE HOUSING CELL

806.2.2 Benches. Where benches are provided, at least one bench shall comply with Section 903.

❖ If a bench is provided within the cell, the bench must be either against a wall or provide back support. Technical criteria, including bench size and space for a transfer, are defined in Section 903.

806.2.3 Beds. Where beds are provided, clear floor space complying with Section 305 shall be provided on at least one side of the bed. The clear floor space shall be positioned for parallel approach to the side of the bed.

❖ If beds are provided in the cell, a 30-inch by 48-inch (760 by 1220 mm) clear floor space must be available beside and parallel to the bed. This will allow for someone to transfer into bed at night.

806.2.4 Toilet and Bathing Facilities. Toilet facilities or bathing facilities provided as part of a cell shall comply with Section 603.

❖ If a water closet, lavatory or shower is provided in the cell, it must be constructed accessible. Security concerns will dictate some alternatives to provide accessible features. In every instance, regardless of toilet and lavatory configuration, adequate space needs to be provided for inmates who use wheelchairs to transfer onto and off of the toilet and have knee and toe clearances under the lavatory. Grab bars may be constructed with an infill plate or continuous mounting bracket for suicide prevention [See commentary Figures C806.2.4 and C604.5(a)].

Figure C806.2.4
ACCESSIBLE HOUSING CELL TOILET AND LAVATORY

806.3 Communication Features. Cells required to have communication features shall comply with Section 806.3.

❖ Communication features in cells are those elements that impart information to people in the facility (e.g., alarms) or for persons to communicate (e.g., pay phones, phones at security glazing).

806.3.1 Alarms. Where audible emergency alarm systems are provided to serve the occupants of cells, visual alarms complying with Section 702 shall be provided.

EXCEPTION: In cells where inmates or detainees are not allowed independent means of egress, visual alarms shall not be required.

❖ The authority having jurisdiction determines when a general emergency alarm system is required throughout a building that contains housing or holding cells. If it is the intent for persons in cells to react or self-evacuate during an emergency situation, both audible and visible alarms must be provided so that they alert persons in the cells. The alarm system must be installed in accordance with NFPA 72. If security personnel dictate how and when persons in the cells will evacuate, the alarm system is not required to notify the cell residents.

806.3.2 Telephones. Where provided, telephones within cells shall have volume controls complying with Section 704.3.

❖ Pay phones may be available in some holding and housing cell areas. At a minimum, these phones must have the volume control requirements in Section 704.3. These phones may also need to meet the pay phone provisions in Section 704.

When phones are part of visitor areas with security glazing, all the phones must have a volume control in accordance with Section 704.3 (see commentary Figure 806.3.2).

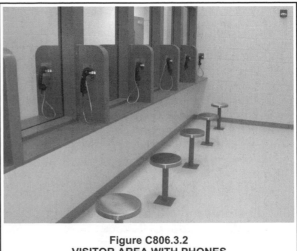

Figure C806.3.2
VISITOR AREA WITH PHONES

807 Courtrooms

❖ The sixth and seventh amendments in the Bill of Rights guarantee all Americans the right to a public trial and trial by a jury. To guarantee the rights of persons with disabilities, it is important that courthouses be accessible. Minimal requirements for the courtrooms are addressed in this section.

Courtrooms are unique spaces. Historically, the judge's bench is raised for reasons of decorum. Often, to facilitate interaction between the judge and the courthouse staff, as well as important lines-of-sight among participants, other portions of the courtroom are also raised. As a result, providing adequate access to all areas of a courtroom can be a challenge.

For additional information on this topic, the U.S. Access Board Courthouse Access Advisory Committee has developed a report that clarifies minimum federal requirements, as well as recommendations for best design practices.

The Access Board organized the Courthouse Access Advisory Committee in 2004 to promote accessibility in the design of court facilities. The committee's November 15, 2006, "Final Report" provides design guidance and best-practice recommendations to achieve access in courthouses, including courtrooms. Available free of charge at www.access-board.gov/caac/report.htm, the report also includes sample plans and educational strategies for disseminating the information to a variety of audiences. Although focused on the design of new facilities, it can also be used as a resource in the retrofit of existing facilities.

807.1 General. Courtrooms shall comply with Section 807.

❖ All parts of a courtroom must be accessible, and the space must meet the general requirements for these areas. For example, the gallery area seating must meet the assembly seating provisions in Section 802 (see commentary Figure C807.1), or the gate in the bar must

Figure C807.1
GALLERY SEATING

meet the provisions in Section 404. Elements particular to courtrooms include witness stands, jury boxes, judges' benches, clerks' stations and other work stations, and assistive listening systems (Section 706), among others. Design is complicated because it must achieve access effectively while preserving traditional and necessary features of courtroom design.

807.2 Turning Space. Where provided, each area that is raised or depressed and accessed by ramps or platform lifts with entry ramps shall provide an unobstructed turning space complying with Section 304.

❖ When a judge's bench area, clerk's station, witness box, jury box or other defined areas is raised or depressed, that area must include a turning space. The intent is that a person could turn around to be able to go back up or down the ramp or onto the platform lift. If the platform includes an accessible work surface, the knee and toe clearances under that work area can be used to provide the turning space.

807.3 Clear Floor Space. Within the defined area of each jury box and witness stand, a clear floor space complying with Section 305 shall be provided.

EXCEPTION: In alterations, wheelchair spaces are not required to be located within the defined area of raised jury boxes or witness stands and shall be permitted to be located outside these spaces where ramps or platform lifts restrict or project into the means of egress required by the administrative authority.

❖ A person who uses a mobility device such as a scooter or wheelchair must be able to testify from within the witness stand or serve as a member of the jury. Typically, half height walls define these areas.

For example, sometimes witness boxes are raised, and sometimes not. If the area is raised, both a turning space (Sections 304 and 807.2) and a clear floor space is required (Section 305). The clear floor space should be positioned so that the person testifying can face in the same direction as anyone else testifying from the witness box. If the space is confined, the alcove provisions are applicable [see commentary Figure C807.3(a)].

Jury boxes are often two levels. Sometimes both levels are raised, and sometimes only the second level is raised. A space for a juror using a wheelchair or scooter must be available within the jury box [see commentary Figure C807.3(b)]. The juror must be able to face in the same direction as the rest of the jurors. If the wheelchair space is confined by the half height wall or the other raised areas, the alcove provisions are applicable. This is different from the wheelchair space provided in the gallery seating because there are no requirements for companion seats, or shoulder alignment with other jurors [See commentary Figure C807.3(c)].

**Figure C807.3(a)
WITNESS BOX**

807.4 Judges' Benches and Courtroom Stations. Judges' benches, clerks' stations, bailiffs' stations, deputy clerks' stations, court reporters' stations and litigants' and counsel stations shall comply with Section 902.

❖ Work station counter or desk surfaces provided within the courtroom must be constructed accessible. What stations are provided depend on the type of courtroom. This includes the counselor's tables and the speaking lectern (see commentary Figure C807.4).

The lectern must be usable by both standing persons and persons using wheelchairs; therefore, the lectern work surface should be adjustable mechanically. In ad-

**Figure 807.3(b)
JURY BOX**

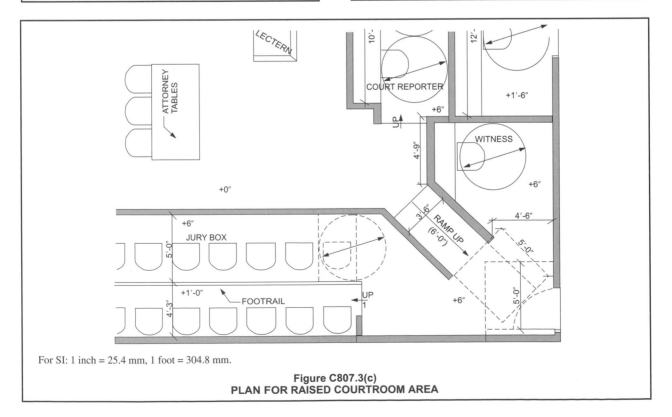

For SI: 1 inch = 25.4 mm, 1 foot = 304.8 mm.

**Figure C807.3(c)
PLAN FOR RAISED COURTROOM AREA**

dition to the work surface and knee and toe clearance requirements in Section 902, it is important to keep a line of sight between the judge and lawyer. The surrounding edges should lower with the work surface.

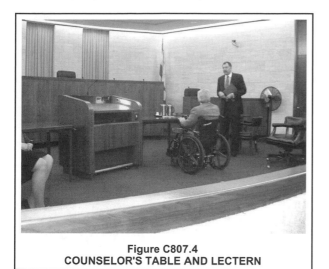

Figure C807.4
COUNSELOR'S TABLE AND LECTERN

Chapter 9. Built-In Furnishings and Equipment

❖ Chapter 9 contains the technical requirements for built-in furnishings and equipment that were not addressed in other chapters. Parts of this chapter are referenced from other chapters, similar to the building blocks in Chapter 3. For example, the work surface section is referenced for the work surfaces in kitchens.

- Section 901 is a general statement about the Chapter 9 criteria being applicable for the special types of elements addressed in this chapter where required by the authority having jurisdiction.

- Section 902 states criteria for fixed dining surfaces, such as bars or banquette tables, or work surfaces, such as study carrels in libraries or check writing stations in banks.

- Section 903 contains technical criteria for benches required in spaces where persons may need to change their clothes, such as a dressing room, fitting room or locker room.

- Section 904 addresses requirements for sales and service counters that are commonly found in grocery stores, banks or mercantile establishments.

- Section 905 provides technical criteria for storage facilities, such as pantries, supply closets or coat closets.

901 General

901.1 Scope. Built-in furnishings and equipment required to be accessible by the scoping provisions adopted by the administrative authority shall comply with the applicable provisions of Chapter 9.

❖ Sections 902 through 905 contain the provisions necessary for accessibility to furnishings and equipment that are built into a building or structure as permanent elements. The elements included in this section are not intended to be a comprehensive list of everything that can be built into a building, but rather a listing of elements typically found in most building types. Elements that are not specifically described in this section, but are similar in nature and similar in use to the elements that are described in this section, must be made accessible to the extent possible for similar elements where specific detailed provisions are stated. Note that these provisions apply to these built-in furnishings and equipment when required by the scoping provisions (see Section 201).

902 Dining Surfaces and Work Surfaces

❖ The requirements in this section establish the necessary dimensions and clearances that must be maintained to provide access to built-in tables or counters that are used for dining surfaces and work surfaces.

Dining surfaces are tables or counters where people consume food or drink, such as fixed tables in restaurants, picnic tables in park shelters, or bars in nightclubs or ice cream parlors. Dining surfaces are typically provided with loose seats, booth seating or fixed stools, but they can also have adjacent standing space.

Work surfaces include tables and counters intended to be accessible surfaces where work can be performed, such as writing, filling out forms, operating a computer, preparing food, reading, personal grooming, etc. Examples include writing counters in banks, admission counters in hospitals, reading and writing surfaces in libraries and classrooms, student laboratory stations and baby changing stations. Counters at visitor areas in courthouses and correctional and detention facilities would be considered a work surface [see commentary Figure C902(a) through (f)].

Seating, counters and work surfaces that must be accessible must be located on an accessible route.

902.1 General. Accessible dining surfaces and work surfaces shall comply with Section 902.

EXCEPTION: Dining surfaces and work surfaces primarily for children's use shall be permitted to comply with Section 902.4.

❖ Built-in work counters and surfaces are designed for a vast number of reasons, built to a wide variety of sizes and shapes, and use many of the available building materials. It is not always necessary for an entire counter or work surface to be accessible, but people with physical disabilities must have access to a portion of these building elements. This is also true for fixed tables with seating. Not only must a percentage of the tables be accessible, but if fixed seating is provided, a loose seat or open space for a wheelchair location must be available at those accessible tables.

The heights for adults are different than for children; therefore, an option that allows for accessible location when tables or work surfaces are designed for children is given in Section 902.4. Examples would be a reading counter in the children's section of a library or work counters or tables in a preschool or elementary classroom.

902.2 Clear Floor Space. Clear floor space complying with Section 305, positioned for a forward approach, shall be provided. Knee and toe clearance complying with Section 306 shall be provided.

❖ In addition to providing counters or work surfaces at an accessible height (Section 902.3), a work surface or dining surface must be on an accessible route and have adequate clearances under that surface. Although some items in this standard have an option of a front approach or a parallel approach, a front approach is required at dining and work surfaces.

The 30-inch by 48-inch (760 by 1220 mm) clear floor or ground space (Section 305) is required at all accessible built-in furnishings to provide maneuvering space that will allow access to the seating spaces at

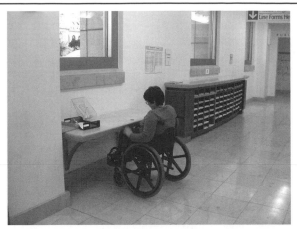

(a) FORM COUNTER

(b) LIBRARY CARRELS

(c) BOOTH SEATING

(d) PICNIC TABLE

(e) VISITOR WINDOW

(f) RESOURCE CENTER

Figure C902
EXAMPLES OF DINING AND WORK SURFACES

counters and work surfaces. If the area under the work surface is confined in some way by items such as walls, a privacy shield, table legs, etc. the provisions for alcoves are applicable. This could result in a minimum width of 36 inches (915 mm).

The space for a person using a wheelchair is permitted to project under tables, counters and work surfaces to the extent described in Section 306. Clearances for a person's knees and toes are required. The arms on a wheelchair or the chest of the person using the wheelchair will limit the amount someone can move forward under a counter or table. If objects are located under the surface adjacent to the knee and toe space (e.g., cable tray, support), it is advisable to protect the person using the surface from injury by padding or rounding any sharp edges or locate these items as far past the knee and toe clearances as practical.

Although not required, design is improved if the clear floor space at accessible furnishings does not interfere with the path of travel for other people using aisles adjacent to accessible features so persons sitting in the wheelchair locations will not be continually jostled. For example, locate the wheelchair seating in a restaurant so that when a person is using that space, people moving to and from other tables or waiters and waitresses serving the tables can have a clear path past the person without bumping them, squeezing past or having to ask them to move.

902.3 Height. The tops of dining surfaces and work surfaces shall be 28 inches (710 mm) minimum and 34 inches (865 mm) maximum in height above the floor.

❖ The height of any type of table top, counter, work surface or similar furnishing is determined by the intended use, as well as by the needs of the person using the wheelchair. These provisions apply to the specific furnishing and do not change because of the particular occupancy of the building.

Dining surfaces can be of a variety of configurations. When booths are installed for accessible seating, the accessible space can be either at the side or end of the table. Tables with booth seating on one side and loose chairs on the other side are called banquettes. If accessible seating is provided at a bar, the length of the accessible section should be a minimum of 60 inches (1525 mm) to accommodate a companion at the same level.

Different types of work require different work surface heights for comfort and ease of use. Light detailed work such as writing requires a work surface close to elbow height for a standing person. Heavy manual work such as rolling dough requires a work surface height about 10 inches (255 mm) below elbow height for a standing person. The principle of a high work surface for light detailed work and a low work surface for heavy manual work also applies for seated persons; however, the limiting condition for seated manual work is clearance under the work surface.

Table C902.3 lists convenient work surface heights for seated persons. The great variety of heights for comfort and optimal performance indicates a need for alternatives or a compromise in height if both people who stand and people who sit are using the same

TABLE C902.3
CONVENIENT HEIGHTS OF WORK SURFACES FOR SEATED PEOPLE[a]

CONDITIONS OF USE	SHORT WOMEN		TALL MEN	
	inches	mm	inches	mm
Seated in a wheelchair				
Manual work				
Desk or removable armrests	26	660	30	760
Fixed, full-size armrests[b]	32[c]	815	32[c]	815
Light, detailed work				
Desk or removable armrests	29	735	34	865
Fixed, full-size armrests[b]	32[c]	815	34	865
Seated in a 16-inch (405 mm) high chair				
Manual work	26	660	27	685
Light, detailed work	28	710	31	785

a. All dimensions are based on a work-surface thickness of $1^1/_2$ inches (38 mm) and a clearance of $1^1/_2$ inches (38 mm) between legs and the underside of a work surface.

b. This type of wheelchair arm does not interfere with the positioning of a wheelchair under a work surface.

c. This dimension is limited by the height of the armrests; a lower height would be preferable. Some people in this group prefer lower work surfaces, which require positioning the wheelchair back from the edge of the counter.

counter area. Service counters serve as duty stations for employees who require knee clearances and may double as temporary work surfaces for persons using wheelchairs having a need to complete forms or work directly with personnel.

902.4 Dining Surfaces and Work Surfaces for Children's Use. Accessible dining surfaces and work surfaces primarily for children's use shall comply with Section 902.4.

> **EXCEPTION:** Dining surfaces and work surfaces used primarily by children ages 5 and younger shall not be required to comply with Section 902.4 where a clear floor space complying with Section 305, positioned for a parallel approach, is provided.

❖ When designing spaces where a high percentage of the users are children, such as schools, libraries, museums or community centers, a designer/owner may want to provide areas specifically sized for the comfort of children. If a designer/owner wants to provide an accessible dining or work surface specifically designed for the use of children from age 6 to 12 years, they must follow the provisions in the following sections. If the children using the surface are 5 years or younger, a counter of any height may be provided as long as a 30-inch by 48-inch (760 by 1220 mm) clear floor space is provided that allows for a side approach. Typically with children of that age, the table height is lower than 26 inches (660 mm), which would not allow for knee and toe clearances.

902.4.1 Clear Floor Space. A clear floor space complying with Section 305, positioned for forward approach, shall be provided. Knee and toe clearance complying with Section 306 shall be provided.

> **EXCEPTION:** Knee clearance 24 inches (610 mm) minimum above the floor shall be permitted.

❖ This child provision allows for consideration of child appropriate sizes. The basic requirement is that a typical adult-sized clear floor space along with knee and toe clearances is provided at the accessible dining or work surface (see Sections 902.2 and 902.3). The exception allows for the height required for the knee space to be reduced to 24 inches (610 mm) instead of the standard 27 inches (685 mm) minimum. This will in turn allow for the lower table/counter service height permitted in Section 902.4.2.

902.4.2 Height. The tops of tables and counters shall be 26 inches (660 mm) minimum and 30 inches (760 mm) maximum above the floor.

❖ This child provision allows for consideration of child appropriate sizes. The lower knee clearances permitted with the exception in Section 902.4.1 will allow for the lower table/counter surface height. The allow-

ances for adult table/counter surface heights are addressed in Section 902.3.

903 Benches

❖ The section on benches is referenced in the requirements for dressing, fitting and locker rooms (Section 803.4) and holding and housing cells (Section 806.2.2).

The scoping provisions may require accessible benches at other locations.

903.1 General. Accessible benches shall comply with Section 903.

❖ For dressing, fitting and locker rooms, the intent is that if a person using a wheelchair needs to transfer, or a person with mobility impairments or balance problems needs to sit down to change any item of clothing, that a seat is available. In a locker room, the bench must be located so that it does not require transfer to the bench to access the accessible lockers. At the same time, the bench is not required to have reach range to the lockers, but it is more user friendly if they are in proximity. As discussed in Section 803, if such spaces, for example storage lockers for bags or purses available for the public in a museum, are not intended to allow for changing, a bench is not required.

For housing and holding cells, for security reasons, sometimes the only seat provided is a bench seat. In a housing cell, a person may need to transfer to the bench for grooming activities.

903.2 Clear Floor Space. A clear floor space complying with Section 305, positioned for parallel approach to an end of the bench seat, shall be provided.

❖ When considering the relationship of clear floor space to the bench, a primary consideration is transfer between a wheelchair and the bench. This can be accomplished by placing the wheelchair at the end of the bench, allowing transfer between two seats that face the same direction. To accomplish this, however, the clear floor space must be located at the open end of the bench so the side of the wheelchair is parallel to the end of the bench [see Figure 903(a)]. Transfer is easier if the seat on the wheelchair and the bench line up. If possible, the clear floor space provided for transfer should be 12 inches (305 mm) back from the back of the seat [see commentary Figure C903.2(a)]. It is also important to recognize the barrier introduced by arm rests at the ends of benches.

Installing a grab bar on a side wall would exceed code requirements and possibly aid transfer to the bench; however, a grab bar should not be installed over the back of the bench. A grab bar on the rear wall would cause a problem with using the wall for back support [see commentary Figure C903.2(b)].

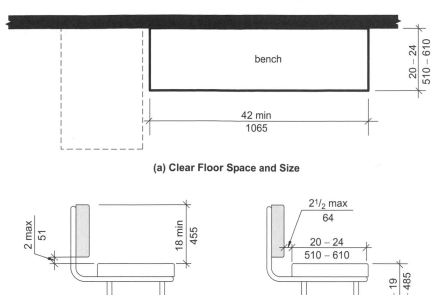

(a) Clear Floor Space and Size

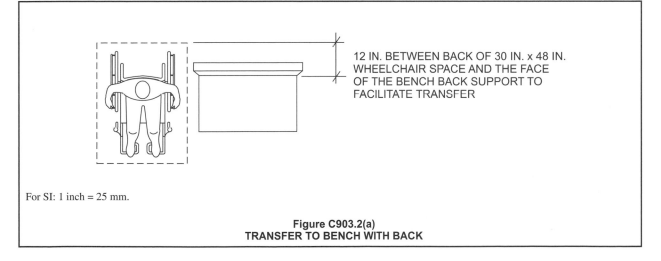

(b) Bench Back Support and Seat Height

Fig. 903
Benches

12 IN. BETWEEN BACK OF 30 IN. x 48 IN. WHEELCHAIR SPACE AND THE FACE OF THE BENCH BACK SUPPORT TO FACILITATE TRANSFER

For SI: 1 inch = 25 mm.

Figure C903.2(a)
TRANSFER TO BENCH WITH BACK

903.3 Size. Benches shall have seats 42 inches (1065 mm) minimum in length, and 20 inches (510 mm) minimum and 24 inches (610 mm) maximum in depth.

❖ The 42 inch (1065 mm) dimension is the overall length of the bench and the 20 to 24 inch (510 to 610 mm) is the seat depth. The length will allow for a person to put their leg up on the bench sideways for assistance in changing clothes. A user may need to brace themselves into the corner for added support, so a much longer bench is not recommended. Remember, the clear floor space for transfer, required in Section 903.2, must be at the end of the bench [see Figure 903(a) and commentary Figure C903.2(a)].

903.4 Back Support. The bench shall provide for back support or shall be affixed to a wall. Back support shall be 42 inches (1065 mm) minimum in length and shall extend from a point 2 inches (51 mm) maximum above the seat surface to a point 18 inches (455 mm) minimum above the seat surface. Back support shall be $2^1/_2$ inches (64 mm) maximum from the rear edge of the seat measured horizontally.

❖ Back support by either a back rest or wall is required for the full length of the bench [e.g., 42 inches (1665 mm) per Section 903.3]. The dimensions for the back rest are given in Figure 903. Although the option of a wall may provide a corner location for support, the option of a back rest may allow for an easier transfer or better proximity to lockers or hooks (see commentary Figure C903.2(a)].

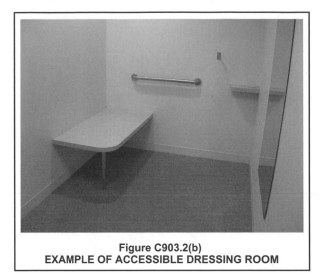

Figure C903.2(b)
EXAMPLE OF ACCESSIBLE DRESSING ROOM

903.5 Height. The top of the bench seat shall be 17 inches (430 mm) minimum and 19 inches (485 mm) maximum above the floor, measured to the top of the seat.

❖ The height of the bench seating area above the floor is critical for the wheelchair user to make a safe and comfortable transfer from the wheelchair to the bench. For a comfortable transfer, the height of the bench seat should be as close as possible to the seat height of the wheelchair. The seat height of most standard wheelchairs is about 17 inches (430 mm).

903.6 Structural Strength. Allowable stresses shall not be exceeded for materials used where a vertical or horizontal force of 250 pounds (1112 N) is applied at any point on the seat, fastener mounting device, or supporting structure.

❖ The structural loads required in this section are to be applied to the bench seat material, as well as to the structural components that support the bench seat. One of the options is for the bench to be fixed to the wall along the long side of the bench. It is not the intent to require all or any of the structural loads to be supported from the wall at the long side of the bench. The only requirement is for the bench to be adjacent to the wall for back support. It is the responsibility of the bench designer to provide the prescribed structural support of the bench. Consideration must also be given to the structural support system to ensure that the system itself does not create an obstacle that will make the bench inaccessible.

903.7 Wet Locations. Where provided in wet locations the surface of the seat shall be slip resistant and shall not accumulate water.

❖ Wet locations such as showers, saunas, steam rooms and pool bathhouses are generally more hazardous because of the presence of moisture and standing water. Wheelchair users quite often use the surface on the bench for support while making a wheelchair transfer. Benches in these types of locations must be made of nonslip materials. The materials must be certified as being nonslip while wet. A material that is considered nonslip only when dry does not comply with the intent of this requirement. Bench seats must also be installed with a minimum degree of slope to allow water to drain off the seat surface. The surface can have a minimum of perforations to prevent water from ponding on the seat. If perforated seat material is used, care must be taken to ensure that the perforations do not become a hazard.

904 Sales and Service Counters

❖ This section addresses all types of sales and service counters where transactions take place at or over the counter. The key is how the customer is expected to interact with the employee at that counter, or if they are expected to access items themselves. Examples are a checkout counter in grocery stores, counters for pick-up such as a drycleaner, reception counters at the front of an office, car rental and airline counters in airports, counters used for viewing merchandise, fast food ordering counters, cafeteria lines, etc.

Simply providing a cash register at a counter is not intended to require the checkout aisle requirements. The provisions in Section 904.4 were written for the standard conveyor belt to bagger type of checkout aisle commonly found in grocery stores. The provisions for service counters or windows in Section 904.3 are intended to cover locations where transactions take place, such as a bank teller window or a hotel check-in counter. The designer should follow the provisions based on the use of the counter and what type of interaction occurs at that location. For example, many drug stores have one or two counters with cash registers at the front of the store. Customers typically bring up several items to purchase that they have gathered from throughout the store. The counter at this location may follow the provisions for check-out aisles, even if they do not have a conveyor belt. However, there are also cash registers at several other locations, such as the photo development window, the cosmetic counter and at the pharmacy. At these locations the customer is typically coming in for an item that is handed to them by the employee. Although someone could take additional items to any of those locations, the number is usually limited to a few items. These locations would most likely be considered sales or service counters.

Food service line requirements in Section 904.5 were developed for cafeteria style dining or portions of fast food restaurants where the customer helps themselves, such as condiment or drink service areas. The portion of the counter where you order the food in a fast food restaurant is most likely a sales or service counter.

904.1 General. Accessible sales and service counters shall comply with Section 904 as applicable.

❖ Where sales counters and service counters are required by the administrative authority to be accessible for use by the public, the provisions of this section apply. Typical scoping provisions are for one at each location or each type when these counters are dispersed. When they are grouped, as in the front of a large store, a minimum percentage is typically required. When not all aisles are accessible, the accessible aisles will be signed.

904.2 Approach. All portions of counters required to be accessible shall be located adjacent to a walking surface complying with Section 403.

❖ Adjacent to the accessible portion of the counter should be a level surface that is part of an accessible route. At a hotel checkout counter, this may be only a small portion. At a cafeteria line or checkout aisle, this may be down the entire line.

If a queue or waiting line defined by permanent walls or rails is part of the access to the sales or service counter, checkout aisles or food service line, the clearances must be maintained in this portion as well.

904.3 Sales and Service Counters. Sales and service counters shall comply with Section 904.3.1 or 904.3.2. The accessible portion of the countertop shall extend the same depth as the sales and service countertop.

❖ A sales or service counter may be accessed by either a parallel or a forward approach. The use of the counter should dictate when a forward approach with knee and toe clearances should be used. An example would be when the customer/employee interaction requires some type of filling out of forms.

This section is applicable at sales or service windows too. Not having a counter surface is not intended to be an exemption from this requirement.

904.3.1 Parallel Approach. A portion of the counter surface 36 inches (915 mm) minimum in length and 36 inches (915 mm) maximum in height above the floor shall be provided. Where the counter surface is less than 36 inches (915 mm) in length, the entire counter surface shall be 36 inches (915 mm) maximum in height above the floor. A clear floor space complying with Section 305, positioned for a parallel approach adjacent to the accessible counter, shall be provided.

❖ Typically, service counters are designed and used from both sides at the same time. An employee will address the counter from one side while the other side is used for customers. Sales and service counters are designed using a vast assortment of materials, and the sizes and shapes are limited only by the imagination of architects and designers. Because sales and service counters can take on many shapes and be constructed to a wide

variety of sizes it is important to establish guidelines that will ensure a portion of the counter will contain an area that is accessible for someone using a wheelchair. The 36 inch (915 mm) height will allow for a standard counter height. The width of the accessible counter must be at least 36 inches minimum. For interaction between the customer/employee, the 36-inch (915 mm) height must be the full depth of the counter. A shelf under a higher window is not adequate (see commentary Figure C904.3.1).

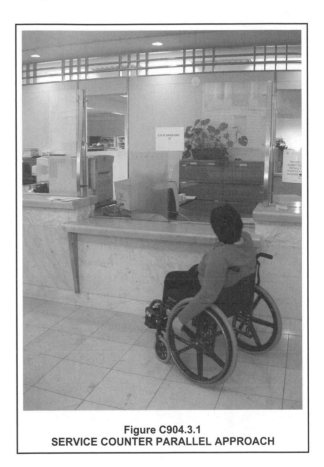

Figure C904.3.1
SERVICE COUNTER PARALLEL APPROACH

904.3.2 Forward Approach. A portion of the counter surface 30 inches (760 mm) minimum in length and 36 inches (915 mm) maximum in height above the floor shall be provided. A clear floor space complying with Section 305, positioned for a forward approach to the accessible counter, shall be provided. Knee and toe clearance complying with Section 306 shall be provided under the accessible counter.

❖ Sometimes a service counter can be the location where someone may need to fill out forms or access information. In these cases, the service window should have a forward approach with knee and toe clearances similar to a work surface (see Section 902 and commentary Figure C904.3.2).

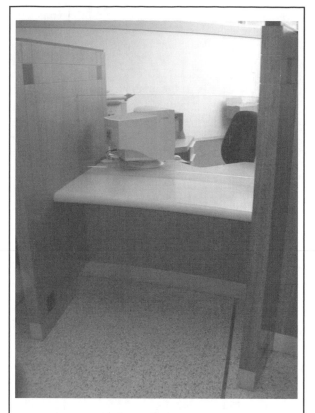

Figure C904.3.2
SERVICE COUNTER FORWARD APPROACH

904.4 Checkout Aisles. Checkout aisles shall comply with Section 904.4.

❖ Accessible checkout aisles, such as those found in grocery stores, must meet the provisions for the aisle, counter and any check writing surface. See the commentary to Section 904 for an explanation of the difference between a checkout aisle and a sales and service counter (see commentary Figure C904.4).

904.4.1 Aisle. Aisles shall comply with Section 403.

❖ The aisle between the checkout counter and any other obstruction, such as a wall or another checkout counter, must have a clear width of 36 inches (915 mm) minimum. If getting into or out of the aisle would require making a tight turn around an obstruction, the requirements of Section 403.5.1 may result in a 42 inch (1065 mm) minimum aisle width.

904.4.2 Counters. The checkout counter surface shall be 38 inches (965 mm) maximum in height above the floor. The top of the counter edge protection shall be 2 inches (51 mm) maximum above the top of the counter surface on the aisle side of the checkout counter.

❖ A 2-inch (50 mm) high ledge is permitted along the edge of accessible checkout counters so that food will not tip off the conveyor belt as it moves forward. The 38-inch (965 mm) high checkout aisle will still allow

Figure C904.4
CHECKOUT AISLE

a person using a wheelchair to be able to see the merchandise.

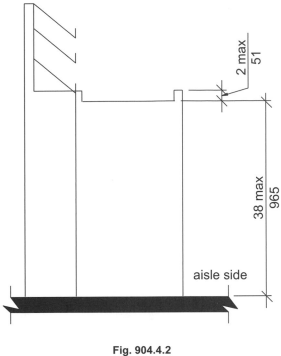

Fig. 904.4.2
Height of Checkout Counters

904.4.3 Check Writing Surfaces. Where provided, check writing surfaces shall comply with Section 902.3.

❖ If a surface is provided for customers to write checks or sign a credit card slip, the height of that surface must be between 28 inches and 34 inches (710 and 865 mm) high. The reference to Section 902.3 does not require any knee or toe clearances under that surface. A side approach would be permitted.

  The intent is not to prohibit an additional check writing surface at a higher level. With the checkout counter at 38 inches (965 mm) in height (Section 904.4.2) it is not possible to meet both requirements at the same location. A small pull-out shelf or fixed shelf at the lower height may be provided for this condition. If a pull-out shelf is provided, it must meet the operable parts provisions in Section 309 and be operable with only one hand.

904.5 Food Service Lines. Counters in food service lines shall comply with Section 904.5.

❖ Unlike the requirements for service windows or work surfaces that require portions of counters to be acces-

sible, the provisions in this section apply to the entire length of the tray slide. The height must be maintained throughout the tray slide without requiring the user to interrupt progress by lifting or moving the tray to another tray slide or to a different level within the same service line.

904.5.1 Self-Service Shelves and Dispensing Devices. Self-service shelves and dispensing devices for tableware, dishware, condiments, food and beverages shall comply with Section 308.

❖ Areas where condiments, napkins and tableware are provided are found in many fast food restaurants and cafeterias. When customers get their own drinks, this area must also be accessible, including the drink machine, cups, lids and straws. The reference to Section 308 requires everything to be within the 15 inch to 48 inch 380 to 1220 mm) reach range (see commentary Figure C904.5.1).

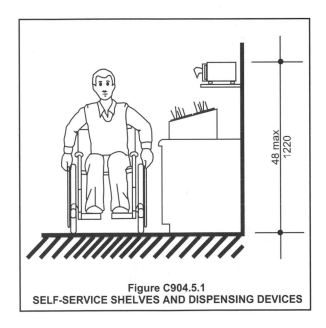

Figure C904.5.1
SELF-SERVICE SHELVES AND DISPENSING DEVICES

904.5.2 Tray Slides. The tops of tray slides shall be 28 inches (710 mm) minimum and 34 inches (865 mm) maximum above the floor.

❖ The height for tray slides is consistent with those for work surfaces; however, knee and toe clearances are not required (See commentary Figure C904.5.2).

  The standard 24-inch (610 mm) maximum reach range should be considered when designing access for the food. Not all portions must be within the reach range (e.g., food layout and suitable utensils can be a factor).

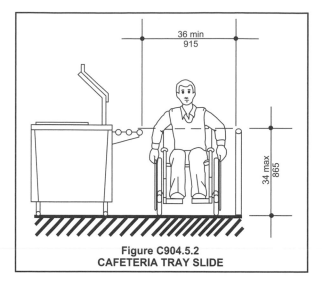

Figure C904.5.2
CAFETERIA TRAY SLIDE

904.6 Security Glazing. Where counters or teller windows have security glazing to separate personnel from the public, a method to facilitate voice communication shall be provided. Telephone handset devices, if provided, shall comply with Section 704.3.

❖ For security reasons, some service windows may have glazing at the window. Examples would be bank teller windows, currency exchanges or sign-in windows at controlled facilities. Security glazing may include voice communication methods such as openings, grilles, slats, talk-through baffles, intercoms, assistive listening systems (Section 706) or telephone handsets. If the system of choice includes telephone handsets, volume controls (Section 704.3) are required.

Visiting areas in judicial facilities and detention and correctional facilities are considered two work surfaces separated by security glazing. Therefore, in addition to proving accessible stations (e.g., typically 5 percent) in accordance with the authority having jurisdiction, all stations must meet the security glazing provisions for both sides [see commentary Figure C904.6(a) and C904.6(b)].

Figure 904.6(a)
SECURITY GLAZING AT VISITOR WINDOW

Figure 904.6(b)
SECURITY GLAZING AT SERVICE WINDOW

905 Storage Facilities

❖ An accessible storage facility is defined as one that complies with the provisions of this section. The components required to make a storage facility accessible are addressed in this section, including the approach, reach ranges and hardware that allows operation by a person with a physical disability.

Example of storage facilities may include shelves, cabinets, clothes rods, mail boxes, storage lockers, etc.

905.1 General. Accessible storage facilities shall comply with Section 905.

❖ The provisions in this section are not intended to determine whether or when a storage facility must be accessible. The provisions in this section are the minimum standards necessary to ensure that a storage facility is accessible when required by the administrative authority.

905.2 Clear Floor Space. A clear floor space complying with Section 305 shall be provided.

❖ To be usable by a person with a disability, storage facilities must have a 30-inch by 48-inch (760 by 1220 mm) clear floor or ground space to position a wheelchair so that the user can reach the stored items. This clear floor space must be on an accessible route (see commentary Figure C905.2).

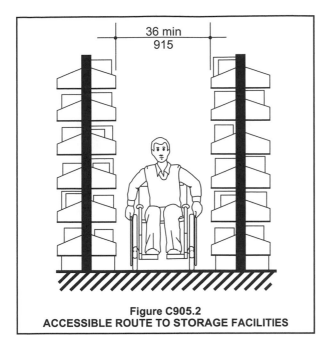

Figure C905.2
ACCESSIBLE ROUTE TO STORAGE FACILITIES

905.3 Height. Accessible storage elements shall comply with at least one of the reach ranges specified in Section 308.

❖ Once a wheelchair is positioned for forward or parallel approach at a storage facility, the facility is still not us-able unless the stored items are kept within reach ranges that allow the wheelchair user to reach and retrieve them. Typically, this would include shelving or clothes rods between 15 inches and 48 inches (380 and 1220 mm) above the floor (see commentary Figure C905.3). Reaching over an obstruction may reduce the high reach to 44 inches (1115 mm). See Section 308 for full requirements.

Providing additional shelves or clothes rods outside of the reach ranges is acceptable.

905.4 Operable Parts. Operable parts of storage facilities shall comply with Section 309.

❖ This reference reflects the more general need to consider those persons with limited physical dexterity. Hardware requiring tight grasping, pinching or twisting of the wrist is undesirable. Touch latches, levers and U-shaped pulls are acceptable because they do not require great dexterity. These issues are addressed in Section 309.4. The general reference to Section 309 results in the operable parts needing to meet clear floor space (Section 309.2) and height (Section 309.3) restrictions, as well as the requirements for the storage element itself already addressed in Sections 905.2 and 905.3.

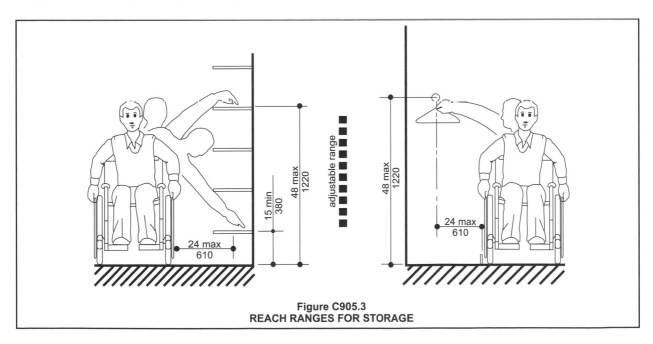

Figure C905.3
REACH RANGES FOR STORAGE

Chapter 10. Dwelling Units and Sleeping Units

❖ Chapter 10 contains the technical requirements for Accessible, Type A and Type B dwelling and sleeping units. See the commentary at the beginning of Sections 1002, 1003 and 1004 for a description of the different types of units and history.

- Section 1001 is a general statement about the Chapter 10 criteria being applicable for the Accessible, Type A and Type B dwelling and sleeping units addressed in this chapter where required by the authority having jurisdiction. This scoping criterion provides information on 'what, where and how many.' Technical criteria in this chapter are the 'how.'
- Section 1002 details technical criteria for Accessible dwelling and sleeping units.
- Section 1003 states technical criteria for Type A dwelling and sleeping units.
- Section 1004 provides technical criteria for Type B dwelling and sleeping units.
- Section 1005 contains criteria for accessible communication features such as those used for emergency evacuations (e.g., fire alarms, smoke detectors) and announcing visitors (e.g., doorbells, voice or visual communication between the apartment and the building entrance).

For each level of accessibility of dwelling and sleeping units, Chapter 10 provides the users all of the technical requirements for the unit. The technical criteria are stated in the section for the specific type of unit or the section gives the user a reference to the location of the technical requirement either in another section of Chapter 10 or one of the other chapters of the standard. A section contained in Chapters 1 through 9 is not used for dwelling or sleeping unit design unless it is specifically referenced in Chapter 10. For example, Section 1003.12.3 provides the requirements for a kitchen work surface in a Type A unit; however neither Section 804.3 nor 902, which address work surfaces in kitchens in other occupancies, is referenced. On the other hand, for an Accessible unit, Section 1002.12 refers the user to Section 804 for the design of a kitchen and Section 902 for the work surface. For the Type A unit work surface, the standards of Sections 804.3 and 902 do not apply; for the Accessible unit work surface they do.

Each of the sections for dwelling or sleeping units is set up in the same order. This allows for easy comparison between Accessible, Type A and Type B units.

- 100*.1 is a general reference to the section requirements.
- 100*.2 is criteria for the primary entrance to the unit.
- 100*.3 is accessible route requirement throughout the inside of the unit.
- 100*.4 deals with the walking surfaces that are part of the accessible route in Section 100*.3.
- 100*.5 is for the doors and doorways within the unit. In Type B units there are separate criteria for the primary entrance door and the other doors and doorways in the unit.
- 100*.6 is a reference to the general ramp provisions in Section 405.
- 100*.7 indicates that a private residence elevator (Section 409) is an option to provide an accessible route within the unit. Passenger elevators and LULAs in accordance with Sections 407 and 408 are also acceptable as alternatives because they result in a higher level of accessibility.
- 100*.8 indicates that a platform lift (i.e., not a chair lift) in accordance with Section 410 can also serve as part of an accessible route within a unit.
- 100*.9 provides technical criteria for the referenced list of operable parts. It is important to note that the items that must meet operable parts provisions are not the same in Accessible, Type A and Type B units. For example, appliance controls, plumbing controls and door hardware are not required to meet operable parts requirements in Type B units.
- 100*.10 states the applicable provisions for laundry facilities installed within the unit. Laundry facilities in a shared or common location for residents must match the level or accessibility for the units they serve.
- 100*.11 contains options for bathrooms. Note that the two alternatives in Type B units are called Option A and Option B. Although some people confuse this nomenclature with Type A units, the Option A and Option B bathrooms are limited to Type B units.
- 100*.12 deals with kitchen requirements within units. Kitchenettes or wetbars must comply as applicable.
- 100*.13 deals with provisions for accessible windows. Type B units do not require accessible windows.
- 100*.14 deals with storage facilities such as closets, cabinets and shelving other than those in the kitchen area. Type B units do not include requirements for storage facilities.

1001 General

❖ Dwelling units and sleeping units are defined in Section 106.5.

A dwelling unit contains independent facilities for living, sleeping, eating, cooking and sanitation (i.e., living room, bedroom, a full kitchen and a bathroom). This group covers all types of units individuals or families think of as their house and a minimal number of transient lodging facilities. Examples are: apartments, condominiums, townhouses, single-family homes and residential type hotel guestrooms.

A sleeping unit is something that is not a full dwelling unit. It can be just a sleeping area, such as a dorm room with access to gang bathrooms and no cooking facilities. A sleeping unit can include either sanitation or cooking, but not both (i.e., the unit is a space to live and sleep, but shares a bathroom outside the unit and/or does not include a full kitchen). This group covers all types of congregate living arrangements and most transient lodging. Examples are: guestrooms in hotels and motels; bedrooms in dormitories, boarding houses, sorority houses, fraternity houses, halfway houses, group homes, monasteries, convents, assisted living facilities and nursing homes; and sleeping cells in jails.

1001.1 Scoping. Dwelling units and sleeping units required to be Accessible units, Type A units, Type B units, or units with accessible communication features by the scoping provisions adopted by the administrative authority shall comply with the applicable provisions of Chapter 10.

❖ The requirements of this chapter are intended to provide the technical criteria for accessibility within dwelling and sleeping units for Accessible, Type A or Type B units when scoped by the authority having jurisdiction (see Section 201). Scoping may also include dwelling or sleeping units that require accessible communication features, regardless of whether the unit is accessible in other ways. For example, an apartment building may have requirements for visible alarm notification appliances (e.g., visible fire alarms and smoke detectors) or entry systems (e.g., closed circuit communication systems) to all floors in a building, including upper floors without elevator access.

The model codes contain scoping criteria for the three levels of accessibility in dwelling and sleeping units. The level of accessibility increases based on the anticipated needs.

The model codes provide scoping criteria for accessibility in all types of places where people live, eat and sleep. Types of dwelling units are addressed, including apartments, condominiums and townhouses. Typically single-family detached homes are exempted, but a home owner may choose to follow these criteria to build an accessible home. The model codes also contain scoping criteria for congregate living facilities, such as assisted-living · facilities, group

homes, shelters, nursing homes, boarding houses, dormitories, convents, monasteries, fraternities and sororities. Even though each person's accommodations may not contain all the element listed in Chapter 10, they must comply with the applicable provisions. For example, a boarding house may have a private or semi-private sleeping room with a private bath, but additional living space and possibly a kitchen area common to a group of rooms. If the boarding house sleeping rooms are scoped for Type B units, the sleeping rooms, bathrooms and all shared/common spaces for resident must have a minimum level of accessibility consistent with Type B unit criteria.

The model code, including ICC A117.1, is working toward coordinating with federal requirements such as the American's with Disabilities Act (ADA) and the Fair Housing Act (FHA). For example, ADA deals with transient facilities such as a typical hotel. A percentage of the hotel rooms must be constructed as Accessible units. FHA deals mostly with permanent housing, such as apartments. Apartment buildings are required to contain Type B units. In some situations ADA and FHA overlap, such as in dormitories and nursing homes. In these situations, the model codes require a percentage of units to be Accessible units and a percentage of units to be Type B units. These examples are illustrations only. For full criteria, see the scoping in the model codes.

ICC A117.1 is certified as a 'safe harbor' document for compliance with the Fair Housing Act Accessibility Guidelines (FHAG). The provisions for Type B units are intended to be consistent with FHAG. The Type A and Accessible units exceed FHAG.

1002 Accessible Units

❖ Accessible units are considered to provide a higher level or accessibility than both Type A and Type B units. Therefore, compliance with the provisions in Section 1002 would exceed Type A and Type B requirements.

For the design of an Accessible unit, the requirements in Section 1002.1 through 1002.14 must be met. The technical criteria are either specifically stated in these sections or the section contains a reference to another section of the standard that contains the applicable technical standard. If a technical standard in another chapter is not referenced, it is not applicable to the design of an Accessible unit.

1002.1 General. Accessible units shall comply with Section 1002.

❖ An Accessible dwelling or sleeping unit must comply with all the provisions in this section. Accessible units are constructed wheelchair accessible. See the scoping documents for when Accessible dwelling and sleeping units are required. Accessible units are typically required in transient facilities such as hotels, or facilities where there is a high anticipation of people who may need these facilities, such as nursing homes.

1002.2 Primary Entrance. The accessible primary entrance shall be on an accessible route from public and common areas. The primary entrance shall not be to a bedroom.

❖ In an apartment type unit, the main entrance is typically into a central living area, so this should also be the accessible entrance for the unit. The accessible entrance cannot be a 'backdoor' entrance, such as a patio door or through a bedroom. This accessible unit entrance must be connected by an accessible route to an accessible building entrance and all public or shared areas intended for the use of the residents of that unit. This includes areas such as the building lobby, mail boxes, garbage chutes or dumpsters, shared laundry facilities and recreational facilities, such as exercise rooms or pools. See also Section 1002.5 for requirements for the accessible entrance door to the unit.

In an efficiency unit or sleeping unit where the main living area is also the bedroom, this entrance may serve as the accessible entrance, and is not considered prohibited by the last sentence of this section. It is not the intent of this section to require an entry vestibule or second room.

In facilities such as hotels or nursing homes, the changing of linens or removal of garbage may be the responsibility of employees rather than residents. In these situations, the areas such as laundry rooms and garbage disposal areas should be regulated under the employee work area provisions and are not required to be accessible to the residents of the dwelling units.

1002.3 Accessible Route. Accessible routes within Accessible units shall comply with Section 1002.3. Exterior spaces less than 30 inches (760 mm) in depth or width shall comply with Sections 1002.3.1, 1002.3.3, 302, and 303.

❖ The accessible route within the unit must meet the provisions for location, turning space and components. However, if an exterior space that is part of the unit, such as a balcony, is less than 30 inches (760 mm) deep, rather than have a turning space (Section 1002.3.2, which references Section 304, including Sections 302 and 303), the floor surface and change in level provisions are applicable. The intent is that the space will still be level with the inside space so someone using a wheelchair could pull out onto the balcony, but the additional space for turning around would not be required.

1002.3.1 Location. At least one accessible route shall connect all spaces and elements that are a part of the unit. Where only one accessible route is provided, it shall not pass through bathrooms and toilet rooms, closets, or similar spaces.

EXCEPTION: An accessible route is not required to unfinished attics and unfinished basements that are part of the unit.

❖ A route must be available to all living spaces within the unit. A route must be available to all stories in the unit as well as any raised or sunken floor areas.

In a congregate living arrangement, this also includes access to shared spaces such as the bathroom and living or eating areas.

When only one route is available to certain spaces, the route should not be through areas that are subject to locking such as bathrooms or closets. This is not intended to prohibit access through spaces controlled by the individual. For example, a master suite with the closet accessed through the bathroom would not be blocking access for the occupant of that bedroom.

Unfinished attics and basements are not required to be on an accessible route because these spaces do not include living space for the unit.

1002.3.2 Turning Space. All rooms served by an accessible route shall provide a turning space complying with Section 304.

❖ Turning spaces are required in each room. This space can be circular or T-shaped. The turning spaces can include knee and toe clearances under fixtures, counters, shelves, etc.

At this time the standard is not specific on whether a walk-in closet or pantry would be considered a 'room' and require a turning space. Best design practice would be to have these spaces a minimum of 60 inches (1525 mm) wide. A turning space can rely on knee and toe clearances under the rods or shelves in the space. However, many of these spaces are typically accessed with a pull-in back-out maneuver. The 36-inch (915 mm) wide accessible route (Section 1002.3) between the shelves or the space between clothes may provide better access. Doors to these spaces must have maneuvering clearances on both sides (Section 1002.5). Storage elements within these types of spaces must have a clear floor space in front (Section 1002.14).

1002.3.3 Components. Accessible routes shall consist of one or more of the following elements: walking surfaces with a slope not steeper than 1:20, ramps, elevators, and platform lifts.

❖ The accessible route throughout the unit should be on level surfaces. When a transition is needed between levels or stories, either a ramp, elevator or platform lift can be used. See commentary to Sections 1002.6, 1002.7 and 1002.8.

1002.4 Walking Surfaces. Walking surfaces that are part of an accessible route shall comply with Section 403.

❖ The reference to Section 403 requires walking surfaces that are generally level to be stable and firm with a clear width of 36 inches (915 mm). For example, carpet must have a firm cushion or no pad. Heavy pile or thick padding under carpets make it difficult for a person using a wheelchair to turn or move forward.

1002.5 Doors and Doorways. The primary entrance door to the unit, and all other doorways intended for user passage, shall comply with Section 404.

> **EXCEPTION:** Existing doors to hospital patient sleeping rooms shall be exempt from the requirement for space at the latch side provided the door is 44 inches (1120 mm) minimum in width.

❖ The primary entrance door should be the main door used to access the unit. Any doors that a person walks through in the unit must also be accessible. This includes doors to all rooms, walk-in closets, bathrooms, balconies, etc. Doors to spaces such as reach-in closets are not required to meet the provisions for Section 404.

Requirements include 32 inch (815 mm) clear width, thresholds, lever hardware, door opening force, bottom door surface on the push side and vision lite locations. A front door with a screen/storm door is not considered doors in a series. If an automatic door is installed, the provisions of Section 404.3 are applicable.

The scoping document specifies that a percentage of the hospital patient sleeping rooms are required to meet Accessible unit requirements. In new construction, doors to Accessible units must meet the provisions in Section 404, including maneuvering clearances. In existing hospital patient sleeping rooms, the additional maneuvering clearance on the latch side of 44 inch (1120 mm) wide doors is not required.

1002.6 Ramps. Ramps shall comply with Section 405.

❖ Ramps that serve as part of the accessible route into or through an Accessible dwelling or sleeping unit must meet the general ramp provisions in Section 405.

Ramps for a change in elevation greater than 6 inches (150 mm) will require handrails on both sides. The local building code should be consulted when guards are required along ramps. Ramps must have a landing at both the top and the bottom, so a ramp cannot extend up to the face of a door. The ramp landing and door maneuvering space (Section 1002.5) are permitted to overlap.

1002.7 Elevators. Elevators within the unit shall comply with Section 407, 408, or 409.

❖ Elevators installed within a single dwelling unit or providing private access to a single dwelling unit are permitted to be passenger elevators, LULAs or private residence elevators. Refer to the referenced standard ASME A17.1 for limitations of use. For an example of a private residence elevator see commentary Figure C1002.7.

Section 1002.3.1 requires an accessible route throughout an Accessible unit. If an Accessible unit is multi-story, elevators or platform lifts (Section 1002.8) can serve as part of the accessible route within an individual unit. Although a common-use elevator is often used for residents to access common use areas in a building (e.g., mail room, lobby, laundry room), it is not the intent to allow the use of a common-use elevator to provide access to multiple levels of the same unit. The accessible route should be contained within the unit.

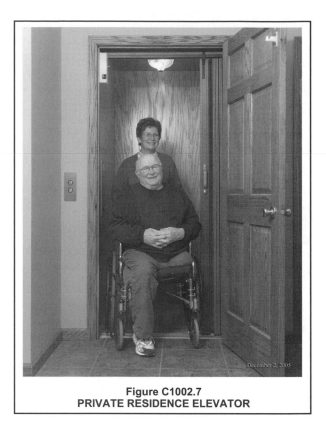

Figure C1002.7
PRIVATE RESIDENCE ELEVATOR

1002.8 Platform Lifts. Platform lifts within the unit shall comply with Section 410.

❖ Platform lifts can be used within individual dwelling units to serve as part of an accessible route between levels or to provide access into an individual unit. The lift must be a platform (wheelchair) lift in accordance with ASME A18.1, not a chair lift (e.g., flip-down seat). Platform lifts may be incline or vertical. The current standard limits the maximum rise to 12 feet (3660 mm). See ASME A18.1 for limitations of use.

1002.9 Operable Parts. Lighting controls, electrical switches and receptacle outlets, environmental controls, appliance controls, operating hardware for operable windows, plumbing fixture controls, and user controls for security or intercom systems shall comply with Section 309.

> **EXCEPTIONS:**
>
> 1. Receptacle outlets serving a dedicated use.

2. One receptacle outlet shall not be required to comply with Section 309 where all of the following conditions are met:

   (a) the receptacle outlet is above a length of countertop that is uninterrupted by a sink or appliance;

   (b) at least one receptacle outlet complying with Section 1002.9 is provided for that length of countertop; and

   (c) all other receptacle outlets provided for that length of countertop comply with Section 1002.9.

3. Floor receptacle outlets.

4. HVAC diffusers.

5. Controls mounted on ceiling fans.

6. Where redundant controls other than light switches are provided for a single element, one control in each space shall not be required to be accessible.

❖ The requirements for operable parts are listed in Section 309. Included are a clear floor space adjacent to the part; that the part be within reach ranges; and that operation of the part not require tight pinching, grasping or twisting of the wrist to operate or more than 5 pounds force (22 N).

The intent is that the person in the space be able to operate the equipment in the room in a normal manner. It is not the intent that the these provisions be applicable to items such as shut-offs for plumbing fixtures or protection switches for electrical equipment, such as the reset switch on a garbage disposal or a circuit breaker box.

Examples of lighting controls are wall light switches or pull cords. Electrical switches could include wall activation switches for garbage disposals, bathroom ventilation fans or cooking hoods. Exception 6 allows for redundant controls to be located in an accessible location. For example, the switch on the range hood can be out of reach range if a wall switch is installed within reach ranges. However, if light switches are offered with 3-way or 4-way operation, all switches must be accessible.

Receptacle outlets are typically the standard duplex wall outlets located around a room or over a counter. Note that there are several exceptions for receptacle outlets. Outlets that serve a dedicated purpose (Exception 1), such as the outlet for a washer/dryer, refrigerator or stove need not be accessible. These items are typically plugged in all the time. The model electrical code requires outlets spaced at a maximum of 12 feet (3660 mm) apart in most rooms. In spaces with very tall windows or along balcony guards, there may not be wall space for the required electrical outlets. Large rooms may need outlets located toward the center of the room. When floor outlets are used, these outlets do not need to be accessible (Exception 3). Exception 2 is most often used when dealing with outlets over kitchen counters. In kitchens, per the model electrical code, one outlet is required over each section of counter top with a maximum spacing of 4 feet (1220 mm). If an appliance or sink is located along a counter top, the counter on each side is considered a separate section, and an outlet must be installed on each side. In a kitchen in an Accessible unit, the sink and the work surface must be at a maximum height of 34 inches (865 mm), although the remainder of the counters can be located at any height, typically 36 inches (915 mm). Accessible outlets could be provided over the sink and work surface. However, with the obstructed side reach range requirements in Section 308.3.2, outlets cannot be located over the standard 36 inch (915 mm) high counter and be accessible. Exception 2 allows for one outlet per counter section to not be accessible if the remainder of the outlets are accessible. An alternative that would provide an accessible outlet is to locate an outlet on the side or front surface of the lower cabinet. This is commonly done on kitchen island counters; however, this will reduce drawer space. This same problem is not typically found in bathrooms because bathroom counter heights are typically between 29 and 34 inches (735 and 865 mm) high.

Environmental controls can include ceiling fans or heating and air conditioning thermostats. A common error for locating the thermostat is to specify the electrical box at 48 inches (1220 mm) high, not noting that the actual control is on the top of the thermostat box, thus placing the control out of the reach range. Exception 4 does exempt the heating and air conditioning diffusers from being accessible. They need to be on or near the floor and near the ceiling to circulate the air in the room effectively. Exception 5 exempts controls mounted on ceiling fans. Typically the on-off and speed for ceiling fans are controlled from a wall switch, but there may be a switch on the fan itself for reversing the direction of the blades.

Appliance controls vary greatly and may include the key pad for temperature and type of cooking (e.g. bake/broil) on ovens, knobs for burner settings on stove tops, door handles to access the interior of the appliance, water/ice dispensers on refrigerators, latches for self-cleaning ovens, soap containers on dishwashers and clothes washers, lint trays on dryers, etc. The specifics for appliance controls in Section 804.6.2 allow some exceptions for appliance doors in kitchens. Laundry equipment is specifically addressed in Section 611.3.

Operating hardware for operable windows includes locks and opening devices for windows that must be accessible. Which windows must be accessible is scoped by the authority having jurisdiction and Section 1002.13. At this time, to meet the operating force requirements, most windows need add-on devices for opening.

Plumbing fixture controls include faucets in showers, tubs and sinks, and flush valves on toilets. Lever type handles are much easier to operate than knobs for those with limited hand mobility or strength. See the specifics in Sections 604.6, 606.4, 607.5, 607.6 and 608.5 for plumbing controls.

Security or intercom systems may include activation keypads or access to a phone or speaker. Refer to Sections 1005.6 and 1005.7 for additional specifics for communication features.

Operable parts on doors are regulated under Section 1002.5 by a reference to Sections 404.2.6 and 404.3.5.

1002.10 Laundry Equipment. Washing machines and clothes dryers shall comply with Section 611.

❖ The standard does not require laundry equipment within the unit; however, if provided, the washers and dryers must meet the same accessibility provisions as in a common laundry room (see Section 611). Stacked washers and dryers typically do not meet the opening requirements in Section 611.4 or the reach range for the operable parts in Section 611.3. It is not required that a person be able to reach into the bottom of the washer or dryer drum. People often use extension arms to reach the clothes in the bottom of the top loader machines. Front-loading washers are becoming more readily available for the home market and may provide a higher level of accessibility. A lower drawer feature can raise the washer and dryer for easier access into the drum [see commentary Figure C1002.10(c)].

When designing the laundry area, several items must be considered. Section 611.2 requires a parallel clear floor space in front of each appliance, centered on that appliance.

When laundry equipment is installed in a room, Section 1002.3.2 requires a turning space within the room, and Section 1002.5 requires maneuvering clearance at the door. To provide a more user friendly space, even though an accessible work surface is not required, if a counter for folding is provided within the room, knee and toe clearances should be available for that work surface. If a laundry sink is provided,

scoping documents typically exempt service sinks from knee and toe clearances because of the needed depth of the sink, but it would be better design to provide a parallel approach to that sink to allow for use [see commentary Figure C1002.10(a)].

When laundry equipment is installed in a closet, the clear floor space can be located 10 inches back from the face of the units (Section 308.3.1) which would allow for the wall thickness, but may necessitate either sliding closet doors or no doors, so the doors will not block the clear floor space [see commentary Figure C1002.10(b)].

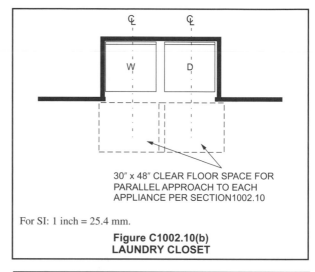

30" x 48" CLEAR FLOOR SPACE FOR PARALLEL APPROACH TO EACH APPLIANCE PER SECTION 1002.10

For SI: 1 inch = 25.4 mm.

Figure C1002.10(b)
LAUNDRY CLOSET

Figure C1002.10(c)
EXAMPLE OF A LAUNDRY ROOM

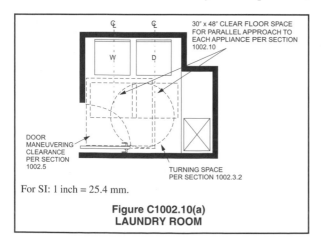

30" x 48" CLEAR FLOOR SPACE FOR PARALLEL APPROACH TO EACH APPLIANCE PER SECTION 1002.10

DOOR MANEUVERING CLEARANCE PER SECTION 1002.5

TURNING SPACE PER SECTION 1002.3.2

For SI: 1 inch = 25.4 mm.

Figure C1002.10(a)
LAUNDRY ROOM

1002.11 Toilet and Bathing Facilities. Toilet and bathing facilities shall comply with Sections 603 through 610.

❖ Every bathroom in Accessible units must be constructed fully accessible in accordance with the requirements in Sections 603 through 610. This includes grab bars installed at the water closet and tub or shower, a water closet that allows for a side transfer, a front approach lavatory and an accessible bathing fixture (i.e., either a tub or shower). Unlike Type A and Type B unit bathrooms, the lavatory may not overlap the clear floor space for the water closet.

1002.11.1 Vanity Counter Top Space. If vanity counter top space is provided in nonaccessible dwelling or sleeping units within the same facility, equivalent vanity counter top space, in terms of size and proximity to the lavatory, shall also be provided in Accessible units.

❖ Accessible dwelling units are commonly scoped for hotels, dormitories, assisted living facilities or nursing homes. In these residential and institutional types of facilities, a counter space is typically provided for a person to place grooming items while using the lavatory. Counters are provided either within a bathroom or immediately adjacent (e.g., lavatory located adjacent to a room with a water closet and tub). The same type of counter space should be available for the use of the person within the Accessible unit as that which is provided in other similar units.

1002.12 Kitchens. Kitchens shall comply with Section 804. At least one work surface, 30 inches (760 mm) minimum in length, shall comply with Section 902.

❖ Kitchens within an Accessible unit must be constructed accessible in accordance with Section 804. This would include a front approach sink and an accessible work surface, along with access to each appliance. The requirement for an accessible work surface in this section is redundant with Section 804.3. Section 1002.3.2 requires a turning space within the room. If the space under the sink or the work surface is used as part of a T-turn, the width must be a minimum of 36 inches (915 mm).

At this time, this standard does not specifically address kitchenettes in Accessible sleeping units (e.g., a hotel room or assisted-living facility room) in this section. Requirements are included in Section 804 for kitchenettes.

1002.13 Windows. Where operable windows are provided, at least one window in each sleeping, living, or dining space shall have operable parts complying with Section 1002.9. Each required operable window shall have operable parts complying with Section 1002.9.

❖ For those windows that must be accessible, it is logical to ensure that the mechanisms that lock and unlock or open and close be positioned for accessibility, including clear floor space, reach ranges and graspability of the mechanisms (see Sections 309 and 1002.9). Examples of required operable windows would be egress windows in bedrooms and windows in spaces where natural ventilation is required. Examples of the types of operable windows include double-hung, sliding, casement and awning windows. At this time, to meet the 5 pounds (22 N) maximum operating force requirement, most windows need add-on devices for opening.

1002.14 Storage Facilities. Where storage facilities are provided, they shall comply with Section 905. Kitchen cabinets shall comply with Section 804.5.

❖ Storage facilities such as closets, bathroom cabinets or pantries must have a clear floor space in front of the storage element. At least a portion of each storage facility provided, such as shelves or rods must be within the 15 inch to 48 inch (350 to 1220 mm) reach range. A standard closet organizer with a high-low rod for a portion of the closet meets this provision. If there are doors or drawers, the latches and knobs must be easily operable by a person with limited hand movement and strength. If this is a reach-in closet, the door does not have to meet the clear width, threshold or maneuvering clearance requirements in Section 1002.5.

Kitchen cabinets should comply with Section 804.5. The special work environment and concentrated amount of storage allows for unique consideration.

1003 Type A Units

❖ Type A units are considered to provide a higher level of accessibility than Type B units, but less accessibility than Accessible units. Therefore, compliance with the provisions in Section 1003 would exceed Type B requirements. Compliance with Section 1002 would exceed Type A requirements.

For the design of a Type A unit, the requirements in Sections 1003.1 through 1003.14 must be met. The technical criteria are either specifically stated in these sections or the section contains a reference to another section of the standard that contains the applicable technical standard. If a technical standard in another chapter is not referenced, it is not applicable to the design of a Type A unit.

1003.1 General. Type A units shall comply with Section 1003.

❖ A Type A dwelling or sleeping unit must comply with all the provisions in this section. Type A units have some elements constructed wheelchair accessible (e.g., 32 inch (815 mm) clear doors with maneuvering clearances, controls within reach ranges) and some elements that allow for planning for those elements to be made accessible (e.g., sink and work space in the kitchen, lavatory in the bathroom). When fully adapted, the Type A units come close to meeting the level of access found in Accessible units. The bathrooms, depending on the configuration, may have a lesser level of accessibility. See the scoping documents for when Type A dwelling and sleeping units are required. Type A units are typically found in large apartment buildings.

Historically the Type A unit had been called the Adaptable dwelling unit in the A117.1 editions prior to 1998. The idea of Adaptable dwelling units was added into the model building codes in the mid 1970s. When Type B units were added, the name of this type of unit was changed to Type A.

1003.2 Primary Entrance. The accessible primary entrance shall be on an accessible route from public and common areas. The primary entrance shall not be to a bedroom.

❖ In an apartment type unit, the main entrance is typically into a central living area, so this should also be the accessible entrance for the unit. The accessible entrance cannot be a 'backdoor' entrance, such as a patio door or through a bedroom. This accessible unit entrance must be connected by an accessible route to an accessible building entrance and all public or shared areas intended for the use of the residents of that unit. This includes areas such as the building lobby, mail boxes, garbage chutes or dumpsters, shared laundry facilities and recreational facilities, such as exercise rooms or pools. See also Section 1003.5 for requirements for the accessible entrance door.

In an efficiency unit or sleeping unit where the main living area is also the bedroom, this entrance may serve as the accessible entrance, and is not considered prohibited by the last sentence of this section. It is not the intent of this section to require an entry vestibule or second room.

1003.3 Accessible Route. Accessible routes within Type A units shall comply with Section 1003.3. Exterior spaces less than 30 inches (760 mm) in depth or width shall comply with Sections 1003.3.1, 1003.3.3, 302, and 303.

❖ The accessible route within the unit must meet the provisions for location, turning space and components. However, if an exterior space that is part of the unit, such as a balcony, is less than 30 inches (760 mm) deep, rather than have a turning space (Section 1003.3.2, which references Section 304, including Sections 302 and 303), the floor surface and change in level provisions are applicable. The intent is that the space will still be level with the inside space, so someone using a wheelchair can pull out onto the balcony, but the additional space for turning around is not required.

1003.3.1 Location. At least one accessible route shall connect all spaces and elements that are a part of the unit. Where only one accessible route is provided, it shall not pass through bathrooms and toilet rooms, closets, or similar spaces.

EXCEPTION: An accessible route is not required to unfinished attics and unfinished basements that are part of the unit.

❖ A route must be available to all living spaces within the unit. A route must be available to all stories in the unit, as well as any raised or sunken floor areas. In a congregate living arrangement, this also includes access to shared spaces such as the bathroom and living or eating areas.

When only one route is available to certain spaces, the route should not be through areas that are subject to locking, such as bathrooms or closets. This is not intended to prohibit access through spaces controlled by the individual. For example, a master suite with the closet accessed through the bathroom would not be blocking access for the occupant of that bedroom.

Unfinished attics and basements are not required to be on an accessible route because these spaces do not include living space for the unit.

1003.3.2 Turning Space. All rooms served by an accessible route shall provide a turning space complying with Section 304.

EXCEPTION: Toilet rooms and bathrooms that are not required to comply with Sections 1003.11.5 through 1003.11.9.

❖ Turning spaces are required in each room. This space can be the circular or T-shaped. The turning spaces can include knee and toe clearances under fixtures, counters, shelves, etc.

In Type A units with multiple bathrooms, only one bathroom must meet the clearances in Section 1003.11. The bathroom that is not accessible does not have to have a turning space within the room. The bathroom that serves as the accessible bathroom is allowed to have the turning space available with the knee and toe clearances planned for under the lavatory (e.g., after the cabinets have been removed), rather than at the time of initial construction.

At this time the standard is not specific on whether a walk-in closet or pantry would be considered a 'room' and require a turning space. Best design practice would be to have these spaces a minimum of 60 inches (1525 mm) wide. A turning space can rely on knee and toe clearances under the rods or shelves in the space. However, many of these spaces are typically accessed with a pull-in back-out maneuver. The 36-inch-wide (915 mm) accessible route (Section 1003.3) between the shelves or the space between clothes may provide better access. Doors to these spaces must have maneuvering clearances on both sides (Section 1003.5). Storage elements within these types of spaces must have a clear floor space in front (Section 1003.14).

1003.3.3 Components. Accessible routes shall consist of one or more of the following elements: walking surfaces with a slope not steeper than 1:20, ramps, elevators, and platform lifts.

❖ The accessible route throughout the unit should be on level surfaces. When a transition is needed between levels or stories, either a ramp, elevator or platform lift can be used. See the commentary to Sections 1003.6, 1003.7 and 1003.8.

1003.4 Walking Surfaces. Walking surfaces that are part of an accessible route shall comply with Section 403.

❖ Section 403 requires walking surfaces to be stable and firm and generally level with a clear width of 36 inches (915 mm). For example, carpet must have a firm cushion or no pad. Heavy pile or thick padding under carpets makes it difficult for a person using a wheelchair to turn or move forward.

1003.5 Doors and Doorways. The primary entrance door to the unit, and all other doorways intended for user passage, shall comply with Section 404.

EXCEPTIONS:

1. Thresholds at exterior sliding doors shall be permitted to be $^3/_4$ inch (19 mm) maximum in height, provided they are beveled with a slope not greater than 1:2.

2. In toilet rooms and bathrooms not required to comply with Section 1003.11, maneuvering clearances required by Section 404.2.3 are not required on the toilet room or bathroom side of the door.

❖ The primary entrance door should be the main door used to access the unit; typically the front door. Any doors that a person walks through in the unit must also be accessible. This includes doors to all rooms, walk-in closets, bathrooms, balconies, etc. Doors to spaces such as reach-in closets are not required to meet the provisions for Section 404.

Requirements include 32 inch (815 mm) clear width, thresholds, lever hardware, door opening force, bottom door surface on the push side and vision lite locations. A front door with a screen/storm door is not considered doors in a series. If an automatic door is installed, the provisions of Section 404.3 are applicable.

Section 404.2.4 requires a $^1/_2$ inch (13 mm) maximum threshold. Exception 1 allows a $^3/_4$ inch (19 mm) threshold at exterior sliding doors. This typically occurs most often at an exterior balcony or deck.

Section 1003.11.1 states that only one bathroom in a multi-bathroom unit must be accessible in accordance with Sections 1003.11.5 through 1003.11.9. Per Exception 2, maneuvering clearance is not required on the inside of the door to the inaccessible bathroom, but is required on the outside of the door.

1003.6 Ramps. Ramps shall comply with Section 405.

❖ Ramps that serve as part of the accessible route into or through a Type A dwelling or sleeping unit must meet the general ramp provisions in Section 405.

Ramps for a change in elevation greater than 6 inches (150 mm) will require handrails on both sides. The local building code should be consulted when guards are required along ramps. Ramps must have a landing at both the top and the bottom, so a ramp cannot extend up to the face of a door. The ramp landing and door maneuvering space (Section 1003.5) are permitted to overlap.

1003.7 Elevators. Elevators within the unit shall comply with Section 407, 408, or 409.

❖ Elevators installed within a single dwelling unit or providing private access to a single dwelling unit are permitted to be passenger elevators, LULAs or private residence elevators. The requirements for private residence elevators found in this section in the 1998 edition of ICC A117.1 have been relocated to Section 409, so that all elevator provisions could be grouped together. Refer to the referenced standard ASME A17.1 for limitations of use.

Section 1003.3.1 requires an accessible route throughout a Type A unit. If a Type A unit is multi-story, elevators or platform lifts (Section 1003.8) can serve as part of the accessible route within an individual unit. Even though a common-use elevator is often used for residents to access common use areas in a building (e.g., mail room, lobby, laundry room), it is not the intent to allow the use of a common-use elevator for access to multiple levels of the same unit. The accessible route should be contained within the unit.

1003.8 Platform Lifts. Platform lifts within the unit shall comply with Section 410.

❖ Platform lifts can be used within individual dwelling units to serve as part of an accessible route (Section 1003.3.1) between levels or to provide access into an individual unit. The lift must be a platform (wheelchair) lift in accordance with ASME A18.1, not a chair lift (e.g., flip-down seat). Platform lifts may be incline or vertical. The current standard limits the maximum rise to 12 feet (3660 mm). See ASME A18.1 for limitations of use.

1003.9 Operable Parts. Lighting controls, electrical switches and receptacle outlets, environmental controls, appliance controls, operating hardware for operable windows, plumbing fixture controls, and user controls for security or intercom systems shall comply with Section 309.

EXCEPTIONS:

1. Receptacle outlets serving a dedicated use.

2. One receptacle outlet is not required to comply with Section 309 where all of the following conditions are met:

   (a) the receptacle outlet is above a length of countertop that is uninterrupted by a sink or appliance; and

   (b) at least one receptacle outlet complying with Section 1003.9 is provided for that length of countertop; and

   (c) all other receptacle outlets provided for that length of countertop comply with Section 1003.9.

3. Floor receptacle outlets.

4. HVAC diffusers.

5. Controls mounted on ceiling fans.

6. Where redundant controls other than light switches are provided for a single element, one control in each space shall not be required to be accessible.

❖ The requirements for operable parts are listed in Section 309. Included are a clear floor space adjacent to the part; that the part be within reach ranges; and that operation of the part not require tight pinching, grasping or twisting of the wrist to operate or more than 5 pounds force (22 N).

The intent is that the person in the space be able to operate the equipment in the room in a normal manner (see commentary Figure C1003.9). It is not the intent that these provisions be applicable to items such as shut-offs for plumbing fixtures or protection switches for electrical equipment, such as the reset switch on a garbage disposal or a circuit breaker box.

Examples of lighting controls are wall light switches or pull cords. Electrical switches could include wall activation switches for garbage disposals, bathroom ventilation fans or cooking hoods. Exception 6 allows for redundant controls located in an accessible location. For example, the switch on the range hood can be out of reach range if a wall switch is installed within reach ranges. However, if light switches are offered with 3-way or 4-way operation, all switches must be accessible.

Receptacle outlets are typically the standard duplex wall outlets located around a room or over a counter. Note that there are several exceptions for receptacle outlets. Outlets that serve a dedicated purpose (Exception 1), such as the outlet for a washer/dryer, refrigerator or stove need not be accessible. These items are typically plugged in all the time. The model electrical code requires outlets spaced at a maximum of 12 feet (3660 mm) apart in most rooms. In spaces with very tall windows or along balcony guards there may not be wall space for the required electrical outlets. Large rooms may need outlets located toward the center of the room. When floor outlets are used, these

outlets do not need to be accessible (Exception 3). Exception 2 is most often used when dealing with outlets over kitchen counters. In kitchens, per the model electrical code, one outlet is required over each section of counter top with a maximum spacing of 4 feet (1220 mm). If an appliance or sink is located along a counter top, the counter on each side is considered a separate section and an outlet must be installed on each side. In a kitchen in a Type A unit, the sink and the work surface must be adjustable to a maximum height of 34 inches (865 mm), while the remainder of the counters can be located at any height, typically 36 inches (915 mm). Outlets could be installed over the sink and work surface so they would be accessible when those areas were modified. However, with the obstructed side reach range requirements in Section 308.3.2, outlets cannot be located over the standard 36-inch (915 mm) high counter and be accessible. Exception 2 allows for one outlet per counter section to not be accessible if the remainder of the outlets are accessible. An alternative is to locate an outlet on the side or front surface of the lower cabinet. This is commonly done on kitchen island counters; however, this will reduce drawer space. This same problem is not typically found in bathrooms because bathroom counter heights are typically installed between 29 and 34 inches (735 and 865 mm) high.

Environmental controls can include ceiling fans or heating and air conditioning thermostats. A common

Figure C1003.9
EXAMPLE OF OPERABLE PARTS

error for locating the thermostat is to specify the electrical box at 48 inches (1220 mm) high, not noting that the actual control is on the top of the thermostat box, thus placing the control out of reach range. Exception 4 does exempt the heating and air conditioning diffusers from being accessible. They need to be on or near the floor and near the ceiling to circulate the air in the room effectively. Exception 5 exempts controls mounted on ceiling fans. Typically the on-off and speed for ceiling fans are controlled from a wall switch, but there may be a switch on the fan itself for reversing the direction of the blades.

Appliance controls vary greatly and may include the key pad for temperature and type of cooking (e.g., bake/broil) on ovens, knobs for burner settings on stove tops, door handles to access the interior of the appliance, water/ice dispensers on refrigerators, latches for self-cleaning ovens, soap containers in dishwashers and clothes washers, lint trays in dryers, etc. The specifics for appliance controls in Section 1003.12.6.1 allow for some exceptions for appliance doors in kitchens. Laundry equipment is specifically addressed in Section 1003.10 with a reference to Section 611.3.

Operating hardware for operable windows includes locks and opening devices for windows that must be accessible. Window accessibility is scoped by the authority having jurisdiction and Section 1003.13. At this time, to meet the operating force requirements most windows need add-on devices for opening.

Plumbing fixture controls would include faucets in showers, tubs and sinks, and flush valves on toilets. Lever type handles are much easier to operate than knobs for those with limited hand mobility or strength. See the specifics in Sections 1003.11.7.5, 606.4, 607.5, 607.6, 608.5 and 608.6 for plumbing controls.

Security or intercom systems may include activation keypads or access to a phone or speaker. Refer to Sections 1005.5, 1005.6 and 1005.7 for additional specifics for communication features that are part of security or intercom systems.

Operable parts on doors are regulated under Section 1003.5 through a reference to Sections 404.2.6 and 404.3.5.

1003.10 Laundry Equipment. Washing machines and clothes dryers shall comply with Section 611.

❖ The standard does not require laundry equipment within the unit; however, if provided, the washers and dryers must meet the same accessibility provisions as in a common laundry room (see Section 611).

Laundry facilities present some complex problems of accessibility to the person in a wheelchair. The reach ranges in Section 308 do not include criteria for accessing things that require bending the elbow joint such as reaching over the top of and into the basket of a top loading clothes washing machine or down and into the front of a front loading washer or dryer. Many

devices are available to aid the user in reaching into these appliances to retrieve clothes at the bottom of the washer basket or rear of the dryer drum.

This standard includes specifics for top and front loading laundry equipment and basically assumes separate pieces of equipment (see commentary Figure C1003.10). Criteria included are clear floor space, height of the door handles and operational requirements for all operable parts (e.g., doors, lint traps) and controls (e.g., time or temperature settings, on/off control). It is not the intent of this standard to prohibit dual use equipment or stacked units if they show equivalent or greater levels of accessibility (see Section 103). Front loading washers are becoming more readily available for the home market and may provide a higher level of accessibility. A lower drawer feature can raise the washer and dryer for easier access into the drum [See commentary Figure C1002.10(c)].

When designing the laundry area, several items must be considered. Section 611.2 requires a parallel clear floor space in front of each appliance, centered on that appliance.

When laundry equipment is placed in a room, Section 1003.3.2 requires a turning space within the room, and Section 1003.5 requires maneuvering clearance at the door. If a counter for folding is provided within the room, to provide a more user friendly space, even though an accessible work surface is not required, knee and toe clearances should be available for that work surface. If a laundry sink is installed, scoping documents typically exempt it from knee and toe clearances because of the needed depth of the sink, but it would be a better design to provide a parallel approach to that sink to allow for use [See commentary Figure C1002.10(a)].

When laundry equipment is installed in a closet, the clear floor space can be located 10 inches (255 mm) back from the face of the units (Section 308.3.1), which would allow for the wall thickness, but may ne-

Figure C1003.10
EXAMPLE OF A LAUNDRY ROOM

cessitate either sliding closet doors or no doors so the doors will not block the clear floor space [See commentary Figure C1002.10(b)]. This standard does not address whether removal of the doors can be considered an adaptable feature.

1003.11 Toilet and Bathing Facilities.

1003.11.1 General. All toilet and bathing areas shall comply with Section 1003.11.4. At least one toilet and bathing facility shall comply with Section 1003.11. At least one lavatory, one water closet and either a bathtub or shower within the unit shall comply with Section 1003.11. The accessible toilet and bathing fixtures shall be in a single toilet/bathing area, such that travel between fixtures does not require travel through other parts of the unit.

❖ Unlike an Accessible unit, when a Type A unit has multiple bathrooms, only one bathroom in the unit must be accessible. In addition, there are provisions that allow for planning for the future installation of grab bars, and installing cabinetry under the lavatory. There are also allowances for lavatories to overlap the clearance for the water closet in Type A units that are not permitted in Accessible units.

Bathroom requirements in Type A units result in a higher level of accessibility than required for Type B dwelling units. Note that the Option A bathrooms (Section 1004.11.3.1) under Type B dwelling units are applicable for Type B units only, not Type A units.

In Type A units, the intent is the bathroom has certain elements that are constructed accessible, and certain elements that are permitted to be adaptable. Because these types of units are typically required where the residents are nontransient, the unit bathroom can be adapted based on the needs of the resident.

Although only one bathroom needs to comply with the standards of Section 1003.11, each bathroom needs to be located on an accessible route (Section 1003.3.1) and have accessible doors (Section 1003.5). The bathroom chosen to be accessible must include a turning space (Section 1003.3.2). Because the exception to Section 1003.11.5 allows for cabinetry to be installed under the lavatory, the turning space can rely on the knee and toe clearance under the lavatory when the bathroom is adapted in the future.

Items specifically addressed for the accessible toilet or bathing room are door swing, blocking, a lavatory, a mirror, a water closet and a bathing facility. Where two lavatories are provided in the same room, only one is required to meet the provisions in this section. Where a bathtub and a separate shower are provided in the same room, only one bathing facility is required to meet the provisions in this section.

The inaccessible bathroom must have blocking in the walls for the future installation of grab bars (Section 1003.11.4); however, the fixture clearances and other items under the other subsection of Section 1003.11 are not required. The exception for Section 1003.3.2 exempts the inaccessible bathroom from having a turning space within the room. Section 1003.5, Exception 2, exempts the door to the inaccessible bathroom from maneuvering clearances on the inside of the bathroom. One of the reason for this is so the Type A unit bathroom requirements would not be less than what is required for Type B unit bathrooms.

1003.11.2 Doors. Doors shall not swing into the clear floor space or clearance for any fixture.

EXCEPTION: Where a clear floor space complying with Section 305.3 is provided within the room beyond the arc of the door swing.

❖ The door to the accessible bathroom must not swing into the bathroom and over the clear floor space for the lavatory, water closet, tub or shower. However, the exception allows that where a 30 inch by 48 inch (760 b7 1220 mm) wheelchair space is provided past the swing of the door, the door can swing over the fixture clearances. With this configuration, someone could enter the room, close the door, and then maneuver to access the fixtures. Based on Section 305.4, the 30 inch by 48 inch (760 by 1220 mm) wheelchair space can include knee and toe clearances under the lavatory.

1003.11.3 Overlap. Clear floor spaces, clearances at fixtures and turning spaces are permitted to overlap.

❖ The clear floor space is the location where a person will sit to access a fixture. These areas are permitted to overlap; however, fixtures can overlap only the clear floor spaces where they are specifically indicated. See the requirements for each fixture to see what fixture overlap is permitted. The turning space in the room and the door maneuvering clearances are permitted to overlap any of the clear floor spaces.

1003.11.4 Reinforcement. Reinforcement shall be provided for the future installation of grab bars and shower seats at water closets, bathtubs, and shower compartments. Where walls are located to permit the installation of grab bars and seats complying with Sections 604.5, 607.4, 608.3 and 608.4, reinforcement shall be provided for the future installation of grab bars and seats meeting those requirements.

EXCEPTION: Reinforcement is not required in a room containing only a lavatory and a water closet, provided the room does not contain the only lavatory or water closet on the accessible level of the dwelling unit.

❖ In Type A unit bathrooms, either grab bars must be installed or the blocking must be provided for the future installation of grab bars at the water closet and bathtub or shower. The reference to water closets (Section 604.5), bathtubs (Section 607.4) and showers (Section 608.3) provides the information for the length and location of the grab bars. Bathtub and shower seat requirements are found in Section 608.4. The blocking must be sized to cover the range for the height of the grab bars and the minimum lengths. Allowance must also be made for the attachment of the grab bars. The escutcheon plates at the ends of the bars are larger than the bars, and a minimum edge distance must be allowed for secure embedment of the screws used to attach the bar to the wall (see commentary Figure C1003.11.4).

Redundant exceptions for grab bars and seats when reinforcement is provided are found in Section 604.5, Exception 3; Section 607.4, Exception 2; Section 608.3, Exception 2; and Section 608.4, Exception 2.

The new vertical grab bar is not required in Type A and Type B dwelling units (Section 604.5.1). The rear grab bar may be shorter when the lavatory is so close to the water closet that it will conflict with the installation (Section 604.5.2).

1003.11.5 Lavatory. Lavatories shall comply with Section 606.

    EXCEPTION: Cabinetry shall be permitted under the lavatory, provided:

    (a) the cabinetry can be removed without removal or replacement of the lavatory;

    (b) the floor finish extends under such cabinetry; and

    (c) the walls behind and surrounding cabinetry are finished.

❖ The lavatory is one of the elements that is permitted to be adaptable in a Type A unit. The base requirement are for a lavatory with a maximum height of 34 inches (865 mm), a clear floor space for a front approach with associated knee and toe clearances underneath the lavatory, and faucets that meet operable parts requirements. Pipes underneath must be padded or configured to prevent accidental contact that may result in injury. This is the same as required in an Accessible unit.

The exception allows for installation of cabinetry under the lavatory or counter top. The intent of other requirements is to ensure that the modification be accomplished with the minimum amount of additional work in the space. Preplanning allows for an easy modification rather than becoming a major remodeling project to make the bathroom look 'finished.' A design with a lavatory supported on a vanity cabinet which must be removed, requiring reinstallation of a lavatory and installation of new floor coverings, new trim, new wall painting, etc. does not comply with this exception.

An alternative would be a pedestal lavatory, if the pedestal will be clear of the knee and toe clearances.

Lavatories in Type B units require a lesser level of access (e.g., parallel approach), but they may use either of the options permitted for lavatories in a Type A unit because this is considered to result in a higher level of access.

The reference to Section 606 in Exception 1 includes all subsections (Section 606.1 through 606.7). Section 606.5 includes an exception to indicate that the requirements for lavatories with enhanced reach ranges are not intended for Type A and Type B dwell-

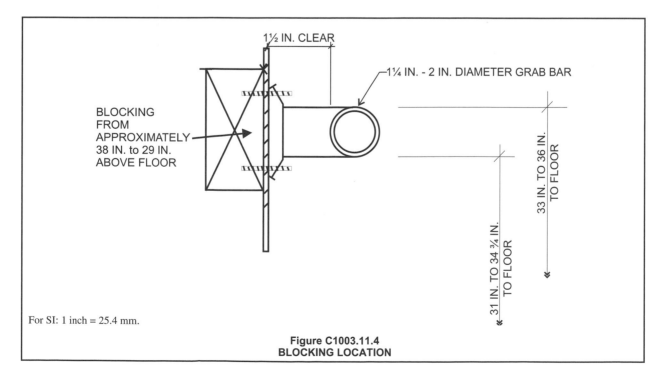

For SI: 1 inch = 25.4 mm.

Figure C1003.11.4
BLOCKING LOCATION

ing or sleeping units. Because towel dispensers and hand dryers are typically not installed within dwelling units and sleeping units, Section 606.7 is typically not applicable.

1003.11.6 Mirrors. Mirrors above lavatories shall have the bottom edge of the reflecting surface 40 inches (1015 mm) maximum above the floor.

❖ The standard lavatory or counter height within bathrooms varies from 29 inches to 34 inches (735 to 865 mm). Counters or wall mounted lavatories typically have a 4-inch (100 mm) high backsplash. The normal eye level of a person using a wheelchair, 43 inches to 51 inches (1090 to 1295 mm), providing an angle of incidence sufficient for a reflection from a mirror with a maximum bottom edge 40 inches (1015 mm) above the floor. This allows for an adequate field of view for the desired bathing or grooming activities while allowing for clearance over the backsplash on the lavatory or counter [see commentary Figure C102(a)].

If mirrors are to be used by both ambulatory people and wheelchair users, design standards recommend 74 inch (1880 mm) height, minimum, at the topmost edge. In rooms with multiple lavatories, it would typically be considered best design practice to make the mirror over the accessible sink the accessible mirror. This section does not require mirrors over lavatories.

1003.11.7 Water Closet. Water closets shall comply with Section 1003.11.7.

❖ The water closet must be located adjacent to a wall. Specifications include two options for a clear floor space around the water closet (Sections 1003.11.7.2 and 1003.11.7.3); where the water closet sits within that clear space (Section 1003.11.7.1); the height of the seat (Section 1003.11.7.4); and the location of flush controls (Section 1003.11.7.5). The location for the blocking in the walls for the future installation of grab bars references back to the general grab bar requirements for water closets in Section 604.5 (Section 1103.11.4).

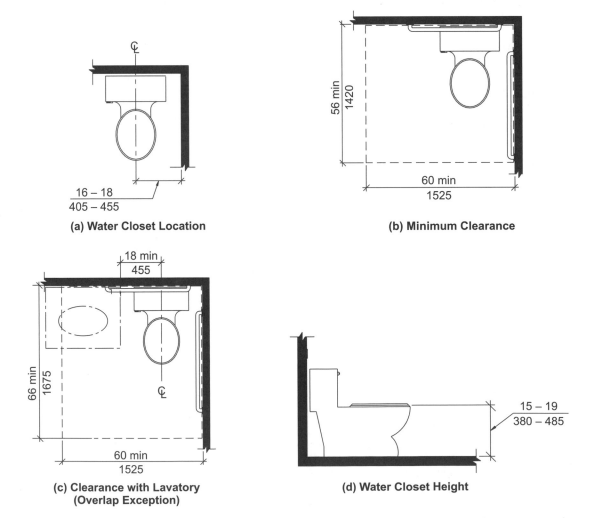

(a) Water Closet Location

(b) Minimum Clearance

(c) Clearance with Lavatory (Overlap Exception)

(d) Water Closet Height

Fig. 1003.11.7
Water Closets in Type A Units

1003.11.7.1 Location. The water closet shall be positioned with a wall to the rear and to one side. The centerline of the water closet shall be 16 inches (405 mm) minimum and 18 inches (455 mm) maximum from the sidewall.

❖ In Type A units the water closet must be positioned adjacent to a wall so the wall mounted grab bars can be installed in the future. The relationship between the wall and the water closet is the same as in an Accessible unit.

Sixteen inches to 18 inches (405 to 455 mm) has been established as the optimal dimension from a side wall or partition to the center line of the water closet to allow optimum bearing and reach for the grab bar. Once everything is installed, this 2-inch (50 mm) tolerance addresses differences that occur between the plumbing rough-in and the finished wall to water closet measurement.

1003.11.7.2 Clearance. A clearance around the water closet of 60 inches (1525 mm) minimum, measured perpendicular from the side wall, and 56 inches (1420 mm) minimum, measured perpendicular from the rear wall, shall be provided.

❖ The 60 inch by 56 inch (1525 by 1420 mm) water closet clearance in a Type A unit is the same as for an Accessible unit (Section 604.3.1). However, clearances and overlap work in conjunction. A second option is permitted under Section 1003.11.7.3 when a 60 inch by 66 inch (1525 by 1675 mm) clear floor space is provided.

The first option is intended to allow for a side transfer. The 60 inch (1525 mm) width with no other fixtures in the space provides approximately 30 inches (760 mm) between the water closet and the nearest wall or fixture. This space allows the wheelchair user to back into the space and accomplish a side transfer from the wheelchair to the water closet [see commentary Figure C604.3.1(a)].

The second option allows for a lavatory to overlap a deeper [i.e., 60 inch by 66 inch (1525 by 1675 mm)] clear floor space. This configuration allows space for a diagonal transfer to the water closet [see commentary Figure C604.3.1(b)]. With the lavatory overlapping the clear floor space for the water closet, there is not adequate space for a side transfer. The 10 inches (255 mm) of extra depth allows for the wheelchair to be positioned facing the water closet. The required clear floor space for the adjacent lavatory (Section 1003.11.5) will provide additional clearance for the wheelchair.

1003.11.7.3 Overlap. The required clearance around the water closet shall be permitted to overlap the water closet, associated grab bars, paper dispensers, coat hooks, shelves, accessible routes, clear floor space required at other fixtures, and the wheelchair turning space. No other fixtures or obstructions shall be located within the required water closet clearance.

EXCEPTION: A lavatory complying with Section 1003.11.5 shall be permitted on the rear wall 18 inches (455 mm) minimum from the centerline of the water closet where the clearance at the water closet is 66 inches (1675 mm) minimum measured perpendicular from the rear wall.

❖ Requirements for clearances and overlap must be viewed in conjunction. The options basically allow for either a side or diagonal transfer to the water closet for a person using a wheelchair. See the commentary for Section 1003.11.7.2.

The overlaps that are permitted are intended to allow for access to the water closet, and for everything a person needs to reach from the water closet (e.g., toilet paper dispensers). Although shelves can overlap the clear floor space, the intent is that shelves must not obstruct access to the water closet or the future installation of grab bars.

1003.11.7.4 Height. The top of the water closet seat shall be 15 inches (380 mm) minimum and 19 inches (485 mm) maximum above the floor, measured to the top of the seat.

❖ Preferences for the heights of toilet seats vary considerably among persons with disabilities. Higher seats are an advantage to some ambulatory persons with disabilities, but a disadvantage for some wheelchair users and others. The allowance for 15 inches to 19 inches (380 to 485 mm) in Type A units is less restrictive than the 17 inches to 19 inches (430 to 485 mm) required in Accessible units (Section 604.4). Seats and filler rings of various thicknesses are available to adapt china-fixture rims, which typically vary from 14 inches to 18 inches (355 to 460 mm) high.

A 17-inch to 19-inch (430 to 485 mm) water closet seat height is based on the assumption that a typical wheelchair seat height, with or without a cushion, would fall within that range. For the easiest transfer, both the seat of the wheelchair and the water closet must be as level as possible. It is easier to transfer "down" to a seat, more strength is required to transfer back "up" to the wheelchair. An upward spring-loaded toilet seat will interfere with the user's transfer.

1003.11.7.5 Flush Controls. Hand operated flush controls shall comply with Section 1003.9. Flush controls shall be located on the open side of the water closet.

❖ The reference to Section 1003.9 means that flush controls must meet all operable parts requirements. The intent is that controls be within reach of a user sitting in the wheelchair, not on the water closet seat; therefore, there is the additional requirement for the flush control to be on the open side of the water closet. This is not intended to prohibit a top-of-tank flush control as long as the control is within reach ranges.

Flush controls for tank-type toilets have a standardized mounting location on the left side of the tank (facing the tank). Tanks are available by special order with controls mounted on the right side.

1003.11.8 Bathtub. Bathtubs shall comply with Section 607.

EXCEPTIONS:

1. The removable in-tub seat required by Section 607.3 is not required.

2. Counter tops and cabinetry shall be permitted at the control end of the clearance, provided such counter tops and cabinetry can be removed and the floor finish extends under such cabinetry.

❖ If the accessible bathing fixture is a bathtub, the bathtub must comply with Section 607. A clear floor space of 30 inches (760 mm) by the length of the tub is required. No fixtures can overlap the clear floor space in front of the tub. See Section 607 for specific requirements.

Section 607.4, Exception 2 and Section 1003.11.4 allow for the exemption of grab bars around the tub if reinforcement is provided.

The exceptions in this section are concerned with the adaptable features for the bathtub. The removable seat is not required. Exception 2 allows for a portion of a vanity to overlap the clear floor space of the tub if this portion can be easily removed should the occupant need the space to access the bathtub.

In Type B units, Option A bathrooms allow a lavatory or water closet in the clear floor space for the bathtub (Section 1004.11.3.1.3.1 and 1004.11.3.1.3.2), but this is not an option in a Type A unit bathroom.

1003.11.9 Shower. Showers shall comply with Section 608.

EXCEPTION: Counter tops and cabinetry shall be permitted at the control end of the clearance, provided such counter tops and cabinetry can be removed and the floor finish extends under such cabinetry.

❖ If the accessible bathing fixture is to be a shower, it can be a transfer shower, roll-in shower or alternate roll-in shower as specified in Section 608. A lavatory can overlap the clear floor space in front of the roll-in shower (Section 608.2.2). Based on the options for lavatories in Section 1003.11.5, if a lavatory is installed in the clear floor space for the roll-in shower, it could have removable cabinetry.

Section 1003.11.4, Sections 608.3, Exception 2, and Section 608.4, Exception 3 are concerned with the adaptable features for the showers. Seats and grab bars are not required if reinforcement is provided.

The exception allows for a portion of a vanity to overlap the clear floor space of a shower if this portion can be easily removed should the occupant need the space to access the shower. This is consistent with the exception permitted for bathtubs. The result is that at roll-in showers, either a lavatory or counter can overlap the clear floor space for the roll-in shower if it has removable cabinetry. At transfer showers, a removable cabinet and counter would be permitted to overlap the clear floor space, but a lavatory would not be permitted.

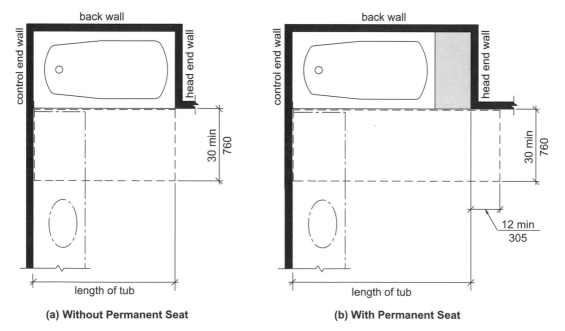

(a) Without Permanent Seat   **(b) With Permanent Seat**

**Fig. 1003.11.8
Clearance for Bathtubs in Type A Units**

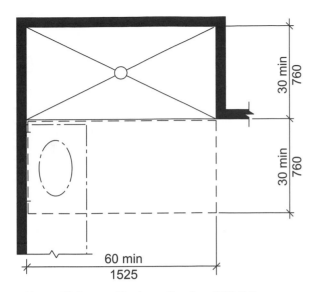

Note: Sink permitted per Section 608.2.2

**Fig. 1003.11.9
Standard Roll-in-Type Shower
Compartment in Type A Units**

1003.12 Kitchens. Kitchens shall comply with Section 1003.12.

❖ Type A unit kitchens include some parts constructed accessible and some elements constructed with accessibility planned for as an adaptable element. See Sections 1003.12.3 and 1003.12.4 for adaptability allowances for work surfaces and sinks, respectively. Accessible unit kitchens require full accessibility at the time of initial construction. If a designer chooses to use some of the Accessible unit requirements for kitchens, this results in a higher level of accessibility and would exceed the Type A unit requirements.

The design of kitchens usable by a person with a disability demands careful consideration and thoughtful planning. Careful location of appliances, plumbing fixtures and cabinetry is essential to achieve the required maneuvering clearances and clear floor spaces required to perform the necessary functions in an accessible and functional kitchen. Careful design will produce a kitchen that is accessible and functionally efficient, and that is easily usable by a person with a disability or mobility impairment, as well as an able-bodied person.

Section 1003.3.2 requires a turning space within the room. If the space under the sink or the work surface (once they are adapted) is to be used as part of a T-turn, the width must be a minimum of 36 inches (915 mm).

At this time, this standard does not specifically address kitchenettes in Type A sleeping units. Requirements for kitchenettes are included in Section 804.

1003.12.1 Clearance. Clearance complying with Section 1003.12.1 shall be provided.

❖ Kitchens include requirements for clearances between cabinets or appliances; the clearance requirements in referenced Sections 1003.12.1.1 and 1003.12.1.2 are different because the two different floor plan arrangements are unique and require different types of spaces for maneuvering.

It is not the intent of these provisions to prohibit other types of kitchen layouts, such as L-shaped or kitchens with islands. If other layouts are used, the key considerations are maneuvering to access appliances, the sink, the work surface and storage elements.

1003.12.1.1 Minimum Clearance. Clearance between all opposing base cabinets, counter tops, appliances, or walls within kitchen work areas shall be 40 inches (1015 mm) minimum.

❖ The minimum clear width between opposing cabinets/appliances, or a cabinet/appliances and wall or other type of obstruction, is 40 inches (1015 mm). This measurement would not include cabinet/appliance handles.

Galley style kitchens are typically laid out with all the appliances, counters and sink in straight lines. The appliances and fixtures can be located along one side of the kitchen, or they can be located along both sides of the kitchen. Unlike a pass-through kitchen (Section 804.2.1), a Type A unit galley kitchen may be open on one or both ends.

The need for a turning space in a kitchen is not intended to increase the 40 inch (1015 mm) width between opposing cabinets. The knee and toe clearances under the work surface (Section 1003.12.3) or the sink (Section 1003.12.4), once they are adapted, may be used as part of the turning space within the kitchen.

1003.12.1.2 U-Shaped Kitchens. In kitchens with counters, appliances, or cabinets on three contiguous sides, clearance between all opposing base cabinets, countertops, appliances, or walls within kitchen work areas shall be 60 inches (1525 mm) minimum.

❖ U-shaped kitchens are kitchens with cabinets and appliances on three contiguous sides. In such an arrangement, 60 inches (1525 mm) clearance is required between the faces of opposing cabinets and appliances to make all sides usable.

Unlike Accessible unit kitchens (Sections 1002.12 and 804.2.2), in Type A units, a galley-style kitchen with an opening on only one end is not considered a U-shaped kitchen and does not have to have a 60-inch (1525 mm) clear floor space between cabinets. The key for a U-shaped kitchen in a Type A unit is the need to be able to turn 90 degrees (1.6 rad) to reach an appliance or use a counter or cabinet on the third wall.

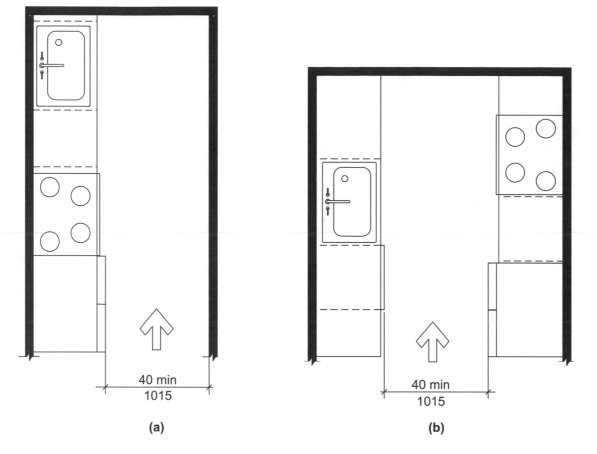

Fig. 1003.12.1.1
Minimum Kitchen Clearance in Type A Units

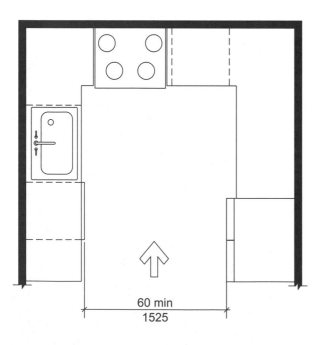

Fig. 1003.12.1.2
U-Shaped Kitchen Clearance in Type A Units

1003.12.2 Clear Floor Space. Clear floor spaces required by Sections 1003.12.3 through 1003.12.6 shall comply with Section 305.

❖ The clear floor space for the work surface, sink, cabinet access and appliances is 30 inches by 48 inches (760 by 1220 mm) (Section 305.3). Where knee and/or toe clearances are provided, the clear floor space can extend underneath, (e.g., under a sink or work surface, or under the door of an oven or dishwasher in the down position). If a space is confined on three sides, the alcove provisions in Section 305.7 are applicable.

1003.12.3 Work Surface. At least one section of counter shall provide a work surface 30 inches (760 mm) minimum in length complying with Section 1003.12.3.

❖ An accessible work surface is a critical component of a kitchen for persons who use wheelchairs. Without an accessible work surface many of the tasks necessary for preparing a meal, such as mixing, chopping, cutting and cleaning, become very difficult, and for some people routine tasks may even become impossible. Although Accessible units require the accessible work surface adjacent to the oven (Section 1002.12

references Sections 804.6.5.1 and 805.6.5.2), Type A units are required only to have a counter surface adjacent to ovens (Sections 1003.12.6.5.1 and 1003.12.6.5.2); therefore, the work surface can be located anywhere within the kitchen. It is not the intent of this provision to require all work surfaces in the kitchen to meet this section. This section is consistent with the general requirements for accessible work surfaces in Section 902.

If the space under the work surface is to be used for a T-turning space, the minimum width of the clearance will be 36 inches (915 mm) instead of 30 inches (760 mm) (see Section 304.3.2).

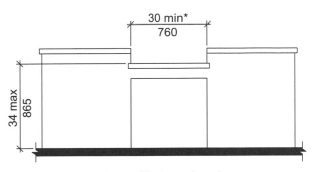

*36 min. (915) if part of T-shaped turning space per Sections 304.3.2 and 1003.3.2

Fig. 1003.12.3
Work Surface in Kitchen for Type A Units

1003.12.3.1 Clear Floor Space. A clear floor space, positioned for a forward approach to the work surface, shall be provided. Knee and toe clearance complying with Section 306 shall be provided. The clear floor space shall be centered on the work surface.

EXCEPTION: Cabinetry shall be permitted under the work surface, provided:

(a) the cabinetry can be removed without removal or replacement of the work surface,

(b) the floor finish extends under such cabinetry, and

(c) the walls behind and surrounding cabinetry are finished.

❖ In addition to installing counter or work surfaces at an accessible height (Section 1003.12.3.2), a work surface must be on an accessible route and have adequate clearances under that surface. Although some items in a kitchen have an option of a front approach or a parallel approach, a front approach is required at work surfaces.

The 30 inch by 48 inch (760 by 1220 mm) clear floor space (Section 305) is required by Section 1003.12.3. If this space is also used for a T-turn, a 36 inch (915 mm) width is required (Sections 303.3 and 1003.3.2)

The space for a person using a wheelchair is permitted to project under the work surfaces to the extent described in Section 306. Clearances for a person's knees and toes are required. The arms on a wheelchair or the chest of the person using the wheelchair will limit the amount someone can move forward under a counter.

Some kitchen designs include a desk type work area so that the accessible work surface is available at the time of initial construction (see commentary Figure C1003.12.3.1). However, the intent of the exception is for the work surface to be one of the adaptable elements in a Type A unit. Planning for the work surface to be made accessible in the future requires a removable cabinet under that portion of the counter and the floor treatment to be installed under that cabinet. The back wall should be finished and the cabinets on each side should be ordered with finished side panels. This way, when the cabinet is removed, the space looks like it was always there. The counter must either be located at the height between 29 inches and 34 inches (735 and 865 mm) at installation, or the counter must be adjustable to that height. Some types of counters can have seams located over the removable cabinet, so they can be reinstalled at the lower height when the cabinet is removed. The idea is that the counter surface for the kitchen or work surface not have to be replaced. Providing an accessible work surface in the Type A kitchen should require minimal effort.

Figure C1003.12.3.1
EXAMPLE OF BUILT-IN WORK SURFACE

1003.12.3.2 Height. The work surface shall be 34 inches (865 mm) maximum above the floor.

EXCEPTION: A counter that is adjustable to provide a work surface at variable heights 29 inches (735 mm) minimum and 36 inches (915 mm) maximum above the floor, or that can be relocated within that range without cutting the counter or damaging adjacent cabinets, walls, doors, and structural elements, shall be permitted.

❖ Different types of work require different work surface heights for comfort and ease of use. Light detailed work such as writing requires a work surface close to elbow height for a standing person. Heavy manual work such as rolling dough requires a work surface height about 10 inches (255 mm) below elbow height for a standing person. The principle of a high work surface for light detailed work and a low work surface for heavy manual work also applies for seated persons; however, the limiting condition for seated manual work is clearance under the work surface.

Table C902.3 lists convenient work surface heights for seated persons. The great variety of heights for comfort and optimal performance indicates a need for alternatives or a compromise in height if both people who stand and people who sit are using the same counter area.

The intent of the exception is to allow adjustment of the counter height from the standard 36 inches (915 mm) to the desired height between 29 inches and 34 inches (735 and 865 mm). [Section 902.3 allows for 28 inches (710 mm).] The intent is not that the counter surface be mechanically adjustable, but rather that it be planned for adjustment of the counter without replacement of the counter or surrounding cabinets. Some types of counters allow for locating seams along the sides of the removable cabinet so that the piece can be reinstalled at a lower height when this area is adapted to be accessible.

1003.12.3.3 Exposed Surfaces. There shall be no sharp or abrasive surfaces under the exposed portions of work surface counters.

❖ Hot, cold and abrasive surfaces may cause harm to people using wheelchair because the ability to feel and react to such hazards may be diminished significantly by paralysis or loss of sensation. This protection can be provided by padding, apron walls, recessing the pipes, etc.

If objects are located under the surface above or adjacent to the knee and toe space (including counter supports), it is advisable to protect the person using the surface from injury by padding or rounding any sharp edges, or locating these items as far past the knee and toe clearances as practical.

1003.12.4 Sink. Sinks shall comply with Section 1003.12.4.

❖ Sinks in kitchens must have knee and toe clearances that allow for a front approach (including protection from the pipes), a maximum rim height of 34 inches (865 mm), and faucets that meet operable parts requirements. If a double bowl sink is installed, these requirements can apply to only one bowl. This allows for the second bowl to be deeper or include a garbage disposal.

If the space under the sink is to be used for a T-turn space, the minimum width of the clearance will be 36 inches (915 mm) instead of 30 inches (760 mm) (see Section 304.3).

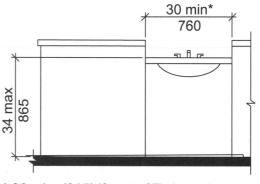

30 min* 760

34 max 865

* 36 min. (915) if part of T-shaped turning space per Sections 304.3.2 and 1003.3.2

Fig. 1003.12.4
Kitchen Sink for Type A Units

1003.12.4.1 Clear Floor Space. A clear floor space, positioned for a forward approach to the sink, shall be provided. Knee and toe clearance complying with Section 306 shall be provided. The clear floor space shall be centered on the sink bowl.

EXCEPTIONS:

1. The requirement for knee and toe clearance shall not apply to more than one bowl of a multi-bowl sink.

2. Cabinetry shall be permitted to be added under the sink, provided:

   (a) the cabinetry can be removed without removal or replacement of the sink,

   (b) the floor finish extends under such cabinetry, and

   (c) the walls behind and surrounding cabinetry are finished.

❖ In addition to being at an accessible height (Section 1003.12.4.2), a kitchen sink must be on an accessible route and have adequate clearances under that surface. Although some items in a kitchen have an option of a front approach or a parallel approach, a front approach is required at sinks in a Type A unit.

The 30-inch by 48-inch (760 by 1220 mm) clear floor or ground space (Section 305) is required. If this space is also used for a T-turn, a 36 inch (915 mm) width is required (Sections 303.3 and 1003.3.2).

The space for a person using a wheelchair is permitted to project under the sink to the extent described in Section 306. Clearances for a person's knees and toes are required. The arms on a wheelchair or the chest of the person using the wheelchair will limit the amount someone can move forward under a counter.

When a single bowl sink is installed, the clear floor space must be centered on the sink. To allow for a double bowl sink with a garbage disposal, the knee and toe clearances and centering are required on only one bowl (Exception 1). Typical sink widths would result in the clear floor space extending under the side of the second bowl (see commentary Figure C1003.12.4.1). If the garbage disposal has sharp edges, protection should be provided as noted in Section 1003.12.4.4.

The intent of Exception 2 is for the sink to be one of the adaptable elements in a Type A unit. Planning for the sink to be made accessible in the future requires a removable cabinet under that portion of the counter, and the floor treatment to be installed under that cabinet. The back wall should be finished and the cabinets on each side should be ordered with finished side panels. This way, when the cabinet is removed, the space looks like it was always there. The sink must either be located at the height between 29 inches and 34 inches (735 and 865 mm) at installation, or the counter must be adjustable to that height. Some types of counters can have seams located over the removable cabinet, so they can be reinstalled at the lower height when the cabinet is removed. The plumber should install the supply and drain lines at a location that would allow for the future lowering of the sink. The idea is that neither the sink nor the counter surface for the kitchen or around the sink would have to be replaced. Providing an accessible sink in the Type A kitchen should require minimal effort.

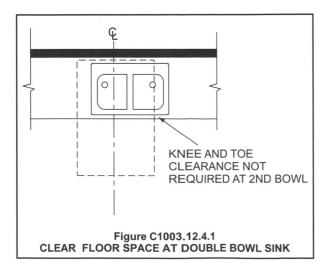

Figure C1003.12.4.1
CLEAR FLOOR SPACE AT DOUBLE BOWL SINK

1003.12.4.2 Height. The front of the sink shall be 34 inches (865 mm) maximum above the floor, measured to the higher of the rim or counter surface.

EXCEPTION: A sink and counter that is adjustable to variable heights 29 inches (735 mm) minimum and 36 inches (915 mm) maximum above the floor, or that can be relocated within that range without cutting the counter or damaging adjacent cabinets, walls, doors and structural elements, provided rough-in plumbing permits connections of supply and drain pipes for sinks mounted at the height of 29 inches (735 mm), shall be permitted.

❖ The top rim of the sink for over-mount sinks or the counter height for under-mount sinks must be at a maximum height of 34 inches (865 mm). This will allow for a 6¹/₂ inch (165 mm) deep sink and still have a 27 inch (685 mm) high knee clearance.

The intent of the exception is to allow adjustment of the counter surrounding the sink from the standard 36 inch (915 mm) height to the desired height between 29 inches and 34 inches (735 and 865 mm). [Section 902.3 allows for 28 inches (710 mm).] The intent is not that the sink be mechanically adjustable, but rather that the counter be adjustable without replacement of the counter or surrounding cabinets. Some types of counters allow location of seams along the sides of the removable cabinet, so the counter and sink can be reinstalled at a lower height when this area is adapted to be accessible. Note that the supply and drain lines must be installed to permit the sink to be adjusted to the 29 inch (735 mm) height.

1003.12.4.3 Faucets. Faucets shall comply with Section 309.

❖ The faucet controls, including the temperature and water flow, hand spray and the spigot swivel, must meet the operable parts provisions of Section 309. Single-lever controls for the faucet typically are the easiest for persons with limited hand mobility to use.

1003.12.4.4 Exposed Pipes and Surfaces. Water supply and drain pipes under sinks shall be insulated or otherwise configured to protect against contact. There shall be no sharp or abrasive surfaces under sinks.

❖ Hot, cold and abrasive surfaces may cause harm to a person using a wheelchair because the ability to feel and react to such hazards may be diminished significantly by paralysis or loss of sensation.

This protection can be provided by padding, apron walls, recessing the pipes, etc. This protection is not intended to be the type of insulation required for steam pipes, hot water heating pipes or other types of system piping.

1003.12.5 Kitchen Storage. A clear floor space, positioned for a parallel or forward approach to the kitchen cabinets, shall be provided.

❖ Kitchen cabinets can be an upper or lower cabinet or within a pantry type unit. The kitchen cabinets must be located so that a person using a wheelchair can get in front of the cabinet by either a front or side approach. The shelves need not be located within reach ranges or the handles meet operable parts provisions. Although not specifically stated, it is the intent that all storage, including drawers and open shelves, be located so that a person using a wheelchair could maneuver to access those spaces. From that point reach extender aids could be used to reach higher or lower objects. Pantry style cabinets, rather than cabinets mounted over work counters, would allow for improved accessibility (see commentary Figure C1003.12.5). Storage in areas outside of the kitchen should comply with Section 1003.14.

Figure C1003.12.5
EXAMPLE OF KITCHEN PANTRY STORAGE

1003.12.6 Appliances. Where provided, kitchen appliances shall comply with Section 1003.12.6.

❖ Specific requirements are listed for dishwashers, ranges, cooktops, ovens, refrigerator/freezers and trash compactors. Many other types of built-in appliances are now on the market, such as warming drawers, built-in microwaves, range hoods, built-in coffee cen-

ters, wine refrigerators, freezers, ice machines, etc. Some appliances may contain multiple elements. For example, a refrigerator/freezer may incorporate an ice maker and a water dispenser. Access should be provided to all appliances in accordance with Section 1002.12.6.1 and 1002.12.6.2.

1003.12.6.1 Operable Parts. All appliance controls shall comply with Section 1003.9.

EXCEPTIONS:

1. Appliance doors and door latching devices shall not be required to comply with Section 309.4.

2. Bottom-hinged appliance doors, when in the open position, shall not be required to comply with Section 309.3.

❖ Appliance controls must meet the clear floor space, reach range and operable parts requirements in Section 309. Section 1003.9, Exception 6 does exempt the redundant controls. For example, controls on range hoods do not have to be within reach ranges if redundant accessible controls are provided.

Per Exception 1, appliance doors and door latches do not have to meet the operable parts requirements for operation with one hand, no tight pinching, grasping or twisting of the wrist or the 5 pounds force (22 N) found in Section 309.4. Typically for doors, because the door seal is necessary for some appliances, such as an oven or freezer, to maintain heat or cold the consideration is for the 5 pounds force. An example of a door latch would be the lever for sealing a dishwasher door, or the latch used when self-cleaning an oven. The hardware used to open an appliance door, such as the handle on an oven, refrigerator or dishwasher, has to meet operable parts provisions. Doors and door latches do have to meet the clear floor space and height requirements in Sections 309.2 and 309.3.

Exception 2 allows for the appliance door, when folded down, to be out of the 15 inch to 48 inch (380 to 1220 mm) reach range in Section 309.3. A dishwasher or range with the door down typically has the door at about 9 or 10 inches (230 to 255 mm) from the floor.

1003.12.6.2 Clear Floor Space. A clear floor space, positioned for a parallel or forward approach, shall be provided at each kitchen appliance. Clear floor spaces shall be permitted to overlap.

❖ Although the 30-inch by 48-inch (760 by 1220 mm) clear floor space at appliances can be a side approach or front approach, how someone would typically use the appliance and could more easily reach must be considered. For example, a side approach to a cooktop allows access to all the burners, but a front approach, because of the difficulty reaching past the kick plates, would probably allow access to only the front burner. Some appliances must have the door open for access (e.g., dishwasher, oven, refrigerator, trash compactor). Clear floor space can use the knee and toe clearances available when the door is open.

1003.12.6.3 Dishwasher. A clear floor space, positioned adjacent to the dishwasher door, shall be provided. The dishwasher door in the open position shall not obstruct the clear floor space for the dishwasher or an adjacent sink.

❖ Locating the clear floor space so the dishwasher is usable is important. If the clear floor space is located immediately in front of the dishwasher, the door in the open position will overlap the clear floor space. By requiring that the clear floor space not be obstructed by the dishwasher door, either the clear floor space must be located past the door, or the door could overlap the toe clearance if there was a minimum of 9 inches (230 mm) clearance under the door when open. It is important to locate the clear floor space so the dishwasher can be easily loaded and unloaded. Often, it is desirable to load the dishwasher from the sink area; therefore, it may be helpful to locate the sink and dishwasher adjacent to each other. Where a dishwasher is located adjacent to the clear floor space for a sink, the single clear floor space can be used to serve both the sink and the dishwasher [see commentary Figure C1003.12.6.3(a) and (b)]. The exception for sink knee and toe clearances in Section 1003.12.4 is still be permitted.

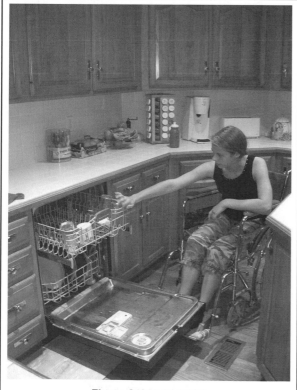

Figure C1003.12.6.3(a)
EXAMPLE OF ACCESS TO DISHWASHER

1003.12.6.4 Range or Cooktop. A clear floor space, positioned for a parallel or forward approach to the space for a range or cooktop, shall be provided. Where the clear floor space is positioned for a forward approach, knee and toe clearance complying with Section 306 shall be provided. Where knee and toe space is provided, the underside of the range or cooktop shall be insulated or otherwise configured to protect from burns, abrasions, or electrical shock. The location of controls shall not require reaching across burners.

❖ A range includes a cooktop and an oven. A range must be located for the parallel approach discussed in Section 1003.12.6.2, not a front approach (See commentary Figure C1003.12.6.4) because the footplates on a wheelchair stop a person from reaching forward past their toes.

A cooktop can be provided with a parallel approach or with a front approach. When a designer chooses to provide a cooktop with a front approach, the cooktop must have adequate clearances for a person's knees and toes underneath, as well as protection from accidental bumps, cuts or burns.

To reduce the chance of accidental scalding or burns, access to controls for the burners on either a cooktop or range must not require reaching across burners. Controls can be provided on the front, center or side of the burners. Access to controls for the oven that is part of the range must also be located so a person using the range does not have to reach across burners to access the oven controls (Section 1003.12.6.5). Sections 1003.12.6.5.1 and 1003.12.6.5.2 require a counter surface next to the oven. This could be the accessible work surface (see commentary Figure 1003.12.6.4). However, best design practice would have a portion of the counter at the same level as the burners [i.e., typical 36 inches (915 mm) height] so that someone with limited strength could slide pots over without a drop down [i.e., work surface is 34 inches to 29 inches (865 to 735 mm) height].

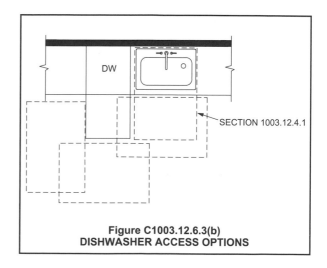

Figure C1003.12.6.3(b)
DISHWASHER ACCESS OPTIONS

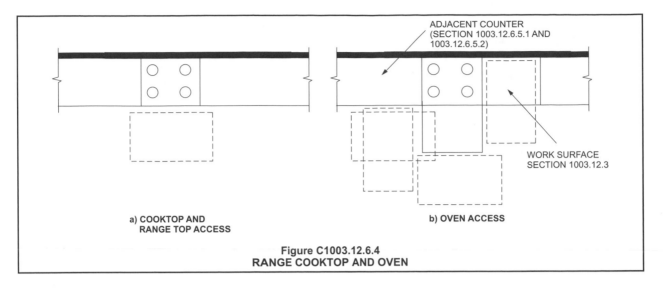

a) COOKTOP AND
RANGE TOP ACCESS

b) OVEN ACCESS

ADJACENT COUNTER
(SECTION 1003.12.6.5.1 AND
1003.12.6.5.2)

WORK SURFACE
SECTION 1003.12.3

Figure C1003.12.6.4
RANGE COOKTOP AND OVEN

1003.12.6.5 Oven. Ovens shall comply with Section 1003.12.6.5. Ovens shall have controls on front panels, on either side of the door.

❖ Ovens may be part of a range, or they may be the wall type. A person must be able to open the oven door fully and reach the oven racks. Therefore, how the oven is used must be considered when determining the clear floor space location. Wall mounted ovens may have better access because the height makes access easier for persons using wheelchairs (see commentary Figure 1003.12.6.5). A person would not have to reach both down and over the door to reach the rack or item in the oven. Another option to increase access would be racks that pull out all the way without tilting.

Access to oven controls that are part of a range must not require reaching across burners (Section 1003.12.6.4). Controls for both ranges and wall ovens must be within reach ranges.

1003.12.6.5.1 Side-Hinged Door Ovens. Side-hinged door ovens shall have a countertop positioned adjacent to the latch side of the oven door.

❖ Though most standard wall ovens come with a bottom hinged door, some manufacturers are starting to offer microwave/oven combinations with a side swing door. If a side opening wall oven is chosen, to facilitate transfer of heavy or hot dishes into and out of the oven, the latch side must be adjacent to a counter space. An accessible work surface located adjacent to the oven could serve as this counter space and could result in improved access for the oven; however, in a Type A unit kitchen, the work surface can be located anywhere in the kitchen [see commentary Figure C1003.12.6.4(b) and Section 1003.12.6.4].

1003.12.6.5.2 Bottom-Hinged Door Ovens. Bottom-hinged door ovens shall have a countertop positioned adjacent to one side of the door.

❖ If a bottom hinged oven is chosen, to facilitate transfer of heavy or hot dishes into and out of the oven, counter space must be located adjacent to the oven. The fold-down type doors are often used as the shelf for dishes, but this is not recommended by the manufacturer. An accessible work surface located adjacent to the oven could serve as this counter space and could result in improved access for the oven; however, in a Type A unit kitchen, the work surface can be located anywhere in the kitchen [see commentary Figure C1003.12.6.4(b) and commentary Section 1003.12.6.4].

Figure C1003.12.6.5
EXAMPLE OF ACCESS FOR A WALL OVEN

1003.12.6.6 Refrigerator/Freezer. Combination refrigerators and freezers shall have at least 50 percent of the freezer compartment shelves, including the bottom of the freezer 54 inches (1370 mm) maximum above the floor when the shelves are installed at the maximum heights possible in the compartment. A clear floor space, positioned for a parallel approach to the space dedicated to a refrigerator/freezer, shall be provided. The centerline of the clear floor space shall be offset 24 inches (610 mm) maximum from the centerline of the dedicated space.

❖ The position for the parallel approach to the refrigerator and freezer must consider how the person using a wheelchair will access the interior with the door open [see commentary Figure C1003.12.6.6(a)].

Refrigerator/freezer choices can have the freezer on the top, on the bottom or side-by-side. If a top freezer option is chosen, a freezer with the bottom of the compartment at a maximum of 54 inches (1370 mm) above the ground (assuming one shelf in the freezer) will meet the freezer compartment requirements. Bottom freezer access is not specifically addressed; however, the intent is if a bottom freezer option is chosen, at least one shelf in the freezer compartment must be 15 inches

(380 mm) minimum above the floor. Bottom freezers are typically pull out drawers, so a clear floor space must be available with the freezer door fully open. Side-by-side refrigerator/freezers provide the easiest access to the freezer compartment; however, then clear floor spaces for both sides must be considered for the unit [see commentary Figure C1003.12.6.6(b)]. Locating refrigerators so the doors swing back 180 degrees (3 rad) can provide greater accessibility for a person using a wheelchair.

Although not specifically mentioned, if a refrigerator has ice or water available through the door or inside the appliance, that feature is considered part of the refrigerator/freezer. Therefore, those elements must also have a clear floor space for access and meet reach range and operable parts requirements.

1003.12.6.7 Trash Compactor. A clear floor space, positioned for a parallel or forward approach to the trash compactor, shall be provided.

❖ The trash compactor is similar to the dishwasher and oven in the fact that it must be open for use. Therefore, the clear floor space should be located so that it does not obstruct the door of the trash compactor in the open position.

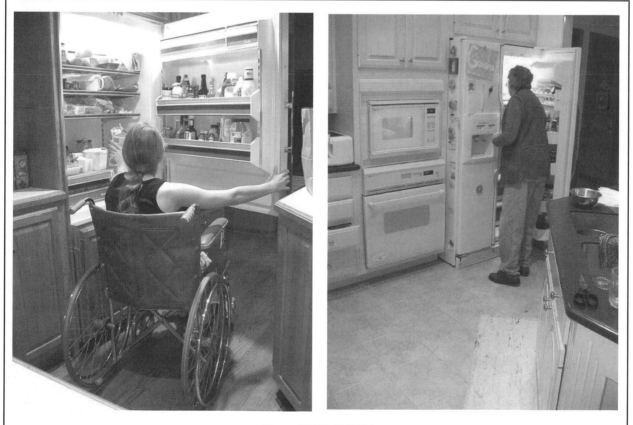

Figure C1003.12.6.6(a)
EXAMPLE OF ACCESS TO A REFRIGERATOR/FREEZER

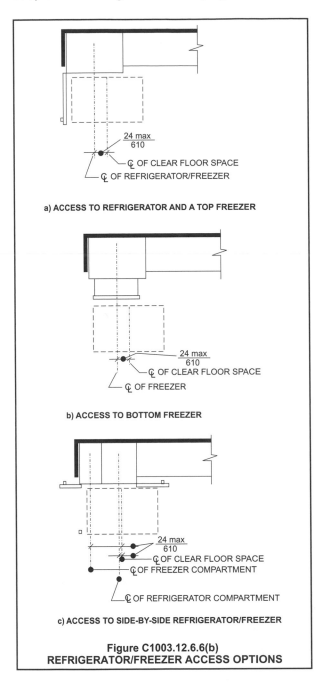

a) ACCESS TO REFRIGERATOR AND A TOP FREEZER

24 max
610
℄ OF CLEAR FLOOR SPACE
℄ OF REFRIGERATOR/FREEZER

24 max
610
℄ OF CLEAR FLOOR SPACE
℄ OF FREEZER

b) ACCESS TO BOTTOM FREEZER

24 max
610
℄ OF CLEAR FLOOR SPACE
℄ OF FREEZER COMPARTMENT
℄ OF REFRIGERATOR COMPARTMENT

c) ACCESS TO SIDE-BY-SIDE REFRIGERATOR/FREEZER

Figure C1003.12.6.6(b)
REFRIGERATOR/FREEZER ACCESS OPTIONS

1003.13 Windows. Where operable windows are provided, at least one window in each sleeping, living, or dining space shall have operable parts complying with Section 1003.9. Each required operable window shall have operable parts complying with Section 1003.9.

❖ For those windows that must be accessible, it is logical to ensure that the mechanisms that lock and unlock or open and close are positioned for accessibility, including clear floor space, reach ranges and graspability of the mechanisms (see Sections 309 and 1003.9). Examples of required operable windows would be emergency escape and rescue windows in

bedrooms and windows in spaces where natural ventilation is required. Examples of the types of operable windows include double-hung, sliding, casement and awning windows. At this time, to meet the 5 pounds (22 N) maximum operating force requirements most windows need add-on devices for opening.

1003.14 Storage Facilities. Where storage facilities are provided, they shall comply with Section 1003.14. Kitchen cabinets shall comply with Section 1003.12.5.

❖ The provisions for storage elements in Type A units are consistent with the provisions in Section 905 for Accessible units. There must be a clear floor space in front of storage facilities, such as closets, bathroom cabinets or pantries, and at least a portion of the shelves and clothes rods must be within reach ranges. The latches and knobs on doors or drawers must be easily operable by a person with limited hand movement and strength. If this is a reach-in closet, the door does not have to meet the clear width, threshold or maneuvering clearance requirements in Section 1003.5.

Kitchen cabinets should comply with the specific provisions in Section 1003.12.5. The special work environment and concentrated amount of storage allows for unique consideration.

1003.14.1 Clear Floor Space. A clear floor space complying with Section 305, positioned for a parallel or forward approach, shall be provided at each storage facility.

❖ A 30-inch by 48-inch (760 by 1220 mm) clear floor space must be provided at each storage element. Centering is not a requirement; rather, the access into the element should be considered. For example, access into a corner closet may be better served by a clear floor space that allows for opening the door and then moving forward to access the shelves. Access to a drawer may be better partially under or adjacent to the drawer to allow for opening the drawer to its full extension. Access can be forward or parallel.

If access to the storage element is confined in any way on three sides, the additional maneuvering clearances required in alcoves may be needed. For example, access to a bathroom cabinet may be confined by walls and a tub; therefore, the clearance width for a front approach needs to be 36 inches (915 mm) rather than 30 inches (760 mm).

1003.14.2 Height. A portion of the storage area of each storage facility shall comply with at least one of the reach ranges specified in Section 308.

❖ At least a portion of each storage facility, such as shelves or rods must be within the 15 inch to 48 inch (380 to 1220 mm) reach range. A standard closet organizer with a high-low rod for a portion of the closet meets this provision. Although some fixed shelves must be located within the reach range, pull-out shelves may improve access.

Because the standard cabinet height in bathrooms is lower than in kitchens, an upper wall cabinet or medicine cabinet can be located within the limits specified in the obstructed reach ranges.

1003.14.3 Operable Parts. Operable parts on storage facilities shall comply with Section 309.

❖ Door hardware or cabinet or drawer latches or pulls must be within reach ranges and be easy to operate.

1004 Type B Units

❖ Accessible and Type A units are considered to provide a higher level of accessibility than Type B units. Therefore, compliance with the provisions in Section 1002 or 1003 would exceed Type B requirements.

For the design of a Type B unit, the requirements in Sections 1004.1 through 1004.12 must be met. The technical criteria are either specifically stated in these sections or the section contains a reference to another section of the standard which contains the applicable technical standard. If a technical standard in another chapter is not referenced, it is not applicable to the design of a Type B unit.

1004.1 General. Type B units shall comply with Section 1004.

❖ A Type B dwelling or sleeping unit must comply with all the provisions in this section. Type B units are intended to be consistent with the Fair Housing Accessibility Guidelines (FHAG) (see Section 101). See the scoping documents for when Type B dwellings and sleeping units are required. Type B units are typically found anywhere people live where four or more units are constructed together. This can include both institutional and residential type facilities.

Historically, the Type B unit was first added in the A117.1 1998 edition. Both the 1998 and 2003 editions of ICC A117.1 have been designated as 'safe harbor' documents for compliance with FHAG by Housing and Urban Development (HUD). Although the 1986 and 1992 editions of A117.1 are also considered 'safe harbor' documents, they did not contain requirements specifically to match FHAG, but did contain criteria for units that provided a higher level of access, Accessible units and Adaptable units. Adaptable units are now called Type A.

Note that Type B units do not include requirements for storage and windows such as to those found in Accessible and Type A units.

1004.2 Primary Entrance. The accessible primary entrance shall be on an accessible route from public and common areas. The primary entrance shall not be to a bedroom.

❖ In an apartment type unit, the main entrance is typically into a central living area, so this should also be the accessible entrance for the unit. The accessible entrance cannot be a 'backdoor' entrance, such as a patio door or

through a bedroom. This accessible unit entrance must be connected by an accessible route to an accessible building entrance and all public or shared areas intended for the use of the residents of that unit. This includes areas such as the building lobby, mail boxes, garbage chutes or dumpsters, shared laundry facilities, and recreational facilities, such as exercise rooms or pools. See also Section 1004.5.1 for unique requirements for the accessible entrance door.

In an efficiency unit or sleeping unit where the main living area is also the bedroom, this entrance may serve as the accessible entrance, and is not considered prohibited by the last sentence of this section. It is not the intent of this section to require an entry vestibule or second room.

In facilities such as hotels or nursing homes, the changing of linens or removal of garbage may be the responsibility of employees rather than residents. In these situations, the areas such as laundry rooms and garbage disposal areas should be regulated under the employee work area provisions and are not required to be accessible to the residents of the dwelling units.

1004.3 Accessible Route. Accessible routes within Type B units shall comply with Section 1004.3.

❖ Type B units differ from Accessible and Type A units in that the accessible route does not require a turning space anywhere within the unit. The accessible route in the Type B units must meet the provisions for location and components only.

1004.3.1 Location. At least one accessible route shall connect all spaces and elements that are a part of the unit. Where only one accessible route is provided, it shall not pass through bathrooms and toilet rooms, closets, or similar spaces.

> **EXCEPTION:** One of the following is not required to be on an accessible route:
>
> 1. A raised floor area in a portion of a living, dining, or sleeping room; or
>
> 2. A sunken floor area in a portion of a living, dining, or sleeping room; or
>
> 3. A mezzanine that does not have plumbing fixtures or an enclosed habitable space.

❖ A route must be available to all living spaces within the unit. The provisions were written assuming a single-story unit; however, this could include multiple stories within an individual unit. In a congregate living arrangement, this accessible route would also include access to shared spaces such as the bathroom and living or eating areas (Section 1004.2).

When only one route is available to certain spaces, the route should not be through areas that are subject to locking, such as bathrooms or closets. This is not intended to prohibit access through spaces controlled by the individual. For example, a master suite with the closet accessed through the bathroom would not be blocking access for the occupant of that bedroom.

In a Type B unit, certain portions of a multi-level unit do not need to be on an accessible route. This includes either a raised area, a sunken area or a mezza-nine within the unit [see commentary Figure C1004.3.1(a) and (b)]. See the scoping documents for exemptions for multistory units.

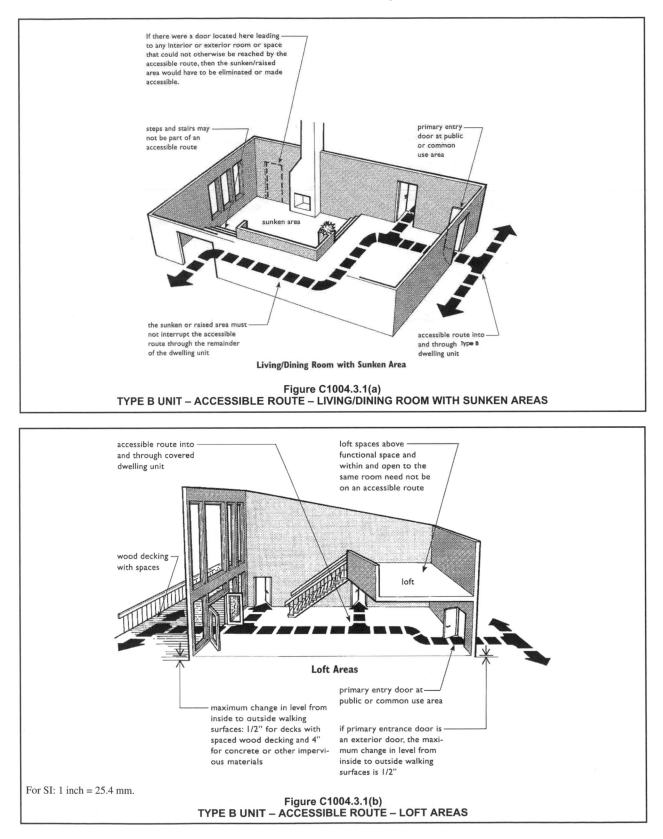

If there were a door located here leading to any interior or exterior room or space that could not otherwise be reached by the accessible route, then the sunken/raised area would have to be eliminated or made accessible.

steps and stairs may not be part of an accessible route

primary entry door at public or common use area

sunken area

the sunken or raised area must not interrupt the accessible route through the remainder of the dwelling unit

accessible route into and through Type B dwelling unit

Living/Dining Room with Sunken Area

Figure C1004.3.1(a)
TYPE B UNIT – ACCESSIBLE ROUTE – LIVING/DINING ROOM WITH SUNKEN AREAS

accessible route into and through covered dwelling unit

loft spaces above functional space and within and open to the same room need not be on an accessible route

wood decking with spaces

loft

Loft Areas

primary entry door at public or common use area

maximum change in level from inside to outside walking surfaces: 1/2" for decks with spaced wood decking and 4" for concrete or other impervi-ous materials

if primary entrance door is an exterior door, the maxi-mum change in level from inside to outside walking surfaces is 1/2"

For SI: 1 inch = 25.4 mm.

Figure C1004.3.1(b)
TYPE B UNIT – ACCESSIBLE ROUTE – LOFT AREAS

Unfinished attics and basements do not need to be on an accessible route because these spaces do not include living space for the unit.

In the scoping provisions found in the model codes and the Fair Housing Act, there are exceptions for multistory units without elevator service, and a second level in multistory dwelling units with elevator access to only the first level. See the scoping documents for specific provisions. See Section 201 and the preface for an explanation of scoping provisions and technical requirements.

1004.3.2 Components. Accessible routes shall consist of one or more of the following elements: walking surfaces with a slope not steeper than 1:20, doorways, ramps, elevators, and platform lifts.

❖ The accessible route throughout the unit should be on level surfaces. When a transition is needed between levels or stories, either a ramp, elevator or platform lift can be used. See the commentary to Sections 1004.6, 1004.7 and 1004.8.

1004.4 Walking Surfaces. Walking surfaces that are part of an accessible route shall comply with Section 1004.4.

❖ An accessible route in public areas must comply with Section 403, including floor surfaces (Section 302), slope, change in level (Section 303) and clear width. Within the Type B unit, walking surfaces need to comply only with the requirements for width and change in level. What this most often represents is that Type B units can have carpets with higher pile and padding than what is permitted in the building corridors.

1004.4.1 Width. Clear width of an accessible route shall comply with Section 403.5.

❖ The general width for the accessible route throughout the unit is 36 inches (915 mm). At framed openings or where a route may narrow, a minimum clear width of 32 inches (815 mm) provides adequate clearance. However, if an opening or another type of restriction along a route is more than 24 inches (610 mm) deep, it must be a minimum of 36 inches (915 mm) wide (see commentary Figure C403.5). This allows for framed openings, pilasters or other minimal protrusions along the accessible route.

For the width requirements at doors, see Section 1004.5. It is not the intent of this section to require the clear widths at turns (Section 403.5.1) or passing spaces (Section 403.5.2) within the Type B unit.

1004.4.2 Changes in Level. Changes in level shall comply with Section 303.

EXCEPTION: Where exterior deck, patio or balcony surface materials are impervious, the finished exterior impervious surface shall be 4 inches (100 mm) maximum below the floor level of the adjacent interior spaces of the unit.

❖ Change in level means a change in elevation between horizontal planes in the direction of travel along an accessible route. The general limits are $^1/_4$ inch (6 mm) maximum change vertically or $^1/_2$ inch (13 mm) maximum with a beveled edge. These provisions are covered in Section 303, which is generally applicable to all floor surfaces on an accessible route. In addition, more than $^1/_2$ inch is considered a tripping hazard for ambulatory persons. See commentary with Section 303.

The exception allows for a maximum 4 inch (100 mm) change between the interior finished floor and the exterior deck surface. This dimension does not include the threshold permitted in Section 1004.5.2.2. This change in elevation is permitted at doors other than the primary entrance. The change is elevation allows for concerns about water infiltration and/or wind resistance for that opening–typically a sliding patio door or a swinging door.

1004.5 Doors and Doorways. Doors and doorways shall comply with Section 1004.5.

❖ Two types of doors are addressed in this section, the door that serves as the primary entrance door to the unit and other doors within the unit intended for people to walk through. This includes doors leading to private areas that are part of the unit, such as attached private garages or balconies.

1004.5.1 Primary Entrance Door. The primary entrance door to the unit shall comply with Section 404.

EXCEPTION: Maneuvering clearances required by Section 404.2.3 shall not be required on the unit side of the primary entrance door.

❖ The primary entrance door should be the main door used to access the unit. Although this may be somewhat interpretive in some units, it is typically the front door to the unit. See Section 1004.2 for additional information.

The primary entrance door to the Type B unit must meet all the provisions for doors that are located along an accessible route (see Section 404). This includes the requirements for 32 inch (815 mm) clear width, thresholds, lever hardware, door opening force, bottom door surface on the push side and vision lite location, which typically results in a 36 inch (915 mm) front door. Door hardware must be installed between 34 inches and 48 inches (865 and 1220 mm) above the floor. A front door with a screen/storm door is not considered doors in a series.

The only exception is that the maneuvering space is not required on the inside of the primary entrance door, but maneuvering space is required on the outside.

If an automatic door is installed, the provisions of Section 404.3 are applicable.

1004.5.2 User Passage Doorways. Doorways intended for user passage shall comply with Section 1004.5.2.

❖ Doors 'intended for user passage' are any doors that a person is expected to pass through to access a space. For example, doorways to rooms or walk-in closets are doorways intended for user passage. Doorways to reach-in pantries or closets are not required to comply with the requirements in this section.

Doors within Type B units must meet the clear width and threshold requirement in the subsections that follow. Maneuvering clearances, level hardware, meet opening forces, etc. are not required.

1004.5.2.1 Clear Width. Doorways shall have a clear opening of $31^3/_4$ inches (810 mm) minimum. Clear opening of swinging doors shall be measured between the face of the door and stop, with the door open 90 degrees.

❖ The opening is measured with the door open 90 degrees (1.6 rad), even if the door can open wider. The intent of the $31^3/_4$ inch (810 mm) dimension is to allow for a 2 foot, 10 inch (865 mm) door. The 32 inch (815 mm) clearance at the primary entrance door (Section 1004.5.1) typically requires a 36 inch (915 mm) door.

Although the standard does not specifically mention door hardware, it is not the intent to include hardware when determining door width clearance.

1004.5.2.2 Thresholds. Thresholds shall comply with Section 303.

EXCEPTION: Thresholds at exterior sliding doors shall be permitted to be ¾ inch (19 mm) maximum in height, provided they are beveled with a slope not steeper than 1:2.

❖ Thresholds and changes in the surface height at doorways are difficult for persons using a wheelchair who also may have low stamina or restrictions in arm movement because complex maneuvering is required to get over the level change when operating the door.

The reference to Section 303 effectively establishes $^1/_2$ inch (13 mm) as the maximum change in elevation for a threshold at a doorway. Where a threshold exceeds $^1/_4$ inch (6 mm) in height, the edge or the threshold must be beveled (see Figures 303.2 and 303.3). This is in addition to the change in floor level in Section 1004.4.2.

Because of the requirements for sliding doors to stay in their tracks for proper operation, a $^3/_4$ inch (19 mm) threshold is permitted at exterior sliding doors. See Section 1004.4.2 for a discussion of sliding doors at patios or balconies. Similar to a $^1/_2$ inch (13 mm) threshold, the edges must be beveled.

1004.5.2.3 Automatic Doors. Automatic doors shall comply with Section 404.3.

❖ Automatic doors are not required within Type B dwelling units, but if installed, they must meet the general provisions for automatic doors in Section 404.3.

This item is not specifically listed in Accessible or Type A dwelling units because the general reference to Section 404 for all doors already requires this.

1004.5.2.4 Double Leaf Doorways. Where an inactive leaf with operable parts higher than 48 inches (1220 mm) or lower than 15 inches (380 mm) above the floor is provided, the active leaf shall provide the clearance required by Section 1004.5.2.1.

❖ At the primary entrance door, a double door with an inactive leaf would require one leaf to meet clear width requirements. Within a Type B unit, at a double door, an inactive leaf can count toward the required clear width of $31^3/_4$ inches (810 mm) if the door latches that hold the door in place are within reach ranges.

1004.6 Ramps. Ramps shall comply with Section 405.

❖ Ramps that serve as part of the accessible route into or through a Type B dwelling or sleeping unit must meet the general ramp provisions in Section 405. See Sections 1004.3.1 and 1004.4.2 for levels within a Type B unit that do not have to be on an accessible route.

Ramps for a change in elevation greater than 6 inches (150 mm) will require handrails on both sides. The local building code should be consulted regarding when guards are required along ramps. Ramps must have a landing at both the top and the bottom, so a ramp cannot extend up to the face of a door.

1004.7 Elevators. Elevators within the unit shall comply with Section 407, 408, or 409.

❖ Elevators installed within a single dwelling unit or providing private access to a single dwelling unit are permitted to be passenger elevators, LULAs or private residence elevators. Refer to the referenced standard ASME A17.1 for limitations of use.

Refer to the scoping documents for requirements when elevators are installed for general access in the building and within individual units. In the model code and Fair Housing Act Accessibility Guidelines, when there are no elevators in the building, multistory units are exempted from Type B requirements. When a common elevator is available in the building, the levels served by the elevator must meet Type B units and must include at least a toilet room (i.e., powder room with water closet and lavatory) and a living space. When an elevator is provided for access within an individual dwelling unit (e.g., a multistory townhouse), the Type B unit requirements are applicable to all levels served by the elevator. In all cases, an accessible route must be provided from the site arrival point, through the accessible entrance, to the elevator.

Another example of elevators being used in relation to Type B dwelling units is when dwelling units are located above other uses, such as parking, business or mercantile.

1004.8 Platform Lifts. Platform lifts within the unit shall comply with Section 410.

❖ Platform lifts can be used within individual dwelling units to serve as part of an accessible route between levels or to provide access into an individual unit. The lift must be a platform (wheelchair) lift in accordance with ASME A18.1, not a chair lift (e.g., flip-down seat). Platform lifts may be incline or vertical. The current standard limits the maximum rise to 12 feet (3660 mm). See ASME A18.1 for limitations of use.

1004.9 Operable Parts. Lighting controls, electrical switches and receptacle outlets, environmental controls, and user controls for security or intercom systems shall comply with Sections 309.2 and 309.3.

EXCEPTIONS:

1. Receptacle outlets serving a dedicated use.

2. One receptacle outlet is not required to comply with Sections 309.2 and 309.3 where all of the following conditions are met:

   (a) the receptacle outlet is above a length of countertop that is uninterrupted by a sink or appliance; and

   (b) at least one receptacle outlet complying with Section 1004.9 is provided for that length of countertop; and

   (c) all other receptacle outlets provided for that length of countertop comply with Section 1004.9.

3. Floor receptacle outlets.

4. HVAC diffusers.

5. Controls mounted on ceiling fans.

6. Controls or switches mounted on appliances.

7. Plumbing fixture controls.

❖ The general requirements for operable parts are listed in Section 309. By a more specific reference to Sections 309.2 and 309.3 (and not 309.4), operable parts in Type B units require a clear floor space adjacent to the part and that part be within reach ranges. The operation of the part does not require any tight pinching, grasping or twisting of the wrist to operate or more than 5 pounds force (22 N).

The intent is the person in the space be able to operate the equipment in the room in a normal manner. It is not the intent that these provisions be applicable to items such as shut-offs for plumbing fixtures or protection switches for electrical equipment, such as the reset switch on a garbage disposal or a circuit breaker box.

Examples of lighting controls are wall light switches or pull cords. If light switches are offered with 3-way or 4-way operation, all switches must be accessible. Other types of switches could include wall activation switches for garbage disposals, bathroom ventilation fans or cooking hoods. Exception 2 exempts any electrical switches mounted on appliances, such as the cooking hoods. The bathroom ventilation fan should be accessible as part of the environmental controls.

Receptacles are typically the standard duplex wall outlets located around a room or over a counter. Note that there are several exceptions for electrical receptacles. Receptacles that serve a dedicated purpose (Exception 1), such as the receptacle for a washer/dryer, refrigerator or stove, need not be accessible. These items are typically plugged in all the time. The model electrical code requires electrical receptacles spaced at a maximum of 12 feet (3660 mm) apart in most rooms. In spaces with very tall windows or along balcony guards there may not be wall space for the required electrical receptacles. Large rooms may need receptacles located toward the center of the room. When floor receptacles are used, they do not need to be accessible (Exception 3). Exception 2 is most often used when dealing with receptacles over kitchen counters. In kitchens, per the model electrical code, one receptacle is required over each section of counter top with a maximum spacing of 4 feet (1220 mm). If an appliance or sink is located along a counter top, the counter on each side is considered a separate section, and a receptacle must be installed on each side. In a kitchen in a Type B unit, the counters can be located at any height, typically 36 inches (915 mm). However, with the obstructed side reach range requirements in Section 308.3.2, receptacles cannot be located over the standard 36-inch (915 mm) high counter and be accessible. Exception 2 allows for one receptacle per counter section to not be accessible if the remainder of the outlets are accessible. An alternative is to locate a receptacle on the side or front surface of the lower cabinet. This is commonly done on kitchen island counters; however, this will reduce drawer space. This same problem is not typically found in bathrooms because bathroom counter heights are typically installed between 29 and 34 inches (735 and 865 mm) high.

Environmental controls can include ceiling fans or heating and air conditioning thermostats. A common error for locating the thermostat is to specify the electrical box at 48 inches (1220 mm) high, not noting that the actual control is on the top of the thermostat box, thus placing the control out of the reach range. Exception 4 does exempt the heating and air conditioning diffusers from being accessible. They need to be on or near the floor and near the ceiling to circulate the air in the room effectively. Exception 5 exempts controls mounted on ceiling fans. Typically the on-off and speed for ceiling fans are controlled from a wall switch, but there may be a switch on the fan itself for reversing the direction of the blades.

For Type B units (unlike Accessible and Type A units), Exception 6 exempts all appliance-mounted controls. Appliance controls vary greatly and may include the key pad for temperature and type of cooking (e.g., bake/broil) on ovens, knobs for burner settings on stove tops, door handles to access the interior of the appliance, water/ice dispensers on refrigerators, latches for self-cleaning ovens, soap containers in dishwashers and clothes washers, lint trays in dryers, etc.

In Type B units, plumbing fixture controls are exempted per Exception 7. Plumbing fixture controls would include faucets in showers, tubs and sinks, and flush valves on toilets, which do have accessibility requirements in Accessible and Type A units.

Accessible windows and window hardware are covered in Accessible and Type A units; however, they are not required in Type B units.

Security or intercom systems may include activation keypads or access to a phone or speaker. Refer to Sections 1005.5, 1005.6 and 1005.7 for additional specifics for communication features that are part of security or intercom systems.

Operable parts on the primary entrance door to the units are regulated under Section 1004.5.1 through a reference to Sections 404.2.6 and 404.3.5. Door hardware on other doors within the unit is not regulated (see Section 1004.5.2).

1004.10 Laundry Equipment. Washing machines and clothes dryers shall comply with Section 1004.10.

❖ The standard does not require laundry equipment within the unit; however, washers and dryer must meet the minimal level of accessibility in Section 1004.10.1. These provisions are less than those in a common laundry room (see Section 611).

When designing the laundry area, several items must be considered. Section 1004.10.1 requires a parallel clear floor space in front of each appliance, centered on that appliance.

When laundry equipment is located in a room, turning spaces and maneuvering clearances are not required as they are for an Accessible unit and Type A

unit. A service/laundry sink does not need be accessible; however, it would be better design to provide a parallel or side approach to that sink to allow for use [see commentary Figure C1004.10(a)].

When laundry equipment is located in a closet, the clear floor space can be located 10 inches (255 mm) back from the face of the units (Section 308.3.1), which allows for the wall thickness, but may necessitate either sliding closet doors or no doors so the doors will not block the clear floor space [see commentary Figure C1004.10(b)]. This standard does not address whether removal of the doors could be considered an adaptable feature.

1004.10.1 Clear Floor Space. A clear floor space complying with Section 305.3, positioned for parallel approach, shall be provided. The clear floor space shall be centered on the appliance.

❖ See Section 1004.10.

1004.11 Toilet and Bathing Facilities. Toilet and bathing fixtures shall comply with Section 1004.11.

EXCEPTION: Fixtures on levels not required to be accessible.

❖ Type B units allow for a minimal access into a bathroom. Bathroom requirements for Accessible units and Type A units provide for a higher level of accessibility.

In Type B units, designers can choose to meet either Option A (Section 1004.11.3.1) or Option B (Section 1004.11.3.2) requirements for the bathroom(s) in the dwelling unit or serving the sleeping unit. The choice for Option A and Option B is available for dwelling units or sleeping units with one bathroom. When there are multiple bathrooms in the unit, Option A clearances would apply to all bathrooms, and Option B clearances would apply to just one bathroom in the unit. All bathrooms must provide blocking for the future installation of grab bars (Sec-

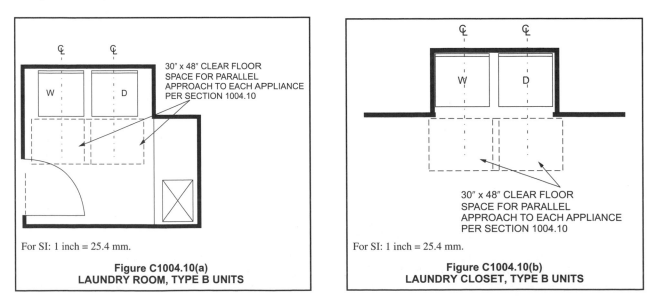

For SI: 1 inch = 25.4 mm.

Figure C1004.10(a)
LAUNDRY ROOM, TYPE B UNITS

For SI: 1 inch = 25.4 mm.

Figure C1004.10(b)
LAUNDRY CLOSET, TYPE B UNITS

tion 1004.11.2). Whichever bathroom option is chosen, the clearances in those bathrooms must also meet Section 1004.11.1.

Once an option is chosen, the requirements are exclusive–no mixing between Option A and Option B requirements. However, requirements for Type A unit and Accessible unit bathrooms provide a higher level of accessibility. Designers could choose to exceed requirements for separate fixtures or the bathroom as a whole (Section 103).

The exception is caused by the scoping provisions in the model code and the Fair Housing Act allowing an exception for the second floor in a multistory unit in an elevator building. Bathrooms on the inaccessible level would not have to meet these provisions. See these documents for specific requirements.

1004.11.1 Clear Floor Space. Clear floor space required by Section 1004.11.3.1 or 1004.11.3.2 shall comply with Sections 1004.11.1 and 305.3.

❖ In Type B units, the designer chooses to comply with either Option A (Section 1004.11.3.1) or Option B (Section 1004.11.3.2) bathroom requirements. In a multi-bathroom unit, only one bathroom is required to comply with Option B. Bathrooms that meet Option A or Option B clearance requirements must also meet the additional requirements in this section (Section 1004.11.1 through 1004.11.1.3).

The reference to the 30-inch by 48-inch (760 by 1220 mm) clear floor space (Section 305.3) appears to be redundant given the specific clearance provisions in Option A and Option B. The intent is to make sure that a space for a person using a wheelchair is available at each fixture.

1004.11.1.1 Doors. Doors shall not swing into the clear floor space for any fixture.

> **EXCEPTION:** Where a clear floor space complying with Section 305.3, excluding knee and toe clearances under elements, is provided within the room beyond the arc of the door swing.

❖ The door to the bathroom must not swing into the bathroom and over the clear floor space for the lavatory, water closet, tub or shower. However, the exception allows that where a 30-inch by 48-inch (760 by 1220 mm) wheelchair space is located past the swing of the door, the door can swing over the fixture clearances. With this configuration, someone can enter the room, close the door and then maneuver to access the fixtures. The portion of the exception, "excluding knee and toe clearances," indicates that even though knee and toe clearances are not required in Type B unit bathrooms, this wheelchair space cannot use any knee and toe clearances that are there.

1004.11.1.2 Knee and Toe Clearance. Clear floor space at fixtures shall be permitted to include knee and toe clearances complying with Section 306.

❖ Provisions in Type B dwelling unit bathrooms are for a parallel approach to fixtures and do not require knee and toe clearances; however, if a designer chooses to provide knee and toe clearances, for example under a lavatory, this would be acceptable.

This provision is not applicable to the exception in Section 1004.11.1.1.

1004.11.1.3 Overlap. Clear floor spaces shall be permitted to overlap.

❖ The clear floor space is the location where a person will sit to access a fixture. These areas are permitted to overlap; however, fixtures can overlap only the clear floor spaces where they are specifically indicated. See the requirements for each fixture to see what fixture overlap is permitted.

1004.11.2 Reinforcement. Reinforcement shall be provided for the future installation of grab bars and shower seats at water closets, bathtubs, and shower compartments. Where walls are located to permit the installation of grab bars and seats complying with Sections 604.5, 607.4, 608.3 and 608.4, reinforcement shall be provided for the future installation of grab bars and seats meeting those requirements.

> **EXCEPTION:** Reinforcement is not required in a room containing only a lavatory and a water closet, provided the room does not contain the only lavatory or water closet on the accessible level of the unit.

❖ If walls are located adjacent to a plumbing fixture, that wall must include blocking so that grab bars can easily be installed in the future. The references are to water closets (Section 604.5), bathtubs (Section 607.4) and transfer and roll-in showers (Section 608.3). The reference to Section 608.4 is for bathtub and shower seats. The following sections include specific exceptions for Type B units.

Section 604.5, Exceptions 4 and 5 — Section 604.5 is concerned with grab bars at water closets. Generally grab bars are required on the side and rear wall. Type B units are the only location where blocking for swing-up grab bars or the installation of swing-up grab bars is permitted instead of the blocking or installation of fixed rear and side grab bars. See Section 604.5.3 for swing-up grab bar requirements. Per Exception 4, within the Type B units required in institutional facilities (e.g., nursing homes) and assisted living facilities, two swing-up grab bars are permitted in place of the rear and side grab bars in recognition of two commonalities in Type B units in these facilities: 1) there may be additional space adjacent to the water closet to allow for nurse assistance; or 2) the occupant may be using mobility aids such as a walker or cane, so the purpose of the grab bar is for assistance in rising or sitting, not transfer. Exception 5 is in recognition that Option A bathrooms in Type B units allow for the water closet to be located between a tub and a lavatory; therefore, a wall is located only behind the water closet. A swing-up grab bar is a viable alternative for the side grab bar. Although a swing-up grab bar is not ideal for transfer, providing a fixed grab bar would block access to the tub. For persons with mobility impairments, Option A configurations allow a person to sit down at or transfer to the water closet, swing up the bar and transfer to the tub. This can reduce the chance of a fall getting in and out of the tub [see commentary Figure C604.5(b)].

Section 604.5.1—Section 604.5.1 addresses requirements for the side wall grab bar at water closets and includes a horizontal and a vertical grab bar. Exception 1 is in recognition that windows are often located in the wall adjacent to the water closet within dwelling units; therefore, blocking for the vertical grab bar is not required in Type A and Type B dwelling units.

Exception 2 is limited to Type B units and is applicable when the side wall does not allow for blocking for a full length side bar. This may occur when the water closet is adjacent to a shower or tub enclosure or the door into the room is on the side wall. Blocking for the shorter bar is acceptable (see commentary Figure C604.5.1).

Section 604.5.2—Section 604.5.2 addresses requirements for the rear wall grab bar at water closets. Exception 2 is limited to Type B units and is applicable when the side wall does not allow for blocking for a full length side bar. This may occur when the water closet is adjacent to a shower or tub enclosure or the door into the room is on the side wall. Blocking for the shorter bar is acceptable (see commentary Figure C604.5.1).

Section 604.5, Exception 3; 607.4, Exception 2; 608.3, Exception 2; 608.4, Exception 2; state that in Type A units grab bars are not required if blocking is installed. A similar exception for Type B units is not needed because the initial requirement is for reinforcement, not the grab bars.

Section 1004.11.2—Some dwellings include a toilet room with only a water closet and a lavatory, often referred to as a powder room or a half-bath. If this toilet room is the only bathroom, it must contain blocking in the walls at the water closet. If other bathrooms are provided, blocking is not required in the powder room. The terminology in the exception to this section follows the scoping provisions in the model code and the Fair Housing Act allow for an exception for the second floor in a multistory unit in an elevator building. See these documents for specific requirements.

1004.11.3 Toilet and Bathing Rooms. Either all toilet and bathing rooms provided shall comply with Section 1004.11.3.1 (Option A), or one toilet and bathing room shall comply with Section 1004.11.3.2 (Option B).

❖ When multiple bathrooms are located within the same unit, a designer can choose to have either all the bathrooms meet Option A bathroom clearances, or one bathroom meet Option B bathroom clearances. When a unit has only one bathroom, a designer still has the choice of Option A or Option B.

Option B bathrooms, with a clear floor space in front of the bathtub, are considered to provide a higher level of access for persons using wheelchairs than Option A bathrooms. On the other hand, physical therapists will advise persons with mobility impairments to sit on a toilet to disrobe and then move to the bathtub. Therefore, the Option A bathroom could be considered more user friendly for a person with mobility impairments.

1004.11.3.1 Option A. Each fixture provided shall comply with Section 1004.11.3.1.

EXCEPTION: A lavatory and a water closet in a room containing only a lavatory and water closet, provided the room does not contain the only lavatory or water closet on the accessible level of the unit.

❖ The general configuration for an Option A bathroom is with the lavatory, water closet and tub along one common plumbing wall (see commentary Figure C1004.11.3.1). The general configuration for an Option B bathroom is with the tub on one side and the water closet and lavatory on the side (see commentary Figure C1004.11.3.2).

If Option A bathrooms are chosen, each fixture in the bathroom must meet the clearance requirements in this section. This provision is silent about the idea of when multiple lavatories or multiple bathing fixtures (e.g., bathtubs and showers) are provided in the same bathroom. This is consistent with the Fair Housing Act. Type B units, Option B bathrooms, Type A unit bathrooms and Accessible unit bathrooms, all of which are considered to provide a higher level of accessibility, do specifically state that one of each fixture must be accessible (i.e., lavatory, water closet and either a bathtub or shower).

The exception allows for a powder room or half-bath to not have clearances if this is not the only bathroom on the accessible level. The wording of the exception is a result of the scoping provisions in the model code and the Fair Housing Act allowing for an exception for the second floor in a multistory unit in an elevator building. Bathrooms on the inaccessible level do not need to meet these provisions. See these documents for specific requirements.

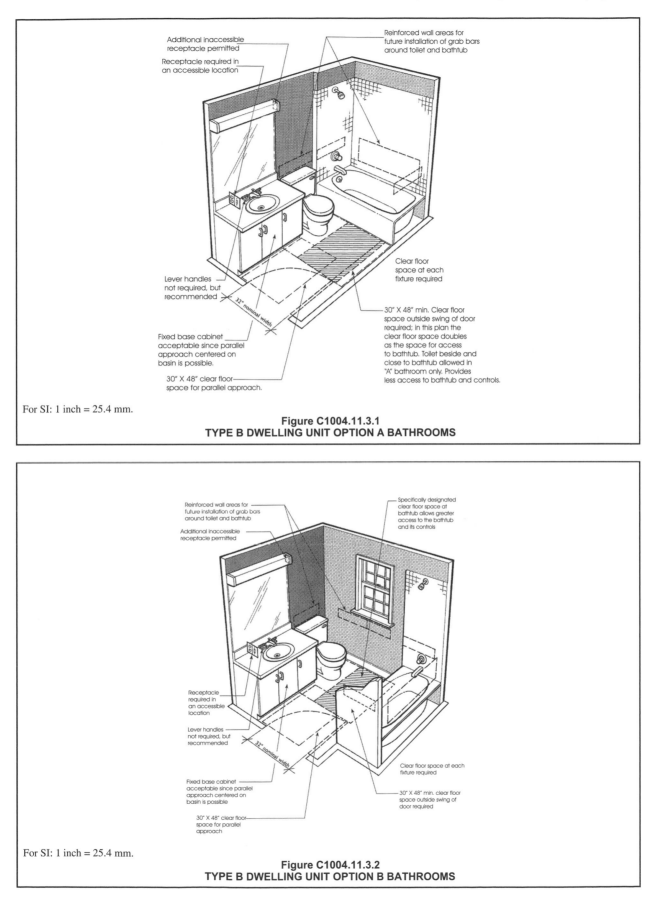

For SI: 1 inch = 25.4 mm.

Figure C1004.11.3.1
TYPE B DWELLING UNIT OPTION A BATHROOMS

For SI: 1 inch = 25.4 mm.

Figure C1004.11.3.2
TYPE B DWELLING UNIT OPTION B BATHROOMS

1004.11.3.1.1 Lavatory. A clear floor space complying with Section 305.3, positioned for a parallel approach, shall be provided. The clear floor space shall be centered on the lavatory.

EXCEPTIONS:

1. A lavatory complying with Section 606.

2. Cabinetry shall be permitted under the lavatory provided such cabinetry can be removed without removal or replacement of the lavatory, and the floor finish extends under such cabinetry.

❖ The clear floor space requirement for Option A and Option B lavatories is the same; however, Option B has an additional height requirement. See Section 1004.11.3.2.1.3.

A 30-inch by 48-inch (760 by 1220 mm) parallel space centered on the lavatory will allow a person using a wheelchair to approach the lavatory and use it for bathing. Because the wheels of a wheelchair typically extend at least 12 inches (305 mm) behind the back of the wheelchair seat, the center of the lavatory must be at least 24 inches (610 mm) from an adjacent wall or other obstruction.

The intent of the exceptions is to allow the more accessible lavatory options permitted in Accessible units or Type A units (see Section 1003.11.5). Although the reference to Section 606 would result in faucets having to meet operable parts requirements (Section 606.4), the specific exception for plumbing fixtures in Type B units in Section 1004.9, Exception 7 would negate that requirement.

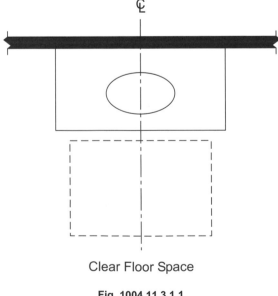

Clear Floor Space

Fig. 1004.11.3.1.1
Lavatory in Type B Units –
Option A Bathrooms

A result of Exception 2 not referencing Section 1003.11.5 directly, is that the Option A bathroom does not have to locate the lavatory at a 34 inch (865 mm) maximum height. However, standard bathroom cabinets typically are constructed with the top of the counter at 29 inches to 34 inches (735 to 865 mm).

The reference to Section 606 in Exception 1 includes all subsections (Section 606.1 through 606.7). Section 606.5 includes an exception to indicate that lavatories with enhanced reach ranges are not required within Type A and Type B dwelling or sleeping units. Because towel dispensers and hand dryers are typically not installed within dwelling units and sleeping units, Section 606.7 is typically not applicable.

1004.11.3.1.2 Water Closet. The lateral distance from the centerline of the water closet to a bathtub or lavatory shall be 18 inches (455 mm) minimum on the side opposite the direction of approach and 15 inches (380 mm) minimum on the other side. The lateral distance from the centerline of the water closet to an adjacent wall shall be 18 inches (455 mm). The lateral distance from the centerline of the water closet to a lavatory or bathtub shall be 15 inches (380 mm) minimum. The water closet shall be positioned to allow for future installation of a grab bar on the side with 18 inches (455 mm) clearance. Clearance around the water closet shall comply with Section 1004.11.3.1.2.1, 1004.11.3.1.2.2, or 1004.11.3.1.2.3.

❖ The water closet clearance requirements for Option A and Option B bathrooms are the same. Although the requirements for the water closet clearances are the same, Option A bathrooms allow a configuration with the water closet located between the tub and lavatory, and Option B bathrooms require the water closet to be located next to a wall.

The water closet must have a clearance of at least 15 inches (380 mm) on the side of the approach and 18 inches (455 mm) on the side away from the direction of approach. The intent is that the location of the future grab bar will be on the far side [see Figure 1004.11.3.1.2(a)].

Accessible and Type A units allow for 16 inches to 18 inches (405 to 455 mm) from the center line of the water closet to the wall. Type B units require 18 inches (455 mm) minimum. For situations where the plans are for a swing-up grab bar, the 18-inch (455 mm) minimum is needed for clearances. However, when plans are for mounting the grab bar on the wall, exceeding 18 inches (455 mm) could place the wall mounted bar past the reach of a person attempting a transfer. In a configuration with the water closet adjacent to a wall, using the complete water closet location and clearances associated with Type A or Accessible unit water closets would result in a higher level of access.

See also the commentary to Section 1004.11.2 regarding the blocking for the future installation of grab bars around the water closet.

There are three choices for the clearances around the water closet. The arrows in Figure 1004.11.3.1.2 indicate the anticipated approach direction to the water closet. The third choice, parallel or forward approach, is intended to allow the Type B dwelling unit to meet the same clearances as required for water closets in Accessible units (Section 604.3.1). Type A unit clearances (Section 1003.11.7.2) would also exceed Type B unit water closet clearances. The designer can use any of the three choices.

1004.11.3.1.2.1 Parallel Approach. A clearance 56 inches (1420 mm) minimum measured from the wall behind the water closet, and 48 inches (1220 mm) minimum measured from a point 18 inches (455 mm) from the centerline of the water closet on the side designated for future installation of grab bars shall be provided. Vanities or lavatories on the wall behind the water closet are permitted to overlap the clearance.

❖ The clear floor space for the parallel approach for water closets in the Type B unit is smaller than that required for Type A units (Section 1002.11.5.2.1). The depth of the space is 56 inches (1420 mm). The width is measured 18 inches (455 mm) from the centerline of the water closet away from the approach and toward the side where the grab bar is to be located and then back 48 inches (1220 mm) over the water closet [see Figure 1004.11.3.1.2(b)].

1004.11.3.1.2.2 Forward Approach. A clearance 66 inches (1675 mm) minimum measured from the wall behind the water closet, and 48 inches (1220 mm) minimum measured from a point 18 inches (455 mm) from the centerline of the water closet on the side designated for future installation of grab bars shall be provided. Vanities or lavatories on the wall behind the water closet are permitted to overlap the clearance.

❖ The clear floor space for the forward approach for water closets in the Type B unit is narrower than that required for Type A units (Section 1002.11.5.2.2). The depth of the space is 66 inches (1675 mm). The width

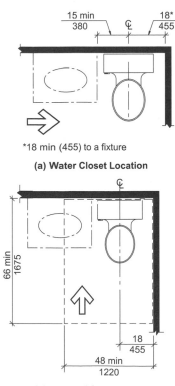

*18 min (455) to a fixture

(a) Water Closet Location

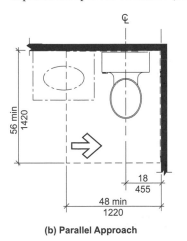

(b) Parallel Approach

(c) Forward Approach

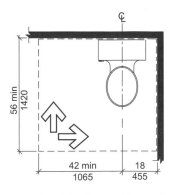

(d) Parallel or Forward Approach

Fig. 1004.11.3.1.2
Water Closets in Type B Units

is measured 18 inches (455 mm) from the centerline of the water closet towards where the grab bar will be installed and then back 48 inches (1220 mm) over the water closet [See Figure 1004.11.3.1.2(c)].

1004.11.3.1.2.3 Parallel or Forward Approach. A clearance 56 inches (1420 mm) minimum measured from the wall behind the water closet, and 42 inches (1065 mm) minimum measured from the centerline of the water closet shall be provided.

❖ The third option for Type B units is intended to be consistent with the clear floor space that is required in Accessible units (Section 604.3). The depth of the space is 56 inches (1420 mm). The width of the space is 42 inches (1065 mm) plus 18 inches (455 mm) for a minimum total width of 60 inches (1525 mm) [see commentary Figure 1004.11.3.1.2 (d)]. Approach can be from either direction.

1004.11.3.1.3 Bathing Facilities. Where a bathtub or shower compartment is provided it shall conform with Section 1004.11.3.1.3.1, 1004.11.3.1.3.2, or 1004.11.3.1.3.3.

❖ Bathing facilities can be either a bathtub or shower. Provisions address a parallel or forward approach to a bathtub and access to a standard shower stall. A bathtub constructed in accordance with Section 607 or a roll-in shower, alternate roll-in shower or transfer shower constructed in accordance with Section 608 would result in a higher level of accessibility.

See Section 1004.11.2 for requirements for blocking at bathing facilities for the future installation of grab bars.

There are three choices for the clearances in front of the bathtub. The arrows in Figures 1004.11.3.1.3.1

and 1004.11.3.1.3.2 indicate the anticipated approach direction to the water closet. The designer can use any of the three choices. Section 1004.11.3.1.3.3 is intended to address a transfer type shower.

1004.11.3.1.3.1 Parallel Approach Bathtubs. A clearance 60 inches (1525 mm) minimum in length and 30 inches (760 mm) minimum in width shall be provided in front of bathtubs with a parallel approach. Lavatories complying with Section 606 shall be permitted in the clearance. A lavatory complying with Section 1004.11.3.1.1 shall be permitted at the control end of the bathtub if a clearance 48 inches (1220 mm) minimum in length and 30 inches (760 mm) minimum in width for a parallel approach is provided in front of the bathtub.

❖ Two options exist for bathtubs with a parallel approach. The figures show a standard 60 inch (1525 mm) length tub. This could also be a 30 inch by 60 inch (760 by 1525 mm) shower stall.

If a 30 inch by 48 inch (760 1220 mm) wheelchair space is available in front of the tub, a lavatory with a parallel approach can be located at the end of the tub [(see Figure 1004.11.3.1.3.1(b)].

Alternatively, a 30 inch (760 mm) wide space for the length of the tub must be provided. A lavatory constructed for a front approach with knee and toe clearances can overlap the tub space [see Figure 1004.11.3.1.3.1(a)]. Installing removable cabinetry under the lavatory consistent with Type A units is also viable (Section 1002.11.5).

1004.11.3.1.3.2 Forward Approach Bathtubs. A clearance 60 inches (1525 mm) minimum in length and 48 inches

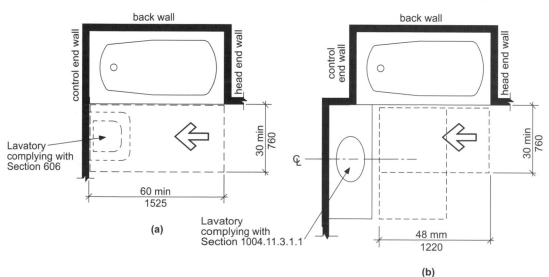

Fig. 1004.11.3.1.3.1
Parallel Approach Bathtub in Type B Units – Option a Bathrooms

(1220 mm) minimum in width shall be provided in front of bathtubs with a forward approach. A water closet shall be permitted in the clearance at the control end of the bathtub.

❖ Figure 1004.11.3.1.3.2 shows a standard 60 inch (1525 mm) tub. This could also be a 30 inch by 60 inch (760 by 1525 mm) shower stall. With a perpendicular approach to the tub, the depth must be 48 inches (1220 mm). A water closet can be located within this clear floor space.

This configuration is often viewed as a good alternative for persons with mobility impairments or the elderly. Physical therapists teach people to sit on the toilet to disrobe, adjust the tub water, and then move into the tub to reduce the chance of falls while getting into and out of the bathtub.

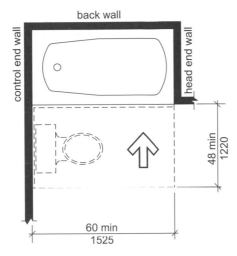

Fig. 1004.11.3.1.3.2
Forward Approach Bathtub in Type B Units –
Option A Bathrooms

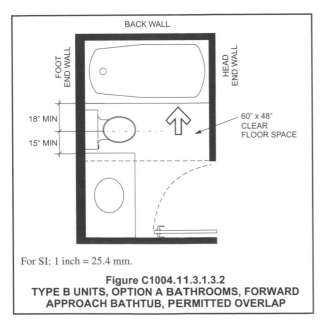

For SI: 1 inch = 25.4 mm.

Figure C1004.11.3.1.3.2
TYPE B UNITS, OPTION A BATHROOMS, FORWARD APPROACH BATHTUB, PERMITTED OVERLAP

The water closet clearances (Section 1004.11.3.1.2) allow for a lavatory to be located 15 inch (380 mm) from the centerline of the water closet on the approach side and 18 inches (455 mm) from the centerline of the water closet to the tub on the opposite side. Therefore, a lavatory could also overlap the clear floor space as shown in commentary Figure C1004.11.3.1.3.2.

1004.11.3.1.3.3 Shower Compartment. If a shower compartment is the only bathing facility, the shower compartment shall have dimensions of 36 inches (915 mm) minimum in width and 36 inches (915 mm) minimum in depth. A clearance of 48 inches (1220 mm) minimum in length, measured perpendicular from the shower head wall, and 30 inches (760 mm) minimum in depth, measured from the face of the shower compartment, shall be provided. Reinforcing for a shower seat is not required in shower compartments larger than 36 inches (915 mm) in width and 36 inches (915 mm) in depth.

❖ The clear floor space requirements for showers in Type B units, Option A bathrooms are similar to what is required for a transfer type shower in Section 608.2.1 (see Figure 1004.11.3.1.3.3). The difference is that an accessible transfer shower must be 36 inches by 36 inches (915 by 915 mm) and this section specifies 36 inches minimum by 36 inches minimum. Therefore, although a larger shower would be permitted, good design practices would consider both a transfer location and access to controls from a possible seat location.

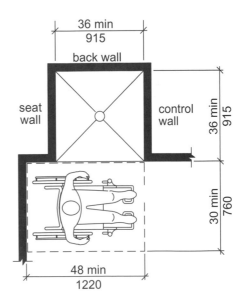

Fig. 1004.11.3.1.3.3
Transfer-Type Shower Compartment in Type B Units

Although reinforcement for the shower seat is not required in larger showers, reinforcement for grab bars is required.

A roll-in shower or alternative roll-in shower would be permitted as alternatives that result in a higher level of accessibility.

1004.11.3.2 Option B. One of each type of fixture provided shall comply with Section 1004.11.3.2. The accessible fixtures shall be in a single toilet/bathing area, such that travel between fixtures does not require travel through other parts of the unit.

❖ The general configuration for an Option A bathroom is with the lavatory, water closet and tub along one common plumbing wall (see commentary Figure C1004.11.3.1). The general configuration for an Option B bathroom is with the tub on one side and the water closet and lavatory on the other side (see commentary Figure C1004.11.3.2).

The base requirement is that if Option B bathrooms are chosen, each type of fixture in one bathroom must meet the clearance requirements in this section. Therefore, when two lavatories are installed in the same bathroom, only one is required to meet clearance requirements. If a separate bathtub and shower are installed in the same bathroom, it is designer's choice which one to make accessible. Per Section 1004.11.2, other bathrooms in the unit do not have to have clearances, but must have blocking in the walls for the future installation of grab bars.

The exception allows for a powder room or half-bath to not have clearances if this is not the only bathroom on the accessible level. The wording of the exception is caused by the scoping provisions in the model code and the Fair Housing Act allowing for an exception for the second floor in a multistory unit in an elevator building. Bathrooms on the inaccessible level would not have to meet these provisions. See these documents for specific requirements.

1004.11.3.2.1 Lavatory. Lavatories shall comply with Section 1004.11.3.2.1.

❖ The clear floor space requirement for Option A and Option B lavatories is the same; however, Option B has an additional height requirement. In an Option B bathroom the lavatory is limited to a 34 inch (865 mm) maximum height. See Section 1004.11.3.2.1.3.

1004.11.3.2.1.1 Clear Floor Space. A clear floor space complying with Section 305.3, positioned for a parallel approach, shall be provided.

EXCEPTIONS:

1. A lavatory complying with Section 606.

2. Cabinetry shall be permitted under the lavatory, provided such cabinetry can be removed without removal or replacement of the lavatory, and the floor finish extends under such cabinetry.

❖ A 30-inch by 48-inch (760 by 1220 mm) parallel space centered on the lavatory will allow a person using a wheelchair to approach the lavatory and use it for bathing. Because the wheels of a wheelchair typically extend at least 12 inches (305 mm) behind the back of the wheelchair seat, the center of the lavatory must be at least 24 inches (610 mm) from an adjacent wall or other obstruction (Section 1004.11.3.2.1.2).

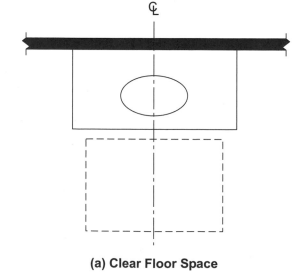

(a) Clear Floor Space

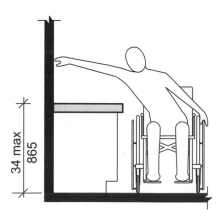

(b) Height

Fig. 1004.11.3.2.1
Lavatory in Type B Units – Option B Bathrooms

The intent of the exceptions is to allow the more accessible lavatory options permitted in Accessible units or Type A units (Section 1003.11.5). Although the reference to Section 606 would result in faucets having to meet operable parts requirements (Section 606.4), the specific exception for plumbing fixtures in Type B units in Section 1004.9, Exception 7 would negate that requirement.

The reference to Section 606 in Exception 1 includes all subsections (Section 606.1 through 606.7). Section 606.5 includes an exception to indicate that lavatories with enhanced reach ranges are required within Type A and Type B dwelling or sleeping units. Because towel dispensers and hand dryers are typically not installed within dwelling units and sleeping units, Section 606.7 is typically not applicable.

1004.11.3.2.1.2 Position. The clear floor space shall be centered on the lavatory.

❖ See the commentary in Section 1004.11.3.2.1.1.

1004.11.3.2.1.3 Height. The front of the lavatory shall be 34 inches (865 mm) maximum above the floor, measured to the higher of the fixture rim or counter surface.

❖ The clear floor space requirement for Option A and Option B lavatories is the same; however, Option B has an additional height requirement. In Option B bathrooms the lavatory is limited to a 34 inch (865 mm) maximum height [see Figure 1004.11.3.2.1(b)].

1004.11.3.2.2 Water Closet. The water closet shall comply with Section 1004.11.3.1.2.

❖ The water closet requirements are the same for Option A and Option B bathrooms. See Section 1003.11.3.1.2.

1004.11.3.2.3 Bathing Facilities. Where either a bathtub or shower compartment is provided, it shall conform with Section 1004.11.3.2.3.1 or 1004.11.3.2.3.2.

❖ One bathing fixture must have clearances in a Type B unit, Option B bathroom. When both a bathtub and a shower are installed in the same room, only one must meet the clearance requirements.

Because of the reinforcement requirements in Section 1004.11.2, reinforcement would be required in any walls constructed around any bathing fixture.

1004.11.3.2.3.1 Bathtub. A clearance 48 inches (1220 mm) minimum in length measured perpendicular from the control end of the bathtub, and 30 inches (760 mm) minimum in width shall be provided in front of bathtubs.

❖ The main difference between the Option A and Option B bathrooms is at the tub. A 30-inch by 48-inch

(760 by 1220 mm) clear floor space must be provided perpendicular to the tub. To ensure access to the controls, the clear floor space must be measured from the end with the controls. There are no options for a water closet or lavatory to overlap this clear floor space.

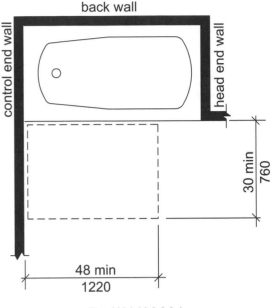

Fig. 1004.11.3.2.3.1
Bathroom Clearance in Type B Units –
Option B Bathrooms

1004.11.3.2.3.2 Shower Compartment. A shower compartment shall comply with Section 1004.11.3.1.3.3.

❖ The requirements for showers in Option B bathrooms are the same as those for Option A bathrooms. See Section 1004.11.3.1.3.3.

1004.12 Kitchens. Kitchens shall comply with Section 1004.12.

❖ The intent of the Type B unit kitchen is that the kitchen is usable by a person using a wheelchair. Consideration must be given for wheelchair access to the general kitchen area, sink and appliances. The Type B unit kitchen does not include some of the access requirements found in Type A units, such as adaptability for front approach at the sink or a work surface, a turning space within the room, or specific requirements for access to the cabinets in the kitchen. A side approach to the kitchen sink is permitted. Type B and Type A units are similar in their requirements for clearances in the kitchen and approach to the appliances. If a designer chooses to use some of the Type A unit requirements for kitchens, the higher level of accessibility that results would exceed the Type B unit requirements.

Careful design will produce a kitchen with a minimal-level accessible and functionally efficient kitchen that is easily usable by a person with a disability or mobility impairment, as well as an able-bodied person.

This standard does not specifically address kitchenettes in Type B sleeping units in this section. Requirements for kitchenettes are included in Section 804.

1004.12.1 Clearance. Clearance complying with Section 1004.12.1 shall be provided.

❖ Kitchens include requirements for clearances between cabinets or appliances; the clearance requirements in referenced Sections 1004.12.1.1 and 1004.12.1.2 are different because the two different floor plan arrangements require different types of spaces for maneuvering.

It is not the intent of these provisions to prohibit other types of kitchen layouts, such as L-shaped or kitchens with islands. If other layouts are used, the key considerations would be maneuvering to access appliances and the sink. Good design practices also look for access to the counters and storage elements. There are no specific requirements for work surfaces and kitchen storage in a Type B unit as there are in Accessible and Type A units (Sections 804.3, 804.5, 1002.12, 1003.12.3 and 1003.12.5). The intent in Type B units is to allow standard kitchen design practices for these elements.

1004.12.1.1 Minimum Clearance. Clearance between all opposing base cabinets, counter tops, appliances, or walls within kitchen work areas shall be 40 inches (1015 mm) minimum.

❖ The minimum clear width between opposing cabinets/appliances, or a cabinet/appliances and wall or other type of obstruction, is 40 inches (1015 mm). This measurement does not include cabinet/appliance handles.

Galley style kitchens are typically laid out with all the appliances, counters and sink in straight lines. The appliances and fixtures can be located along one side of the kitchen, or they can be located along both sides of the kitchen. Unlike a pass-through kitchen required for an Accessible unit (Sections 1002.12. and 804.2.1), a Type B unit and Type A unit (Section 1003.12.1.1) galley kitchen may be open on one or both ends.

1004.12.1.2 U-Shaped Kitchens. In kitchens with counters, appliances, or cabinets on three contiguous sides, clearance between all opposing base cabinets, countertops, appliances, or walls within kitchen work areas shall be 60 inches (1525 mm) minimum.

❖ U-shaped kitchens are kitchens with cabinets and appliances on three contiguous sides. In such an arrangement, a 60 inch (1525 mm) clearance is required between the faces of opposing cabinets and appliances to make all sides usable.

Unlike Accessible unit kitchens (Section 1002.12 and 804.2.2), in Type B units and Type A units (Section 1003.12.1.2), a galley-style kitchen with an opening on only one end is not considered a U-shaped

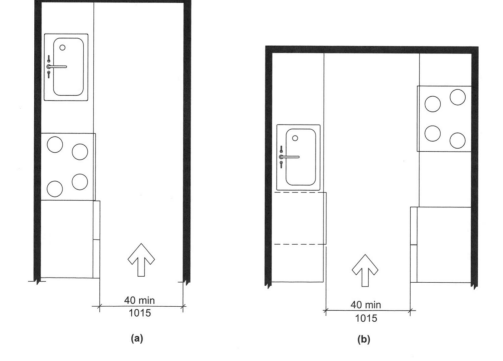

40 min
1015

(a)

40 min
1015

(b)

**Fig. 1004.12.1.1
Minimum Kitchen Clearance in Type B Units**

kitchen and would not have to have a 60-inch (1525 mm) clear floor space between cabinets. The key for when a U-shaped kitchen is required in a Type B unit is the need to be able to turn 90 degrees (1.6 rad) to reach an appliance or use a counter or cabinet on the third wall.

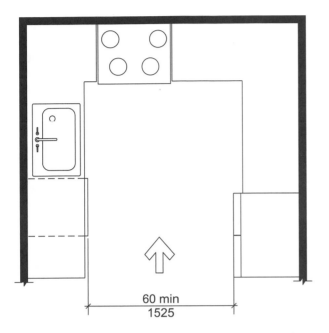

Fig. 1004.12.1.2
U-Shaped Kitchen Clearance in Type B Units

1004.12.2 Clear Floor Space. Clear floor space at appliances shall comply with Sections 1004.12.2 and 305.3.

❖ The clear floor space for the sink, dishwasher, cooktop, oven, refrigerator/freezer and trash compactor must be 30 inches by 48 inches (760 by 1220 mm) (Section 305.3). The intent is that all built-in appliances, not just the ones specifically listed, have a clear floor space. For example, if a built-in microwave is provided in the kitchen, a clear floor space is needed.

Although either a forward or side approach is permitted, a centering of that space is required only at cooktops and sinks. The intent is that the clear floor space be located to allow access to the appliance, and should be located based on how the appliance is used. For example, access to the dishwasher may be from the side to allow for the door to be opened and the racks slid out. The clear floor space can overlap the door as long as it does not obstruct the door–a designer can use toe clearances under the door. Clear floor spaces can overlap. Using the same clear floor space for the sink and an adjacent dishwasher allows someone to rinse the dishes and put them into the

dishwasher without moving (see commentary Figure C1004.12.2.2).

Note that Section 1004.9 exempts appliance controls from operable parts requirements.

1004.12.2.1 Sink. A clear floor space, positioned for a parallel approach to the sink, shall be provided. The clear floor space shall be centered on the sink bowl.

EXCEPTION: Sinks complying with Section 606 shall be permitted to have a clear floor space positioned for a parallel or forward approach.

❖ Although some items in a kitchen have an option of a front approach or a parallel approach, a parallel approach is required at sinks. Whether the sink is a single bowl or double bowl, the clear floor space must be centered on the unit (see commentary Figure C1004.12.2.1). As a plumbing fixture, Section 1003.9 Exception 7, exempts the faucets from operable parts requirements.

The intent of the exception is to allow a kitchen sink that is required in an Accessible unit (Sections 1002.12, 804.4 and 606). The sink must be constructed accessible including a rim height at 34 inches (865 mm) maximum, clear floor space for a front approach, knee and toe clearances, pipe protection and faucets with operable parts. Although not specifically mentioned in the exception, the Type A dwelling unit sink (see Section 1003.12.4) allows for a sink that is designed to be adaptable to be accessible, and would also exceed Type B unit requirements for sinks.

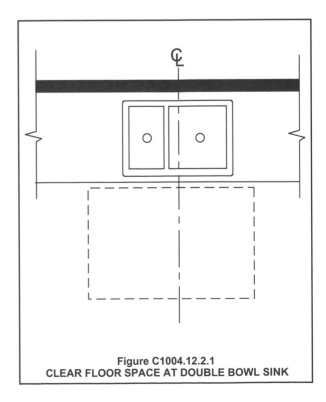

Figure C1004.12.2.1
CLEAR FLOOR SPACE AT DOUBLE BOWL SINK

1004.12.2.2 Dishwasher. A clear floor space, positioned for a parallel or forward approach to the dishwasher, shall be provided. The clear floor space shall be positioned beyond the swing of the dishwasher door.

❖ Locating the clear floor space so that the dishwasher is usable is important. If the clear floor space is located immediately in front of the dishwasher, the door in the open position will overlap the clear floor space. By requiring that the clear floor space be positioned beyond the swing of the dishwasher door, either the clear floor space must be located past the door, or the door could overlap the toe clearance if there was a minimum 9 inch (230 mm) clearance under the door when open. It is important to locate the clear floor space so the dishwasher can be easily loaded and un-

loaded. Often, it is desirable to load the dishwasher from the sink area; therefore, it may be helpful to locate the sink and dishwasher adjacent to each other. Where a dishwasher is located adjacent to the clear floor space for a sink, the single clear floor space can be used to serve both the sink and the dishwasher (see commentary Figure C1004.12.2.2).

Controls for a dishwasher are exempted from the operable parts requirement per Section 1004.9, Exception 6.

1004.12.2.3 Cooktop. A clear floor space, positioned for a parallel or forward approach to the cooktop, shall be provided. The centerline of the clear floor space shall align with the centerline of the cooktop. Where the clear floor space is positioned for a forward approach, knee and toe clearance complying with Section 306 shall be provided. Where knee and toe space is provided, the underside of the range or cooktop shall be insulated or otherwise configured to prevent burns, abrasions, or electrical shock.

❖ A standard range includes a cooktop and an oven. A range must be located for the parallel approach, not a front approach [see commentary Figure C1004.12.2.3(a)] because of the footplates on a wheelchair stopping people from reaching forward past their toes.

A cooktop can have a parallel approach or a front approach. When a designer chooses a front approach, the cooktop must have adequate clearances for a person's knees and toes underneath as well as protection from accidental bumps, cuts or burns.

Controls for a range or cooktop, as well as the associated hood, are exempted from the operable parts requirement per Section 1004.9, Exception 6.

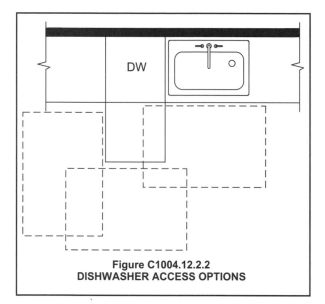

Figure C1004.12.2.2
DISHWASHER ACCESS OPTIONS

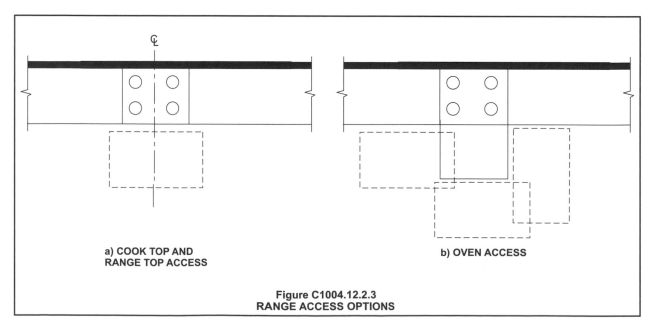

a) COOK TOP AND
RANGE TOP ACCESS

b) OVEN ACCESS

Figure C1004.12.2.3
RANGE ACCESS OPTIONS

1004.12.2.4 Oven. A clear floor space, positioned for a parallel or forward approach to the oven, shall be provided.

❖ A standard range includes a cooktop and an oven. Access to the ovens can be either a parallel approach or a front approach [see commentary Figure C1004.12.2.3(b)].

Usability of the oven must be considered when choosing placement and options. A person must be able to open the oven door fully and reach the oven racks. Wall mounted ovens may provide better access for persons using wheelchairs or persons who have difficulty bending down. Although most ovens have a bottom hinge door, some manufacturers are starting to offer microwave/oven combinations with a side swinging door. Other options that increase access include racks that pull all the way out without tipping, or doors that can support the weight of a full pan.

Placement of the oven next to a counter surface or accessible work surface assists in transfer of hot dishes out of the oven, but is not required in a Type B unit, as it is in an Accessible unit (Sections 1002.12.2, 804.6.5.1 and 804.6.5.2) or a Type A unit (Sections 1003.12.6.5.1 and 1003.12.6.5.2).

Controls for a range or wall oven are exempted from the operable parts requirement per Section 1004.9, Exception 6.

1004.12.2.5 Refrigerator/Freezer. A clear floor space, positioned for a parallel or forward approach to the refrigerator/freezer, shall be provided.

❖ The position for the parallel or forward approach to the refrigerator and freezer must consider how the person using a wheelchair will access the interior with the door open.

Refrigerator/freezer choices can have the freezer on the top, on the bottom or side-by-side. Side-by-side refrigerator/freezers have the most accessible freezer compartment; however, clear floor spaces for both sides must be considered for the unit (see commentary Figure C1004.12.2.5). Bottom freezers are typically pull out drawers, so a clear floor space must be available with the freezer door fully open. While not a requirement in Type B units, Accessible unit and Type A unit requirements (Sections 804.6.6 and 1003.12.6.6) look for a parallel approach with a maximum of 24 inches (610 mm) between the centerline of the compartment and the centerline of the clear floor space. Locating refrigerators so the doors swing back 180 degrees (3 rad) can result in greater accessibility for a person using a wheelchair.

Although not specifically mentioned, if a refrigerator dispenses ice or water through the door, or inside the appliance, that feature is considered part of the refrigerator/freezer. Therefore, those elements must also have a clear floor space for access.

1004.12.2.6 Trash Compactor. A clear floor space, positioned for a parallel or forward approach to the trash compactor, shall be provided.

❖ The trash compactor is similar to the dishwasher and oven in the that it must be open for use. Therefore, the clear floor space should be located so that it does not obstruct the door of the trash compactor in the open position.

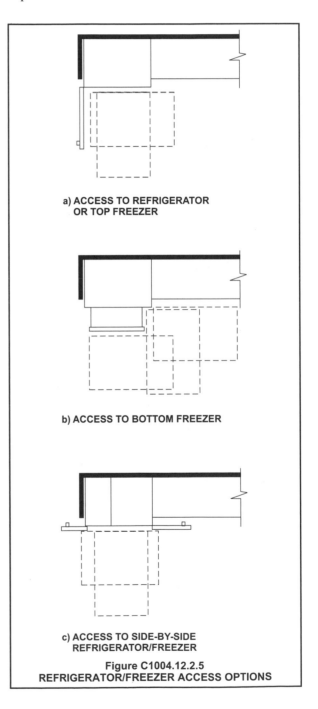

a) ACCESS TO REFRIGERATOR OR TOP FREEZER

b) ACCESS TO BOTTOM FREEZER

c) ACCESS TO SIDE-BY-SIDE REFRIGERATOR/FREEZER

Figure C1004.12.2.5 REFRIGERATOR/FREEZER ACCESS OPTIONS

1005 Units with Accessible Communication Features

❖ Section 1005 contains criteria for accessible communication features such as those used for emergency evacuations (e.g., fire alarms, smoke detectors) and announcing visitors (e.g., doorbells, voice or visual communication between the apartment and the building entrance).

Sections 1005.2 through 1004.5.4 work together for the emergency alarm system. Sections 1005.5 through 1005.7 deal with communication between entrances and occupants.

1005.1 General. Units required to have accessible communication features shall comply with Section 1005.

❖ The provisions of this section are the technical criteria for accessible communication features within dwelling units when scoped by the authority having jurisdiction (see Section 201). Scoping may include dwelling units that are not accessible in other ways (i.e., other than Accessible units, Type A units or Type B units). For example, an apartment building may have requirements for visible alarm notification appliances (e.g., visible fire alarms and smoke detectors) or entry systems (e.g., closed circuit communication systems) to all floors in a building, including upper floors without elevator access.

The model codes have scoping criteria for accessibility in all types of places where people live, eat and sleep. Types of dwelling units are addressed, including apartments, condominiums and townhouses. Typical single-family detached homes are exempted, but a home owner may choose to follow these criteria to build an accessible home. Scoping criteria for accessible communication features typically include apartments, condominiums and townhouses–all of which are typical dwelling units. Scoping criteria may include other types of places where people live–congregate living arrangements such as assisted living facilities, group homes, shelters, nursing homes, boarding houses, dormitories, convents, monasteries, fraternities and sororities. Scoping for transient type lodging, such as hotels and motels, is often addressed separately, but may also include provisions for accessible communication features.

1005.2 Unit Smoke Detection. Where provided, unit smoke detection shall include audible notification complying with NFPA 72 listed in Section 105.2.2.

❖ In occupancies with sleeping areas, occupants must be notified in a fire so they can promptly evacuate the premises. Dwelling unit or sleeping unit smoke detection is typically provided by a single-station or multiple-station smoke alarm.

A single-station smoke alarm is a self-contained alarm device that detects visible or invisible particles of combustion. Its function is to detect a fire in the immediate area of the detector location. Where the single-station smoke alarms are interconnected with other single-station devices, they are considered a multiple-station smoke alarm system. Single-station smoke alarms are not capable of notifying or controlling any other fire protection equipment or system. They may be battery powered, directly connected to the building power supply or a combination of both.

Multiple-station smoke alarms are self-contained smoke-activated alarm devices that can be interconnected with other devices, so all integral or separate alarms will operate when any one device is activated.

Model codes typically specify where dwelling or sleeping unit smoke detection will be required within a dwelling or sleeping unit. In dwelling units, this is typically outside each sleeping area, in each sleeping room and on each story in a multistory unit. In congregate living arrangements requirements are similar. In hotels, dormitories or other types of sleeping units, the smoke alarms must be in sleeping rooms and in any room between the sleeping room and the entrance to the unit (e.g., living area of a suite). Smoke alarms must be interconnected within the unit (i.e., activation of one smoke alarm will set off all smoke alarms within the unit).

For successful smoke alarm operation and performance, single- and multiple-station smoke alarms must be listed in accordance with UL 217 and installed to comply with the model code and NFPA 72, which contains the minimum requirements for the selection, installation, operation and maintenance of fire warning equipment for use in family living units. Model codes and NFPA 72 use the term "smoke alarms" rather than "smoke detectors" because they are independent of a fire alarm system and include an integral alarm notification device.

This section requires that the unit smoke detectors have an audible notification in accordance with NFPA 72. NFPA 72 requires a minimum average ambient sound level for smoke alarms in the private mode to be greater than 45 dba at 3 meters, and 10dba above average ambient sound level or 5 dba above the maximum sound level (NFPA 72, Section 7.4).

1005.3 Building Fire Alarm System. Where a building fire alarm system is provided, the system wiring shall be extended to a point within the unit in the vicinity of the unit smoke detection system.

❖ In residential facilities, a building fire alarm system, dwelling unit smoke alarms and a sprinkler system are parts of on overall fire protection system for a building. These elements are considered part of the active fire safety provisions. They are directed at containing and abating the fire once it has erupted, as well as providing notification to occupants and emergency responders to emergency situations. The requirements are generally based on what the building is used for, and the height and area of the building. These are factors that most affect fire-fighting capabilities and the relative hazard of a specific space.

Building fire alarms include both audible and visible alarm requirements (see Section 702) and are intended to serve as a general evacuation alarm system. Model codes typically require a building fire alarm system in apartment buildings that have basement dwelling units, apartment buildings four stories or higher, and apartment buildings with 16 or more apartments. Check with the authority having jurisdiction for specifics. Activation of the smoke alarms within a unit and the building fire alarm system are typically independent.

This section requires that when there is a building fire alarm system, the wiring be extended into each unit in the area of one of the smoke alarms. The intent is that the resident of that unit can request standard smoke alarms be switched out to smoke alarms that have both audible and visible alarms, rather than just audible. With the wiring in place, the smoke alarms in the unit can be hooked up so the activation of the building alarm system will also activate the smoke alarms in that unit. Because multiple-station smoke alarms are already interconnected, the wiring from the building alarm system need be extended to only one smoke alarm. It is not the intent for the activation of the smoke alarm to activate the building alarm system.

It is not the intent of this section to require wiring for full visible alarm coverage within the dwelling unit in permanent residential facilities. See the scoping provisions of the model codes for coverage of the building alarm audible and visible alarms. Model codes do scope a certain number of sleeping units in transient lodging and assisted living facilities to have full visible and audible alarm coverage.

1005.4 Visible Notification Appliances. Visible notification appliances, where provided within the unit as part of the unit smoke detection system or the building fire alarm system, shall comply with Section 1005.4.

❖ Requirements for visible alarms within the unit and the public spaces and common spaces in the building are intended to alert individuals with hearing impairments of a possible emergency situation. The model codes scope where visible alarm coverage is required; therefore, this section does not require visible alarms, but indicates that when they are installed they should meet the provisions in the following subsections.

1005.4.1 Appliance. Visible notification appliances shall comply with Section 702.

❖ Both the required visible alarm coverage in the public and common areas of the building and the smoke alarms with a visible component should meet the applicable provisions in NFPA 72. NFPA does not require the same area coverage, flash rate or intensity for the visible notification in the smoke detectors as it requires for the visible appliances in the building alarm system.

1005.4.2 Activation. All visible notification appliances provided within the unit for smoke detection notification shall be activated upon smoke detection. All visible notification appliances provided within the unit for building fire alarm notification shall be activated upon activation of the building fire alarm in the portion of the building containing the unit.

❖ Once the dwelling unit smoke alarms are connected to the building alarm system, the dwelling unit smoke alarms should activate when there is either smoke detected within the unit or when the building alarm system is activated.

The intent is that a resident can request installation of smoke alarms with both visible and audible notification (e.g., flashing lights and horns) within their unit as a reasonable modification. The wiring that allows for the preplanning for this is required by Section 1005.3. Because the smoke alarms have their own power, this should not increase the power requirements for the building alarm system.

1005.4.3 Interconnection. The same visible notification appliances shall be permitted to provide notification of unit smoke detection and building fire alarm activation.

❖ This section clarifies that the lights in the smoke alarms can serve to notify the dwelling occupants of both smoke within the unit and the general building evacuation alarm.

1005.4.4 Prohibited Use. Visible notification appliances used to indicate unit smoke detection or building fire alarm activation shall not be used for any other purpose within the unit.

❖ The lights in the smoke alarms for alarm notification should not be used for other purposes, such as means of egress emergency lighting, or other types of emergency notification, such as tornadoes warnings.

1005.5 Unit Primary Entrance. Communication features shall be provided at the unit primary entrance complying with Section 1005.5.

❖ When the authority having jurisdiction requires communication features at individual dwelling unit entrances, those systems shall comply with the notification and identification requirements listed in the subsections that follow.

1005.5.1 Notification. A hard-wired electric doorbell shall be provided. A button or switch shall be provided on the public side of the unit primary entrance. Activation of the button or switch shall initiate an audible tone within the unit.

❖ The doorbell, as an operable part, should have a clear floor space and be located within reach ranges. Best design practice allows for an adjustment of the tone and/or volume of the bell within the unit for persons with hearing losses. The adjustment in tone rather than just volume would be beneficial for persons with hearing loss in a specific range.

1005.5.2 Identification. A means for visually identifying a visitor without opening the unit entry door shall be provided. Peepholes, where used, shall provide a minimum 180-degree range of view.

❖ Visual identification could be by the use of a peephole, a door with inset lites or side lites, or a video monitoring system–anything that allows for a person inside the unit to see who is outside without opening the door. If a peephole is used, the eye height of an average person in a wheelchair is 43 inches to 51 inches (1090 to 1295 mm), so that range would be considered an accessible height. A door can have both a high and a low peephole. The bottom edge of door lite glazing must be below 43 inches (1090 mm) (Section 404.2.11).

1005.6 Site, Building, or Floor Entrance. Where a system permitting voice communication between a visitor and the occupant of the unit is provided at a location other than the unit entry door, the system shall comply with Section 1005.6.

❖ When the authority having jurisdiction requires communication features at a building entrance or similar location, those systems must comply with the interface requirements listed in the subsections. Systems at these locations typically involve a phone, intercom, video relay or some combination of these.

1005.6.1 Public or Common-Use Interface. The public or common-use system interface shall include the capability of supporting voice and TTY communication with the unit interface.

❖ For a persons visiting in the building, the option of some type of TTY system, either built in or a portable that could be plugged in, must be considered because either the visitor or the person living in the unit could be hearing impaired. TTY specifications for phone systems are found in Sections 704.4, 704.5 and 704.6.

1005.6.2 Unit Interface. The unit system interface shall include a telephone jack capable of supporting voice and TTY communication with the public or common-use system interface.

❖ For persons living in the building, the option of some type of TTY system, either built in or a portable that could be plugged in, must be considered because either the visitor or the person living in the unit could be hearing impaired. TTY specifications for phone systems are found in Sections 704.4, 704.5 and 704.6.

1005.7 Closed-Circuit Communication Systems. Where a closed-circuit communication system is provided, the public or common-use system interface shall comply with Section 1005.6.1, and the unit system interface in units required to have accessible communication features shall comply with Section 1005.6.2.

❖ Two-way communication systems are used at security entrances, for closed circuit entry systems, from areas of refuge, etc. These systems must be available for persons with hearing impairments. Persons with hearing impairments will need TTY capability the same as required for the public or common-use interface. For additional information on two-way communication systems, see Section 708.

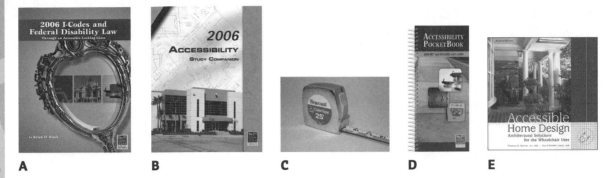

Don't Miss Out On Valuable ICC Membership Benefits. Join ICC Today!

Join the largest and most respected building code and safety organization. As an official member of the International Code Council®, these great ICC® benefits are at your fingertips.

EXCLUSIVE MEMBER DISCOUNTS

ICC members enjoy exclusive discounts on codes, technical publications, seminars, plan reviews, educational materials, videos, and other products and services.

TECHNICAL SUPPORT

ICC members get expert code support services, opinions, and technical assistance from experienced engineers and architects, backed by the world's leading repository of code publications.

FREE CODE—LATEST EDITION

Most new individual members receive a free code from the latest edition of the International Codes®. New corporate and governmental members receive one set of major International Codes (Building, Residential, Fire, Fuel Gas, Mechanical, Plumbing, Private Sewage Disposal).

FREE CODE MONOGRAPHS

Code monographs and other materials on proposed International Code revisions are provided free to ICC members upon request.

ICC *BUILDING SAFETY JOURNAL*®

A subscription to our official magazine is included with each membership. The bi-monthly magazine offers insightful articles authored by world-renowned code experts, plus code interpretations, job listings, event calendars, and other useful information. ICC members may also enjoy subscriptions to a bi-monthly newsletter and an electronic newsletter.

PROFESSIONAL DEVELOPMENT

Receive "Member Only Discounts" for on-site training, institutes, symposiums, audio virtual seminars, and on-line training! ICC delivers educational programs that enable members to transition to the I-Codes®, interpret and enforce codes, perform plan reviews, design and build safe structures, and perform administrative functions more effectively and with greater efficiency. Members also enjoy special educational offerings that provide a forum to learn about and discuss current and emerging issues that affect the building industry.

ENHANCE YOUR CAREER

ICC keeps you current on the latest building codes, methods, and materials. Our conferences, job postings, and educational programs can also help you advance your career.

CODE NEWS

ICC members have the inside track for code news and industry updates via e-mails, newsletters, conferences, chapter meetings, networking, and the ICC Web site (www.iccsafe.org). Obtain code opinions, reports, adoption updates, and more. Without exception, ICC is your number one source for the very latest code and safety standards information.

MEMBER RECOGNITION

Improve your standing and prestige among your peers. ICC member cards, wall certificates, and logo decals identify your commitment to the community and to the safety of people worldwide.

ICC NETWORKING

Take advantage of exciting new opportunities to network with colleagues, future employers, potential business partners, industry experts, and more than 40,000 ICC members. ICC also has over 300 chapters across North America and around the globe to help you stay informed on local events, to consult with other professionals, and to enhance your reputation in the local community.

For more information about membership
or to join ICC, visit www.iccsafe.org/members
or call toll-free 1-888-ICC-SAFE (422-7233), x33804

INTERNATIONAL CODE COUNCIL®

People Helping People Build a Safer World™

8-61804-06